The Roosevelt Family

of Sagamore Hill

THE MACMILLAN COMPANY
NEW YORK · CHICAGO
DALLAS · ATLANTA · SAN FRANCISCO

THE MACMILLAN COMPANY
OF CANADA, LIMITED
TORONTO

THE FAMILY

LEFT TO RIGHT: Quentin, the President, Theodore, Jr., Archie, Alice,
Kermit, Mrs. Roosevelt, Ethel

The Roosevelt Family

OF SAGAMORE HILL

HERMANN HAGEDORN

NEW YORK

The Macmillan Company

1954

Permission to quote copyright material is acknowledged to publishers and authors as follows: John Day Company—*Theodore Roosevelt— a Hero to His Valet*, by James E. Amos, copyright 1927 by James E. Amos; Harvard University Press —*Collected Letters of Theodore Roosevelt*, 8 vols., ed. Elting E. Morrison, copyright 1951–1954 by the President and Fellows of Harvard College; Houghton Mifflin Company—*Pedestrian Papers*, by Walter S. Hinchman, copyright 1928 by Walter S. Hinchman; The Macmillan Company—*Roosevelt—The Story of a Friendship*, by Owen Wister, copyright 1930 by The Macmillan Company; G. P. Putnam's Sons—*All in the Family*, by Theodore Roosevelt, Jr., copyright 1929 by Theodore Roosevelt, Jr.; Fleming H. Revell Company—*The White House Gang*, by Earle Looker, copyright 1929 by Fleming H. Revell Company; Charles Scribner's Sons—*The Autobiography of Theodore Roosevelt*, copyright 1913 by Charles Scribner's Sons; *Crowded Hours*, by Alice Roosevelt Longworth, copyright 1933 by Charles Scribner's Sons; *Letters to Kermit from Theodore Roosevelt*, copyright 1946 by Charles Scribner's Sons.

To my grandchildren

Susan Marie Hagedorn and Michael David Parfit

When you, Susie, who are now eight, are grown up and have children
of your own, I believe that you will want to be the kind of mother that
Mrs. Roosevelt was, loving, strong and understanding, ready always to
listen and to laugh, keeping promises, bringing the heroes of poetry and
history into your children's lives, waking the love of God in their hearts,
and so shaping their minds and spirits that they may be capable of sustaining the privileges and the responsibilities of freedom.

And when you, Mikey, who are seven, are twenty-seven and thirty and
thirty-seven and have a family, I believe that you will want to be as tender,
true and gay a father as Theodore Roosevelt; a playmate to your children,
as young as they in a race or a roughhouse, yet always helping them to
grow in strength, compassion and courage; expecting the best from them,
yet never too hard on them when they fall short; summoning them ever to
richer adventure, higher service, and yourself leading the way.

Being as you are, Susie and Mikey, yourselves and nobody else, you
will not be imitating either of these great people and, insofar as you did,
you would be unlike them, since they themselves imitated nobody. But
you will draw from the Source from which they drew their power, and if
you follow their motto—*Fear God and take your own part*—the world will
feel the impact of your lives.

Contents

Book I

THE GROWING FAMILY

1887–1901

Chapter I

THE WIND, blowing across the Bay, still had winter in it, for all the calendar's insistence that spring was a week old. The high two-seater with the fringed top was open to the wind, but the chill air was nothing to what they had experienced on the passage from Liverpool on the *Etruria*; and at the end of the three-mile drive was home. That would mean much to Theodore Roosevelt, who loved his Long Island hilltop and had been away from it for five months. What it meant to Edith Roosevelt is beyond surmise. Her emotions would be complex, with breathless anticipation mixed, perhaps, with the memory, insistent and sharp, that Theodore had planned the house not for her but for another, whom he had passionately loved. That other had died before the first stone had been laid for the foundation, but he had named the house for her. "Leeholm" had since given way to "Sagamore Hill." Memories gave way to actuality, through the years, but not so easily.

Alice Lee's child had greeted her new mother in New York, the afternoon before, at the home of Theodore's unmarried sister Anna: a bright-faced child of three, in her best dress and sash, with a bunch of pink roses in her arms almost as big as herself. This child was her child now, Edith recognized, and she was determined to love her as her own.

The horses trotted eastward past stately houses—one with white pillars, impressively on an elevation overlooking the Bay. Edith remembered Tranquillity, the spacious house where the Roosevelts had for years spent their summers. She had had a memorable visit there twelve years before when she was fourteen and Theodore seventeen. The name was ironical. Countless cousins, assembling there with their friends, had fairly rocked the old walls.

3

The carriage clattered up hill and down dale along the shore of the Bay, swinging sharply to the left, at last, between a picturesque old cemetery sloping up a hillside on the right, and, on the bay-side, a rambling colonial house where Washington had once stayed after he became President. Beyond it were salt marshes, teeming with wild life. They were now on the peninsula known as Cove Neck, that jutted like a gigantic thumb, a half-mile across, a mile and a half long, north into Long Island Sound. Even in late March, with the rolling pastures still brown and the trees bare, its unspoiled rural quality was satisfying to sight and feeling alike. To Theodore it was home, all of it, since Sagamore was in its midst.

The carriage swung to the right, up an old wood road, then to the right again, sharply, in short loops up a steep hill that slowed the horses to a walk that became a pull, exacting even in the crisp March air. At the top, a left turn and a hundred yards of straight-away gave Edith opportunity to survey the house, half brick, half frame, that was to be her home.

She had seen it before, but not with the eyes that now sought to devour every detail and, at the same time, the exciting whole. The elaborate structure, so sedate, even heavy in its lines, fairly shouted jubilee in its colors, with the shingles of the upper stories a mustard yellow above the bricks, and the trim, rose-pink, intended to harmonize the whole, and not doing it too well. On the peak of the southern gable, the wide antlers of an elk, already weathered and gray, proclaimed a huntsman's habitat.

Under a wide porte-cochère, the horses, trotting again, came to a halt. Edith had crossed that porch before; but once only, arriving for a hunt ball, a year and a half before, when Anna Roosevelt had been the hostess—plain-faced, vivacious, brilliant and great-hearted "Bamie," who could hold fifty guests in the hollow of her capable little hand, besides a twenty-two-room house and the servants it took to run it. How like Theodore Bamie was in her love for people and her delight in bringing them together for talk and merriment! How together they had made the air vibrate! Edith knew she could never compete with Bamie in the subtle arts of hospitality; and shuddered, perhaps, at the thought of even trying.

No maids, starched and beaming, threw open the wide door as on that other occasion. The house was closed for the winter and the door was opened from the outside.

The paneled hall was dark except for white-shrouded game-heads thrusting their muffled majesty into the echoing abode of silence. There were dark stairs rising out of darkness to deeper darkness. But the library at the right of the front door was warm with broad windows looking over the crest of the hill southeastward to a weathered hay-barn that was said to go back almost to the Revolution. A portrait of Theodore's father, bearded and kindly, gave the room gravity. You could feel the solicitude with which this wise and devoted man was watching the progress of his ebullient son. Edith had no fear of what he was seeing or would see.

Across the hall from the library was the room that, Edith knew, would be peculiarly hers—the drawing-room, with its white wood-work, its furniture shrouded too in sheets that could not entirely dispel its decorous air of elegance and of formal ladies calling, and saying very little, stiffly, in very many words. She remembered the dining room, perhaps, more vividly than the other rooms, for it was there that Bamie and Theodore had sparkled most entrancingly: the fireplace across one corner, the doorway to the hall across another, and, through the window and the trees, a view of the lodge and the stable where Theodore kept his horses. Everywhere, under their white canopies, were game-heads. This, over the hall fireplace, Theodore would explain, was a buffalo-head he had first encountered beside Little Cannonball Creek in Dakota. The antlers under that white canopy had adorned a white-tail deer in the Bad Lands; those others, an elk in the Bighorns of Wyoming. Theodore took more pride in those game-heads than in any of the books he had written or the political achievements that had already carried his name across the continent. They meant manhood to him, manhood won at a price: tokens of triumph of character over physical inadequacy, testimony to daring, strength, endurance, straight aim and steady nerves, none of them innate, all laboriously acquired.

Upstairs, the bedrooms were successions of snowdrifts with everything that had meaning or beauty, white-shrouded, and even the wall-papers, in the dim light of the shuttered rooms, indistinguishable. It was as though they were passing through a tomb on their way to a home. Sleeping Beauty and the Prince, waking a half-hour ahead of the rest of the household, might have found the castle a little like this.

5

The bare, gently rounded hill to which he would give the name of Sagamore had been a part of Theodore Roosevelt's life since he was fifteen. He had idled over it through the lazy summer days, spotted the birds which hovered and sang in its treetops and coverts, repeating the bird-notes over and over until he could set them down, for the record, in terms of vowels and consonants; deployed his battalions in imaginary Agincourts on the eastern meadows, luxuriated in a boy's "long, long thoughts" on the western slope when the sun set the Bay afire, and the first white star broke through the afterglow. When he married Alice Lee it was to Sagamore Hill that he brought his bride of less than a week, for her approval of its purchase.

Day-dreaming in the long grass at fifteen, sixteen, seventeen, he would not have been the boy he was, filled from top to toe with ancient legendry, if the old Sagamore Mohannis had not romantically entered his musings, with the other Long Island chieftains who had held war councils on the hilltop. The venerable chief had signed away his tribe's rights to the land two and a half centuries before, and Theodore would, no doubt, have been thrilled beyond measure if he had known that some day he would own the yellowed deed of transfer, and set it, framed, on the mantel-piece of his study. The sagamore had deeded the land to one Joseph Cooper who passed it on to the Youngs family, one of whom, Captain Daniel Youngs, had entertained the first President, and another, Thomas, ninety years later, had, in December 1880, two months after Theodore's marriage, given a future President the first of three deeds for a total of 155 acres, conveying the two others three years later. What he received in return was the customary "One Dollar, lawful money of the United States, and other considerations," which in this case meant $10,000 cash, a mortgage for $20,000, and the right to remove the growing crops and the crops stored in the "farm barn," the only building on the bare, treeless hill. Theodore sold 28 acres to Bamie and 32 to his Aunt Anna Gracie, his mother's sister, the cherished guardian spirit of the nursery in the brownstone house in New York where he had been born.

Theodore set the architectural firm of Lamb and Rich—later Rich and Lorenzo—of 486 Broadway, to work on plans; first, for a "stable and lodge," then for a house. He was beginning to be a personage in New York State politics; he was married; he wanted a home for his young wife and elbow-room for a growing family. The architects gave it to him. The agglomeration of gables and dormers, piazzas, chimneys and colored glass that they designed was nothing if not spacious. The ten bedrooms on the second floor and two on the third, besides maids' rooms, suggested a program of family increase which might well have frightened a young wife about to have her first baby. Happily, carved in wood over the broad door leading into the house from the west was the motto from the Roosevelt family crest: *Qui plantavit curabit*—*He who has planted will preserve*—which, under the circumstances, must have seemed comforting.

The house that Lamb and Rich designed was nothing to soothe the eye or melt the spirit with subtle harmonies of proportion or grace of line. "I did not know enough to be sure what I wished in outside matters," Theodore wrote the editor of *Country Life in America* thirty years later. "But I had perfectly definite views what I wished in inside matters, what I desired to live in and with; I arranged all this, so as to get what I desired in so far as my money permitted; and then Rich put on the outside cover with but little help from me. I wished a big piazza . . . where we could sit in rocking-chairs and look at the sunset; a library with a shallow bay window looking south, the parlor or drawingroom occupying all the western end of the lower floor . . . big fireplaces for logs. . . . I had to live inside and not outside the house; and while I should have liked to 'express myself' in both"—the phrase was the Editor's —"as I had to choose I chose the former." So the architects gave him on the outside what self-respecting men of substance of the 1880's valued more than beauty, and what architects were summoned to express: solidity, first of all; dignity, hospitality, comfort, the social stability of the owner, and permanence. The foundations were twenty inches thick; joists, rafters and roofboards were in proportion. Long Island's gales were not going to shake this house, if Mr. Lamb and Mr. Rich could prevent it. Theodore's desires regarding fireplaces were fully covered, moreover, with four on the first floor, four on the second, and a dumb-waiter for firewood rising from the cellar to feed them. Apart from the satisfaction of crackling logs and dancing flames, Theodore was assuming—quite correctly, as the event proved—that even two hot-air furnaces in the cellar might need supplementing.

Taken all in all, it was quite a house that the architects designed for the well-to-do young man who was cutting so wide a swathe in New York politics. But before he could sign the contract for its construction an event occurred which made the plans appear tragically ironic and irrelevant. On February 13, 1884, Alice, his wife, gave birth to a daughter, in his mother's house on West 57th Street in New York, and died the next day. The fact that his mother died the same day, in the same house, gave the tragedy a suggestion of cosmic malevolence.

To return to Albany, a week after Alice's death, and plunge again into its political Donnybrook was one thing; to face, on his table, the plans for the house on Sagamore Hill that they had worked over together, was another. The queries of the architects regarding estimates and contracts were, no doubt, respectful, hesitant, even hushed. But how could he reply to such before he had faced the basic questions, and found answers that were as rational as anything could be in a universe that must have seemed to him at the moment devoid of meaning or order? What now? Life must go on, of course. But how—and where? A house on Sagamore Hill? A house anywhere? Without Alice? He had four walls and a roof in the Bad Lands of Dakota. That was all he wanted or would ever want, and he would go there as soon as the legislative session was over, lose himself in the primitive life of the frontier, among primitive men; hunt, ride, eat, sleep; forget he had ever known happiness, since he would never know it again. At last, it would seem to him as though Alice Lee had been no more than a lovely dream, in which he would find solace.

No. The situation wasn't as simple as that. There was their child, to remind him always that Alice Lee had been a reality, the one enchanting reality of his life. He could not shut the door of his heart on their baby. He might leave her with Bamie for a while, but ultimately he must give her a home. And he could not bring her up on the frontier. She must grow up among his friends and her mother's friends, in close touch with both families. For her, he must have a base in the East. Where? Where, except among the aunts and uncles and cousins at Oyster Bay? Where, indeed, except in the house that Alice had planned with him and looked forward to? This would still be her home, and her name would be a part of it forever—"Leeholm."

The plans that Lamb and Rich had made took on meaning

again. The queries of the architects became rational to him, queries he had to answer, and could answer. He examined estimates, and they became something other than the jumbled irrelevancies of a nightmare. Finally, he read a contract in which Theodore Roosevelt, party of the first part, and John A. Wood & Son, carpenters, of Lawrence, Long Island, party of the second part, agreed to the building of a house in Oyster Bay, at a total cost of $16,975. On March 1, 1884—two weeks after Alice's death—he signed it.

3

During the two years that followed, Theodore shuttled back and forth between New York and the cattle-herd in Dakota Territory in which he had invested a large part of his patrimony. He threw himself into the hardy life of the frontier, in the saddle all day, hunting or on the roundup, entering into the struggle for law and order in a community that boasted one of the most efficient horse-rustling rackets between the Mississippi and the Rockies. But his heart was in the East, with his baby at Bamie's, and the house, rising slowly, all too slowly, on Sagamore Hill.

He always stayed with Bamie on Madison Avenue, when he was East, and had a tacit understanding with her that he was to have fair warning when Bamie's friend, Edith Carow, was coming for a meal, or overnight, so he could arrange to be elsewhere.

There was a story behind that, of course.

Theodore had known Edith almost as long as he could remember; since he was three, in fact, and Edith was in the cradle. The Carows lived next to his grandfather on Union Square, and Edith and Theodore's sister Corinne had been wheeled side by side in baby-carriages in the Square. Edith had come and gone constantly in "Thee's" and "Conie's" house, a half-dozen blocks north on Twentieth Street; and Theodore, in Europe when he was nine, had been inclined to be sentimental about her. When "Edie" visited at Tranquillity, the year that "Thee" turned seventeen, it was she he was generally rowing in the smallest boat and the roughest water he could find. She was a girl you could talk to about books and birds and animals, and collecting specimens on the banks of the Nile and meeting odd and delightful human beings in Dresden.

Edith, three years his junior, knew almost as much about books as he did. She had discovered early the New York Society Library on University Place in which her father owned a "share." All the Carows, it seemed, were avid readers, drawing out 648 books over one 28-month period in the late Eighties, or six books a week. The family taste was varied, ranging all the way from Browning's poems, a life of Alfred de Musset and Thoreau's "The Maine Woods," to "The Gilded Age," "Cherry Ripe" and "The Wayward Woman." Which books were Edith's choice is not recorded.

The girls at Miss Comstock's private school on West Fortieth Street, overlooking Bryant Park, couldn't make Edith out. She was pretty, they admitted, wore expensive clothes and wore them well, but she didn't seem interested in the chatter, the tableaux and the parties that thrilled them. She was forever slipping away somewhere with a book.

"Girls," remarked one of her schoolmates in desperation one day, "I believe you could live in the same house with Edith for fifty years and never really know her."

Edith, composed and self-sufficient, would have been inclined to regard that less as a criticism than as a compliment, and to smile with an almost Oriental detachment. People would never have much luck trying to find out what Edith was thinking when she felt there was a reason for them not to know.

Theodore knew her, if anybody did, but it is doubtful if, at eighteen and nineteen and twenty, even he knew the depths of those still waters. They were friends; they enjoyed each other's company. When there were parties, Theodore was Edith's escort. Their friends recognized the relationship and assumed that, when the time came, they would marry; and gathered that Theodore and Edith assumed it too. There was no engagement, nor even, probably, an "understanding." Before Theodore went to college, or shortly after, they had a quarrel; but what it was about they never told. They were still boy and girl—Edith only fifteen—both high-spirited and proud, and neither yet mature; Theodore, dramatically romantic, Edith, unsure of herself, hypersensitive, inclined to suffer agonies over imaginary slights and, like Kipling's famous cat, to "walk by her wild lones." "Her ladyship," as Theodore spoke of her occasionally in his letters to his sisters, had her "good days," moreover, and her "bad days," which may have had a part in their separation.

Theodore met Alice Lee at the home of a classmate, the beginning of his Junior year, and was so swept off his feet by her demure charm, her gaiety and her quick intelligence, as to say to himself that he had never been in love before. Certainly he had never before experienced the flood of passion that Alice awoke in him. Edith went to Chestnut Hill for the wedding on Theodore's twenty-second birthday and by no flutter of an eyelid indicated that it mattered more to her than to any of the other guests. But Alice, settling down with Theodore on West 45th Street, asked her sister-in-law, Corinne, why it was that, with all Theodore's other friends so cordial, she couldn't seem to get anywhere with Edith Carow.

Four years had passed. Alice was dead. People were talking about Edith's aloofness. Apparently, they said, she had made up her mind never to marry. Over a period of a year or a year and a half she and Theodore managed to avoid meeting at Bamie's. Why they should have wanted to evade each other is not clear. They had met frequently during his marriage and apparently felt no strain. Theodore recognized, perhaps, since Alice's death, a new and deeply disturbing reaction toward Edith Carow. The door he had closed would not stay closed. Yet, by all that was holy, it must. Edith, too, could shut doors if she had to, though never so rigorously as Theodore.

One day there was a slip-up somewhere. Edith stayed at Bamie's later than she expected, or Theodore came home earlier; or, perhaps, he returned from the ranch without letting Bamie know. In the hall, suddenly, he and Edith confronted each other. Taken unawares, neither had time to put up any defenses. The door they had closed and put their backs against dissolved in the blazing light that suddenly suffused them.

Perhaps neither spoke; or, more likely, Edith said, "Good evening. How do you do?" and was out of the door and down the steps before Theodore caught his breath.

But they did not try to avoid each other after that.

4

Theodore continued to shuttle back and forth between New York and Dakota, punching cattle and hunting; writing articles on ranch-life, charmingly, and a biography, superficially; besides taking a flier in the publishing business, to nobody's satisfaction. He was out of politics and saw no chance of getting back.

The house on Sagamore Hill was completed—to the point, at

least, where he could move in. Bamie deserted her own house in New York to take command of Sagamore, and soon a stream of guests was justifying the twelve bedrooms. All that was society on the North Shore, or played polo or followed the hounds, sooner or later climbed the winding road through the locust grove on horse-back or in their surreys and high-wheeled traps, and drew up under the porte-cochère.

Life was gay at Sagamore those first years of its existence, gay when Theodore was there, and gay when he wasn't. He was spend-ing next to nothing at the ranch, he wrote Bamie, and he wanted her to invite all their friends and give them a good time. Bamie took him at his word and reported to him on the "jolly parties" at Sagamore. When he was there he joined in the fun. There were dances that spread from the parlor into the hall and out on the broad west piazza; dances that old ladies would still be talking about sixty-five years later.

He rode, he chopped wood, he followed the artful fox. He liked the challenge and excitement of hunting to hounds, the speed, the risk, the combination of physical capacity, daring and skill re-quired. He liked the colorful picture; the riders in pink coats on horses as eager for the sport as their masters, the pack baying and no less intent on the chase, the gallery of smartly dressed women in drags and tandems to wish their husbands, brothers or lovers some-thing better than a broken neck. That spring and fall of 1885 he rode seven or eight times, and only twice was not in at the death.

One sparkling day the Meadowbrook and Essex hunts met at Sagamore Hill, with thirty-five horsemen in the field, hard riders all. At a five-foot fence that had staggered the best of them Theo-dore's horse struck the top rail and rolled over on his side on a pile of stones. Theodore's face was dripping blood, but he remounted and, by hard riding, managed to be in at the death, not a hundred yards behind the leaders, "no thing of beauty and an object of considerable concern to his friends," as the New York *Times* put it next day, "but thoroughly pleased with himself." He viewed the affair, indeed, as mainly comic in character. He was always willing to pay the piper when he had had a good dance, he told his friend, Henry Cabot Lodge, and now and then it was good to drink the wine of life with brandy in it. A friend, seeing him ride back to Sagamore Hill after the hunt, noted the court plaster covering most of his face, but assumed he had merely been scratched, since he

12

stopped to greet little Alice, who was at the stable with her nurse, and, when she fled in terror from his bloody visage, pursued her, laughing. After Theodore had entered the house, a prominent physician, who had taken part in the hunt, galloped up, his horse in a lather, and asked anxiously whether Theodore had come home, and how he was getting along.

The guest reported what he had seen.

"Why, man," exclaimed the doctor, "he broke his arm when his horse went down!"

5

Meanwhile, Theodore was seeing Edith now and again, and their friends were beginning to exchange comments about it. Fanny Smith, who had grown up with Corinne and Edith and Theodore and was quicker than most people to discern hidden currents, gathered that Theodore was shocked at the thought that he could love any woman besides Alice; and that Edith was shocked too. Both had grown up in the tradition of romantic love. A man loved a woman, a woman loved a man, unto death—and beyond. Of course, men and women were constantly remarrying, but the ideal remained, and, if you considered yourself in the great tradition, you held to it—if you could. To be able to love another after the loved one had died—and within a period of less than two years—was a kind of infidelity that Theodore had not dreamed he could be guilty of. His world rocked under his feet. Could a man of loyalty and honor, such as he believed himself to be, experience what he was experiencing? Edith shared his dismay. But on the 17th of November, 1885, they became engaged.

They kept the news to themselves, dreading the lifted eyebrows of their friends. Meanwhile, the death of Edith's father brought her family financial reverses, and her mother took her and her sister Emily abroad, where ladies in straitened circumstances could live "respectably," even comfortably. Throughout that spring and summer of 1886, Theodore was in the Bad Lands, returning East to accept a Republican nomination for the mayoralty of New York and to fight a campaign in which defeat was inevitable. Early in November he wrote his friends that he was about to sail for England to marry Edith Carow, and was out of the country before the chatter could affect him. They were married in London, early in

13

December, a delightful Englishman, Cecil Spring-Rice, as best man, and Emily Carow as the other witness.

They had just returned from a four-month honeymoon on the Continent when, that March day in 1887, Theodore took Edith for the first time to Sagamore Hill.

Chapter II

THEY WOKE the sleeping house in May, spending happy days placing Edith's furniture and the handsome dining-table, sideboard and chairs they had picked up in Florence before news reached them that Dakota's worst winter in fifty years had almost wiped out Theodore's substantial cattle investment. They had had dark moments in Italy wondering whether they would have to sell Sagamore Hill and live for a time on the ranch. But, with a baby coming, a Dakota winter was out of the question, and, in the fragrant airs that blew across the hill, Edith took gaily the harsh fact that she would have to run the house on just about one half of what Bamie had spent when she was its mistress.

It was no time before they were settled, with a cook in the kitchen, a waitress, a chambermaid and (in charge of Alice) a factotum from the Carow family, Mary Ledwith, called "Mame," who had come from Ireland in a sailing-vessel and had guided Edith's infant steps. For a couple who had thought that their future fortunes were so desperate that only a long hibernation in the wilderness could restore them, the set-up was substantial, and to a later generation might seem fairly luxurious. But the household pay-roll was barely sixty dollars a month. There were a farmer, Noah Seaman, and a boy, whose wages together equaled those of the servants. Two "woolly horses," as Theodore described them, did yeoman's work on the farm, and there were two riding-horses, Sagamore, a magnificent hunter whom Theodore cherished as one of his dearest possessions, and Caution, who doubled as a buggy-horse and nearly upset Theodore and Edith on one of their first drives. There was a dog, Peter, and what Theodore called a "jolly" rowboat. That was Sagamore Hill when its new life began in May, 1887.

It was a very satisfying life, and from the first the rowboat played a big part in it. Theodore would row Edith to a distant headland where they would have their lunch, or to a great marsh, filled with lagoons and curious winding channels through which the tide ran like a mill-race; or to Lloyd's Neck, with Theodore portaging the skiff across into Huntington Harbor, a tough haul. They would read Browning to each other, or Matthew Arnold, or Thackeray, or Clough, of whom Edith was fonder than Theodore. "Ideal" days —and if there were blisters and stiff muscles afterward, who cared?

Theodore wrote Bamie of "spasms of sociability" in which the "male oysters" participated, with riding, tennis and rifle-shooting: but, on the whole, the newly wedded pair spent the summer quietly, "befitting our straitened finances." Edith was glad of an excuse to await the baby alone with Theodore and books, or alone with books when Theodore was chopping in the woods or in his study on the top floor writing a biography of Gouverneur Morris, answering the critics of his recently published life of Thomas Hart Benton or "giving the mugwumps something to howl over." She needed books as she needed air and food, consumed them and absorbed them, adding their life to hers.

Alice, bright, lovable, and in what her father called "uproarious health," made an adorable third. A photograph taken that year reveals an imperious young lady in a pose comically like the one captured by the great John S. Sargent in his portrait of her father as President. Here was assurance; here was command. Theodore was her slave. Carrying her down to breakfast pig-a-back every morning became a ritual, resulting shortly, he wrote Bamie, in Alice's "invoking me, with unintentional irreverence, as 'Now, pig'!"

Another cherished delight that Alice claimed on all occasions was "playing Sagamore" (referring to the horse, not the hill), and Theodore wrote of "cavorting and prancing with that young lady on my back," one Sunday morning on the piazza, "until I feared I would incapacitate myself for church." When the weather kept her indoors, Theodore built her innumerable houses of blocks, peopling them with imaginary beings whose picturesque personalities and dramatic adventures made the little girl's eyes shine. The independent young lady was not easily coerced, even in fun. On the eve of one of her departures to visit her grandparents at Chestnut Hill, "looking just like a little white penguin," Theodore wrote his sister, all her father's efforts to work on her feelings brought nothing but a gleeful smile.

16

Out of her big Irish heart, that summer of 1887, Mame summed up the happy trio on Sagamore Hill: "Such a lovely family!"

2

It ceased being a trio at two-fifteen in the morning of September 13th when the baby arrived, a boy, weighing eight and a half pounds. They called him Theodore, as a matter of course. "We were pretty nearly caught badly," his father wrote Bamie. The doctor, J. West Roosevelt, who happily also lived on Cove Neck, arrived in time, but not the nurse; and Theodore's beloved Aunt Annie Gracie came "across lots" and took charge. So it was a family party. Alice was in heaven, with "my own little brother," and would not let her rocking-chair be moved from the cribside. "*My* little brother's a howling polly parrot," she boasted, which her father agreed was a truthful observation.

The baby ate and slept and grew; a "very merry lovable little fellow," who soon was crawling about the floor, his father wrote Bamie, "just like one of Barnum's little seals. According to his lights he plays more vigorously than anyone I ever saw."

3

The children were not alone on Sagamore Hill in experiencing the pangs and satisfactions of growth. Home for Theodore was a place where guests were always coming and going, bringing each his or her contribution of personality or ideas or both. He needed people to talk to and to draw out, and to utter his opinions to on a thousand subjects, from politics to birds, the beauty of the blood-root "glowing like a tender flame" on a neighboring hillside, the idiosyncrasies of the weasel and the shortcomings of the Democratic administration in Washington. He had a new project, moreover, that he was full of, since it promised to satisfy his passionate Americanism, his love of heroic action and his hope—"I suppose," he wrote a friend, "a mere dream"—to write "some book that would really take rank as in the very first class." It was a history of the winning of the area between the Alleghenies and the Mississippi, and he was beginning to gather material for it. All these matters were boiling in him and setting the lid dancing. He wanted to talk and talk and talk. And did.

There were house-guests in quick succession, as well as neighbors dropping in for tennis or a bout on the rifle-range and staying for dinner or tea with duets in the evening. Edith liked people, but not in a steady stream or too many at a time. She was by nature reserved; she shrank from strangers. She had her definite likes and dislikes, moreover—on excellent grounds, as a rule—and sharply resented intrusion of any sort. Her idea of home was a place to withdraw into from the noise and push of crowds and the inquisitive eyes of people who were always trying to find out what you were thinking, and criticizing you because you foiled them. Home was a place for books and pictures and children and open fires, and evenings when your husband read aloud to you or told stories of the hunting-trail and of queer frontier characters who were his friends.

Their differing conceptions of what a home should be constituted a major point of adjustment those first years of their marriage. Edith remembered it twenty years later. "One should not live to oneself," she wrote her son Theodore. "It was a temptation to me, only Father would not allow it. Since I have grown older and realize that it is a great opportunity when one has a house that one can make pleasant for younger—and also older—people to come to, I have done better."

All the adjustments were not on her side. Edith, from the first, saw to that, as Theodore himself testified in a letter he wrote his eldest son at the time of his engagement, as a special word of counsel to the girl he was to marry: "Greatly though I loved Mother, I was at times thoughtless and selfish, and if mother had been a mere unhealthy Patient Griselda I might have grown set in selfish and inconsiderate ways. Mother, always tender, gentle and considerate, and always loving, yet, when necessary, pointed out where I was thoughtless, instead of submitting to it. Had she not done this, it would in the end have made her life very much harder, and mine very much less happy."

So, in the painful give-and-take of intelligent and fearless personalities, both grew, and their comradeship deepened.

4

Theodore was in Washington in October, 1889, having accepted a post on the United States Civil Service Commission, when he received a telegram from home saying that a second baby, which had not been expected for several weeks, had arrived and was a boy. He took the next train to New York, but arrived at the East 34th Street ferry too late to catch the last train to Oyster Bay. Undaunted by the time-table or the low state of his exchequer, he crossed to Long Island City and chartered a special train—to Edith's affectionate fury!—arriving at Sagamore at four in the morning.

When "the little brother in a blanket," as Ted called Kermit, was christened, Ted was more vocal than the baby. What was "the man" wearing "Mame's clothes" for? The reference was to the Reverend Washburn's surplice. When the baby cried, Ted announced, "Baby bruvver Kermit miaous," and was removed across the hall to the library before his penetrating comments completely broke up the solemnity of the occasion.

Alice mothered the newcomer. Ted eyed him with suspicion, but recognized an elder brother's responsibility. Whenever Kermit wandered off into forbidden territory, Ted pursued him officiously and dragged him back, literally by the neck, an act of authority which the younger failed wholly to appreciate. Kermit had more of his mother's qualities than his father's, preferring the dimness of a shaded room with his mother, any day, to the brightness and activity of outdoors with anyone else.

Ted, on the other hand, loving, high-tempered but never bearing grudges—and looking, in his big spectacles, like a wiry, very active brownie—was his father's shadow. He haunted the big room on the top floor which filled the western gable. Theodore had chosen it as his work-shop, partly because it was more detached from the comings-and-goings of the household than the library near the front door, partly for the elbow-room he craved for his restless body and the vistas his hungry eyes required of woods and fields on one side, the Bay on another, the Sound and the blue line of Connecticut on a third. For the good of his soul he needed wide views, and all things spacious.

The architects' plan had designated the room archly as "the den," but Ted called it the "gun-room," and the name stuck. There was a case against the wall, in fact, filled with his father's firearms. Thirty years later, Ted remembered the three shot-guns—two of them ancient, almost prehistoric—and the collection of modern rifles; the Arab scimitars in frayed plush scabbards on the wall, the glass-covered groups of birds his father had collected in Egypt

19

as a boy of eleven, the brace of inlaid dueling pistols in a mahogany box and another brace of six-shooters with carved ivory butts— "relics of the time when Father as a young man wished to dress as well as act the part of a dashing young cattleman." The game-heads on the wall, the skins on the floor, were alive to the boy, and he listened entranced to the stories his father told of the adventures that had made the trophies worth the winning.

Opposite the gun-case was a door leading to the crawl-space between the rafters and the floor that seemed to Ted and Alice, and later to their brothers and sister, a mysterious and dangerous cavern of no-one-knew-what treasures, since, scattered about it, were cartridge boxes, leather cases, ramrods, old pistols, and all the paraphernalia a sportsman accumulates. Its musty smell and the stifling, dry, hot air in summer only added to its charms for children who learned early that life was meant for adventure.

Theodore let Ted and Alice browse through his illustrated books, his "Paradise Lost," his "Nibelungenlied," with heroic warriors in combat, and told them of Washington crossing the Delaware, and of Lincoln and Farragut. He romped with them, night and morning, slipped them the icing off his cake at tea-time when their mother wasn't looking, played with them in the old Revolutionary hay-barn, climbed trees with them or took them down the sharp declivity of Cooper's Bluff, Ted happily returning "piggy-back." "He delights in carrying a tin sword, at present, even in his romps," Theodore wrote Edith's mother, Mrs. Carow, who, with her other daughter, Emily, was living in Italy. "It is an awe-inspiring sight to see him, when Alice has made a nice nest in a corn-stack, take a reckless header in after her, with sword and spectacles, showing a fine disregard both of her life and his own."

"Ted is such a piece of quicksilver," Edith wrote Bamie, "that I am in constant anxiety about his life and limb. Theodore thought his neck was broken the other day and declares he will never live to grow up."

Ted loved his father with all his affectionate heart. At Sagamore, the faithful Mame overheard him talking to himself in his bed shortly before his father was due, on one occasion, to arrive from Washington, and stopped to eavesdrop. "A little mufstache," he was murmuring, "and white teeth, and black hair, very short." Something was obviously wrong with his color-sense, for his father's hair was sandy-colored. "A nice smell of cologne," Ted went on.

"And wears glasses and gray trousers. And white feet with bones in them and red slippers. And that's my Papa."

Next to his father, Ted adored Alice, welcoming her with wild rapture on her returns from her periodic visits to the Lees, her mother's people at Chestnut Hill. The conversations between the two had their comic passages. Once, when the children were failing to quiet down at night, Mame threatened to call their father.

"Yes, Mame," Ted agreed affably. "Call Misser Roosevelt."

"Ted, you little goose," exclaimed Alice, "don't you know that Mr. Roosevelt's papa?"

"Ted is Misser Roosevelt too!" Ted responded jubilantly. Then, suddenly overcome by his own physical shortcomings, he added, "But Ted got no mufstache! Oh, Mame, Mame," he wailed, "Ted got nuffin' but a mouf!"

Mame, one day, overheard Ted and Alice debating the question of their mother's name. Alice said it was "Mother," but Ted insisted it was Edith. Neither was quite clear about her status, Alice expressing great surprise, Edith noted in her journal, "that I was not papa's sister."

There was a week, when Ted was two and a half, when Theodore and Edith knew the terror of the shadow of death. "It has just been heart-breaking," Theodore wrote Bamie, "to have the darling little fellow sick; and the first forty-eight hours I really look back to with a shudder. When he would rally at times and come out of his stupor, and begin to say the cunning things he always says, in his little, changed sick voice, it was about as much as Edith and I could stand."

5

Life took on a new excitement for parents and children alike when a little sister, Ethel, joined the family on Sagamore Hill in August, 1891.

The great event brought the inevitable query.

"How do little babies come?" asked Alice.

Edith executed the customary manœuvre. "God sends them. No one knows exactly how."

"Will we be angels when we get to heaven?" Ted asked, with apparent irrelevance.

21

On this safer ground, his mother could speak with assurance. "Then," said Ted, "we will help God make the little babies."

Ted was maturing rather too quickly, insisting, at four, on his mother's reading him everything that Alice was talking about— Grimm's fairy tales and the Arabian Nights, Longfellow's "The Arrow and the Song," Scott's "Young Lochinvar" and the stag hunt from "The Lady of the Lake"—and was reading his primer "quite nicely," his mother thought, by the time he was five. But she was worried at his nervousness. "It is really painful at times to see how his brain works," she wrote Bamie. "Everything seems to whiz like a clock that has something the matter with it." A certain "irregular independence" of his eyes, which his father had noted when he was born, became a definite squint. He suffered from headaches, which spectacles did not relieve. The family oculist talked of an operation, but Edith shrank from it in horror. "It would be mortal agony to me," she wrote Emily, "to see the knife touch Ted's eyes."

Ted's abnormally quick mind inclined him to look down on Kermit, who had just begun his lessons and was pretending he did not really need them. "Do you think a very young person," asked the elder, from the vantage-ground of a two years' seniority, "can learn his lessons all by himself under the bed?"

Kermit, pale and yellow-haired, was dreamy and detached. Edith wrote her sister of his "big dark eyes, full of poetry, of which he has not a particle in his nature." "Above all his fine toys, his favorite gift"—at Christmas—"was a dustpan he had been begging for, for the last three months, not a toy but a good serviceable size." But "the dreaming eyes of wonder," his mother referred to in another letter, meant more than she had imagined. At three, the moon entranced him and he asked his father to get it for him, insistently repeating, "Better get the moon, Father." He was a good deal of a hermit. "He never need retire to a cloister for a life of abstraction from outside interests," Edith wrote Emily. "I believe I am the only person he really cares for." But he adored a white bunny that had shed most of its fur and another white-furred doll which his mother had brought him from the Alaska Exhibit at the World's Fair in Chicago, and was always bringing them votive gifts of pebbles or flowers.

Ted fairly glowed in his assurance of superior wisdom. Kermit asked his mother whether God made the wasps, and instantly answered his own question. "Course not, because he would get stung."

"Kermit, you little goose," Ted broke in, "God just says, 'Let there be wasps,' and they come."

The children all had measles, the winter that Ted was five. When Mame commented, in Ted's hearing, on the fact that he had got over the attack more quickly than the other children, he remarked, "I just let the measles come in to see the house, but not to stay."

While Alice and Ted were recuperating, their father made them a ram and a monitor apiece, out of pasteboard, and, with the addition of a dozen little lead toy ships that Ted had, fought the battle of Mobile Bay for them with Admiral Farragut as hero. "They were, of course, absorbed spectators," their father wrote his mother-in-law. "In the battle Ted's monitor was sunk; and, as soon as I left to dress, Ted began the battle over again, Alice looking on from the bed. This time Ted intended that Alice's monitor should sink, while Alice was alert to see that no such variation took place."

As the crisis of the battle approached, Ted, running actively round, announced, "And now bang! goes a torpedo, and Sisser's monitor sinks!"

Alice would not have it. "No, it didn't sink at all!" she insisted. "My monitor always goes to bed at seven, and now it's three minutes past!"

6

Alice worried Edith, suffering intense pain in her ankles and having to wear braces. She was a good sport about it, and the other children regarded the braces as rather a mark of distinction. But she was "looking white and wretchedly," most of the time, Edith wrote her sister. "My only comfort is in the recollection of what Theodore was as a child."

Alice also presented temperamental difficulties. More than most children, she was skittish in the face of discipline and disinclined, Edith wrote her sister, "to do anything unless she is made to." Edith attributed the child's tendency to revolt to her periodic visits to the Lees, who exercised the prerogatives of grandparents to expend in three weeks, on a dead daughter's entrancing child, a half-year's accumulated hunger to have a part in her life. "I do dread getting her upset from all her sweet little ways," Edith wrote Bamie, "by that unavoidable visit."

Alice was delightfully unpredictable. At nine, she decided she was tired of being a girl, gave up her intention (frequently announced in mixed company) of shortly having twins, and decided that she wanted to wear trousers and possess a monkey. But at ten, she began to grow up. "She is no longer the quiet and mousy person," Edith wrote Bamie, "but a great romping girl who comes home full of stories about her school. More seems to happen in those two hours!" "I read her some poetry, generally Scott's, before dinner, which she really delights in," Theodore wrote his sister, during a period when Edith was ill and confined to her room, "and she then chatters away and tells me all the children have done, with a really considerable sense of humor."

Never, in these hours of happy fellowship, alone together, did he speak to Alice of her own mother. Never once, indeed, at any time, would he speak of her to their child. That door in his heart was locked, and Alice would never find the key.

She did not, in fact, look very hard. Life was too exciting in the present to let her wonder much about the past.

7

Ethel was a character from the beginning, with a will of her own and a sharp sense of what was right and what wasn't, so far as she was concerned. Theodore described her at fourteen months as "a jolly, naughty, whacky baby, too attractive for anything, and thoroughly able to hold her own in the world." At two, the little girl seemed to her mother "the merriest baby you can imagine and so fat she waddles when she tries to run . . . very bright but not in the least nervous like Ted . . . just a sturdy Dutch baby with quick intelligence." At three, Ethel was "too overpowering," her mother wrote Emily, "for any but those with strongest physique and robust health to grapple with. . . . She orders everyone around . . . and will beat me if I refuse her the box of cream . . . and then kiss me the next second." She ate a toadstool and swallowed a bottle of nitre without noticeable effect that summer, and clamored to be allowed to "pick strawberries from the cherry-tree." Theodore called her "Elephant Johnnie." When she was moved into what her mother called "the gregarious nursery," she made her own way against Alice and the two boys, ruling Kermit with a rod of iron, though he was two years her senior.

All the children, Edith wrote her sister, "do have the most happy times together," and were at one in their devotion to their father and mother, Alice with the others. When, the summer that Ted was approaching five, Edith was about to leave Sagamore to be with Theodore in Washington for a week, the boy lay across the library table pretending to read a book but actually struggling to suppress the tears.

The father's occasional visits to Sagamore in the summers were occasions of breathless anticipation. "I wish you could see the children all dancing on the piazza when I drive up after an absence," Theodore wrote Mrs. Carow, "and the politeness with which they strive to ignore the attractive looking bundle which they know contains toys."

8

When Archie was born one April midnight in Washington, in 1894, he made so little fuss about it that Mame, sleeping upstairs with the other children, was unaware of the event. Theodore climbed the stairs to tell her. Ted awoke and waked Alice and they sat on Mame's bed, "chattering like parroquets," their father wrote Bamie, "and hugging two darkey ragdollies which they always take to bed." When he let them slip downstairs and for a minute hold the new baby, they agreed that it was "better than Christmas."

Kermit, four and a half, wasn't so sure, but Ethel was overjoyed. "Lend me that little Archibald baby," she commanded. When, finally, Kermit too had held the new little brother, he admitted that he loved him, "because," he explained, "he has such berry tiny feet." But he insisted that he still preferred the cherished "dushtpan."

Kermit developed trouble in his knee the summer after Archie was born, and the weight of the brace he was given wore perceptibly on the boy's strength and spirit. "It is heart-breaking," Theodore wrote Bamie, "to see the poor little fellow sitting still and looking at the other children play." The Gracies, Theodore's Aunt Annie and her husband, living on an adjoining estate, offered Kermit refuge for a while from the hullabaloo of the Sagamore nursery. Mame went with him, his mother visited him twice a day, and now and again the other children paid him a call. The result was all that Edith hoped for. "My little Kermit is so good and patient," she wrote Bamie. "The other day, he said 'Mother I am so glad you haven't this. I shouldn't like you to be uncomfortable. I would rather be so myself.' "

Kermit, at five, revealed an inquiring mind and a quick imagination. After inspecting a Cupid he asked his father "why that little boy has nothing on but a tape measure?" He had a child of his fancy whom he called Peter, besides his real doll, a muslin owl called Bogey Boy. One day Peter "died." "Peter," Kermit explained to his mother, "could just walk and talk a little and was cunninger than Bogey Boy, just as Archie is cunninger than Ethel or me." He was in perpetual rows with Ethel, who had a way, her father noted, of "doing everything and managing everybody." The summer that Ethel was three she and Kermit celebrated their father's arrival from Washington for a midsummer visit by a row that was worthy of the occasion. When Ethel finally bit Kermit, that young man stood on his head and thumped her with his steel brace.

But a year later the story was different. Their father was reproving them together one day, speaking especially sternly to Kermit. As he reached down and shook the boy by the shoulder, the tears started streaming down Ethel's cheeks. She touched her father's arm. "Shake *me*, Father," she begged.

Alice's Grandfather Lee gave Edith a substantial check for the children, and she bought them a pony-cart. "It is like a little nest," she wrote Emily, "and they go off chirping like a family of birds."

Chapter III

FATHER, mother, children, it was a very happy family.

The father was a busy man, acting as spark-plug of the Civil Service Commission, fighting the spoilsmen in Congress and the executive departments, going over the country to tell the people what the struggle was all about, pushing ahead his history on "The Winning of the West" as opportunity offered; and doing it all without missing a chance to read to the children or romp with them, mornings and evenings, or take them on rambles, week ends, in Rock Creek Park.

With it all, he wasn't too well, physically, suffering frequently from heavy colds which often became bronchitis and held on for months at a time until, in one case, his heart was affected. A pillow-fight with the children occasionally brought a return of the asthma he had supposedly overcome during his Dakota years. But his energy was undiminished, though his girth was increasing. He played as strenuously as he worked. One afternoon, when his niece Eleanor, his brother Elliott's daughter, was a visitor at Sagamore, "he was a bear," Edith wrote Emily, and "pounced" on the children with such effect "that he tore all the gathers out of Eleanor's frock and both button-holes out of her petticoat."

The mother of the family was as busy as the father. Happily, a snapshot survives, showing Edith, at this point of the family story, in white muslin and balloon sleeves, the long skirt belted at the narrow waist, and, on her chestnut hair, a sailor-hat with a dark band —a slender and very lovely figure under the arching boughs of the Sagamore roadway, with the sun sparkling in the leaves and casting dappled shadows on the road. But her leisurely mood in the picture is deceptive. With five children needing physical care, teaching, companionship, endless sewing and intelligent upbringing generally, her days were packed to the limits of her strength. For in

27

the practical matters of day-to-day living Theodore was not much of a help. Edith recognized this particularly when the family was on its semi-annual migrations between Sagamore Hill and Washington. "Fathers are no help whatever when the family is traveling," she told Ted's wife, many years later. Once, when she was ill, Theodore volunteered to conduct the transfer from Oyster Bay to a temporary abode in New York. He got the five children and two nurses safely by train to Long Island City and across the ferry to East 34th Street. "Then," he told Edith later, "everything became confused." He was walking toward the horse-car, holding Ted and Kermit by the hand, when Ted slipped and fell face down in an enormous puddle. By the time the boy had detached himself from it he was mired from head to foot; his clothes caked; his face and hands unrecognizable, his hair thick with mud. One glance sufficed to tell Theodore that this was a case far beyond any wiping off with handkerchiefs. What to do? What in heaven's name did one do in such circumstances? A good-natured policeman, observing his plight, came to his rescue and scraped the worst of the mud off the boy with a penknife. By the time this operation had been completed the nurses and the three other children had disappeared, and Theodore reached the family lodgings with Ted a "sight" and the rest of his party mislaid.

"The best advice I can give you," Edith told her daughter-in-law, "is always to let your husband go by another train, so you will have nothing to attend to but the children."

Theodore gladly admitted her superior ability on such expeditions as in other matters. "Sweetest and best of wives and mothers," he described her to Mrs. Carow a month after Ted's fifth birthday, "and I really believe I shall be always just as much in love with her as when we were married." Edith's devotion to Theodore defied the years no less. When in 1894 the reform element in New York City offered the fighting Civil Service Commissioner the nomination as Mayor, Edith refrained from offering advice. But when Theodore, surmising, perhaps, that she preferred staying in Washington where they had established themselves, made a home and had many friends, indicated that he would refuse the nomination, she supported his decision. Only after he had given the committee his answer did she recognize how much he had really wanted the nomination and how much her own too evident, though unspoken, inclinations had determined his decision. In an agonizing letter, she wrote Bamie that she had "failed him" and "helped to spoil some years of a life which I would have given my own for." If only she had known how much the offer meant to him, "I should have thrown all my influence in the scale, and helped instead of hindering him." Theodore had been "so sweet and good" about it, she added, but she was "utterly unnerved, a prey to the deepest despair." Theodore was away for a day or two, she ended, and she would have herself in hand by the time "the darling" got back.

Edith suffered from neuralgia and required more rest than she ever permitted herself. When servants and children together became for the moment too much for her, she found refuge on warm days at Sagamore in a wistaria-covered arbor two hundred yards north of the house, known as "The Nest," overlooking the wide expanse of the Sound. It was a haven of quiet to flee to with a book or a basket of sewing when Mame for an hour or an afternoon stood ready to bear the brunt of the children's innocent and ingenious pandemonium.

She had no such refuge in Washington and had to get her revitalizing hour of quiet on a sofa with one of the children occasionally gently caressing her aching forehead. But for all the busyness of her days, and the headaches, she enjoyed Washington and would not forego the intellectual give-and-take of the dinner-parties once or twice a week when Henry Adams and John Hay, the Cabot Lodges or "Czar" Reed, the powerful Speaker of the House, were frequently among the other guests. With her delicate beauty and gentle spirit; her liking for people, coupled with reserve, that were complementary elements of her charm; her wit, her gift for laconic utterance and evocative listening, she was a perfect foil for her militant, occasionally dogmatic and over-forceful husband, and was a favorite in Washington society. The dinners they themselves gave were simple, making up in intellectual sparkle what they lacked in champagne.

She was as ardent a reader as her husband, and her taste was as catholic as his, though its major direction was different. Theodore liked Sienkiewicz, and the gorier the better; Edith liked Mrs. Gaskell and Jane Austen. Edith left no record of what she thought of Theodore's smiters and hackers, but Theodore was heard to remark that, after reading Jane Austen, he was always conscious that "duty done was a rainbow to the soul." They were companions in the open as well as in the world of books, riding daily when they were at Sagamore and the weather permitted. "Diamond" and "Pickle" were their riding-horses, and when Edith was alone at Sagamore she drove them, hitched to their high-wheeled trap. "They prefer taking opposite sides of the road," she wrote Emily, "but are as good as horse angels."

She never failed, once or twice a week, to write her mother or her sister in Italy, telling them the week's news of the children, their little ailments, and their quaint sayings and doings, describing the clothes that she or Mame or Margaret, the second nurse, was making for them, rejoicing over the happy fortunes of relatives and friends or lamenting their sorrows; and relating crisply the latest gossip of Oyster Bay or Washington. The references to Theodore were the usual references of any wife to any husband—his comings and goings, the dread of parting—"My heart fails when I think of leaving Theodore here"—the joy of reunion. The letters bear eloquent testimony to her impartial love for all the children. Every solicitous or playful reference to Alice indicated that her stepdaughter was no less precious to her than her own children. Edith was, in fact, in frequent touch with Mrs. Lee, Alice's grandmother, and welcomed her to Sagamore Hill for lengthy visits. Mrs. Lee became a kind of adopted grandmother to all the children, who, except for one visit of Mrs. Carow, when they were very small, knew no other grandmother.

The third in importance in the family was Mame, capable, crotchety, and devoted. There was something about Mame in every letter Edith wrote her mother or her sister—her aches and pains, which were many; her devotion, which was constant, and the complications caused by the occasional visits of her sister "Car," even more crotchety than Mame. Exasperated by the rows that Mame was always having with the other maids, the "wars and rumors of wars," as she put it, she recognized that Mame would always be "a difficult element" in her household, and cherished her in spite of it, tending her like a daughter when she was ill, even to the most menial service. Most often her comments took the form of "Mame is very well and happy," or "Mame is wonderful. Long may she wave."

2

A happy family . . . a quiet life, from day to day, with no particular excitement for the children except Christmas and birthdays and the return in spring to Sagamore after the winter exile in Washington; and happily no world-shaking events to agitate their elders. Yet the children's lives were saturated with romance. It was in their exciting father, his fund of thrilling experience, his apparent omniscience. "His knowledge," Ted remembered in later years, "stretched from babies to the post-Alexandrian kingdoms and, what was more, he could always lay his hands on it. It made little difference in what channels the conversation turned. Sooner or later Father was able to produce information which often startled students of the theme under discussion." There was romance in their father's stories of *his* father and his work for the wounded in the Civil War, and of his mother's brothers in the Confederate navy, his stories of his ranching days, his hunting trips, his pursuit of cattle-thieves, his adventures with Indians, bad men and grizzly bears. There was romance for the children in their lovely mother, too, in their father's devotion to her and in her accounts of her childhood in the Carow house on Union Square not far from their Great-grandfather Roosevelt's; romance, triply distilled, in the books their father or mother read to them before the blazing fire.

The house itself exuded romance; the game-heads on the walls, the framed original illustrations for their father's hunting-books. Each room, each piece of furniture, however insignificant in itself, seemed to the children to have a history. Their parents' colossal bedroom set had won a prize at the Centennial Exposition in Philadelphia and been bought there by their grandfather. This chair had been acquired "the year your brother Kermit was born," which put it back in the Dark Ages, or this rifle, perhaps, belonged "to the time I met Captain Seth Bullock in Deadwood." Here was a footstool "from your great-grandfather's house on Fourteenth Street," or a rosewood desk "that belonged to your great-aunt Kermit." In their mother's room was a tall mirror that had been so rare a thing when it hung in the Fourteenth Street house that strangers had come to the door asking to be allowed to see it. There was a rug of beaver-skins taken near their father's ranch-house on the Little Missouri in Dakota Territory; and a hide, painted by some Indian artist, giving the Sioux version of the battle of the Little Big Horn. Not a trophy hung on the wall or lay underfoot but had a story.

It seemed to Ted in later years that Sagamore was "the off-spring of the years as surely as is a reef of coral." Each article, he added, "tells a story in the same fashion as the rings in the trunk of a great tree."

There was perennial romance for the children on the eighty acres surrounding the house, the gardens, the fields, the woods, stretching almost unbroken to the Bay and the Sound. A favorite haunt in the woods, a quarter of a mile from the house, was the "wood-pile pond," so named because the winter's firewood which Theodore and the hired man cut was piled there. The children loved the noisome bit of stagnant water and black mud—the pig-sty drained into it —for the countless turtles warming their backs on the rotting logs or paddling slowly through the thick water, their heads, Ted always remembered, "sticking out of the green scum like small periscopes." The old hay-barn, set on a corner where three fences met, was a source of perpetual delight, as was the rambling stable back of the house and architecturally akin to it, being born of the same Victorian fancy. The stable was the domain of Seaman the superintendent, Hall the coachman, and of the crusty old Negro gardener named Davis, and was full of "musty corners and promising mysteries," Ted remembered—old harness, saddles, eel spears and a hundred other "oddments" fascinating to a boy's imagination. Seaman and Hall were friends and playmates; but Davis, bent with age, wrinkled as a withered apple, and hung with rumors of tragedy, was an irritable old party who, for obvious reasons, was known to Alice, Ethel and the boys as "Old Let-it-be."

3

Theodore initiated the children in the wonders, joys and exactions of outdoor life as soon as they could walk. Birds were, from the first, more than just birds to them. They were indigo-buntings or thistle-finches, Baltimore orioles that nested in the young elms around the house, or orchard-orioles in the apple-trees near the garden. The children learned early to recognize beauty when they saw it, in the shy mayflower and the trailing arbutus, the shadblow and the anemones, the laurel and the locust, as in the splendor that flamed over the Bay at sunset. The farm activities were an important element in their lives. In a letter to Bamie, Theodore wrote of Ted, at six, associating himself "on intimate terms of mutual affection and respect" with the men who were harvesting the wheat. To all the children the cows and pigs were personalities, and they were at a loss to understand Mame's hurt feelings when they named a pig for her. Other pets came and went, a guinea-pig and a white rabbit at one time harmoniously occupying a single cage. Horses were a part of their lives, almost from birth, the horses their father and mother rode and their own pony, General Grant, presented to Alice by her Lee grandparents and named after the pony her father had loved in his boyhood. Pony Grant was deeply cherished, except on one occasion when he meditatively started to munch Ted's up-tilted straw hat as the three-year-old was hugging one of his forelegs. His father never forgot the "howl of anguish" the boy set up on the evident assumption that the pony had decided to treat him like a radish. The first of a long line of dog-friends was a Scotch terrier named Jessie, offspring of one of their father's ranch dogs, who rounded the children up when they tended to wander too far into the eighty acres of the farm. Theodore and Edith were alike disinclined to preach *safety-first* to their children, girls or boys. "We have found a large hollow tree," Theodore wrote Bamie when Ethel was just under three, "the hollow starting from a huge opening twenty feet up. The other day, with much labor, I got up the tree, and let each child in turn down the hollow by a rope."

Theodore taught the children to swim by dropping them off the dock into deep water. Ted accepted the ordeal without a qualm, keeping himself up and going like a very active frog. The Spartan custom, however, appalled ten-year-old Eleanor when she visited her cousin Alice. She took her courage in her hands, however, and jumped—and never forgot the good-natured ducking she received as a reward when she came up, sputtering. Alice herself took to the swimming naturally, but shrank from diving. Her father would be treading water a few feet from the float on the edge of which she crouched, trembling. "Dive, Alice," he ordered. "Now, dive!"

"Yes, Father," she would quaver and, finally, more afraid of him than of the water, would flop in.

A tradition developed at Sagamore that, after every diving lesson, Alice's tears brought a perceptible rise in the water-level.

Alice was not the only one of the children whom their father held up to the mark. Theodore was determined to toughen Ted early and took him on tramps through the woods which not only tested the boy's spirit but were occasionally beyond his strength. To Ted his father was a combination of deity and friend, his mythical heroes brought to life, King Arthur and Daniel Boone rolled into one, wearing plus-fours and golf-stockings but no less heroic for that. He could not bear the thought of falling short of what his father expected of him, pushing himself to the limit of his endurance and suffering a wear-and-tear on the nerves which his mother noted with grave misgivings. But Theodore, remembering his own struggle for health and vigor, and grateful to his own father for resisting the temptation to coddle him under the affliction of his boyhood asthma, brushed her warnings aside, convinced that he knew better than she what a boy needed to become a man.

The thrill of the hunt entered early into the children's lives. In an early draft of one of his hunting-stories, Theodore gives a sketch of Ted, one pleasant fall morning, five years old and still in kilts, looking around for adventures worthy of his mettle. "He had just abandoned the nursery, where he found insufficient interest in the society of three-year old Kermit or of Kermit's intellectual peer, Peter, the guinea-pig; and of course the baby—the then baby—didn't count. So he walked down to the porch and looked longingly at the hired man . . ."

A few minutes later, as Theodore was settling himself down to a piece of writing he was engaged on, Ted bustled into the "gun-room" to tell him in great excitement that the hired man had seen a coon in one of the trees near the pond. The news was important since Davis, the colored gardener, had complained about some wild creature which had carried off a number of chickens.

Theodore picked a rifle out of his cabinet and trotted down the road with Ted at his heels, clasping the butt. They found the coon asleep in a hollow of a big blasted chestnut some forty feet from the ground. He was altogether too near the chicken coops to remain where he was, and Theodore brought him down. Ted pounced on him gleefully and they returned to the house, each holding a hind leg of the quarry.

On a cold Thanksgiving Day, two years later, Theodore was in the woods with Ted and Kermit chopping out a bridle-path which had become choked with fallen timber. On their way home after sunset their large yellow dog, a male whom the children insisted on calling Susan, treed a possum. Their father had in the past been reluctant to kill "such an absurd creature" and had come to regret his tender feelings. This time he shot. As the possum fell to earth, Kermit remarked, "This is the first time I have seen a fellow killed."

He felt, it seemed, "as if it was much like any other homicide," his father wrote Bamie, "but much approved of it."

4

Theodore and Edith taught all the children, girls as well as boys, the importance not only of hardihood but of obedience. Neither had any hesitancies about corporal punishment. They found that they did not have to administer it often—and Theodore was invariably the agent of its application—but recognized an "absolute necessity" to let children know that at need a heavy hand would come into action. Each child, in turn, they found, had to feel the hand once before he understood that his father would unhesitatingly apply it if he had to. After that, Theodore and Edith observed that firmness and justice, coupled with a meticulous regard for promises, generally forestalled any further necessity for extreme measures.

Both Theodore and Edith believed in robust righteousness, and let poetry and fiction re-enforce their own teachings and the Biblical passages they cherished, notably one about doing justly, loving mercy and walking humbly with your God. There was a quotation from Browning that Theodore hammered into the children early in support of the New Testament injunction about being "doers of the word and not hearers only." It was from "The Flight of the Duchess" and had brought a turning-point in his own childhood. There was a certain young duke, a poor scion of an illustrious line, whose ambition was etched in acid in the lines:

> "All that the old dukes had been, without knowing it,
> This duke would fain know he was, without being it."

Those lines had brought Theodore up short when he was a boy, and he passed them on to his children. It was all right to dream heroic dreams, but they would do well to start early to translate them into action.

"The Pilgrim's Progress" was familiar to all the children long before they could read and, all his life, Ted associated the book with the comfortable upholstered rocking-chair in a corner of his mother's room, in which she sat as she read it. A shabby brown sofa in the library, on which he would sit with his father when he read aloud, similarly brought back memories of "Ivanhoe."

While Theodore was dressing for dinner, evenings, he would teach

35

the children poetry inculcating love of country and admiration for heroic action and, by day, unostentatiously and casually hammered in those "pioneer" virtues he never missed a chance of recalling to his fellow citizens. Accompanying his father to the Civil Service Commission's office, Ted had his first lessons in history at the point of his father's umbrella, drawing battle-maps in the dust of the street. In her own fashion, Edith backed up her husband, not with stories or homilies or historical dramatizations, but by the impression she gave the children that the brave, the disciplined, the considerate thing was the self-respecting thing to do. The day-by-day example of both parents interpreted their precepts beyond any mistaking.

Both combined intuition and understanding of child psychology with sincere respect for each child as an individual. Neither commanded; they advised. Freedom, they knew, was the inalienable right of childhood, and they gave the children all they could safely deal with. They expected truthfulness. "The truth, the truth! Be quicker with the truth!" the father would exclaim when one of the children might try to evade an unhappy fact; but, on unimportant matters, both the father and mother were careful never to expect or demand too much. They respected the plans the children made and possessed a quick understanding of times and seasons when, and when not, to cross them with their own or look the other way. Long after, a contemporary of their children, Earle Looker, drew a picture of Quentin's mother: "She knew that her adult motives could not entirely be her guide," recognizing those moments when outside suggestions would be rejected and bring the opposite effect of what she desired. "Her judgment in these matters was keen because she was alive to the hourly changes of pitch of childhood spirit." So deep was the children's recognition of her intuitive understanding that one of her sons was heard to remark, "When Mother was a little girl, she must have been a boy!"

In all that the father and mother taught the children, directly or through songs and stories, of the need of courage and moral stamina, they never failed to stress the importance of that combination of strength and tenderness which must neither suffer wrong nor inflict it. The children must stick up for their own rights; but also they must be compassionate to the weak and quick to defend them against any who sought to harm them. The first aspect of the injunction penetrated ahead of the second. Shortly after Theodore

36

told his eldest that he must be willing to fight if anyone insulted him, wails of grief were heard coming from the nursery. Edith ran upstairs and, finding Kermit howling in a corner, demanded an explanation of Ted.

"Kermit insulted me," he declared.

"How did he insult you?"

"He took away some of my blocks."

"What did you do?"

"I hit him over the head with my rabbit," the rabbit being a mechanical toy.

Theodore made clear to all the children, but especially to the boys, that a willingness to stand up for their rights, essential as it was, was not enough. There must be initiative also, even aggressiveness, in well-doing. There must be no cheating, no cutting of corners; but there must be drive. He used a figure, borrowed from the football-field: "Hit the line hard; don't flinch or foul, but hit the line hard." The words sank deep into the children's subconscious.

Ted became greatly excited when his mother told him that the cuckoo laid its eggs in other birds' nests and the bad little cuckoo pushed out the little birds that belonged there. He fastened his eyes on his mother, crying, "I will get a sword and *thrust him through!*"

"Where do you suppose," Edith asked Bamie, "children pick up such expressions?"

Where, indeed?

In so strenuous a household someone was always getting hurt, and learning to take it in his stride. Theodore himself took a fall again and again in the local polo matches, returning home with his face battered and bleeding. He was inclined to bleed heavily when he bled, and Edith became accustomed to seeing him bathed in gore. The summer of Ted's fourth birthday, his father one day noticed that the windmill that pumped the water for the house had stuck. He got an oil-can, and climbed the sixty-foot derrick. Just as he reached the top, the wind veered. The paddle swung round and, as Theodore himself described it, twenty years later, "took off a slice of my scalp."

He climbed down blindly, and by the time he reached the ground his face and shoulders were drenched with blood.

In the front hall he met Edith. The gory sight, which might have sent another woman into hysterics or a faint, did not appear to affect her in the least. "Theodore," she said in a bored voice, "I wish you'd do your bleeding in the bathroom. You're spoiling every rug in the house."

5

The growth of the family—they were seven when Archie joined them—had delights, not one of which Theodore or Edith would have missed at any price, but the price was proving pretty high, even though the Lees provided everything for Alice. Theodore had inherited about $125,000 from his father, of which about a third had gone glimmering in the Bad Lands. His $3,500 salary as Civil Service Commissioner was modest even by the standards of the 1890's, and they had not only to rent a house to live in, but move the household back and forth twice a year, itself a staggering item. The problem became no easier when Theodore accepted a reform administration's appointment as president of the New York Police Board, and settled in the city for the winter. "Theodore and I will not have two pennies to put together if we stay here," Edith wrote Emily. "It is expensive even to breathe."

Edith admitted to her sister that she and Theodore had had their financial troubles, "though we are much ashamed of it. It takes a great many pounds of beefsteak at twenty-five cents a pound to fill three little mouths," not to speak of the two chickens a week in soup that Ethel required.

The friends who were inclined to think Theodore cocksure, and convinced of the righteousness of his own actions in all places and at all times, would have been surprised to know of the black moments of doubt which he occasionally suffered. Had he really done wisely in devoting himself to writing and the public service? "The trouble is that my career has been a very pleasant, honorable and useful career for a man of means," he wrote Bamie, "but not the right career for a man without the means." If they ran behind, another year, he added, there was nothing for it but to sell Sagamore Hill, a terrifying prospect. "Theodore says the children will have reason to reproach him for not having entered a money-making profession," Edith wrote her sister when Ted was three, "but this, of course," she added, "is nonsense." Edith herself wanted not less public service of him, but a more dependable continuity of it than appointive office provided. Her dream for him was election to Congress, "but I fear," she wrote, "that is a dream never to be realized."

Edith ran the family finances. Theodore had never had to make his own livelihood, and money had none of the reality to him that a horse had, or a rifle, a deer, a bird, a spoils politician, or a frigate sunk a hundred years under the waves. It was a constant marvel to him that Edith should know so much about this mysterious, this elusive thing and, with a sigh of relief, he gave her full charge of his own share of it, claiming for himself each morning only such an amount as he might need to carry him through the day. A friend met him in a bookshop in the act of buying a book and laughing at the discovery that he had only twenty-five cents in his pocket. "Every morning," he told his friend, "Edie puts twenty dollars in my pocket, and, to save my life, I never can tell her afterward what I did with it!"

Edith's account books give in detail the story of the finances of the Sagamore Hill family. The wages Edith paid in 1890 were fantastically low by the standards of the succeeding generations (as her granddaughters would ruefully note), but she paid them to an astonishing number: a farmer, a gardener and a coachman; a cook and a waitress; a nurse; a maid, a chambermaid, a laundress and a furnaceman. For this magnificent establishment she averaged only $210 a month, but the establishment obviously had to be fed, and fed well. The meat bill in 1890 ran from $29 in September to $119 in May. The local grocery bills, with the bills from Park & Tilford in New York, from whom Edith bought her staples, ran from $35 up. Coal and wood cost up to $300 a year. Milk came under the farm expense at Sagamore, but in Washington ran to $35 a month. With babies arriving and all the children having the usual ailments, doctors' bills were high—in 1890, a total of $383; the next year, $556. Regarding clothes the account book is reticent. The Altman bills seldom ran over $30 a month, which was remarkable in view of Edith's rapt interest in clothes, revealed by her letters to Emily, which were full of detailed descriptions of the clothes she was having made and the bargains she had secured. Once, after the Spanish War, when the family fortunes mended, she plunged, paying $188 at Altman's for a "beautiful dinner gown" reduced from $325; but as a rule she was sternly economical, taking out her joy in clothes in minute descriptions of ingenious adjustments, that she and the seamstress made to the children's clothes and her own. She had, in fact, no choice.

When Theodore, to his great relief, sold a field to his Uncle James, Kermit, aged four, asked his mother why he had done it.

"To get bread and butter for the bunnies," Edith answered.

The boy was much impressed. "If we hadn't *any* bread and butter, I know Auntie Bye would sell *her* field, for she loves us berry much." Auntie Bye was Theodore's beloved "Bamie," and the children were devoted to her.

6

Summers at Sagamore were always what Theodore called "the seventh heaven of delight" for the children, for Cove Neck fairly seethed with cousins. Each of the Sagamore children had a cousin his own age at "Yellowbanks," the home of Theodore's cousin Emlen Roosevelt, or at "Waldeck," where the J. West Roosevelts lived. Alice had the Emlen Roosevelts' daughter Christine and Ted her brother George. Kermit had George's brother John; Ethel, the West Roosevelts' Lorraine; and Archie, her brother Nicholas. Frequently other cousins came—Elliott Roosevelt's Eleanor or Corinne Robinson's Teddy or Monroe or Corinne the second, or others farther removed. Eleanor was a good deal on Edith's mind. "Poor little soul, she is very plain," she wrote Bamie. "Her mouth and teeth seem to have no future, but, as I wrote Theodore, the ugly duckling may turn out to be a swan."

Life at Sagamore took on a new thrill for "the bunnies" and their cousins, with its guiding spirit—never fuller of "life and energy," Edith thought—able to be with them week ends, and occasionally mornings and evenings. Whenever he had a day off he went for a ride or a row with Edith, or took the children to the beach where Roosevelt cousins from adjoining estates generally joined the Sagamore family and added to the excitement. The bathing-suits were in keeping with the period: Theodore's, a one-piece garment buttoned down the front, with little half-sleeves coming just below the shoulders; Edith's including pantalettes that came down to her ankles, and, covering them, heavy skirts.

When Theodore was in charge there was generally the familiar game of "stagecoach," with original trimmings, one child as "the whip," another as the "nigh leader," a third "the off-wheeler," a fourth "the old lady passenger," and so on, in the thrilling story which "the grown-up of buoyant temperament and inventive mind," as Theodore described himself, would improvise. As a particular object was mentioned, the child representing it was supposed to dive off the float. When, finally, Theodore uttered the word "stage-coach," everybody was supposed to go overboard, and the water fairly foamed with vigorously kicking little legs. For Theodore there was a moment of interest, unshared by the children, while he made sure "that the number of heads that came up corresponded with the number of children who had gone down."

Occasionally, at dusk, Theodore and Edith liked to slip out of the house and, escaping for an hour from all family responsibilities, enjoy a dip alone. For both, those stolen hours were forever memorable and, fifty years later, Edith, writing her eldest son of hearing "a chorus of evening song from the wood thrushes in Turnip Patch Woods," recalled "the days when Father and I used to walk up the path thru the woods after bathing, just at the hour when their songs were particularly musical."

It was the year that Ted was nine that Theodore gave him his first gun, a Flobert rifle. Ted was roaming about the farm somewhere when his father arrived with it, and became aware of his good fortune only when he went to the room where his father was dressing for dinner. He fell on the rifle with a delight that was matched by his father's. "I wanted to see it fired to make sure it was a real rifle," Ted wrote in his book of family memories. But . . . it would be too dark to shoot after supper "and Father was not dressed to go out at the moment." The elder picked up the rifle and slipped a cartridge into the chamber. "You must promise not to tell Mother." Readily enough, Ted promised, whereupon his father fired the rifle into the ceiling. "The report was slight, the smoke hardly noticeable and the hole in the ceiling so small that our sin was not detected."

That summer his father taught Ted to use the precious gift on the family target-range across a gully to a butt of rough logs with a pit dug nearby. "It was almost as exciting to be snuggled down in the pit and hear the bullets strike the butt as it was to shoot. When practice was over, we children used to dig the spent bullets out of the bank and keep them as treasures."

Periodically, Theodore and Edith gave Bamie, in England, vignettes of the children: Kermit, "turning somersaults on the manure-heap, indeed a joy forever, in his overalls, a cap like a second-rate French cook, a pair of shabby tennis shoes, and, as his hands are poisoned, a pair of exceedingly dirty gloves," but improving in health all the time, laying aside at last the plaguing brace; Ted, riding Pony Grant "with much pluck and an atrocious seat"; Archie, "the sweetest thing you ever saw, perfectly friendly with cows, dogs and horses" and "trying to make his skin-horse say its prayers"; a family picnic with Alice steering one boat and Edith another, and Ted, on the way home, "slumbering peacefully in the bilge water."

Edith's sketches went deeper than Theodore's and said as much about herself as they said about "the bunnies." "Alice is the dearest child, my right hand and companion"; at eleven already a personality, herself and no one else. "Alice would spend her last cent to give Theodore pleasure but I doubt if she could bring herself to make him a pin-cushion." Edith could never be sure what would amuse her. "I took her to 'Robin Hood' and it was a flat failure." Any imposition of discipline put her back up. "Two weeks ago a law like unto the laws of the Medes and Persians, that she should write a letter every Sunday, came into existence, and was baptized in tears. Alice grows like a weed and Ted grows like a Century Plant, that is, not at all visibly, yet they continue great comrades, and Alice is quite lost if he goes off with the other children. . . . Ted is more like his father every day and Kermit more like himself . . . a funny little fellow, very affectionate, and still babyish, with 'goblin gleams.' Very few outsiders care for him, but if they like him at all they like him very much. Ethel is a general favorite—the greatest little water-baby you can imagine," yet "the most capable little body and, if I lie down on the sofa, she will come and rub my ankles with her pretty little hands." As for Archie, "his face is like a full moon and he is as 'sassy' as Bre'r Rabbit. . . . I call him the fairy child and tell Margaret"—Mame's assistant—"if she heats the shovel and puts him on it he will fly up the chimney."

Ethel was overheard one day teaching Archie the social graces: "Now, Archie, put your hand on your stomach and bow." Solemnly the boy put his hand on his stomach and bowed. From day to day, the children unfolded new devices to keep their parents out of the ruts of routine. Kermit was losing his baby teeth but developed the habit of keeping the rocking tooth in place until its removal could serve worthily the cause of family entertainment. That was generally at the Sunday morning service in church. During the sermon he would give the final yank and hold the gory specimen up for the admiration of the family and of neighboring worshipers. Occasionally, he brought a lump of clay with him and whiled away a weary hour modeling varied and assorted devils. But when the family physician, Theodore's cousin and close neighbor, West Roosevelt, died suddenly, Kermit's sensitive spirit was plunged in grief. "Oh, Mother," he cried, "I wish we had the water of life to give to our friends."

Kermit, Ethel and Archie devised a game of tag adapted to the peculiar conditions of their captivity during the pastor's customary long prayer, poking each other and then crossing their fingers, which made them secure against an immediate counter-poke. Mrs. Roosevelt took it all in her stride. "I always find it well," she said, "to keep my eyes closed during prayers."

The children adored her, Alice no less than the others. In a letter to Emily, Edith gave a picture of her return after a brief absence. "As I got to the top of the hill they gave a wild shriek and the two boys and Ethel rushed from the piazza across the grass. Then came Alice, holding Archie's hand. As she got near me, she let go of him and flew to me and he at once tumbled over in a horrid heap."

"Such darlings!" their father wrote Bamie. "And how impossible to tell how any of them will turn out!"

Kermit, more imaginative than the other children, sensed the joy his father had in them all. When Ted, at seven and a half, declared that he was going to be a soldier some day, Kermit solemnly announced, "I'll just be a plain man with bunnies, like Father!"

Chapter IV

EDITH, conducting her household at Sagamore Hill, bringing up her children and binding up their bruised legs and arms, had the story of her husband's work in the Police Department spread out before her in news-stories, editorials and cartoons, in the daily press. Theodore was making an extraordinary commotion. "The papers are full of his doings," Edith wrote Bamie. Sensitive, even shy, she shrank from the daily reports of conflict. "Mrs. Roosevelt doesn't like me to get into public rows," Theodore told Father Belford, the vigorous and able young priest of the little Catholic church in Oyster Bay. "She says I am not at my best in them."

He grinned, no doubt, as he said it, suspecting that, as usual, Edie was right. But what was he to do when he had such "crooks" or "muttonheads" to deal with?

All day long, he lived in a continuous struggle with "vile crime and hideous vice," as he described it to Bamie, but his letters reveal how little of the dust and smoke of the day's battle clung to him. Sagamore Hill, to which he returned frequently on the last train— bicycling the three miles from the station to the house—gave him a bath in addition to that which the high-walled, narrow tin tub provided. The natural world about him was alone a kind of purification. "The country is so beautiful!" he wrote his sister. "All the locust trees in bloom, and so the whole landscape is streaked and patched with frothy white, against the beautiful rain-fed greens of spring." More deeply, the contact with Edith and the children seemed to cleanse him of the foulness he dealt with at police headquarters, returning him refreshed to face the stench and slime.

Theodore lamented that he saw too little of the children—"little more than a glimpse" in the morning, though in the evening there was generally time for a romp with Archie, a little game with Ethel,

President of the New York City Police Board

a moment, while he was dressing, with Ted and Kermit, and at dinner, a talk with Alice, all of twelve now, and as tall as Edith.

His enemies in the Police Department could not conceive what his home-life meant to him. They had him "shadowed" when he stayed in New York overnight, hoping to catch him "off his guard." His friend Jake Riis was with the Police Commissioner when he heard of it, and noted the angry flush. "What!" Theodore cried, "and I going home to my babies?" His anger died in a sad little laugh of pity and contempt.

2

At Sagamore, meanwhile, friends came and went, staying for a day, a week, a month—men and women with quick minds and spirits akin to Theodore's, who entered into the children's lives and, in their presence, at meals, talked of war or the hunting-field, of political stratagems and struggles, and of great men, dead and living. There was the Englishman, Cecil Spring-Rice, the beloved "Springy," who had been Theodore's best man at his wedding and was a rising personage in the British diplomatic service; the Scot, "Bob" Ferguson, affectionately known as "Fergie," younger son of a Scottish laird, described best, Kermit thought long afterward, in terms of Robinson's "Richard Cory,"

> "A gentleman from sole to crown,
> Clean-favored and imperially slim,"

but never able quite to adjust his sensitive, valiant spirit to the world in which he lived; the German, Speck von Sternberg, precise and cold-blooded, yet devoted to all the family, "the little baron," as Edith spoke of him, who had made up his mind that Theodore was marked by destiny to be President of the United States and repeated his prophecy at each step upward of Theodore's career; the American, Henry Cabot Lodge, the "scholar-in-politics"—too deep in politics, some thought—widely read, astute, devoted. These were the most cherished of the many who, those years, visited at Sagamore Hill, though there were hundreds of others, including numberless attractive and stimulating women whose insights contributed to Theodore's and Edith's education as much as to their children's.

The table talk was over the children's heads, of course, but the sparkle of it was not lost on them. Their father bubbled with ideas, many of them challenging; he had a remarkable vocabulary, moreover, and delighted in using it to castigate his enemies or to characterize some "amiable old fuddy-duddy with sweetbread brains," who had crossed his path; he had a quality of wit, besides, which inspired wit in others. The mother of the family held her own—a priceless counter-weight to her husband's occasionally irresponsible ebullience—as witty as the father; with a touch of acid on occasion, and never forgetting, as Theodore was inclined to do, the part that interested listening might play in the social give-and-take.

3

At nine Ted began his career at the Cove School on the little peninsula of Cove Neck, from which Sagamore Hill rose to its 160-foot eminence, and, his father noted, accepted his new experience "with happy philosophy." Some of the children of other landholders who lived on the Neck the year round went to the little one-room school, but they were far outnumbered by the children of the gardeners and grooms and coachmen on the estates roundabout, so the instruction had a thoroughly democratic background. The fact that Ted was small for his age, and wore spectacles, put him at a disadvantage with boys more robust, but he held his own. Ted—described by his father to "Springy" as "exceedingly active, normally grimy" and devoted to Kipling's poetry—was always getting into fights, the details of which he and his father used to discuss. "We always told him everything," Ted wrote twenty years later, "as we knew he would give us a real and sympathetic interest." The boy was discovering that life could be puzzling. Some of the attitudes he had learned at home to take for granted, he found, were subject to ridicule. This idea that you were courteous to girls, protective to the weak and kind to animals seemed "sissy" to many of his school-mates. Ted was satisfied that the ideas he was getting at home were right, but what about this "sissy" business? He put the matter up to his father.

"You can be just as decent as you wish," his father told him, "provided you are prepared to fight." He spoke of his own father, who had made him want to be both decent and manly and had pointed out that, if he were manly enough, no one would long laugh at his being decent. It had worked, in his own case, Theodore pointed out, in college and among the cowboys of the Dakota Bad Lands. "If you fight hard enough," he added, "you are perfectly certain to secure the respect of your playmates for your virtues."

A month after Ted's entrance in the school, his father wrote Bamie that Ted had "just despatched in single fight a fellow-American citizen named Peter Gallagher." Thenceforward, so far as Ted was concerned, the Cove School was safe for decency.

47

Ted was emulating his namesake in other ways. The 1896 presidential campaign was in full swing, and Theodore, as his policework permitted, was, now and again, campaigning for William McKinley, the Republican candidate. He and Edith had a way of treating the children as equals and, at mealtimes, he gave the family full reports of what he had experienced. Only Alice and Ted were old enough to understand what it was all about, but those two drank it in. That autumn, Alice came upon Ted, on the kitchen porch, with a loaf of bread in one hand and a piece of money in the other, eloquently demonstrating the fallacy of the free coinage of silver to an audience of the hired men and house servants.

Alice remembered, long afterward, the excitement of election night. She was supposed to be in bed, but actually crouched breathless on the floor of the upstairs hall with her nose between spokes of the balustrade. There was no telephone in the house, but at last, late, she heard the crunch of carriage wheels in the gravel and, shortly after, excited voices indicating that McKinley had been elected.

4

Winter at Sagamore brought its own delights, with coasting and snowball fights and sleigh-rides. In Washington, Theodore had learnt from a Norwegian employee of the Smithsonian Institution the use of skis, or "Norwegian snowshoes," as they were known, and brought the boys a new thrill.

Winter was the time for open fires—and did they need them at Sagamore!—with Theodore telling stories of his hunting adventures or acting them out with the children, with himself as the big bear and the children as the cubs, or Edith reading "Sir Patrick Spens" or some other stirring ballad, with their father, perhaps, adding "Sheridan's Ride," or "The Sinking of the Cumberland." If the children missed the meaning occasionally, they caught the rhythm—and the ardor—and it helped them grow up.

In New York, the children's father was in a knock-down and drag-out fight with a colleague on the Police Board and in danger of being legislated out of office; but at Sagamore Hill he made preparations for Christmas, taking Ted into the woods to help him find just the right tree and setting it up happily with him in the "gunroom." The weatherman did his part and brought snow, and the thermometer dropped to zero, but roaring wood-fires kept at least the living-rooms warm—and who cared if the bedrooms and the halls were icy?

Christmas Eve, Edith took Alice and Ted in the wood-sled to the little frame Episcopal church in Oyster Bay, to join in the Christmas carols. A feature of the service always was the singing of a hymn beginning, "It's Christmas Eve on the river; it's Christmas Eve on the bay," which seemed to belong peculiarly to Sagamore's corner of creation, and survived nostalgically in the children's memories.

"It was bitterly cold next morning at six o'clock," Edith wrote Bamie, "and, as you know, my room is not cozy, but we huddled around a bright fire and I muffled Archie in my blue shawl. Bob [Ferguson], with a sofa blanket decently but scantily draping his legs, was most picturesque, and Theodore in his old brocade wrapper, which only flourishes on such occasions, was not far behind him. After breakfast we had the big presents in the gun-room, where the climate was like nothing but the North Pole. After lunch we succeeded in getting warm by playing 'pillow-dex,' very idiotic but very funny." "An ideal Christmas," Theodore wrote a friend, after New Year's. "The children had as lovely a time as children could."

5

Theodore was back in Washington the following spring, as Assistant Secretary of the Navy, and the family followed in the fall. It was an exciting and anxious time for the country, and for the Roosevelts. Spanish rule in Cuba had driven the Cubans to revolution. Conditions on the Island were desperate. Theodore himself was advocating intervention, and the war-fever was rising.

The middle of November, a fourth boy arrived in the Roosevelt family. "Archie by no means approves of Quentin," Theodore wrote Bamie. "The others love him." "Quentin is the merriest, jolliest baby imaginable," Edith wrote in her "Baby Journal." Edith's recovery was swift, but grippe set in, dragging on, month after month, through successive relapses. By the middle of February her condition was grave and Theodore was in a turmoil of apprehension, not knowing from day to day whether she would live or die. An operation, early in March, revealed an abscess, revealing also, once more, Edith's indomitable valor. "She behaved heroically," Theodore wrote Bamie, "quiet, and even laughing," as he held her hand while the preparations were being made. The operation proved successful but, even three weeks later, Theodore wrote Brooks Adams, Edith was only slowly "crawling back to life."

National and family tribulations mingled that winter to confuse life for young and old. "I went away from the house and sted away from the hous a month," Kermit wrote his "dear Aunt Eamily." "Isent it sad about the Maine sinking?"

Meanwhile, Ted was sick, suffering from devastating headaches whose cause five Washington doctors had failed to determine. Alice, now fourteen, was proving a handful, moreover, "running riot" with the boys and girls in Washington, her father wrote Bamie, and Edith too ill to keep her in check. "She always had a string of a dozen boys at her heels," Edith subsequently wrote Emily, "and, being a large and handsome girl, was very conspicuous." Alice did not accept correction gladly and was shipped, on a day's notice, to Bamie, who had married Commander Cowles of the United States Navy and was living in her Madison Avenue house in New York while her husband was on sea-duty. Auntie Bye gave Alice, Theodore recognized gratefully, "exactly what she needed," a diet of lectures and concerts, guaranteed to sober up the liveliest teen-ager. "I have just had a letter from Alice," Edith wrote Emily, "saying it was 'worse than boarding-school,' little knowing, poor child, that that was why I sent her."

A few weeks after Alice's departure Ted also was sent to Auntie Bye's. His father's friend, Dr. Alexander Lambert, examined him and wrote Theodore that the boy was on the verge of what in adults would be called "nervous prostration," and would require a nurse to enforce a rigid regimen of diet and exercise. In no uncertain terms, the forthright, warm-hearted physician told Theodore that he had pushed the boy too hard, and would have to lay off. In humility of spirit, Theodore showed the letter to Edith, "who," he wrote Lambert, "is now well enough to feel the emotions of triumph. Hereafter I shall never press Ted either in body or mind. The fact is that the little fellow, who is peculiarly dear to me, has bidden fair to be all the things I would like to have been and wasn't, and it has been a great temptation to push him."

"As I look back," Edith wrote Ted, thirty years later, recalling the early ailments of her children, "you fared worst, because Father tried to 'toughen' you, but happily was too busy to exert the same pressure on the others!"

With all the family difficulties, Theodore that spring had a grim problem of his own to solve. In case war came, could he, who had urged intervention in Cuba, stay out of it and keep his self-respect? The decision came in pain. In a letter to Emily, Edith noted that he was finding sleep difficult to capture and hold. It was, altogether, Theodore admitted, "a hard winter."

By the time war came, early in April, he had made his decision, offering to raise a regiment of mounted riflemen with his friend Leonard Wood as colonel, and himself as second in command. His friends rose in protest. With a key post in Washington, six children and a wife barely recovered from her illness, he had no business to go to war, they declared. His chief, the Secretary of the Navy, the President himself, begged him not to go. Only Edith, at last convalescing, recognized that he was right, that, having urged the war, he must be in it.

His offer to raise a regiment was accepted. Early in May, he resigned his Navy post and prepared to join his men, already in training in Texas.

"Father went to war last thursday," Kermit informed his Aunt Emily, the middle of May. "I sted up untill he left which was at 10."

Chapter V

JUNE DAYS, long in the nature of things, were interminable that year for Edith, shepherding her enchanting and unpredictable flock, with only a fraction of her mind at Sagamore and all the rest with Theodore on this greatest of his adventures. He had always dreamed of some day putting body, mind and spirit to the ultimate test of war. Well, he was having his chance at last, and she might as well face the implications.

She had often been at Sagamore without Theodore; for whole summers, indeed, while he was Civil Service Commissioner, since his work would keep him in Washington, except for his vacations, and these he had frequently spent at the ranch, or hunting in Montana or Wyoming, to get himself toughened up after the confining winter. But this time it was different. It had merely been quiet, those other summers, and, to her, quiet was always welcome. But there was no quiet now, not for her. Everything in the house spoke, upstairs and down, loudest in the library and in the gun-room, spoke with Theodore's voice. His "darling Edie" rang in her ears all day long.

Where was he now? In camp? At sea? Already in Cuba, fighting? Leonard Wood, the Rough Riders' colonel, would be as eager as Theodore to get where the fire was hottest. At last, news came that the transports had put to sea, followed by days of dreadful suspense with no definite reports and only terrifying surmises regarding the elusive Spanish fleet. Then the landing under hostile fire, and, two days later, the headlines: WOOD AND ROOSEVELT IN BATTLE'S FRONT, LEADING THEIR MEN TO VICTORY. Like troubadours the correspondents smote the lyre; in the case of the New York *Herald*, Richard Harding Davis: "After ten or fifteen minutes of hot work the firing fell off some, and Lieutenant Colonel Roosevelt ordered his men back to the trail, narrowly escaping a bullet himself which struck a tree at one side of the road."

Did Edith's heart skip a beat?

The *Times,* next day, chanted further details: ROUGH RIDERS PROVE HEROES. THEIR FIRST BATTLE MARKED BY MANY ACTS OF BRAVERY. There was an account of Theodore leading the right wing in an attack on a blockhouse. Snatching a rifle and ammunition belt from a wounded soldier as, "cheering and yelling with his men," he led the advance. How like Theodore, and how he must have loved it! "For a moment the bullets were singing like a swarm of bees all around them, and every instant some poor fellow went down."

One imagines, at that point, she laid the paper down, or turned to the editorial page, perhaps, to release the sudden tension in her throat. But there she found what might well have accelerated the heart-beats again: *For Governor, Theodore Roosevelt.* The editor was commenting on reports that the reform element in the Republican Party, the so-called Independents, were planning to confound the Easy Boss, Senator Tom Platt, by nominating for governor this "leader of the desperate charge in the Cuban chaparral."

The idea was exciting but not much comfort to a woman on a Long Island hill-top, reading of the advance of the American forces toward Santiago, and of the imminent assault.

The days crawled by. Then again there were headlines: ROUGH RIDERS IN THE VAN, "clear in front of the general advance, fighting like demons."

2

"The news of the battle of Santiago has come," Edith wrote Emily, "but not the list of our losses, so the suspense is hard and I am grateful that you are not here to share it. Alice is a great comfort for she is very sympathetic and yet persistently looks upon the bright side."

For the sake of the children, she was saying to herself, she must not break down. "The three older children suffer greatly from apprehensions," she wrote Emily, but they "must just take it as best they can. I happened to read Ethel's letter to her father the other day and in the end she had written, 'He shall give His angels charge over thee.'" Would Emily not read the 91st Psalm every night? Edith would be reading it. Together, perhaps . . .

She was still feeling the effects of her illness, the previous winter, and recognized, when she gave way at all, how hard it was to pull herself together again. The women in the Civil War had lived through "four years of this," she said to herself; surely she could keep herself in hand. "I should not cable you of a wound," she wrote Emily, "only in another case. Do not believe until you get a cable from me. I can hardly write it, but it may make your mind easier."

From "Fergie," in Theodore's regiment, Edith received a first-hand report of the San Juan fight and of Theodore, "like Shadrach, Meshach & Co. in the midst of the fiery furnace—unharmed by the fire and sniffing the fragrant air of combat. I really believe firmly now that they can't kill him." The mystical assumption was all right, so far as it went; but Edith, in her heart, had no such assurance, though "Fergie" added that, to all intents and purposes, the campaign was over.

In the newspapers, Theodore was the center of the stories and the comment, "the hero of San Juan Hill." How Theodore always managed to get to the front in everything he undertook! It had been so in the Assembly, on the Civil Service Commission, on the Police Board, and in the Navy Department; and now the regiment and, more than the regiment, the whole American Army besieging

54

Santiago. What was it that made him, sooner or later, the leader of every fight he got into? His self-assurance? His capacity to see things in black and white where most people see lavender or gray, so that every fight he fought took on the character of a holy war? Partly, no doubt. But mainly, it was a kind of genius for action that he had, that had all the driving force of other kinds of genius. It could be cruel, even ruthless. He would have gone into the war if it had killed her, and never doubted he was doing right. How people had pleaded with him not to go! He wouldn't listen. He couldn't. He had to be free to do what he thought was right, or collapse inwardly and be just a walking shadow the rest of his life.

Where was he now? Under fire? Down with fever, perhaps?

Edith bought a new horse, whose name—God bless him!—was Cuba. She took the children to a birthday party at the West Roosevelts for their four-year-old Nicholas, Archie's alter ego. She gathered together the press stories, piling up daily. "I have had such a sticky evening pasting up Theodore's scrap-books. They were getting ahead of me."

She had a golden morning when Santiago fell, for she assumed that the troops, having achieved what they had been sent to do, would be brought home. Nothing happened. Days passed, then weeks; weeks of waiting and of dread; waiting for the morning papers, and the mailman; dread of the blue-coated messenger-boy, pushing his bicycle up the road from Oyster Bay and bringing her the little yellow slip of paper that would tell her the worst.

She grew thin, pale, and tight-lipped. Her heart, in fact, was acting up, and proved on examination to be enlarged. In the St. Hilda Society, where the women of the church met Thursdays to sew for the wounded, she let no one know the terror in her heart, but Mrs. Washburn, the rector's wife, guessed it, and one day impetuously took her in her arms. "Your husband is a hero, my dear. But you are three."

Edith said to herself, no doubt, "How ridiculous! I wish nice Mrs. Washburn wouldn't get sentimental."

July crept past. Edith admitted that she could bear to have only "dear friends or amusing rattles" about her. But the children gave her diversion of a sort: Kermit falling foul of poison ivy and suffering badly; Archie "ordering Mame about," Edith wrote Emily, "so she hardly does a thing for the other children and does not even mend the stockings, which means that they fall to my share!" And so "many people" were sending her "such kind notes," among them one from Jake Riis, telling of the elevator-man at the Police Department saying, "I speak for Mr. Roosevelt in my prayers every night, blamed if I don't!" Occasionally, wounded Rough Riders, home on furlough, came to tell how the men "adore Theodore," how he had a charmed life and how he had trudged eight miles through the mud and over a mountain, "carrying a bag of beans on his back to his men."

August came and Edith had a birthday, which was always a momentous occasion for the children; and, a few days later, Ethel had hers. So life at Sagamore went on. Then, one day, Theodore was in the war news again. He had led a group of officers in a round robin to Shafter, the commanding general, pleading that the troops be sent north before the fever decimated them. The War Department was outraged; there was talk of a court-martial. But the troops were ordered home, and—by all things wonderful!—to Montauk Point, at the eastern end of Long Island.

3

"I am expecting momently to hear of Theodore's arrival," Edith wrote Emily on a mid-August Sunday, "and, after all our rains, today is divine—just fit for a homecoming."

The message took twenty-four hours in coming. The transports, steaming slowly up from Cuba through the midsummer calm, came over the horizon Monday morning. While Edith waited at Sagamore with growing impatience, a scene unfolded which the newspapers next day would describe for her in all its dramatic and colorful detail. Even Theodore's ancient enemy, the New York *Evening Post*, cast off its prejudices to give its own warm picture of the returning hero, "straight and strong . . . with a bright eye and a strong grasp of hand . . . like a boy home from school for the long vacation, throwing a word here and a word there, appearing to be too happily excited to do more than speak and listen in great hurry; wanting the news in a word, to tell in a breath as much as a deliberate man could tell in an hour—just like a boy, for all the world like a boy who had thrown his lessons to the winds and forgotten that there was an end to his holiday."

There was no doubt at all about the Colonel being in a hurry. He was on his way to a telephone.

The bell that tinkled shortly after at Oyster Bay tinkled in the village, not at Sagamore Hill, which had no telephone. Theodore's message to Edith, relayed by a boy on a bicycle, asked her if she couldn't come to Montauk at once.

She required no urging. The leisurely Long Island Railroad carried her westward an hour to Jamaica and then eastward four or five hours in the dust and heat of plush-upholstered seats along the south shore to the very tip of the Island.

Jake Riis, at Montauk for the New York *Sun*, met her at the end of the exhausting journey with the word that yellow fever had been discovered among the returning Rough Riders. The regiment— officers and enlisted men alike—had been sent to a detention camp for quarantine and would presumably not be released for three days.

Edith's heart sank, but at the Red Cross station nearby, an unnamed young officer, "to whom I shall always be grateful," Edith wrote Emily next day, noted her plight and took pity on her. He slipped off into the darkness and returned shortly with the supposedly quarantined Colonel.

Edith and Theodore had an hour together. "Theodore looks well but very thin," Edith wrote. The fugitive returned to the detention camp, returned as surreptitiously as he had come, happily undetected by any officious sentry. He had risked a good deal for this hour with Edie, since the War Department would have given its metaphorical eye-teeth for an excuse to trim this "insubordinate" celebrity down to what it regarded as his proper dimensions.

Edith spent the night in the "hut" of the Red Cross agent, transferring herself next morning to a grimy boarding-house on the dunes, called House No. 3, where she was given a dingy room with bed-linen that had already been slept in, staying four days, she wrote Emily, to help in the hospital, and hungering to stay longer. "There are so many chinks to fill. The devotion of the Rough Riders' men to me is quite touching. They follow me about like a bodyguard."

4

Edith, reading the papers at Montauk while Theodore fumed under the quarantine, became aware that the end of one chapter meant the opening of another, promising to be no less exciting. The papers were full of the new national hero. Would he accept a nomination for governor? He hadn't said that he would, but neither had he said that he wouldn't. The regular Republicans were after him, as well as those Independents who had launched his boom two months before. The very politicians who, two years previously, had been set to legislate Theodore out of his police commissionership, were now clamoring for his nomination for governor. Even the wily Tom Platt, who had fought Theodore tooth and claw, had sent an envoy to Montauk Point to sound him out. Edith, who did not forgive as easily as Theodore, savored their change of heart, no doubt, with just a touch of malice.

5

The Rough Riders disembarked at Montauk Point on a Monday, but it was Saturday before the quarantine had been lifted, and Theodore was given a four days' leave to greet his children. The news of the father's imminent arrival fairly shook Sagamore Hill. Before their mother had departed for Montauk, the children had been eager to hang the outside of the house with bunting, but their mother had demurred. That wouldn't really be good taste, would it? Other people might decorate their houses for the Rough Riders' colonel, but not they. The children, dejected, withdrew to consider what they might do in the face of such obviously inadequate grown-up thinking, returning to their mother, after many hours, with their home-made banner of welcome. On a huge piece of cardboard they had painted in script, of a variety such as only a child can produce, the words *In Honor of Colonel Roosevelt's Return*.

Their mother agreed that such a tribute was proper. Thereupon they fastened the placard to a long stick and planted it proudly where it would catch their father's eye.

The news that the Colonel of the Rough Riders was arriving did not reach the citizens of Oyster Bay until the middle of the afternoon. Houses were hurriedly decorated, the village band was assembled and a red, white and blue banner, bearing the words *Welcome, Colonel!* was strung across Audrey Avenue from the office of the *Oyster Bay Pilot*. A pile of barrels, boxes and other combustible material was collected and saturated with kerosene.

As the train pulled in with its whistle wide open, the band burst forth, but the roar from fifteen hundred throats drowned it out.

Cannon thundered, whistles screeched, revolvers and muskets blazed, in a manner more suggestive of Dakota than of Long Island's sedate North Shore. Someone touched off the bonfire, adding its roar to the tumult.

"The crowd seemed mad with enthusiasm," the New York *Herald* reported next morning. "Women and children were brushed aside like feathers." The station platform was "a solid mass of howling, pushing humanity. The streets were crowded and all the vacant lots filled. The crush was so great that a little girl, caught in the crowd, was literally stripped of her frock."

The three clergymen who constituted the welcoming committee had difficulty in reducing the tumult to a point where the address of the Reverend Washburn could be heard. The hero's response was brief and warm.

It took all three ministers, together with the train conductor, to open a lane for the Roosevelts to the two-seated, tasseled surrey that was to convey them to Sagamore Hill. "I had no idea," Edith wrote her sister, "there were so many people in Oyster Bay."

Chapter VI

IF THEODORE expected the peace and quiet he was accustomed to find at Sagamore, he was disappointed. A steady stream of newspapermen and politicians, neighboring cousins and other visitors, came and went. The children were put to it to understand what it was all about.

"Where is the Colonel?" a reporter asked Archie, in the midst of the turmoil.

"I don't know where the Colonel is," was the bewildered response, "but Father is taking a bath."

The New York *Herald* next morning described comically but with no suggestion of irony the national hero's relation to the political winds whistling about him. "Colonel Roosevelt is not talking politics, while he is resting at his country place," ran the news story, under an Oyster Bay date-line, "except to those politicians who are journeying here to learn whether he will be the Republican candidate for Governor."

There were three or four such callers that hot August Sunday, and he was non-committal with them all. His Cuban experience had for the moment dampened his political ambitions, or cast them into a new perspective. He wanted a chance to think about it all, to talk to Edie about it, to set this prospect of greater eminence and more exacting responsibilities against the background of his family life. What were his friends thinking about his relation to the governorship? A friend like Cabot Lodge, who knew politics as few knew it? Or, on the other hand, a friend like Grant La Farge, architect, son of the great painter, John La Farge, who knew nothing of politics but had the artist's capacity "to see life steadily and see it whole?"

He wired Lodge and La Farge, begging them to come to see him as soon as possible.

La Farge, witty, serene, urbane, arrived late that Sunday afternoon. The house "was packed and jammed," he remembered, a quarter-century later, "crowded as only Sagamore Hill could be crowded. All the world was there."

"You will have to put up with what you can get," Edith warned him. She found an attic room to which Kermit and Archie had retreated. The boys were tumbled out and the guest, in his own words, "was tumbled in."

At dinner, "such a crowd!" La Farge remembered. "Officers and soldiers, politicians, friends and neighbors." He sensed "something political going on." After dinner, "the crowd broke up in little groups, talking together. I retreated to my lair."

The night was stifling. He lit the one candle in the room and lay down on his cot to read. After several hours, he was beginning to doze when he heard footsteps in the narrow hall, followed by a gentle knocking and a loud whisper: "May I come in, Grant? You're not asleep?"

It was an odd figure that appeared in the candle's flicker: Theodore, clad only in his underwear, his bear-skin slippers and his spectacles.

"I want to talk with you, Grant," he began without further preamble. "They want me to run for Governor and I want to know exactly what you think about it. I've had a bully time. I've been in the legislature, I've been Civil Service Commissioner, Police Commissioner and Assistant Secretary of the Navy. I've had just about everything I've tried for. Now I've been in this war. I've had fighting. Here's all this fuss now about the Rough Riders and me. I've reached the crest of the wave. Now I'll probably begin to go down."

"Pshaw!" exclaimed La Farge. "The Lord only knows where you'll fetch up! The wave has carried you this far. It can carry you still farther. As for the governorship, of course, take it! My political opinion isn't worth much, but I know you're headed for big things."

"But, Grant," his visitor insisted, "it may be the top now. And I may begin to go down." He was pacing back and forth. "All you people who believe in me, well, you may be disappointed. It may be too hard for you to see." He paused. "One by one, you might all leave me when I begin to go down. Tell me, Grant, if it *should* be the top of the wave and I do begin to go down, it won't make any difference to you, Grant, will it?"

61

His friend reassured him, and said to himself, when the troubled hero had padded off to bed, that he knew a little better than he had before what it was that made people follow Theodore Roosevelt.

2

The house-guests departed after breakfast, Monday. Theodore shook himself free of the reporters, drove Edie in the surrey to the Episcopal church in the village for a Red Cross meeting, and went for a swim with the family in the afternoon, leaving instructions with the maid regarding two delegations he was expecting. The maid got her wires crossed. The water of Cold Spring Harbor was exceptionally refreshing, and the politicians were getting restless on the porch and very thirsty indeed. Theodore, in an old slouch hat, a flannel shirt and wrinkled trousers that had once been white, finally strolled up from the woods with Edith and one of the boys and was still apologizing to the group on the porch for his tardiness when the screen-door opened and a clergyman, tall, thin, well-groomed and severe, emerged from the house. Would Mr. Roosevelt be so good as to see his committee in the library? They had been waiting some time and would not detain him more than a moment.

Roosevelt entered the house and a few minutes later reappeared, escorting the clerical group to their carriage. By the time the visitors were out of earshot, he was back on the porch, his arms lifted over his head.

"Here's a pretty mess you political fellows have got me into! I told the maid I was expecting a delegation of Chicago politicians and she must not fail to take you into the library and serve you drinks. You come, and she puts you on the porch and takes the dominies into the library! She plants rye, bourbon and cigars between the Congregational minister and the Episcopal rector and makes the dominies believe that I, when I'm alone, sit surrounded by these influences, morning, noon and night!" He was shaking with laughter as he led the politicians into the library. "I gather," he added, "that the clergy have left a few drops."

"The house is besieged with reporters and delegations," Edith wrote Emily that afternoon. "When we came up from bathing

62

just now, two men were waiting in front of the house, more were on the piazza, more in the library and a crowd of mixed sexes surrounding Quentin at his bench, besides a camera fiend taking snapshots at the house from the fence of Smith's field! It is something horrid but will not last long."

Cabot Lodge arrived late the following afternoon. He had opposed Theodore's going to war, but admitted cheerfully how deadwrong he had been. All next day, on the lawn, moving their chairs as the shade moved, the two friends talked. Theodore was not too impressed by the acclaim in the press; emotions, he pointed out, never lasted long and had a way of going in reverse. He wanted to be governor and yet . . . He presented his dilemma to Lodge in terms wholly different from those in which he had presented it to Grant La Farge, though the basic problem was the same; for the sake of the greater prize might he not lose all that he had already won?

Anyway, his heart was with his regiment. When he read in the press that there was an increase in sickness at the camp, he cut his leave by twelve hours and returned to Montauk. "My place is with the boys."

3

Edith did not get many letters from her husband during the weeks that followed—"I am in horrible disfavor," he wrote Lodge—but the newspapers kept her informed of his doings. PLATT'S FRIENDS SHOUT ROOSEVELT, ran the New York *World* headline. The *Herald* spoke of a "stampede." Meanwhile, the Independent Republicans, more interested in destroying Platt than in electing Roosevelt, and as determined as the Platt machine to use the new national hero for their own ends, gave contradictory accounts of their interviews with him, and of his intentions. Between the amateurs and the professionals there was more than a chance that the Roosevelt boom might be torn to shreds.

A week before the regiment was to be mustered out, Edith took Alice, Ted, Kermit and Ethel for a twenty-four-hour visit to Montauk. The day was sparkling, with the deep blue of the September sky over the dunes, the wide, white beaches and the pounding surf. Alice, fourteen and a half, felt herself every inch "the Colonel's daughter," and the rough men of the mountains and plains made much of her. "Our visit to Montauk," Edith wrote Emily, "was a great success. Ted and Kermit slept in Theodore's tent, one on his cot, the other on his air mattress, while poor Theodore occupied the table." She and the girls had a room in a house on the bluff. They had their luncheon both days at the Colonel's mess, "and met all the officers, such attractive handsome young fellows some of them were," Edith wrote, "and just about twenty-one years old, so I felt about a hundred!"

When the regiment was mustered out, the middle of September, the Colonel returned to Sagamore Hill, bearing the regimental flags entrusted to him by the Secretary of War; the pony, Texas, he had ridden in the San Juan fight; and, in a crate with bars, the regimental mascot, a bald-headed eagle, which the children greeted as a priceless addition to their own army of pets. With the Colonel came a half-dozen Rough Riders, mainly the Eastern college men with a few Westerners thrown in, followed during the ensuing weeks by a succession of other attractive if somewhat bewildered plainsmen.

A correspondent of the Albany *Journal* gave a highly colored picture of "rough-riding men from the Bad Lands" going up and down the road that "picks a circuitous way up the hillside . . . their trappings rattling with the jog of the horse and the cased butts of their pistols sticking menacingly out of their hip pockets," not saying where the riders acquired the horses or the "trappings," except by theft from the United States Army, which might have had something to say about it.

One cowboy actually did wangle a horse out of his superiors and rode all the way from Montauk Point, a two days' journey, but the rest came and went prosaically by the Long Island Railroad and, from the depot, by hack or the Sagamore Hill "phaeton" or surrey. The children regarded them as half mythical beings before whom even the eldest stood palpitating and breathless. "If I was in love with one Rough Rider," wrote Alice, long after, "I was in love with twenty, even though I did have a pigtail and short dresses." There were picnics and tennis and swimming and hikes, which some of the visitors, still fighting the Cuban fever, endured rather than enjoyed; and all day long there was such talk of great things and common things, sparklingly intermingled, as only Sagamore Hill, it seemed, could know.

A number of the Colonel's Rough Riders had their part in the "jubilee" which Oyster Bay held in an old apple-orchard not far from the railroad station, less than a week after they were mustered out. As Roosevelt mounted the platform, the band burst forth, comically, with "Listen to the Mocking Bird." A man in an apple-tree called for "Three cheers for the old Rough Rider!" and they were given with zest, Edith, on the platform with the children, cheering with the rest.

Prominent citizens spoke, with the Democrats if possible more eulogistic even than the Republicans. Then came the hero's turn: "You have known me since I was a very small fellow. You know whatever is good or evil in me, and I made up my mind that, if you wanted to hear me, you had the first call." He told of his appreciation of the way in which politics had been kept out of the gathering. "Like my regiment," he added, "no politics and no religion."

A titter ran through the crowd, and Edith, the *Herald* reporter noted, laughed "heartily."

The Colonel flushed. "Hold on!" he interpolated. "I mean there was no religion in the regiment, except as with all good Americans. All, according to our several creeds, tried to serve God and our country."

There was a second interruption, provided by Archie, aged four, announcing in loud tones to all and sundry that he had his new shoes on.

His father told the story of the regiment, "raised, armed, equipped, mounted, dismounted, landed in Cuba and put through two victorious fights, all in fifty days." There were cheers and a tiger when he ended, followed by the presentation of a sword for which funds had been raised by public subscription. Altogether, it was "great fun," Edith wrote Emily.

5

It meant much to Theodore to receive the acclaim of his fellow townsmen; much, to introduce his Rough Riders to his neighbors and his family; to take the boys he had come to love, afoot or on horseback, across the countryside, clothed in the deep green of the late summer; to let the warmth of his hospitality express, as no words he could have framed could do, what he thought of their valor and their fortitude in Cuba, and their personal devotion to him. It was a joy to be with Edie again, her health restored, and to note how slender and girlish she still was after almost twelve years of married life and the bearing of five children. It was relaxation to every fibre in him to be with the "bunnies," to romp with them in the barn, play "stagecoach" with them on the dock, tell them stories, find answers for their engaging and unexpected questions.

But he could give them all—his neighbors, his friends, Edith, the children, only scattered moments. The world was beating on his door, wanting attention. Political storms were rising, within the Republican Party in the state—the "independents" against the "regulars," and, among the "regulars" themselves. Letters came pouring in—and piling up—not by the dozen or the hundred, merely, but by the bag. Letters were everywhere—in the gun-room and the library, covering tables, bulging out of drawers, heaped on chairs.

The Colonel was not given to wailing, and he went out of his way to speak appreciatively of the "exceedingly kind and complimentary people" who were making a galley-slave of him, but what could you say, he demanded, of "the concentrated bedlamite" who asked him to read his essay on "Duties of an American Citizen" and tell him "how it could be strengthened," or the editor who asked him for a short article of 5,000 words or so, and asked for it at once, since he might be too busy to undertake it later? The harassed celebrity went in search of a secretary, found one in the attractive seventeen-year-old daughter, Amy Cheney, of the editor of the Oyster Bay *Pilot,* Albert L. Cheney, and with her plunged into what he called, with feeling, "the battle of the letters."

The mail was, in fact, only a part of their ordeal. The Colonel had made a contract with Charles Scribner's Sons for a book on the Rough Riders, and, at intervals, the publishers sent a special stenographer from New York to Sagamore Hill to take down the story. It became one of Amy Cheney's responsibilities to cool that elderly lady's fevered brow when, on her arrival, the Colonel was nowhere to be found and, after an hour, was discovered in the barn pursuing the children over the hay.

For all the work, the interruptions, the callers who came for thirty minutes and were held captive by their host for three hours, the importunate reporters, the occasional letter that the Colonel would crunch in his hand and answer in cold fury as he strode up and down the gun-room, the new secretary felt no sense of rush or strain.

The gun-room was open to the children, and they invaded it as they pleased, never failing to find a welcome. Ted had a museum in a kind of china closet, where he kept specimens of bugs and butterflies which required periodic attention and which he guarded carefully from his younger brothers, especially Archie, who saw no reason for his defensiveness and said so, pungently. Archie was the most frequent visitor and the most persistent, making ingenious excuses for staying in the room when his father was dictating and occasionally offering to take dictation himself. "Now, Archie," his father would answer, "only two at a time, please."

Amy noted that all three boys copied their father, using words that were characteristic of him and pronouncing them in his fashion, distinctly and emphatically. "Thank you very much for the marble. It's bully! And it's good of you to let me have it." Ted had a way of referring to the younger boys as "the children" which did not help maintain a peaceful atmosphere.

His father took it all with a humorous patience that never seemed to lose sight of "first things," though he could sweep the children into the hall and down the stairs when he had to. Promptly, every afternoon at four, the Colonel would suspend work and, shortly after, Amy would hear strange noises rising from the floor below where he was playing bear with baby Quentin.

6

Edith came to the gun-room rarely, and then, perhaps, only to lay a coat of her own over Amy's shoulders when the chilly days came. But she had her characteristic part in the action nevertheless. The little secretary, wide-eyed and keen-witted, noted that Edith Roosevelt, in contrast to her ebullient husband, was always "doing things without making any noise about it. It wasn't so much the things she did; it was the effect her presence had on us all." She never seemed to raise her voice, or give an order, but let no one think she was not alert to what was going on! The servants were obviously well trained and worked happily, "because they loved to work for people who were so appreciative of their efforts." The whole atmosphere seemed one of order and harmony except when Archie rummaged in the seamstress' work-basket or Ted got careless with his pet toads and snakes.

With all her self-effacement, Amy noted, the Colonel's wife was no devoted *me too,* over-awed and over-shadowed by her self-assertive and dynamic spouse, and there were occasions when she would deal with him with a determination matching his own. One rainy day Ted, who had not yet fully recovered from his break-down, six months before, came in from the woods, covered with mud and soaked to the skin. He had been warned against such exposure, and his mother took him to his father for the reprimand that the boy knew he had coming to him. His father let him have it with both barrels, and longer than Edith thought necessary or effective. Enough was enough. She spoke a quiet word that put an end to the boy's ordeal, the Colonel subsiding into silence before a wisdom he had learned by painful experience to be superior, in some matters, to his own.

The Colonel's little secretary, sitting at the table before the open fire-place, set diagonally in the east wall of the gun-room, gave no hint, as she turned out the letters, that her pretty blue eyes saw more than the alphabet dancing up and down under the play of her fingers. Anybody, indeed, could have seen the warm humanity under the greatness of the man who was her "boss." But only a penetrating imagination, a mature mind and loving heart could have recognized that this self-forgetting woman who carried so intelligently and so steadfastly her responsibilities to her husband, her children and her household, was mistress of her own soul, a slave to no one, "free as a bird."

7

Politics and the penalties of being a national hero were not the only problems which confronted the Colonel of the Rough Riders that September as he resumed his life with his family on Sagamore Hill.

There was Alice.

Her residence with Bamie had not worked out exactly as Theodore and Edith had expected. After her first fierce protest that it was "worse than boarding-school," Alice had found that life with

Auntie Bye was interesting, even exciting. Anna Cowles, competent, entertaining, gracious, with a heart as big as her brother's and a will to match, had for several years served as official hostess for her cousin, J. Roosevelt Roosevelt, when he was secretary to the American Legation in London. In the best sense, she was a woman of the world, a *grande dame*. She might be plain to look at, but she was fascinating to talk to. She knew everybody in society on both sides of the Atlantic and lived with a degree of unostentatious elegance that to Alice was new and alluring. There was a butler; there were dinners, formal and informal, with a glittering table, champagne, and guests whose names figured in the society columns, Burke's Peerage, or the journals of literature, science and government. Alice was too young to attend the dinners, but she observed from a discreet distance what was going on, drank in the details from Auntie Bye's lips and decided that this was the world she was made for, the world in which she intended to live. How bleak and colorless beside it seemed the life at Sagamore Hill! How provincial, how almost vulgar!

The experience gave substance and meaning to a sense of independence which had hitherto been merely instinctive. The revolt of a child against her elders achieved the dignity of a conflict of philosophies.

She knew now what she wanted and what she didn't want. When her father and mother talked again, that summer, of sending her to boarding-school, she told them that she wouldn't go. They argued with her. She stood fast. They laid down the law. She countered with an ultimatum: "If you send me to boarding-school I will humiliate you, I will do something that will shame you. I tell you I will."

Theodore and Edith knew what was behind those firm lips, those flashing eyes, and beat a retreat. "I have engaged a governess for Alice," Edith wrote Emily early in October, "who will, I think, prove a great comfort."

She did, indeed, evolving a method of teaching Alice which was as unorthodox as Alice herself, and thoroughly effective. Her governess worked off her superabundant energy in the fields and woods, on foot and on horseback, for hours at a time. When the fourteen-year-old was ready to drop, Miss Young would then and there begin the daily teaching of a subdued and receptive pupil.

Chapter VII

THE ROSY PICTURE, painted by enthusiasts, of the Rough Rider picking the nomination off the bough amid a tumult of cheers darkened when, less than a week before the convention was to be held in Saratoga, his opponents in the Party threw a bombshell. Roosevelt, they declared, was ineligible for the governorship, since he was by his own assertion no longer a resident of the state. As proof they presented an affidavit that Roosevelt had signed six months before, for tax purposes, claiming Washington as his residence.

The newspapers had a field day, the Democrats took hope, Sagamore Hill rocked under the blast, and the townspeople of Oyster Bay rose indignantly in defense of their hero, "mad, thoroughly and honestly mad," wrote the correspondent of New York's *Commercial Advertiser.* "Didn't we give him a reception 'cause he was a fellow-townsman," asked one antique citizen, "an' didn't we give him a sword? I'll show 'em whether he's a fellow-townsman or not!" The town clerk was kept busy, answering telephone calls and telegrams.

While the convention, the next afternoon, was listening to Elihu Root as he presented the tax case on the basis of Roosevelt's personal files, a group of New York reporters found the candidate at Sagamore Hill, in white flannels and a loose negligé shirt, coming downstairs with a flock of children at his heels—and left him, a half-hour later, "calmly sauntering over the lawn with his wife, seemingly unconcerned about the doings in the Saratoga convention."

Returning to Sagamore Hill at eight-thirty that evening, to tell the Colonel that he had been nominated by a three-to-one vote, the newsmen found him in the library with Edith and Alice, absorbing two telegrams that had just come from Saratoga. The first: "Reading by Root of tax correspondence produced profound sensation and wild enthusiasm"; the second, stating that the man who had made the original charge had withdrawn it. The effect on Roosevelt was to put ginger into his reaction to his nomination. "A word to my opponents," he said, and the way he bit off the words revealed for the first time how deeply the attack on his integrity had cut. "When they find what they deem a mistake or an error of judgment on my part, let them go ahead; but, when it comes to a question of my probity or honor, they may just as well make up their minds at the outset that they will be safer to be sure of the facts before they say anything."

2

The nomination raised the hum of Sagamore Hill to a new pitch, as the hack-drivers brought new relays of politicians and reporters.

The children, who had never been kept in the dark about the family's occasional financial crises, assumed that all the activity had something to do with their father's function as bread-winner.

Kermit, aged nine, encountering a newspaperman browsing in the library, asked him if he knew where his father was.

The reporter explained vaguely that he was "somewhere," and evidently very busy. The boy's ingenuous response was entirely serious. "Father has to work hard to get us all food."

The feature-writers who came seeking to present a picture of this "man of the hour" in his own setting had a hard time of it. One such individual succeeded in getting ten minutes of actual talk with the candidate, spread over a period of three hours and all three floors of the house, besides considerable acreage outside—"the longest exchange of words being four minutes by the watch in a remote corner of the piazza"—but he gave the readers of the New York *Times'* illustrated magazine an authentic and revealing portrait. First, the background: "not a large house," architecturally without pretensions but "homelike and pleasing, a very proper abode for a man of long descent, who needs no ladder to climb into the world of society"; "a man's house throughout," dominated by its "master" in every corner, most definitely in the study, with its books—history, back to Polybius and Herodotus, poetry, big game hunting, adventures, travel—its bronzes, "depicting hunting life,"

71

the "rich, glossy skins" of big game underfoot, the game-heads in the adjoining hall, the "quaint fireplace in which logs were burning."

In this setting, the man: the "athletic figure" in white flannels, with "pink necktie and tawny moustache giving the only touches of color": the "action, spring, energy, enthusiasm" of him—"the older Theodore Roosevelt gets, the more the fire increases"—a keen and prophetic observation—the "restless eyes, half hidden by the gold-rimmed spectacles," the "rush" in him, subsiding at will apparently into complete repose.

The writer caught him on the wing, in the hall. "Shall we talk now or will it be better later on?"

"Now!" the Colonel answered decisively. "Now! It will probably be worse later on."

3

Roosevelt was formally "notified" of his nomination at Sagamore Hill by a committee of Republican wheel-horses. As the carriages drove up the steep drive through clouds of dust, Roosevelt, the *Sun* reporter noted, "ran to the edge of the veranda and waved his hand high over his head, just as a boy would hail a party of other boys who were going to join him to go off on a lark," arriving at the foot of the steps "by the time the first carriage got there, and assisting the occupants to alight, shaking each by the hand."

Theodore presently led the party around to the west porch, where a big ellipse was formed with the nominee standing with his back to the house, facing the Republican Party's inevitable choice when mellifluous speech was in order: handsome, white-whiskered Chauncey M. Depew, president of the New York Central Railroad, who, the week before, had swept the convention with a speech in favor of Roosevelt. Edith came out of the house from a side door and took her place at Depew's left. Alice stood nearby.

Depew gave a brief review of the candidate's career from the New York Assembly to the slopes of San Juan Hill, against the background of national and international issues, speaking, the *Sun* man noted, "as he might have talked if Theodore Roosevelt and he had been alone on the veranda together" and he were telling the Colonel about the convention.

"Mrs. Roosevelt leaned against the balustrade, with her hands clasped," the *Herald* reporter observed. "While her husband was being addressed by Dr. Depew, she smiled, with her eyes cast down. Rarely did she look at her husband, who stood with his right hand on his thigh and his left holding his typewritten speech."

Roosevelt, obviously nervous, stressed national issues in his response, since they were nearer his heart than state issues and, on such an occasion, easier to handle than the Party's dubious record on the Erie Canal. He pledged himself "to enforce strict honesty at home," to which no one could object, but he did it, the *Sun* man recognized, with an "aggressive earnestness," a "deliberate, almost fierce emphasis" that could have given no comfort to the political wire-pullers present. There was a passage in his speech, moreover, that served notice on Platt that he would wear no man's collar— but, if anyone scented gunpowder in the air, no one mentioned it. Edith was heard to ask the rising young Republican State Chairman, Odell, whether her husband's speech was "satisfactory."

"Entirely so," he answered, "very satisfactory." But he himself had his knife out for Platt, and his eye on Platt's seat on the machine.

4

The campaign opened with a crowd of seven thousand packing New York's Carnegie Hall from floor to roof, and all the state's Republican worthies on hand to give the candidate a send-off. "The house was jammed," Edith wrote Emily, "and there was a large overflow meeting outside. I was glad I had gone for there was so much enthusiasm that I had no opportunity of feeling as nervous as I usually do when I hear Theodore."

Edith, that October, saw her husband only for flying moments, but had ample opportunity to know what he was up to. The *Herald* told of the candidate's *Lightning Dash Through Two Hundred Miles of Hudson Valley . . . Horrid with Barbed Wire and Warring Factions.* THOUSANDS CHEER THE ROUGH RIDER.

It sounded wonderful, and Edith, devouring the stories before the fire in the library, might have been justified in thinking the election won and Theodore's triumph complete. But there were undercurrents which the partisan newspapers failed to record. The county chairmen knew what was in the air. The candidate was talking about national issues, and the voters wanted to hear about matters nearer home.

The Tammany boss, Richard Croker, happily came to Roosevelt's rescue by letting it be known that his thumbs were down on the renomination of a certain Democratic judge, for no reason except that the judge had insisted on maintaining his independence of the boss who had originally elected him. This was Roosevelt's meat, directly in line with his own record as a fighter for decent government, and he jumped at the chance that so legitimate a moral issue gave him. The public responded instantly. People might not understand why all the fuss about the Philippines, but they understood common honesty.

ROOSEVELT WINS VOTES, the *Sun* told Edith, two weeks before Election Day, reporting a series of speeches through the "southern tier" of counties. TRIUMPH FOR ROOSEVELT. *Buffalo Beside Itself in Enthusiasm for the Colonel.* Next day: ROOSEVELT MARCHING ON. *Great Outpouring of People in Rochester.* From Utica and other upstate cities came similar reports. Everybody and his wife was wanting to see and hear the Colonel of the Rough Riders. It was "Teddy!" everywhere. "Hooray for Teddy!" "Teddy, we're wid yer!"

Did "Teddy" sound strange in Edith's ears? None of his friends dreamed of calling him anything but "Theodore"; nor did she.

For a wife who had never watched her husband campaign for elective office, it was all fairly breath-taking, and if she didn't wholly relish the familiarity of the greetings, she was thrilled at the public response. The details were even better than the broad strokes of the headlines—the crisp addresses, dealing directly with the issues; the crowds pouring in on Theodore everywhere; the friendliness, the gaiety and Theodore's bubbling humor in response; the occasional heckler and Theodore's swift, generally friendly, now and again savage come-back.

The children shared what Alice long afterward described as "the indescribable excitement of our father running for office." The issues? Alice and Ted cared scarcely more about them than did Kermit, Ethel or Archie. "Father" was *right,* and his Democratic opponent, an undistinguished judge named Van Wyck, was *wrong.* That was all there was to it. (Occasionally, Theodore himself seemed to share that impression.) Alice and the other children seized upon the campaign songs and, tramping through the woods

74

or over the fields around Sagamore, sang the words at the tops of their voices, feeling like an army going to battle.

Theodore came back from upstate for the final week of the campaign. He had a day of rest at Sagamore, and he needed it. "Theodore is under such a strain," Edith wrote Emily, a week before the election. "Last week he made a hundred and two speeches, most of them in the open air." After a day of rest he was off again, returning to Oyster Bay only in time to cast his own vote.

5

That evening, Theodore had dinner alone with Edie and Alice. Two reporters, arriving a little after eight, found them together in the library, the Colonel and his daughter reading by the light of a tall oil-lamp with a pleated silk shade on a table near the fire, and Edith doing "fancy work" beside another table and a second lamp with a shade of fluted glass. It might have been any evening in any American family anywhere, and the correspondents did not noticeably change its mood when they reported excitedly that the Democratic papers in New York had conceded the Colonel's election.

The Colonel was skeptical, but shortly other newsmen brought corroborating reports, setting Edith and Alice off on a jubilee which woke Ted and Kermit, sleeping over the kitchen. The only placid person in the house was the Colonel himself. Why was there no word from Odell, the state chairman?

One of the reporters volunteered to go to the telegraph office to try to have the wires cleared for the message from Odell which he was certain was there. When the young man returned at one in the morning with Odell's announcement of the victory, he found that the Governor-elect had gone to bed. In response to the bell, insistently rung, a very sleepy statesman in a red dressing-gown appeared, one hand holding a kerosene lamp above his head and the other rubbing his eyes.

"You're elected by eighteen thousand!" the reporter shouted exultantly.

"Am I? That's bully!" Thereupon the Governor-elect invited the young man to warm himself at the embers in his study, but not for long. In ten minutes, the flaring lamp was guiding the future Governor up the stairs and back to bed.

A *Sun* reporter, driving out from town to Sagamore Hill in the small hours, came upon groups of men tramping home through the inky dark. As the light of the carriage lamp fell faintly upon them they would raise their voices in an irregular shout for Roosevelt. From up and down the road and from other roads across country, other shouts would answer, some loud and clear and others faint as dying echoes, "just as the voice of a rooster at early dawn will set other roosters crowing for miles."

The jubilation, thus heralded, went on all day. The children in the school caught the general contagion and started their morning exercises with a demonstration their teachers had difficulty in bringing under control; the gray-beards on the street buttonholed their friends to tell them that they had known, when "Teddy" was a boy, that he would be Governor some day. "Even that queer bird, the Oyster Bay anti-Roosevelt voter," noted the *Sun* reporter, "stands on his front doorstep and laughs at himself for a fool in response to the gibes of his fellow-citizens passing in the street."

At Sagamore Hill, Theodore, in his roughest knickerbockers and hobnailed shoes, filled his lungs with the smoke-filled autumn air. It was good to have leisure again, to steal away from the mountain of letters in the gun-room and romp with the children or read to them again, or canter over the fields and through the woods with Edith in her new blue riding-habit and black fedora. "Edith looks as young and pretty as she did fifteen years ago," he wrote Emily, "though it makes her angry when I tell her this."

Winter came early that year, and the Governor-elect dug out his skis and happily skimmed the slopes around the house, when he was not tobogganing with Alice or Ted or the others, or playing parchesi indoors with Kermit, who was suffering from erysipelas and wearing a mask.

When, one day early in December, Lindsay Denison of the *Sun* called at Sagamore Hill to tell the Governor of certain political shenanigans intended to trap him, he found Roosevelt in the woods, cutting down a large hickory. His coat was off, Denison wrote subsequently, "and it was good to see the muscles working under the damp folds of his gray flannel shirt. The blows made the stout trunk tremble; in ten strokes it was toppling. As the Governor leaped out of the way of the 'kick-back' of the scored trunk, and stood grimly smiling at the roar and the crash of the mass of top branches striking the ground exactly where he intended them to strike, he made his only comment on the news he had heard: 'I wish,' he said, with the exaggerated solemnity which is the joy of all with whom he talks familiarly, 'I wish some folks we know could be made into firewood.' "

7

For the Sagamore Hill family, Christmas that year began the afternoon of Christmas Eve, at the Cove School. Shortly after three, the schoolhouse bell, to the accompaniment of squeaky machinery and energetic rope-pulls, announced the arrival of the Governor-elect, dressed informally in a gray coat and knickerbockers, and carrying a gray campaign hat in his hand. The little platform at one end of the schoolroom was flanked with Christmas trees hung with presents and cornucopias and decked with tinsel. At their base lay more presents—sleds, skates and express-wagons, picked by Edith after diligent inquiries.

When Edith and Alice too had come, the school-children, including Ted and Kermit, marched into the room in single file and slipped into their seats. The Reverend Mr. Russell offered an invocation, after which a number of children, including the redoubtable Peter Gallagher whom Ted had engaged in single combat two years before, recited "pieces," all martial, in honor of the Rough Rider. They culminated in a poem by a second Gallagher, predicting, with the tumultuous approval of the children,

> "We'll send you to the White House
> For the gallant deeds you've done,"

a sentiment which, the *Herald* correspondent noted, brought a flush to the Colonel's cheeks and gave his wife obvious satisfaction.

Ted had been expected to speak a piece, but he was just recovering from the grippe and had been excused. Kermit, however, with downcast eyes, rattled off "Higglety Pigglety Went to School," making his bow before the last line was off his lips and scurrying back to the security of his seat.

The Governor-elect, sitting in the rear of the schoolroom, was called upon for the customary speech, and, as he strode up the aisle between the desks, was aware of hoarse whispers from his own

77

offspring: "Father, don't speak long! Think of the poor children!"

He kept his face straight, but only barely. He said nothing to the children about the Christ-child or the Christmas spirit, but gave them in the simplest terms the philosophy of his own "strenuous" life and of his children's up-bringing. "Don't let anyone impose on you. Don't be quarrelsome, but stand up for your rights. If you've got to fight, fight, and fight hard and well. To my mind, a coward is the only thing meaner than a liar. Be brave, but be gentle to little girls, and to all dumb animals. . . . The boy who maltreats animals is not worth having his neck wrung.

"There are two things," he continued, "that I want you to make up your minds to: first, that you are going to have a good time as long as you live—I have no use for a sour-faced man—and next, that you are going to do something worth while, that you are going to work hard and do the things you set out to do."

It was more or less what he had said for the past ten Christmases and would say again for many of the next twenty in varying words but always with the same conviction. The applause and stamping of feet, when he was through, shook the school-house.

Now came the great moment. Someone handed the presents to the Colonel, who called the name of a pupil and, as the child appeared, delivered the gift. There was a sleigh for Peter Kern, skates for James Gallagher, a doll for little Mary Gallagher, a printing press for Bobby Dann and for each of the rest a present and a hearty word.

It was all very simple and very American. In ten thousand communities during that Christmas season there were similar exercises, with the local ministers speaking gentle words and an eminent citizen giving the presents. The only difference in Cove Neck was that the eminent citizen happened to be a national hero and the Governor-elect of a great state.

8

A week later, on the last day of December 1898—and it had been quite a year for the Roosevelts—Theodore and Edith took their children, their maids and a truckload of baggage by train to Albany and the gloomy pile that was the official residence of the Governor of New York.

Theodore's inauguration next day stirred Edith to the depths.

"It was a most solemn and impressive ceremony," she wrote her sister. "I could not look at Theodore or even listen closely or I should have broken down."

She had refused in advance to follow the custom that demanded that the new Governor's wife shake the hands of the guests attending the inaugural reception. Would the guests be affronted? She would take care of that. As she stood next to Theodore, both her gloved hands were occupied holding against her white chiffon waist Bamie's gift of green and brown orchids and Corinne's Roman hyacinths and lilies of the valley. The six thousand who filed past her were so captivated by the affability of her smile and the beauty of the flowers that they never noticed that the new Governor's wife had chosen to preserve her right hand for the practical uses of life.

Chapter VIII

RIDING ALONG the wooded roads of Cove Neck and the pleasant back country, the following spring, snatching what recreation he could from the daily exactions of the letter-writing public, the Governor thought about the future and was puzzled. His friend Lodge had put a bee in his bonnet. The Vice-President, Garret A. Hobart, might not want to run again—and the second place on the ticket might be Roosevelt's, if he wanted it. The idea rather stirred him. He enjoyed being governor; but would he be re-elected, with all the chances there were in New York politics for pulling boners of one sort and another and bringing the roof down on him? Of course, a lot of people were talking about the presidential nomination for him in 1904, even organizing clubs to boom his candidacy. But that directly depended on his re-election as governor. Besides, 1904 was a long way off. At the moment he had a following. But who, he asked Lodge, had ever known "a hurrah to endure five years?" The issue was more than a matter of personal ambition. He had laid out a "scheme of life," as he called it. Since he would not be leaving his children any money to speak of, he was in honor bound to leave them a record of honorable achievement. The Vice-Presidency was an honorable post. There might be something in it.

Edith disagreed, not vociferously, but with steel in her dissent. Theodore was made to be President, she was convinced, and what Vice-President had ever subsequently been elected to the top office? The Vice-Presidency was a side-eddy, and Theodore must not drift into it. Possibly she had another, deeper reason for her opposition. She loved her husband with a love that saw into the farthest recesses of his being, cherishing the imperfections together with the virtues because they were all of the essence of the enchanting Paul Bunyan-ish creature that he was, and she knew that the inaction of the Vice-Presidency was not for him. She did not say much, perhaps, at the time; she was not given to saying much at any time; but she had ways of communication other than words, and no one failed ever to know what was on her mind if she felt it was important that they should be informed.

Perhaps, on the quiet waters of the Sound, or on some shaded beach where they spread out their picnic-lunch, far removed from little pitchers with big ears, Edith asked her husband how, in the name of wonder, with his passion for his country and his instinct for seeing what needed doing and getting it done, could he imagine himself sitting around Washington for four years, doing nothing?

He would write history, he pointed out, perhaps.

Write it, when everything in him would be insisting on making it? More likely (his companion, perhaps, told him) he would burn up with frustration, or, outraged at administrative inaction, make indiscreet speeches, get himself into awful public rows, turn his best friends against him, become a factional leader and ruin all his prospects of ever becoming President.

Did she tell him something like that, those spring days, floating on the smooth waters of the Sound? Perhaps. Sharp insights of that sort, no doubt, were behind her determination that he should not let himself be lured into that particular quicksand. There were excellent lieutenants, he had often pointed out, who made very poor captains. Perhaps Edith reminded him that that was true also the other way round, and a man who was by nature a captain might be a disaster as a lieutenant. In every position he had held he had instinctively claimed the driver's seat, and the lesser men had made way; even, of all places, in the armed forces, where rank was sacrosanct. You couldn't do that sort of thing with the Presidency of the United States.

Perhaps he protested that he was the most loyal of subordinates, and the Round Robin had been only a technical violation of discipline, and, anyway, it had saved thousands of lives. Perhaps. Across a half-century one can hear still the serio-comic note of injured innocence; and see, too, under her broad-brimmed Leghorn hat, Edith Roosevelt's enigmatic smile.

By the time he pulled the boat up on the pebbly beach, he was ready, no doubt, to toss all thought of his future like a coin in the air, not caring how it came down, heads or tails. Politics in America were hopelessly kaleidoscopic, he had a way of saying. On the crest of the wave today, in the trough tomorrow, tossed up on a reef the day after. With even honest voters as jumpy at forthright action as they were, it was only a question of a year or two before he might be out of politics entirely. He did not care a whole lot, really, except for the children. He could always take the editorship of *Harper's Weekly* that had been offered him. Life would be interesting whatever he was doing, and he would manage somehow to make a living.

2

Meanwhile, the "hurrah" showed no sign of subsiding. Even the President, metaphorically speaking, joining in it, inviting him to the White House to get his views on Cuba and the Philippines. Politicians, seeing a national figure "emerging," hurried to Sagamore Hill to climb on the band-wagon; office-seekers came in hordes, and newspaper men, seeking a "big story" and clamorous to get it.

One of the drivers of what the *Times* called "the crab-like vehicles which ply lazily between Oyster Bay and Sagamore Hill" commented on the Governor's methods of handling the invasion. "He most always steams out to the porch to see 'em," he said, "but before they've had a chance to say six words he grabs their hands in goodbye shakes. Yes, he shakes 'em right back into my wagon, an' we are well out of the grounds before they catch their breath again." But the influx of visitors was too much even for this ingenious technique. An outpost was detailed to stand guard at the Oyster Bay depot to question every traveler who indicated that he was bound for Sagamore Hill, and the hack-drivers were asked not to take "suspects" to the Governor's home. Visitors who dodged the outpost, shunned the hacks and climbed the hill on foot, were met at the door by a poker-faced maid who gave her imagination free rein regarding the Governor's whereabouts.

Once more the busy Governor had time, when the back of the day's correspondence was broken, for a romp with Quentin or a swimming lesson for Archie or Ethel, or a ride with Kermit or Ted, or a set of tennis with Alice or a row on the Sound with Edith. Occasionally, the children begged—and seldom in vain—for an obstacle-race around and through the old barn, or for "stagecoach" at the dock on Cold Spring Harbor or for that dizzy slide down Cooper's Bluff which had become the traditional initiation for newcomers to Sagamore, old or young. Cooper's Bluff was a sandy incline, two hundred feet high, sloping at a sharp angle to the beach. Theodore's shy niece, Eleanor, had memories, forty-odd years later, of "Uncle Ted" lining up a dozen cousins, taking the lead, and the lot of them going down holding on to each other until someone fell or the speed became so great that the line broke. In some way, she remembered, rolling or running, they reached the bottom, occasionally to be carried by the impetus into the water. Eleanor was desperately afraid, the first time she essayed the descent, but found it actually not so bad as she had expected. The climb back was an ordeal of another sort, and took a long time, since the climbers slid back one foot for every two they ascended.

Not only Cooper's Bluff but all of Cove Neck was adventureland for the children. None was more conscious of it than Archie, aged five, for whom the woods had denizens undreamed of by his elders. Caught by the darkness with a former Rough Rider whom he was guiding through the twilit woods, Archie urged his stalwart companion just to follow his white head and not be afraid of bogies. They wouldn't hurt him.

3

The Fourth of July was always the children's own day at Sagamore. It began for the father of the family that first year of his governorship at four in the morning, "by the thoughtfulness," as he put it to a reporter later in the day, "of some youngster" —obviously one of his own—"with a bunch of giant fire-crackers"; but he restrained his impulse to reach for the hair-brush when he remembered similar "thoughtfulnesses" in his own boyhood. The Roosevelt children had strong views regarding a "safe and sane" observance of the nation's independence, which their father shared. But their elder playmate recognized the perils of gunpowder in inexperienced little fingers. Ignoring the Cuban fever which had racked him for three days running, keeping the punk-sticks lighted and forestalling casualties, he supervised all morning, from the piazza, what a *World* reporter called "the operations of a fire-cracker brigade, with Teddy, Jr., at the head of seventeen miniature rough riders from Cove Neck."

All evening he set off rockets, Roman candles and swishing, blazing pinwheels for an audience of thirty-three children gasping and squealing, dodging and shouting around him. "An enormous picture of Theodore in fireworks had been presented to us," Edith wrote Emily, "accompanied by the national salute of twenty-one bombs which quite overcame some of the smaller children." The long grass on the western slope was so dry that it caught fire a dozen times, and the father required all the exuberant energy of the children to help him put out the spreading flames.

Surely, when the last rocket had rushed up and burst in a shower of stars and the last Roman candle had feebly expelled its final fiery ball, he gathered the children in a great circle round him on the ground and told them of prairie fires that he and his cowboy companions had battled in the Bad Lands, splitting a steer and dragging the carcass at the end of a rope tied to a saddle, smothering a blaze here, only to see another rise roaring elsewhere, menacing cattle, horses, men, and the lonely ranchhouses where women stood watching, holding their children close. He knew how to tell such a story so boys would feel the sting of the smoke in their eyes and girls would see the flaming waves rushing nearer and nearer.

4

Between the morning's firecrackers and the evening's fireworks, Roosevelt's neighbors in Oyster Bay made their own enthusiastic contribution to the speculation regarding his future. At their Fourth of July observance, the Reverend Mr. Washburn, rector of the Episcopal Church, was sure that destiny had picked Oyster Bay to be the home town not only of a Governor of New York but of a President of the United States. The Reverend John L. Belford, the Roman Catholic priest, young, sensitive and outgoing, disclaimed the gift of prophecy but chanted a strong "Amen!" which brought cries of "Amen!" "Good!" "Right!" from every part of the audience.

Roosevelt, on the gaily decorated stand, tried not to look conscious or to show how pleased he was at this evidence of his neighbors' trust in him. "The Governor's expression," reported the New York *Times* next morning, "was ludicrously like that of a boy trying to keep an impassive face while something pleases him." For all he could do, his lips broke into a broad smile and he dropped his head. When Father Belford, referring to a recent Western tour from which the Governor had just returned, spoke of "the rumble we knew was sure to come from wherever he stood," the Colonel gave up all pretense of coyness and joined in the crowd's laughter. Ted, with him on the speaker's stand, was grinning from ear to ear, and Kermit climbed out of the carriage where he had been sitting with his mother, Alice and the other children, and made his way to the stand to join in the fun.

Altogether, it was a great day for Oyster Bay. The meeting had been rather an impromptu affair, stimulated by jealousy of Sea Cliff, which was having a flag-raising, and Glen Cove, which had advertised a "jubilee." Democrats and Republicans had come together, the clergy had been lined up, and the town's 3,000 inhabitants had bought what bunting and flags were available. Every store in town was closed except the saloons, the livery stable and the Chinese laundry. Flags were everywhere, even wrapped round the telephone poles. The farmers came in from the country round-abouts—the men with strong, beaked noses and bristly beards, stalwart convictions on moral, political and religious questions and a weakness for horseflesh—bringing their wives and daughters in their two-seated buck-boards. From their estates on the shore came the "swells" in their high traps, some drawn by four horses; and the "summer people" of Center Island, who crossed the Bay in sailing skiffs or launches. Sauntering in on foot came the village ancients, telling each other the good advice they had given the Governor the last time they had met on the street.

A stand had been put up among venerable apple-trees in Audrey Park, a flat, grass-grown area opposite the railroad station where the jubilee for the returning Rough Rider had been held the year before, and two or three thousand people were crowded round it. The Oyster Bay band got off to a bad start, but when its members finally agreed as to what they were playing, blared enthusiastically. The Baptist clergyman, delivering the invocation, was fairly drowned out by a volley of firecrackers across the street. The band played "Hail, Columbia!" and the Governor arrived, pushing his way through the crowd, just in time to hear the Methodist parson read the Declaration of Independence.

The Catholic father's large-hearted reference to his Protestant colleagues on the stand struck a note that the Governor picked up at once as "the spirit of true Americanism."

The gathering was, in fact, in its every aspect as American as the flags that draped the stand; the mixture of townspeople, farmers and "swells," of Democrats and Republicans, greeting a neighbor who happened to be Governor of the State, and hailing him for President regardless of party affiliation; the peanut vendors, the pink

85

lemonade, the firecrackers in the distance, the local band happy in dissonance, the star-spangled wooden platform in the grove crowded with prominent citizens in their Sunday clothes, the starched collars of the men in the audience, the white piqué skirts, blouses and stiff straw hats of the women; the girls in fresh white dresses with pink and blue ribbons, the babies in arms, the babies toddling; the group of irreverent youth perched in the apple-trees, cat-calling at everything, even the Declaration of Independence.

Roosevelt felt at home with these people. He too had sat in those apple-trees on Fourth of July gatherings, as a boy, he reminded them. "I grew up among you, cast my first vote here, and I shall keep my residence here." But he felt at home not only because they were his neighbors and he knew hundreds of them by name. He would have been similarly at home in a crowd like this in Ohio, Illinois, or Kansas. He knew what they were thinking about, what they wanted out of life, what was good in them and what was evil, as he knew what was good and what was evil in himself. He knew they wanted no spread-eagle stuff from him. On this Fourth of July in the year 1899 this crowd wanted meat to chew on—thoughts about government and their own relation to it, about the qualities needed in political life—the moral qualities, not only in the leaders but in the average citizen—about the new industrial and international problems looming on the horizon of a new century.

He gave it to them, challenging the best that was in them, promising them no material benefits but setting their souls to work. He spoke of the many duties they must face together: "the duty of being true to ourselves; the duty of bringing up our children to be good citizens; the duty of striving to ameliorate the conditions under which the less fortunate have to live; the duty of so combining sanity with our philanthropy that we may be equally removed from hard-hearted indifference, on the one hand, and the even worse bane of foolish Quixotism, on the other"; the duty of "bringing order out of chaos in the Philippines."

The crowd took in every word, underscoring his points with shouts of "Good!" "That's right!" In front of the stand, a white-haired, shrunken old man, wrapped in a plaid shawl and crouching in a chair, brought his feeble hands together from time to time; and on the limbs of the apple-trees nearby, boys at intervals called, "Teddy! You're all right!" Yesterday and Tomorrow, both, were with him.

86

When he had finished and the applause had died away, the audience surged forward to shake his hand. The folks of Oyster Bay liked this neighbor of theirs, and he liked them. They felt close to each other, they and he, not only as neighbors but as fellow Americans.

5

September brought the dreaded departure from Sagamore, the long looks backward as the carriage made its way down the winding road under the locust-trees, the state Capitol at Albany, and the spacious, if gloomy, wastes of the Executive Mansion. By the time the family were again in the one place that was and ever would be home to them, Lodge's intimation regarding the Vice-Presidency had become something that combined a boom, a conspiracy, and a popular uprising. The public was for it, with cheers; so, for various reasons which indicated his instinct for self-preservation, was Platt. Roosevelt himself was against it; it was not his kind of job; he wanted to be re-elected governor; besides, the unanimity of the magnates in wanting him to take the Vice-Presidency proved to him that he might yet be needed in the governor's chair. But he was intrigued, nevertheless. Reason said sternly that the post of greater usefulness was the governorship, but he enjoyed, perhaps, being tempted. He would not say *Yes,* but the way he said *No* left a door open.

The family was together at Sagamore Hill, early in June. When, two weeks later in Philadelphia, Roosevelt marched up the aisle of the convention hall, through a tempest of applause, to take his seat with the New York delegation, surprise was expressed because he did not remove the broad-brimmed black campaign hat that shaded his set face. The hat annoyed the Party's powerful chairman, Mark Hanna, who liked to see statesmen in uniform, which meant a frock coat and top hat, and he turned to Lodge sitting beside him. "Teddy ought to be spanked."

"Why Roosevelt wore the hat," remarks one of his biographers darkly, "must be left to the psychoanalysts." Happily, the services of the soothsayers may in this case be dispensed with. Theodore wore the hat, in the first place, no doubt, because he liked that kind of hat. He failed to remove it that particular morning for the simple reason that he had a hole in his head that he wanted to avoid comment on, as long as he could. How the hole got there

87

is a bit of history that Elon Huntington Hooker unfolded to Hamlin Garland, twenty-odd years later. Ten days before the convention, Theodore, home from Albany for a week end at Sagamore, had led his children and a number of guests, his assistant state engineer, Hooker, among them, in a scramble up and down steep heights in the Cove Neck woods. At one point, Alice had found herself on top of a cliff from which she could not get down. As her father was rescuing her, a piece of rock, dislodged from the ledge, fell upon his head, cutting a deep gash.

Roosevelt went to the national Republican convention in Philadelphia resolved to refuse the nomination. When he returned to Sagamore Hill he was the vice-presidential nominee. What intervened to change his mind is one of the fascinating half-told tales of American history. But the important event of the convention for him and for the nation was not his nomination. It was his emergence as a leader of the political thinking of a new generation. The younger men in the party were sick of the old figures, the Hannas, Platts, Quays and Depews, seeing all public life in terms of "the protection of infant industries"; aging men, afraid of everything that might conceivably threaten the only treasure they knew anything about. These delegates felt their hearts lift as Roosevelt, seconding McKinley's renomination, appealed again and again not to the caution in them but the courage. The vistas he opened before their eyes were spacious. He spoke of "the great nations of the earth" and, they knew, counted his own among them, "glorious in youth and strength," looking into the future "with fearless and eager eyes, rejoicing as a strong man to run a race." America did not stand "in craven mood," he said, asking to be spared the task, cringing as it gazed on the contest. "We challenge the proud privilege of doing the work that Providence allots us, and face the coming years high of heart and resolute of faith that to our people is given the right to win such honor and renown as has never yet been granted to the peoples of mankind!"

Here was youth calling to youth, vision to vision, daring to daring. The thunders that followed his peroration were nothing to the roars that greeted his nomination an hour later, drowning out the band playing the Rough Riders' theme-song, "There'll Be a Hot Time in the Old Town Tonight," overwhelming for the moment even Edie's apprehension and grief. As his name was "shouted, drowned, taken up, swept out of sight time and again by the wild spontaneous roars and tumults of applause," the reporter of the New York World noted, "the wife of the man who has been the inspiring figure at this great convocation was unable to resist the terrific force that was expending itself in shouts and shrieks of exultation. With just a little gasp of regret, Mrs. Roosevelt's face broke into smiles, as she, once for all, accepted the situation with a grace worthy of a true patriot." Edith insisted in a letter to Emily, later that day, that the enthusiasm, though "tremendous," had not moved her in the least. "I had hoped to the last moment that some other candidate would be settled upon. I am trying to look at the bright side," she added. Theodore would "get the rest that he sadly needs" and "an easy time" for the next four years, "assuming that the election goes rightly, of course." The salary would be two thousand less than they were getting at Albany, but they wouldn't have to entertain, so she wouldn't have to have any new clothes. There was *some* balm in Gilead.

The townspeople were at the Oyster Bay station prepared to give their hero an appropriate welcome when the train on which he had left Long Island City reached Oyster Bay. But he did not turn up, and missed the cheers, having stopped on the way to visit Jake Riis, sick abed at Richmond Hill.

Chapter IX

"*IT WAS* a hard four days at Philadelphia," Roosevelt wrote Elihu Root, a few days after his return to Sagamore. It was a token of what the summer was to be. The telegraph operator at Oyster Bay could not handle the messages that came for the vice-presidential candidate, and Roosevelt worked for days, far into the night, dictating his acknowledgments. Distinguished callers came, and he received them. Photographers came, and he obliged them, on foot and on horseback. But when two men with cameras crept out of the underbrush near the water's edge and snapped his children bathing, he lost his temper, threatening to take "legal steps" if necessary. He would not have the innocent freedom of his children violated. "I am a public man and free game," he said to Jake Riis, "but my house is my castle. In my home I will be let alone."

Roosevelt went west to a Rough Rider reunion, and on his way home stopped off at Canton, Ohio, McKinley's home town. The President asked him to be his guest overnight. Roosevelt, who knew well enough that presidential invitations were, by tradition, not refusable, nevertheless demurred. He had to get home. A promise was involved. There had been weeping and wailing when he had told his children that he would have to be at the Rough Rider reunion in Oklahoma City on the Fourth of July, and nothing but his assurance that he would be with them for a deferred celebration at the end of the week had quieted the tumult. He could not break a promise like that, not even for the President of the United States or a national election.

The elm-shaded road to Cove Neck was a shambles when Roosevelt drove up from the station that Saturday afternoon, and he dreaded to think what the wild midsummer storm the day before might have done to the Sagamore trees. But he found them all standing. The children, surrounded by cousins and friends, were waiting for him with enough gunpowder in the house to blow it into the Bay. They had been as loyal to their own promise as he to his, and had kept all their fireworks against his coming. A sudden thunderstorm threatened the deferred celebration, and a dozen young faces fell; but there was a happy ending after all. "Thanks to the rain," Roosevelt remarked to the correspondents who flocked into his study after dinner, "we will probably now be able to preserve the house, and we will trust in Providence to prevent injury to the youngsters."

Promptly at eight, the father of the family set the first rocket soaring toward the stars. Rockets followed rockets, pinwheels whistled, whizzed, sputtered and spat, fire-crackers cracked, crackled or boomed, lifting tin cans in air, and Roman candles popped fiery balls of every conceivable color. Into the circle of illumination, as the hours passed, groups of townspeople advanced out of the darkness, with no sense of trespass on their side or the Governor's. This man, silhouetted for a moment, now and again, against the brightness of red or blue or yellow fire, might be the Governor of the state and the Republican candidate for the Vice-Presidency, but chiefly he was their neighbor. It was a family party, indeed, but with all the town a part of the family.

For two hours Sagamore Hill was a fountain of sparks. The house survived, and all the children went to bed intact.

2

Roosevelt was back at Sagamore less than a week when he had to climb into his striped trousers and freshly pressed cutaway to receive officially the less than startling information that he had been nominated for the Vice-Presidency. Contrary to Republican custom, Mark Hanna had arranged the notification of the presidential and vice-presidential candidates on the same day. The "cowboy," Hanna remembered, according to the New York *World,* had "the habit of taking the center of the stage and getting himself talked about to the exclusion of others." What more effective way of thrusting him into the background than to notify him on the same day on which McKinley was to have the center of the stage?

Once more everything in Oyster Bay that had wheels wound up through the woods from the Cove. The surreys, buggies, buckboards and farm-wagons bulged with Republican statesmen from all the states, a territory or two, one of the new "possessions," Hawaii, and the District of Columbia, accompanied by other Party worthies, mainly from New York.

Whatever solemnity Senator Wolcott of Colorado and his fellow politicos of the Notification Committee may have felt, as they climbed gingerly out of their rickety conveyances, Roosevelt speedily dispelled, greeting them under the porte-cochère with a handshake and a word that made each feel that, though the candidate might be glad to see everyone, he was obviously interested chiefly in him. Roosevelt had a gift for creating such an impression, all the more effective because it was wholly unconscious.

Edith, in figured China silk trimmed with narrow black velvet ribbon and black lace, seemed to observers almost as glad as her husband to greet these none too sparkling strangers. In a year and a half she had learned to enjoy being the Governor's wife and was not shy any more. She was "becoming somewhat reconciled," moreover about her husband's candidacy, Theodore had written Lodge. That was as much as he knew about it. Reconciled or not, she was not one to tell the world.

"Now, gentlemen," said Roosevelt in crisp, business-like fashion, leading the way to the piazza, "let us proceed." He took his place by the living-room window, facing the gentleman from Colorado and the semi-circle of committee-men and guests, the men in frock coats, the women brightly gowned and providing points of vivid color. Nearby were Ted and Kermit, "looking up to their father with simple adoration," the *World* reporter noted, "the unconscious tribute of a great love, for the junior Roosevelts think that the ages have never produced their distinguished father's equal." Up the grassy field from the Bay a soft breeze brought comfort to perspiring statesmen with wilting collars.

The Senator spoke of the "pleasant duty" that was his, the "unanimous" and "spontaneous" character of the action of the convention, the need of the Empire State of the Governor's services, and the greater need of the nation. He spoke of the candidate's striking Americanism, his "bright and glorious record," in which every young man in the country found "an incentive to better things and higher ideals."

Roosevelt's response was according to pattern, spoken characteristically, with sharp enunciation and emphasis, and happily brief.

92

Once again, the election was "much more than a mere party contest." Once again, there was "a parting of the ways" with "prosperity and high honor" on the Republican road, and "misery," "disaster" and "shame" on the Democratic. If anyone regarded the acceptance-speech as actually the trumpet-call that the candidate might have been expected to sound, no one at the meeting said so loudly enough for any reporter to hear. Roosevelt had done better from the back platform of his train, on his recent trip to the West. The address was redeemed by the impulsive step forward that the Governor took, at the end. "Here, Ned," he said, addressing the Senator, "it is not to the National Committee that I want to say this. This is to my friends—friends," he added quickly, "of my own state who are here." Much as he felt honored to have the vice-presidential nomination, he added, "you cannot imagine how badly I feel at leaving the men with whom I have worked for civic decency and righteousness and honesty in the politics of New York."

Those remarks, the New York *Times* reporter observed, pleased everybody, though William Barnes, Jr., the new chairman of the Republican State Committee, "that loyal follower of Senator Platt," was seen to "pass his hand over his face as the Governor referred to his efforts in behalf of better politics."

Then followed a scene which another generation would regard as so commonplace as to be taken for granted, but which, that hot day in July, 1900, seemed even to the representative of the sparkling and up-to-the-minute New York *Sun,* worth a column of amazed comment. The Governor announced that some "misguided photographers" wanted to take pictures, but not even he was prepared for the array of cameras that suddenly confronted the porchful of notables. Everyone expected a picture for the historical record, of course, but what was this unseemly scramble of persons carrying all manner of impertinent black boxes?—"some that the operators carried around by their lids; others on stilts; others unfolded out of queer, self-supporting cases." The photographers manœuvred for position, scrambled hither and yon and deliberately got in one another's way; fat photographers and thin ones, some meek and some "as important as the Chief of Police in a village that has two policemen."

The galaxy of notables was amused, and then bored. "Gentlemen," cried the Governor in his most solemn manner, "have mercy! Our collars are going, going, going!"

The photographers fell over one another in their effort to be obliging. A prepossessing young woman directing the efforts of one of the photographers wooed Senator Wolcott, securing shots which a later generation would accept as sufficiently "candid." A man with a pointed beard broke through the line with an enormous box with a lens four inches across, and hid under a huge black cloth. On the porch the boredom deepened and the Governor was showing signs of revolt when Ted, Kermit, Archie and Ethel saved the day, appearing from the direction of the dining-room with trays bearing croquettes, salmon and sandwiches.

Tea was the only beverage served. The Indiana committeeman, taking his cup from Mrs. Roosevelt, urged her to join her husband on his forthcoming campaign trip. "Come and bring all the children," he urged, "and we'll show you Western hospitality."

Mrs. Roosevelt protested. The entire family? That would be too great an imposition even by Western standards.

"That's all right," the Hoosier insisted. "We want to see you out there and if necessary we'll hire a hotel."

The warm heart gave an extra beat, no doubt, under the benediction of the grateful, if non-committal, smile.

3

The family on Sagamore Hill saw little of the husband and father that summer but had ample opportunity to know where he was and what he was doing and saying. The papers were full of him. While the President, on the front porch of his house in Canton, Ohio, preached to visiting delegations the gospel according to Senator Mark, his team-mate carried the fight to the people between the Alleghenies and the Rockies. That was "enemy country" where the silver tongue of William J. Bryan, again the Democratic candidate, still made the senses swoon; the "cowboy statesman" was needed to remind the public that the Party which had brought prosperity was able to maintain it, and that American troops were a better assurance of freedom to the Filipino than bloodthirsty Moro chieftains or ignorant politicos, strutting their hour until Germany or Japan was ready to take over.

From the eastern seaboard to the Middle West came the news-stories, editorials and cartoons that Edith Roosevelt pasted that summer into the folio ledger that had succeeded the modest scrap-books of the earlier years. They told of two triumphant but desperately arduous campaign-tours, the first through the Middle West, the second and longer through the mountain states. Like a circus Roosevelt was taken from city to city and state to state, with a half-dozen set speeches a day and countless platform talks. Not the least of his ordeals were the bands, all under the illusion that his favorite tune was "A Hot Time in the Old Town Tonight." That theme-song of the Rough Riders pursued him from New York to Montana. At every whistle-stop there was a band and, at the stops where he made scheduled speeches, generally two or three competing with each other and with him—and all playing "A Hot Time in the Old Town Tonight."

The chronicle of that summer is in the headlines of Edith Roosevelt's clippings:

RANGE GREETS ROOSEVELT
ROOSEVELT IN WYOMING
WYOMING IS STIRRED UP
ROOSEVELT ROUSES BUTTE
IDAHO HEARS ROOSEVELT
ENTHUSIASM AROUSED IN UTAH

"Tis Tiddy alone that's runnin," commented Finley Peter Dunne's priceless Mr. Dooley, "an' he ain't r-runnin', he's gallopin'."

"I have occasional notes from Theodore," Edith wrote her sister, "and follow his progress in the papers. He is evidently enjoying the trip in spite of the great fatigue. His voice holds out and all the meetings have been successful." As for the Vice-Presidency, she wrote, "I hate even to think of it, and can't feel reconciled at all."

4

Edith was torn that summer between solicitude for Theodore and the pain of getting Ted ready to leave the parental roof. Ted was to go to Groton School that fall, and his mother spent the scorching midsummer weeks on the piazza, marking his clothes, his bed linen and towels and everything else that he was taking with him. "Getting Ted ready for school is rather sad work for me," she wrote Emily, "and has to be done with a very smiling face for fear of working on his feelings unduly." For Ted was dreading the wrench as much as she. The middle of September, Edith prepared to take him to the school. Theodore was to have done it, but Theodore was in the mountain states making hay for the Party, day in, day out, at a cost to his own physical resources that made Edith's blood boil. "I should feel worse about taking Ted away," she wrote Emily, "if I did not have Theodore on my mind."

A week later she wrote: "You can't think how we miss Ted. The house seems so empty without him." At Groton, there was a great emptiness, also—in the pit of Ted's stomach. He was desperately homesick, consoled only by the little volume of Frank Stockton's "Rudder Grange" that he had been accustomed to read curled up on a chair in his mother's room, and that Edith had thrust into his trunk at the last minute. Early in October, life began to look up for him again. He was going out for his dormitory football team and, three weeks later, was its captain. He was, in fact, exhibiting both pluck and a good temper. A prefect, who put him on the carpet for "scrapping" in study-hours, returned later to say that perhaps he had been unduly severe. "Oh, no matter," Ted answered. "It will make me remember not to do it again." Ted was learning quickly to stand on his own feet.

When, shortly after, Edith heard that a neighbor who had sent a boy to boarding-school had withdrawn him because he was homesick, she gave a scornful snort. That wasn't the way children were brought up at Sagamore.

5

Meanwhile, two thousand miles away, the vice-presidential candidate was continuing to address his fellow-countrymen, and the papers saw to it that his wife missed none of the colorful details. As the Governor and his party entered Colorado, which was recognized Bryan territory, she had occasion, more than once, to catch her breath.

ROOSEVELT IN DANGER, *Fierce Fighting in the Streets*, were the New York headlines. Edith's reaction was characteristic. "Tomorrow I shall get Theodore's letter about it," she wrote Emily, calmly. A prideful wife and adoring children might take new heart from other headlines, in the best tradition of romantic fiction, telling how the husband and father "courageously refused to be driven from his tour."

The papers that flowed in a steady stream into Sagamore that summer and autumn were filled with other stories of the candidate, less factual and all calculated to burn into the public mind the picture of a latter-day sun-god. Once more, Mr. Dooley gives the authentic flavor: "He niver stops. In Wounded Knee he busts a broncho that has kilt almost th' entire male popylation; busts it so har-rd 'twud dhraw a baby cerredge without wakin' the occupant. He finds a poor ranchman whose punchers is off on a dhrunk, an' he goes out an' rounds up thirty thousan' head iv cattle in less thin an hour. Afther that he r-rides off to th' cow town, finds th' cowboys, takes their guns away fr'm thim, bates thim into subjiction an' swears thim all in as mimbers iv th' Christian Indeavor Society."

Roosevelt's own summary was more prosaic. "I have had a very hard trip," he wrote his brother-in-law, Douglas Robinson. Aside from "half a dozen first-class horseback rides, I do nothing but fester in the car, and elbow to and from stagings where I address my audiences."

"Poor Theodore! I can't bear to think of him," Edith wrote Emily early in October. "I don't really feel as if he owed the party all the work he has done." Two weeks later she wrote, "I am just going down to meet Theodore, or what is left of him." A good deal, she found, was left. "Theodore is very hoarse but looks wonderfully well. I do not see how he has stood the fatigue and excitement." It was Edith, in fact, who showed the strain more than Theodore. "I have grown so thin with the anxiety of this campaign that the bones in my neck show. If all goes well I hope to gain a few pounds."

6

The Republican Party celebrated the return of its hero with a display of fireworks and a mass-meeting in Madison Square Garden that brimmed over into the adjoining park. "I bought a new hat for the occasion," Edith wrote her sister. "Brown velvet with a white plush crown, almost entirely covered with a bird. It tips low over my forehead and, alas, cost sixteen dollars!"

Alice and Kermit were with her at the meeting which, she wrote, was "really a triumph." But the significance of the cheering in the city's greatest auditorium, or of the milling crowds around a dozen spell-binders in the Square itself, was nothing to that of the ninety thousand men, shouting "Teddy, Teddy, Teddy!" as they passed in review before the vice-presidential candidate, in a pouring rain, in New York, the Saturday before election.

Roosevelt drove up Broadway in the downpour, through cheering crowds, and, by the time he reached the reviewing-stand in Madison Square, his hair was flat on his forehead, his eyeglasses dripped water, and his hat flapped about his wrist. Alice was on the stand waiting for her father, and defied the elements at his side. The Party bigwigs, it seemed, had been so assured that God was a Republican that they had provided no shelter against rain. For seven hours, protected only by his blue raincoat and cape, Roosevelt stood in the chill November deluge, bareheaded, as the human river flowed by.

When a reporter asked him solicitously next day at Sagamore Hill whether the drenching he had taken had not brought on a cold or a touch of rheumatism, Roosevelt hooted, as though the idea were too absurd to be considered. "Rheumatism? Cold?" he exclaimed. "Why, I never felt better in my life! There isn't a twinge in a single muscle. In fact, I believe the shower-bath did me good. I hope the same was true of those gallant men who showed their mettle by marching." He paused, musing. "Tell me honestly," he went on, "do you really think that such a demonstration under any conditions whatsoever, could make a man sick?" He did not wait for an answer. "No, No! It's not that sort of thing that gives a man a cold. The atmosphere may be chilly but your flesh keeps warm when you get a welcome like that."

7

If, after the Sound Money parade, any doubt remained in anybody's mind how the election would go, the Tammany boss, Richard Croker, and his mayor, Robert A. Van Wyck, removed it when the mayor's fat and bumbling chief of police, William S. Devery, issued a directive to his subordinates telling them to disregard at the polling places the deputies of the State Election Bureau. Since the function of the bureau was to secure orderly elections, free of intimidation and fraud, the Devery message meant one thing and one thing only.

It was a situation made to order for Roosevelt. Nothing that he himself might have imagined could have suited better his temperament, his habit of mind or his liking for dramatic action, or could have fitted better into the picture that the public, across the country, had of him as the valiant civic reformer.

He did not act at once, though the order struck at his own authority as governor of the state. He waited, in fact, for twenty-four hours. What could be more appropriate, or effective, than to dramatize on Election Day itself the fundamental right of the citizen to vote as he saw fit and to have his vote honestly counted?

Monday evening, in his study at Sagamore Hill, with the opening of the polls less than twelve hours away, Roosevelt took the mayor in hand. In terms as direct as the English language could make them, he wrote him that he, the Governor, would not "fail to call to summary account" anyone, including the mayor, "guilty of intimidation, or connivance at fraud, or of failure to protect every legal voter in his rights."

He gave his letter to the press, and the news was on every breakfast table from Maine to California, Tuesday morning, giving the voter a final picture of the vice-presidential candidate which no self-respecting citizen could argue with or laugh off. Roosevelt might seem to one voter too "jingoistic," to another too "impetuous," to a third too much "the big I AM," and each, on the surface evidence might make a case. But what could you say against a governor who could crack down on a city's officials so simply, yet so effectively, and do it apparently just in the nick of time?

The story was as potent in Iowa and Oregon as in New York, for everybody knew about Tammany. So, thanks to the zeal of the unregenerate, Roosevelt went into the election in shining armor, with his spear clear through the Tiger.

8

Roosevelt drove to the polls in his two-seated surrey, known in the family as the "express wagon," driven by Frank Hall the family coachman, and bringing with them Noah Seaman, the farmer, and "Pop" Davis, the crotchety old colored gardener, who had driven the Governor to Norwich-town twenty years before when he cast his first vote. As the candidate entered the polling place in Fisher's Hall, one flight up from the street, he seemed abstracted and strode toward a booth before he realized that he had no ballot. The clerks were busy with other voters, and it was not until a voter, coming out of a booth, saw the situation that James Mills, one of the clerks, handed the Governor a ballot. Two minutes later Roosevelt deposited it with Ed Franklin, jocosely known as "the Democratic Party in Oyster Bay."

"Theodore Roosevelt, 180," sang out Franklin, "has just voted."

An old man, Charlie Bayliss, who had voted for every Republican since John C. Frémont, buttonholed Roosevelt and told him all about it. Other neighbors joined them and the talk became lively; Ed Franklin pounded on the ballot-box. "Less order, please, less order!"

Everybody laughed, and Franklin hastily amended his admonition, explaining that the clerks could not hear the calling of the numbers.

Roosevelt turned and raised his hat with a characteristic flourish. "Good day, gentlemen," he said. "I had better escape before I am charged with inciting a riot."

He was stopped on the stairs by a young man who had late football news, and remained there five minutes or more flattening himself against the wall to make room for people going up and going down. On the sidewalk he stopped for a talk about certain fences that needed fixing at Sagamore. Then he went home.

To the newspapermen, he seemed, that evening, wholly detached from the excitement that seemed to possess everyone else. Calling at Sagamore Hill after supper, to give him the early reports, they found him in evening dress, with Edith and Alice and Bob Ferguson. The house showed no indications of flurry or thrill. It still had no telephone, and the Governor had again refused to let the telegraph companies string special wires. The telegrams that came from Republican headquarters and from personal friends came the hard way, by bicycle from Oyster Bay.

The reporters, gathered in his study, produced returns from a sufficient number of states to indicate the trend, and offered congratulations. Roosevelt raised a deprecating hand. "Please don't. I don't really feel that I am subject for congratulation." He paused, his head shaking doggedly. "This election tonight means my political death." He paused again. "Of course, gentlemen, this is not for publication."

Late in the evening a *World* reporter brought him word that the Republicans had carried New York by 150,000.

"Isn't that fine?" Roosevelt exclaimed. "By the way, what was the score in the Princeton-Columbia game?" Whereupon he turned to young Ferguson and talked football and bear-hunting. He went to bed at midnight, with the result still suspended.

At two in the morning, Edward Marshall of the *World*, who, as a correspondent in Cuba, had been shot in the spine in the Rough Riders' first fight at Las Guásimas and was still on crutches, was roused from his bed at the Octagon House in Oyster Bay and told by his editor to let Roosevelt know that the last doubts of a Republican victory had vanished. With a brilliant youth named Perry from the New York *Sun*, he started in a buggy for Sagamore Hill. The three-mile drive developed unexpected hazards. At the bend of the Cove Neck Road an exceptionally high tide had left a thirty-foot catboat behind. The catboat, looming ghostly in the darkness, proved too much even for a livery-stable horse. By the time the animal had been restored to something resembling sanity the east was graying. It was five o'clock before the last obstruction had been removed and the buggy drew up under the Sagamore porte-cochère.

Marshall hunched his way up the steps on his crutches and rang the bell. He had borrowed a coachman's coat with buttons like saucers and was a spectacle which the sleepy Vice-President-elect, clad only in his nightgown, could not immediately identify. Marshall gave his news. Roosevelt bustled him into the house, thrust a chair behind him and ran upstairs. The reporter was conscious of figures coming and going in the upper hall and then of excited voices; and stomped out on the porch again, recognizing that this might be a moment when even a newspaperman might prefer to be not too near the heart of a family who might appear unconcerned in public but, being what they were, could not help being deeply moved.

The dawn was brightening when, a few minutes later, Roosevelt, now clad in a flannel shirt and battered knickerbockers, joined the newspapermen. All his teeth were demonstrating the sincerity of his "I am delight—" when the chill November wind swept young Perry's hat off. The horse was still skittish, and the reporter did not dare leave him to pursue his hat; Marshall, on his crutches, was helpless in the situation; and the thirty-mile gale swept the hat westward into space.

The Vice-President-elect did not hesitate. He dashed after the hat, catching it finally after what Marshall subsequently described as "very creditable leg-work," when it lodged against the fence at

101

the foot of the western slope. When Roosevelt had returned with it, he stood beside the buggy, dusting the hat lightly with his fingers. Holding it out, rather at random, toward no one in particular, he began to speak of the days ahead, the needs of the nation and its opportunities at home and abroad. Marshall noted in his eyes "an almost wondering look of realization," even of exultation.

The reporter swung himself awkwardly into the buggy. "Goodbye, Mr. Vice-President."

In the white light of early morning Marshall could see a dull flush slowly rising in Roosevelt's cheeks. The rugged features took on new lines of aspiration and determination, and the shoulders settled as though already they were conscious of the weight of new and limitless responsibilities. As the Governor turned to go up the steps into the house, Marshall said to himself that here, unshaven, disheveled, in torn shirt and flapping knickerbockers, was a man of destiny.

But the young *Sun* man, trying to keep his skittish horse in order, had no such thoughts. The eyes he turned on the Colonel were friendly but sophisticated, and almost patronizing. "Hurrah for Teddy!" he cried.

Roosevelt turned and flashed his teeth in an appreciative grin.

Chapter X

FOR THE six remaining weeks of his term as governor, Theodore went back and forth between Albany and Sagamore Hill, accompanied generally by Edith, leaving the children in charge of the faithful Mame and Alice's capable governess, Miss Young.

The decision to keep Sagamore as the family base that winter had been made mainly for reasons of economy. With the vice presidential salary two thousand less than the governor's and Ted at an expensive school, Edith was back at the old business of counting pennies. Alice looked unfavorably on the idea of hibernation at the end of a branch line, with all her Cove Neck friends in New York for the winter, but Edith, as usual, showed her the cloud's silver lining. "I tell Alice," she wrote Emily, "that, after a winter of country air and early hours, we shall be such a beautiful family that we shall strike Washington dumb." Alice, like the Persian poet, would have preferred to take the cash and let the credit go.

The news from Ted sounded like reports from a war. From the genial editor of the humorous weekly, *Life,* Edward Sanford Martin, who had had it from his own son, also at Groton, Theodore learned that Ted had "licked all the boys in his form." Such belligerency seemed even to Theodore to be going a bit strong and he was inclined to be apologetic. Ted was not quarrelsome, he assured Martin, and he was certainly not a bully. The reports, he assumed, referred to "amicable wrestling and boxing bouts." He admitted that he himself was responsible for some of Ted's "fighting proclivities," but most of them, he insisted, "came naturally." Kermit and Archie were not, in the least, fighters like Ted, "although I think I have succeeded in instilling into them the theory that they ought not to shirk any quarrel forced upon them." To another correspondent he added a delicious, defensive touch by pointing proudly to his belligerent son's singing in the choir.

"Kermit is very difficult to manage," Edith wrote her sister. With Ted off at school, he was feeling his oats. He came into his mother's room one morning with a request that he be allowed to change his room which, Theodore wrote Emily, he thought "too small for a person of his size and social importance in the family . . . an impossible request and, when persisted in, with accents of injury, it aroused Edith's wrath. After some preliminary remarks the dialogue grew heated and ran much as follows:

"*Towhead:* 'Well, I *would* like to change my room. It's too small.'

"*Edith: (with impassioned earnestness)* 'Change your room! Of course not. It's a *very* nice room. I suppose you would like to change your parents too?' (*This question would have been an unwary one if Ethel had been the offender, as in her moments of darkness that young lady would be quite capable of answering in the affirmative.*)

"*Towhead: (Mutter that he was friendless and unappreciated as compared with the rest of the children.*)

"*Edith: (strong in a sense of injury).* 'You're not little Nobody's dog!' (*A proposition under which Kermit collapses; but at that moment the condition of his nails attracts Edith's attention, and she continues with a sense of having already combléed "—overpowered —" him with benefits*) 'Why it's only day before yesterday I gave you a nail brush!' " . . . .

Kermit and Ethel had got over their early inclination to hit each other over the head with whatever came handy and were bosom friends in every type of unholy mischief. They were "not at all good to Archie, who is an inoffensive little boy," Edith wrote her sister, "but the trouble is that Ethel is so flattered when Kermit condescends to play with her that she is only too delighted to do anything that he suggests."

Ethel and Kermit were having Bible lessons together that year and were both impressed unfavorably by Joseph's conduct in telling his brothers of the dream presaging his future dominance over them.

"I think that was very foolish of Joseph," Kermit remarked.

"So do I, very foolish," Ethel chimed in, "and I do not understand how he could have done it."

"Well," mused Kermit after a pause, "I guess he was simple, like Jane in the Gollywogs."

The two were absorbed in their garden and their various and assorted menagerie. Their guinea-pigs bore distinguished names. "Admiral Dewey" and "Bishop Doane" were favorites, with "Fighting Bob Evans" and "Father O'Grady" close runners-up. The fact that the name and the sex failed frequently to harmonize was a matter of complete indifference to the children, Archie, aged seven, running into the house on one occasion and electrifying a mixed company by announcing, "Oh, oh, Father O'Grady has had some children!"

Of all their pets, Kermit and Ethel gave their hearts in deepest devotion to several large barnyard hens they had named after characters in the books their mother or their father had read to them. Unexpectedly, one day, Kermit brought the barnyard into the table-talk. Theodore and Edith were commenting on how badly the President's wife was looking, when Kermit was heard observing to Ethel, as though no one else were within earshot: "Oh, Effel, I'll tell you what Mrs. McKinley looks like. Like Davis' hen dat died—you know de one dat couldn't hop on de perch."

Yet the little boy had moments of astonishing maturity. Overhearing his mother comment on the commotion a cousin of hers was making because her son was facing hostile bullets in the Philippines, he remarked, "Just suppose you had made us all miserable, Mother, the year Father went to the war?"

2

The galleries of the Senate Chamber, on March 4, 1901, were already packed with visitors, when Edith and the children, accompanied by Bamie, Corinne and their husbands, took their places in the gallery. Alice, just seventeen, very mature, and dressed, according to one reporter, in "cadet blue with military trimmings," and according to another in a "red dress, trimmed with black velvet," contributed to the picture obviously. The reporters were no less divided on the matter of Edith's attire, described by one of them as a "dark tailor-made suit with a tight-fitting jacket and a small velvet toque," and by another as a "costume" of "light tan cloth combined with darker brown fur, white lace and blue panne velvet," with "a hat of white chiffon, trimmed with black velvet and pompons of chiffon." Readers could take their choice, and still may. Ted's attire was wholly individual, consisting of the

105

trousers of one suit, the coat of another and the waistcoat of a third. To his mother's exclamation of dismay, on his arrival from Groton, he had responded in righteous indignation: "Now, mother, you know you wrote me to come in my best clothes; and these are the best—the best coat and the best trousers and vest, too." The coats of the boys and Ethel were plastered with McKinley and Roosevelt buttons, flags and other patriotic emblems.

Five lively children nearly fell over the rail in their excitement and fairly split the seams of their kid gloves as their father entered the Senate Chamber, escorted by a senator and a representative. The papers next day spoke of the shoulders thrown back, the face bronzed by the hunting-trip to Colorado from which he had just returned, the play of the muscles visible under the tightly buttoned frock-coat, the dark red carnation in his buttonhole.

"He was very quiet and dignified," Edith wrote Emily. "Spoke in a low voice and yet so distinctly that not a word was lost."

Once more he struck the note of his seconding speech in the Republican convention, speaking of "great privileges and great powers," and the responsibilities that go with them, adding in tones quivering with earnestness, "As we do well or ill, so shall mankind in the future be raised or cast down."

Mankind. Not just the United States or the North American continent, or even the Western Hemisphere. Mankind. The Americas, Europe, Asia, Africa, Australia, the whole wide world. It would sound reasonable enough to a Senate audience a half-century later, reluctant though it might be to draw the inferences. But to the pomp and power of the United States as it sat gathered in the Senate Chamber, that March day, the astonishing prophecy seemed as inconsequential as the rain beginning to patter on the skylight overhead. No one probably bothered to ask himself what "Teddy" was aiming at. Oratory was oratory, inaugural oratory was inaugural oratory, and you weren't supposed to reach beyond the warm emotion it gave you.

"A great work lies ready to the hand of this generation." What specifically the Vice-President meant he did not say. But the great theme which possessed him was none other than to make the youthful energy, the humanitarian impulse and the wealth and power of America—her greatness, in a word—count for the advancement not only of her own people but of all peoples everywhere.

It was a new statement for a new generation of the thought that has haunted Americans since the nation was founded, tucked away, of all places, in a vice-presidential inaugural address.

3

Even with a policeman all her own to guide her and her "retinue" of nineteen members of the assembled clan, Edith waited twenty minutes in the rain for a cab to take her and the children to the White House for the inaugural luncheon. She found Quentin there ahead of her with Pinckney, their colored factotum. Quentin had declared that he was "not going to hear Father pray at the Senate" and, having refused to promise that he would not talk during the ceremony if his mother insisted on his going against his will, had been left with his aunt in the house that Bamie had newly rented. When Edith reached the Executive Mansion, Quentin had just convulsed Mrs. Elihu Root by his reply to her arch query if he knew what his father was as a consequence of the morning's ceremonies. "Just Father," he had answered.

Ted distinguished himself in a different way. "He drank two glasses of champagne," Edith wrote Emily, "thinking it was bad fizzy water, and being very thirsty. Happily, it took no effect whatever, which speaks volumes either for Ted's head or the President's champagne."

Chapter XI

EXCEPT FOR Ted, the family was together again at Sagamore by the middle of March. The Senate had adjourned. Until December, when the new Congress was due to convene, Theodore noted with dismay, his official duties as Vice-President were done. That, multiplied by four, was what he had to look forward to. What was even worse, there was nothing in view even after this four-years period of honorable idleness should come to an end. Of course, there was a good deal of talk of his heading the Republican ticket in 1904, but all the precedents were against it. He might be senator, of course, but it was "very unlikely," he wrote a friend, that he would be "able to go on in politics." He might, of course, study law, but the prospect did not excite him.

Governor Odell, Roosevelt's successor at Albany, tried in vain, the week that Ted was home for his spring vacation, to get the Vice-President to come upstate for a dinner with all the state's Republican personages. He had already missed two days of Ted's home-coming, Theodore answered, because of public engagement which he could not dodge. "Now if I went up to Albany I should have to miss two days more and give up divers sprees we have planned together and which he has four small cousins coming out to share. I really do not feel it would be quite a square deal to do it. Ask your own son!"

Theodore had an intimacy of fellowship with the children, based in part on their recognition that, for all his occasional sternness when sternness was required, he could be trusted to wink at infractions of the rules when no principle was involved. When he returned at ten o'clock one night from a trip with Edith to Buffalo to open the Pan American Exposition, Kermit, in high feather, was up to greet him and exchange experiences with him while his father ate a late snack. Edith, who stood for no such nonsense as children staying up to all hours, had stopped off at Albany to visit friends, and Mame had looked the other way. The revolt ran right down the line. Ethel had put an alarm clock under her pillow to be sure to wake up but slept through its wild buzz, as did Quentin. Archie woke up sufficiently to murmur to his father the important news that he had found a new turtle just as small as the treasured specimen he already possessed.

The next morning, Quentin made up for what he had missed by following his father around wherever he went, accompanied by Black Jack, his own little dog, and carrying on a running comment while his father was dictating letters to a stenographer. Theodore admitted to Ted that the little boy had added "an element of harassing difficulty to my effort to answer my accumulated correspondence," but it did not occur to him apparently to tell the child to go elsewhere.

"Archie and Quentin," their father wrote a friend, "are as cunning as they can be, though they still do not know any more than the innumerable guinea-pigs which the little boys are at present breeding in the cellar." For other friends Theodore painted the picture of his two youngest, "marching solemnly through the room in a procession of two—Archie with a wooden musket on his shoulder and a small hatchet in his breast, and Quentin clad in a straight blue frock without any waist and a broomstick on his shoulder. Archie announced that they were hunting ogres and that he was the fairy king, and Quentin chimed in with, 'And I'm de fairy colonel; I'm de second highest.' Evidently in his mind even in fairyland a colonel was an exalted personage who ranked well up behind a king."

Like Kermit, Quentin, aged three and a half, had his moments of unexpected maturity, as when he was heard to remark to his nurse, quoting from some ballad that had been read to him, "You are the most unpleasant beast I e'er have looked on yet."

The Vice-President of the United States was relegated to the doghouse a month later when he took the children with a flock of neighboring cousins on an all-day picnic. After a luncheon of what Ted recalled as "baked clams and cinders, sandwiches and sand," the father took the children for a walk, leaving the mothers in a contented knot in the shade, sewing and chatting. Looking for shells satisfied the children for a while but the day was warm and what they wanted to do was to go bathing. But there were both boys and girls—and no bathing suits. "In a zealous but possibly not altogether well-considered effort to add to the general enjoyment," the Vice-President wrote Bamie, he permitted three or four of the children to go wading with their clothes on, with the result that before long they were swimming. "I wish you could have seen the more than Roman austerity with which Edith and Laura"— Mrs. J. West Roosevelt, the other mother involved—"received me when I herded the bedraggled procession back to them."

Ted never forgot the long row home, with his mother ostentatiously borrowing an elder cousin's coat to wrap around Kermit, and his father rowing very hard, saying nothing and "pretending that he was not there."

When they reached Sagamore, Edith declared, "Come with me, children. You must each of you have some Jamaica ginger to keep off colds."

Jamaica ginger seemed to the children a particularly noisome medicine and, when their mother had gone upstairs, they flocked around their father begging him to intercede for them.

A quarter-century later, Ted remembered his father's quizzical expression. "Children," he said, "I don't dare interfere. I shall be very fortunate if she doesn't give me ginger too."

A comically similar incident, involving adult guests, took place on a chilly day shortly after, when the Roosevelts' childhood friend, Fanny Smith, spent a week end at Sagamore with her husband, James Russell Parsons. The latter went for a hike with his host and returned, announcing that he had persuaded Theodore to have a swim. Archie, nearby, exclaimed, "Mr. Parsons is going to hear from Mother!"

He heard from his wife also. "Jim, how *could* you be so foolish?" she cried indignantly when they were alone in their room.

"Well," he answered, "I knew we'd have to do it sooner or later, and I thought I might as well be the hero of the occasion!"

What with the children, and picnics, and riding and rowing with Edie, and reading by a wood-fire in the evening, and friends coming for week ends and everything in the world to talk about and all the time in the world to talk about them, the Vice-Presidency, as the spring came to Sagamore, did not seem so bad after all. He "revelled," Roosevelt wrote his friend, William Howard Taft, "in the fresh, green sprouts on tree and bush, in the red of the blossoming maples and the sweet scent and coloring of the mayflowers." The robins, meadow-larks, song sparrows, field sparrows, vesper finches, blue-birds and redwings, were all "in full note." Ten days later he was writing Ted: "The cherry-trees are in full bloom; the peach trees just opening. The mayflowers and bloodroot have gone, the anemones and bellwort have come and the violets are coming. All the birds are here, pretty much, and the warblers troop through the woods." His enjoyment of it all had an undercurrent of guilt. What a life of "unwarrantable idleness" he was leading! He must get after this business of studying law, so he might have a profession when his term as Vice-President ended.

2

The fear that his influence on young men of high purpose whose affection and trust he cherished would begin to wane in the inactivity of the Vice-Presidency and be reduced to zero by the time his term ended, impelled Roosevelt to invite undergraduates from Harvard and Yale to Sagamore Hill that spring, to discuss with him and other veterans in the fight for good government, the possibilities of what Roosevelt described "as the cause of applied decency in public life."

Roosevelt took the project with a good deal of seriousness, going through some soul-searching to find out how best to help these young men recognize the importance of doing the little, humdrum elementary jobs of good citizenship in order to condition themselves to grasp the larger opportunities for service when later they came their way. That was how he himself had accomplished what he had. Not by genius; he had no particle of genius, he was convinced, or even any unusual talent; he had merely done the commonplace, not very difficult things which in theory most men agreed should be done by everyone: the point was, you didn't need exceptional gifts to render notable, even exceptional service; anyone with a fair amount of common sense, courage, integrity and physical hardihood could render it. He'd tell the boys that, if he was sure, when the time came, that they were in a frame of mind to recognize that he was sincere and not merely exhibiting "that particularly obnoxious form of pride that apes humility."

The group came for luncheon, late in June, and fore-gathered afterward on the spacious piazza that had been the scene of the two notification ceremonies and would yet witness a third. The eagerness of the young men to do their part in politics and government stirred Roosevelt. Men like these, idealists with their feet on the ground, were badly needed in the state and the nation, as well as in the political work required in the cities to undergird the social welfare agencies. "The most practical kind of politics," he pointed out, "is the politics of decency." "Political misgovernment is an annoyance on Fifth Avenue," one of his elder guests pointed out incisively, "but on the East Side it's a pestilent disease."

Through the long, warm afternoon and far into the evening the veterans, led by Roosevelt, presented the need and the opportunity to the young men they hoped to enlist, and the young men responded. The stars were bright in the summer sky when the visitors finally shook hands with the Vice-President under the porte-cochère and scrambled into buggies and surreys to catch the last train for New York.

"Yesterday was a field day," Edith wrote Emily, "twenty-five for lunch, and by dinner-time four more had arrived. The children and I took our lunch in a basket in Smith's field and dined with Aunt Lizzie. It was considerable of a strain on the establishment and I am glad it is over."

3

As early as April, Theodore had laid plans for a cruise in Great South Bay in July, with Ted, Kermit, and some of their cousins, for some fishing and shooting if possible. The boys were breathless with anticipation for weeks in advance, and it was a dark moment when Theodore's friend, Paul Morton, president of the Santa Fe Railroad, announced that he was planning to visit the Roosevelts during the particular week for which the trip had been scheduled. Caught between the magnate and the boys, Roosevelt stood by the boys. "On Monday I start with two of my own sons and four of their little cousins for a four days' shooting trip," he wrote Morton, "and it would break their hearts if I abandoned it."

The expedition in the sloop *Showabase* was all that he and the boys had hoped for. If the burden of the years was light upon you, the mere living on a boat for four days and nights was itself an adventure of a high order. Theodore carried through his part with unfeigned enthusiasm, and would not desert the ship even in response to an urgent invitation from his uncle, Robert Barnwell Roosevelt, writer, diplomat and pioneer conservationist, who had a summer cottage at Sayville, on Long Island's South Shore. He was acting the part of "nurse and governess," he explained, having six boys with six guns aboard one boat, and it was not an outfit that he felt he could, with safety, leave.

"It was a most courageous undertaking on Father's part," Ted wrote twenty-odd years later, "and the fact that we all returned uninjured speaks volumes for his discipline. Kermit was so small that, when he shot, Father had to support the gun. We wandered about the marshes and were bitten by mosquitoes. We sat patiently in eelgrass blinds and felt the thrill that comes when the first birds circle down half-seen in the gray of early dawn." He remembered the splash of the waves at night against the schooner's sides. "The faint cries of the night fowl filled us with as wild a longing as ever Stanley or Lewis knew."

Apart from a father's natural devotion to his offspring, Theodore had an objective delight in them, on the expedition, that had literary overtones. Ted and Kermit, running barefoot along the shore, "each with a Jim Crow hat, and, aside from this, exactly two garments apiece, busily collecting fiddler crabs in the marsh," seemed to him straight out of William Allen White's "Boyville." "I felt," he wrote its author, "that Piggy would have hailed them as his own brothers."

From Boyville's point of view the ultimate word on the expedition was spoken by one of the participants, the ten-year-old son of Theodore's sister Corinne. "My, but Uncle Ted is bully!" he exclaimed on his return home. "He never asked me to wash once!"

4

A new element was added, that summer, to the customary Sagamore program of tennis and riding and rowing and bathing and "stagecoach" on the raft and wild snap-the-whips down Cooper's Bluff, and bruised knees and poison ivy and tumbles off Pony Grant's successor, the long-suffering Algonquin. Alice was seventeen, and going to dances at the Seawanaka Yacht Club on Center Island. Alice, tall, slender, lovely to look at and quick-witted, was demonstrating daily the charm, the courage and the independence of mind she had inherited from both parents. She was fully aware that Today was not Yesterday, that times were changing and changing fast, and that American social life was taking on European trimmings. Her stepmother, to whom she was devoted, regarded the social standards of her own youth as fixed and unassailable; her father, whom she adored, and who was going forward by leaps and bounds in his economic and political thinking, was more Victorian than Victoria in the field of social habits and customs. Alice tried out her budding sophistication on the family, puffed a cigarette, and nearly blew the roof off the house.

The sense of detachment from the life of "the family" which her months with Auntie Bye, three years before, had begun, was sharpened by the fact that she was "grown-up" and therefore in a class apart from "the children." The friends she visited had other customs than those that governed Sagamore Hill or even Auntie Bye's home, and some of them attracted her. But when, on a visit to friends in the Adirondacks, in August, her jaw suddenly started to ache furiously and she was hastily shipped to Roosevelt Hospital in New York, she was glad enough to find herself again in the warm family embrace. Her father was in Denver making an address at the quarter-centennial celebration of Colorado's statehood, but her stepmother was at the hospital when she arrived. The family physician, Dr. George Brewer, put her instantly under ether and discovered an abscess in the bone, the consequence, it seemed, of an inadvertent kick in the lower jaw that a little girl had given her a year previously in the course of a fancy dance. The abscess loosened all her front teeth. "The lightest breeze," Alice remarked later, "would have made them wave." Edith stayed with her night and day.

Theodore, writing Lodge, gave a picture of "Little Rosamund's month of misfortunes," with Alice in the hospital, all the other children down with "awful colds,"—Could it have been a consequence of four days in wet sneakers on the cruise?—Ted and Quentin undergoing "slight surgical operations," and himself suffering from bronchitis that got no better on his Western speaking tour. He omitted several items—another operation on the faithful Mame, his own narrow escape in the West from pneumonia, or Kermit's personal little tragedy, his three guinea-pigs having vanished from their boxes, "leaving," Edith wrote Emily, "no trace behind. Kermit, broken-hearted, asked me to tell Theodore and Ethel and beg them not to mention the guinea-pigs to him."

114

Altogether, it had been quite a month on Sagamore Hill.

Alice had never before been a patient in a hospital, and found the experience absorbing. She was about ready, after a week, to be taken home, when her father, who had returned from Colorado to find more trouble brewing at Sagamore, arrived at the hospital. He brought Quentin, who had developed an abscess in his ear as a result of his cold. The condition was not dangerous in itself, "but the treatment for five days," Edith wrote Bamie, "was the most agonizing imaginable. It took the Doctor, myself and two nurses to give it, he fought and struggled so incessantly, and his shrieks of pain I shall never forget." Meanwhile, at Sagamore, Kermit developed earache. Edith suffered a new fright, and returned home, while Theodore, still fighting his bronchitis, spent successive nights in the hospital to keep the children company. Ted came next, not as a patient but to help Alice and Quentin pass the time. It was a family party of a new sort, tying them together with new bonds.

Before Quentin was back at Sagamore, his father was off again on a speaking tour that was to take him as far west as Minnesota, and back east to Vermont. Edith took Alice and the other children to the Tahawus Club in the Adirondacks to give them all some mountain air to hasten their recuperation. Theodore would join the family around September 10th for four or five days of hiking and fun, before they all returned to Sagamore the middle of the month.

Chapter XII

A FANATICAL anarchist named Leon Czolgosz thrust his hand across the Roosevelt family's pleasant plans. Wrapped in a handkerchief, the hand held a revolver which, on September 6th, at a public reception at the Pan American Exposition in Buffalo, sent two bullets into President McKinley.

Theodore heard the news at a political rally on Isle La Motte in Lake Champlain. Appalled and grief-stricken, for he had come to have a kind of younger-brother feeling for the President, he hurried to Buffalo. The President, he was assured by the physicians in charge, three days later, was out of danger and on the way to recovery. There was no reason why the Vice-President should not join his family in the Adirondacks.

"Theodore arrived," Edith wrote Bamie, "naturally much relieved at the rapid recovery of the President. It has really been a most trying position for him. . . . Rain is pouring," she added, "and we are planning to camp out tonight." Then, in a postscript, "Ted shot a buck on Tuesday." It was his first, and he was filled with pride.

That afternoon, Theodore and Edith, with Miss Young, the governess, Kermit and Ethel, accompanied by James MacNaughton, the president of the Tahawus Club whose cottage they were occupying, two guides and two young Harvard law students, Herman and Beverly Robinson, tramped to what was known as the Flowed Lands, five miles up the trail to Mount Marcy. Canoes took the party to two cabins at the upper or western end of Colden Lake, one for the men, the other for Edith, the governess and the children. "We had a delightful day," Edith wrote her sister, "for, in spite of the rain, the woods were beautiful and we dried ourselves before blazing fires and enjoyed the good supper the guides cooked for us."

Edith, who did not take to the strenuous life as wholeheartedly

116

as her husband, did not dream, as she tossed uneasily on her camp cot, of the tragic excitement that was stirring the doctors and officials in Buffalo through the hours of the night. In high spirits, shortly after nine o'clock, following breakfast in the kitchen of the men's cabin, the party separated—the Vice-President, with Mac-Naughton, the Robinson boys and the guides, taking the trail up the mountain, while Edith, with Miss Young and the children, returned by way of Avalanche Lake to the cottage at what was known as the Upper Works.

Once Edith, helping one of the children down the rough trail while Miss Young was helping the other, stepped aside to make way for a guide striding swiftly in the direction of Mount Marcy. She thought nothing of it but, after he had passed, said to herself, "I ought to find out why that man is going up the trail." She called back to Miss Young to ask. "Oh," the governess answered indifferently, "he has a message for one of the party on Mount Marcy."

Edith was troubled, but Theodore's assurance had put all anxiety for the President out of her mind. "It must be for one of the Robinson boys," she thought.

The Vice-President and his party reached the summit at twenty minutes past twelve, and found themselves in clouds that broke now and again to give them tantalizing vistas of blue ridges drifting in and out of the mist. In their descent they reached Lake Tear of the Cloud at two o'clock and were sitting about on rocks and stumps, having their lunch beside a little brook, when, some distance away, a woodsman, Harrison Hall, appeared out of a thicket, coming up the trail. "There wasn't a thought in my mind but that the President would live," Roosevelt told his friend J. J. Leary many years later, "and I was perfectly happy until I saw the runner coming. I had had a bully tramp and was looking forward to dinner with the interest only an appetite worked up in the woods gives you. When I saw the runner I instinctively knew he had bad news, the worst news in the world."

The woodsman handed him a slip of paper. Roosevelt withdrew a step or two. The message was from Elihu Root, the Secretary of War. "The President appears to be dying," it ran, "and members of the Cabinet in Buffalo think you should lose no time in coming."

Roosevelt stood in silence a moment, then told his companions what the note had said. "I must return to the club at once."

As they were preparing for the descent, MacNaughton took the elder Robinson to one side. "You go first," he said, "and be sure to go slowly and carefully. We don't want any broken legs on this trip." With the young man in the lead and the Vice-President next, they started down the mountain. At the Flowed Lands the party separated, Roosevelt proceeding to the Upper Works with Harrison Hall, and the rest returning to Camp Colden.

No fresh word had come from Buffalo when Theodore arrived at the cottage at six that evening, "wet and hungry," Edith wrote, "but in fine condition after his scramble." No news in this case was definitely good news. He took the precaution, however, of sending a messenger to the main clubhouse at the Lower Works, ten miles away, where the nearest telephone was, to pick up any messages which might have arrived subsequent to the one delivered to him that afternoon, and directed him to arrange for relays of horses in case he should, after all, be called to the President's side. But, Theodore remarked to Edith, there appeared no reason at the moment for him to hurry back to Buffalo. "I'm not going unless I am really needed. I have been there once and that shows how I feel. But I will not go just to stand beside those people who are suffering and anxious. I am going to wait here."

They went to bed at nine o'clock. At eleven, there was a sharp knock at the cottage door. It was his messenger, with a sheaf of telegrams, relayed by telephone, to the Lower Works. All said the same thing, with deepening anxiety: the President's condition was causing the gravest apprehension. The Vice-President must come at once. A special train would be waiting at North Creek.

Edith knew the road to the railroad: none too easy by daylight in good weather, and God knew what, at night, rutted deep by a wild rainstorm two days before. Even if her husband reached civilization in safety, what assurance was there that the evil thing which had struck down one President might not strike at the next in succession? Yet a girl, employed at the Upper Works, noted, in the general confusion, how calm both the Vice-President and his wife seemed. Of all the family only Archie seemed to be upset, wailing that his father was going away to be shot like Mr. McKinley.

Relays of swift horses and daring drivers bore Theodore thirty-five miles through the pitch-black night over roads dangerously washed by the heavy rains. He reached the railroad at five-thirty in the morning. The telegram he sent Edith from Ballston, an hour later, was bare and impersonal: "President McKinley died at 2:15

118

this morning. Theodore Roosevelt." Nothing more; no suggestions or directions for her own movements or the children's; Edie would know what to do. No hint of the turmoil of mixed emotions he was himself experiencing. Edie would know all about that too. You didn't have to spell out things for Edie. It was a great comfort.

2

While Theodore was speeding to Buffalo, Edith, with five children, Miss Young and the maid—Alice had gone to visit Bamie elsewhere in the mountains—was off in a carryall on the long drive which her husband had taken in wild haste twelve hours previous.

As the horses jogged down the mountain roads, Edith—so sedate outwardly, so absorbed in keeping the children from falling out of the carriage or getting so bored on the long drive as to become altogether unmanageable—was surely inwardly a riot of emotions in conflict. Pride in Theodore and his capacity to carry the heavy responsibility which had been thrust upon him, dominated, no doubt, the inner tumult; but against her assurance at intervals beat a kind of dread she had never known. Until the President had been shot —the President! That was Theodore now!—until Mr. McKinley had been shot, her imagination had never conceived the possibility of the treacherous assassin lying in wait for Theodore. But, since that tragic day, she had not had an easy moment until he had joined her at Tahawus. And now that he himself stood in the post of danger, would she ever really be able to breath freely again?

Few if any in the day-coach of the slow local, meandering southward from North Creek, guessed that the simply dressed woman, surrounded by baggage and a host of active, curly-haired children, was the new "First Lady of the Land." The tedious journey gave her little rest, but ample time to worry about Theodore. The daylight was beginning to deepen. He must be in Buffalo by this time . . . if all had gone well. That *if* . . . Would that henceforth be always in the back of her mind?

A New York *Herald* reporter, who boarded the train at Saratoga at six o'clock, brought her the news she most wanted to hear. The President had reached Buffalo in safety, at two o'clock that afternoon, and had taken the oath of office an hour and a half later.

Her face lighted up and her soft brown eyes shone. "Are you

119

quite, quite sure?" she asked. The reporter assured her that he had the facts. "Oh, thank you," she replied, "thank you so much for letting me know."

At Albany, she herded her brood aboard the Hudson River night-boat. As the dingy old *Adirondacks* steamed slowly southward, sleep eluded her, and she was exhausted when the boat docked at the foot of Canal Street early next morning. No one was waiting to receive the heavily veiled woman leading her youngest down the gangplank.

Only one cab was in sight, a battered vehicle, described by a reporter as of the "nighthawk variety." Before the sleepy driver could tumble off the box to open the cab door, Edith, the boy and the nurse were inside. A swarm of reporters closed round and peered in at the windows.

The First Lady was tired and nervous. Please. She had nothing to say. The children were all well and they were going directly home to Oyster Bay. No, she was not going to Buffalo, or, so far as she knew, to Washington. "I do not know what plans my husband may have made for me."

That was all. The other children and Miss Young came down the gangplank and jumped into a second cab that followed the first to the Long Island ferry at East 34th Street.

What Edith had said about the children was less truth than a defensive parry to discourage further questioning. Archie had come down with a bad case of tonsilitis and Quentin's ear was acting up again. From the ferry-house she tried to call Dr. Brewer on the telephone to have his judgment on Quentin, and found to her dismay that he had gone on his vacation; ironically, to the Tahawus Club. That was, somehow, the last straw. "That poor child couldn't even see his doctor," was the way she put it, thirty years later; and the memory of the ordeal lingered in the words, "We got out to Oyster Bay"; implying, "Don't ask me how."

The time of her arrival had happily not been announced, and there were no friends or neighbors at the railroad station to harry her with expressions of sympathy so mingled with congratulations that any word she might say in reply would be bound to be mis-construed. She could not face the prospect of rambunctious children inside the house and importunate reporters outside, and let the chil-dren, the governess and the nurse have Sagamore to themselves while she herself stretched out through most of a showery Sunday

120

at Aunt Lizzie's (Uncle James' widow), at Yellowbanks. The emotional turmoil and the long journey, Edith admitted, had left her "thoroughly worn out." She had a way of knowing the point at which too much became too much, and had learned to wait for the depleted energy to be restored. She knew she would need all she could summon. A wire from Theodore had asked her to meet him in Washington for Mr. McKinley's funeral. Of course, on that occasion, if ever, she must be at his side.

The quiet hours in Aunt Lizzie's comfortable old house gave Edith her first opportunity to get the story of Theodore's trip to Buffalo and the place and manner of his taking the oath of office. It was all in the black-bordered papers, sedately in the New York *Times*, colorfully in the *Sun*, luridly in the *Herald*—from the moment of Theodore's leaving Tahawus to his final, earnest personal addition to the oath: "And so I swear."

The *Sun* told the story in its single-column headlines:

OUR PRESIDENT
Roosevelt Takes the Oath in Buffalo
Touching Scene
All Those Present Showed Deep Emotion
The New Administration Will be Conducted
On McKinley Lines
Cabinet Asked to Stay

The *Herald* man at North Creek had interviewed Mike Cronin, the reckless driver of the last of the three relays that had borne the new President from the Tahawus Club to North Creek, and broken all records for the sixteen-mile run. At a ticklish section of the road, where a spill meant a hundred-foot drop, Mike had asked his passenger if he were afraid. "Not at all!" had been the reply. "Push ahead. If you're not afraid, I'm not. Push ahead!"

How like Theodore! How like him, too, Edith mused, perhaps, to enter the place of power at a wild gallop through the pitch-black night.

Yet with what dignity he had gone through the ordeal at Buffalo, insisting on paying his respects to Mrs. McKinley as a friend before taking the oath as President. How sensitive he had been in refusing —even peremptorily, as he had—an official escort for his call at the house of mourning, in order not to dramatize the passing of the power and the glory from the dead man to himself. Surely Edith's throat choked up at the picture of hard-headed Elihu Root in the library of the Ansley Wilcox house, about to ask Theodore to take the oath, standing silent for three painfully long minutes until he could bring his voice under control.

Theodore too had been moved almost to tears. The *Times* gave the picture of him: the long frock-coat, "fitting his athletic figure to perfection," the trousers, "almost a solid gray," the waistcoat, buttoned high, with the thin gold watch-chain across it, the black four-in-hand tie knotted under the turn-down collar, the patent leather shoes, heavy-soled and square-toed. Where had Theodore got all those clothes? He had certainly not had them at Tahawus. He must have drawn heavily on his Buffalo friends.

If the hours at Aunt Lizzie's gave Edith a chance to catch up a little on Theodore's movements, it gave her an opportunity also to adjust herself to the destiny which had so abruptly changed the course of her husband's life—and her own. "I do dread the constraint and confinement of this new position for him," she wrote Emily that day, "and coming in such a tragic way." What was it going to do to their family life? To their relations to each other, and to the children? What was it going to do to Alice, just coming into womanhood? How would Ted, on his own at school, deal with the burden of being the President's son? And the younger children? Would they be mauled over and flattered and spoiled?

There was a battle ahead; she could see that, and she might as well face it. The mild publicity she had had to endure as the Governor's wife, or the Vice-President's, was nothing to what she would suffer as the wife of the President. Saturday's New York *Herald* gave her a foretaste of what to expect. A full-page story: FACTS ABOUT THE ROOSEVELTS—A NAME HONORED IN HISTORY. *Theodore Roosevelt in Public and Private Life.* Private? What private life would any of them have now? It had been hard enough to keep the sob-sisters of both sexes off the premises when Theodore had been only a candidate for the Vice-Presidency, living three miles from a country village at the end of a bumpy branch line. How would Theodore and she be able to protect them from the sentimentalists and the exploiters who swarmed over the White House?

Well, Theodore had always wanted the Presidency, and she had wanted it for him. The frightening thing was just the suddenness of the event. Theodore would handle the sob-sisters. With his bare hands, if necessary.

Some such thoughts, no doubt, were passing through Edith Roosevelt's mind as she lay back, surrounded with newspapers, and let the reservoir fill up at Aunt Lizzie's, that lazy Sunday afternoon.

3

Surely, it was a comfort to her next morning to note in the papers that that Sunday had been for Theodore, also, a kind of God-given prelude of quiet to the years of pressure and responsibility that obviously lay ahead of them both, relaxing the nerves, strained by the experiences of the past ten days, and giving both a chance to put the inner house in order. For once, the apostle of the strenuous life, the man who could not spend a day at Sagamore without cutting down a few trees, rowing several miles on the Sound, playing three or four sets of tennis, riding, swimming, or taking the children tearing down Cooper's Bluff, had not been strenuous at all. He had attended the simple and deeply moving private services for the late President and accompanied the body to the City Hall where it was to lie in state, but, shrinking from the incongruous applause that had greeted his every appearance on the street, had spent the rest of the day at the Wilcox house.

4

At the hour that Theodore left his friend's house, early Monday, to take the train that was to bear the dead President's body to the national capital, Edith was at the Oyster Bay station with Ted, boarding another train, on her way to the severest ordeal she had had to face since fate had swept Theodore and herself to the dizzy heights on which they found themselves: her initial appearance as First Lady of the Land. There was an escort from the State Department on the New York side of the ferry, with a carriage that took her to a milliner for a heavy crepe veil, and the dress-shop known as Hollander's for a ready-made black dress. "It was necessary that I should be suitably dressed," she wrote Emily. "Alas, alas, I had to pay $135. for it!" At a men's furnishing store she bought a mourning band for Ted's hat, and a band for his left sleeve.

Bamie had arranged to open her house so Theodore and Edith and Ted could stay there before the White House would become available, and had come down from her home at Farmington,

Connecticut, to join Edith and Ted at the Pennsylvania Railroad ferry-house at West 23rd Street. A semi-circle of reporters and photographers eyed the party hungrily, but the stationmaster kept them at a distance; all but one, who approached Ted with the seductive query: Was he more pleased to have his father President or to have shot his first deer?

It was the forerunner of a thousand silly or malicious traps that would be set for young Theodore and his brothers and sisters in the next seven and a half years. The fourteen-year-old stepped lightly over it, with a look behind his glasses that was half indignation and half contempt. "I have no time to answer such questions," he said.

Edith, thirty years later, described her journeying to Washington that day as "one of the saddest things" she had ever done. "It is perfectly splendid to go in on a wave of triumph, but it is very far from being splendid to go in with sorrow, loss, and confusion of all kinds."

She arrived at the Cowles house at 1733 N Street, Washington, shortly before five that afternoon, and the great flag hanging at half-staff from a second-story window almost touched her head as she entered.

At half past eight the funeral train from Buffalo reached the Pennsylvania Station, but it was an hour later before Theodore reached the Cowles house. He gave a quick glance at the flag, draped now in black, and ran lightly up the steps. If Ted or Auntie Bye or her gruff naval husband were present when Theodore and Edith met for the first time since he had become President, they never told of it. There was possibly not much to tell. When two people meet, having as much to say to one another as Theodore and Edith had, that evening, silence is likely to be a better conductor of the incommunicable than speech.

5

They went together to the services in the White House, entered together the house that was to be theirs now for three and a half years; perhaps for seven and a half. As they entered, Edith felt less assured than her husband. He knew he was a match for the men who were assembling there to do honor to a dead President and to bend a critical gaze on his successor. She was not so sure.

These weather-worn politicians were shrewd and dangerous. Ted, who was with her, dressed in a dark suit with a bow of crepe on his left arm, was grave, courteous and interested in everything. Observers noted his "strong and sturdy" figure, "his modesty of demeanor and appreciation of the solemn occasion," and the dignity with which he bore himself, "resembling his father and," like him, "looking seriously at the world through a pair of gold-rimmed spectacles." Those who shook hands with him commented how strong his grip was for a boy of his age.

While the Roosevelts were waiting in the Blue Parlor, General John M. Wilson, who had been President Cleveland's military aide, entered to say that the ex-President had arrived and would like to pay his respects. Would it be agreeable to the President if he did it now?

"I shall be delighted," Roosevelt exclaimed, adding quickly, as the general turned to go, "Hold on! I'll go with you." He found the former President in the Red Parlor and they greeted each other warmly. They were good friends, in spite of their political differences and the harsh and occasionally unjust things Roosevelt had said in the heat of three presidential campaigns. They had learned to respect each other when Cleveland was governor of New York and Roosevelt a member of the Assembly, a regard which had been deepened when the younger man was Civil Service Commissioner during Cleveland's second term. Their words were perfunctory but their voices were warm: Cleveland's "I wish you success in your Administration, Mr. President," and Roosevelt's "Thank you. I shall always consider it an honor to have served under President Cleveland." As Roosevelt turned to speak to others who were crowding about him, the former President greeted Edith with a fatherly warmth that made her feel that she could share the burden that was on her heart.

"Oh, Mr. Cleveland," she cried, "my husband is so young!" He was, in fact, six weeks short of forty-three.

His kindly smile reassured her. "Don't worry. He's all right."

She remembered the words all her life. "I don't think," she said thirty years later, "that anything could have given me as much support and satisfaction."

There was a service in the East Room and another in the rotunda in the Capitol and then Theodore was again on the train, speeding westward to Canton, Ohio, for the final exercises at the grave in the late President's own home town.

Edith returned to the White House with Bamie that afternoon to offer her condolences to Mrs. McKinley, who was too broken to see anybody, and came away with the sense that, under the shadow of death, the Executive Mansion was the "gloomiest" place she had ever been in. She knew only one way to make it bearable, and sent a telegram to Sagamore—"Send down as many of the children as you possibly can"; and had a second thought, and went after them herself.

"I suppose in a short time I shall adjust myself," she wrote Emily in pencil on the train, "but the horror of it hangs over me and I am never without fear for Theodore. The secret service men follow him everywhere. I try to comfort myself with the line of the old hymn, 'Brought safely by His hand thus far, why should we now give place to fear?'

"Theodore looks wonderfully well," she added, "and the response of the country to him is most gratifying. The Cabinet stand by him to a man."

Speeding northward through the dusty September landscape, the cloud's silver lining, which she never tired of seeking, revealed itself. "For me the life will be far easier than that of the Vice-President's wife," she wrote. "For one thing, I shall not have to count the pennies, for another I shall have no calls to make, and I won't have to fight Theodore to make him accept invitations to dinner." There was some compensation certainly for having your husband President of the United States.

6

A week after Edith left Washington, a procession of vans drew up at the east entrance to the White House with the lares and penates of the Roosevelt family, and at nine o'clock that evening Edith herself arrived, bringing Kermit and Ethel and such members of the Sagamore Hill menagerie as the children could carry in their arms. Kermit was trailing clouds of glory, having been in an accident on the way through New York. With Henry Pinckney, the colored family servant, he had been driving uptown in a cab to meet his mother at "Fergie's" house at 159 Lexington Avenue. A southbound trolley-car had made the horses skittish, struck them and smashed a wheel of the carriage. Kermit had taken it all, in the press reports, "as though collisions with electric cars were frequent happenings in his young life."

The President was on the north portico of the White House to receive the rapturous greetings of the children and, with their mother, led them into the house that was to be their home. Neither Kermit nor Ethel was unduly oppressed by the dignity of the historic Mansion, and both were shortly comporting themselves as though they had always lived there.

The mother flung open the windows and let the warm September air into the dowdy, Victorian rooms. To fit her large family into the five bedrooms of the residential portion of the house—two of them rather small—find room for the housekeeper, governess and maid, and reserve a room or two for the occasional guests the family would not—at any price—do without, required imagination and quick thinking. The Clevelands, confronting a similar problem, had made an extra bedroom out of a storeroom in the basement. Mrs. Harrison had thrown partitions across the wide hall stretching the entire length of the second floor and Mrs. Cleveland had taken them down again; so there were precedents for whatever the new First Lady decided to do.

"Every household arrangement—both my own and those I found here," she wrote Emily, "had to be readjusted amid many doubts. . . . To me the shadow still hangs over the White House and I am in constant fear for Theodore, which I suppose is not quite justified."

For days she shifted furniture, sent horsehair monstrosities of the Rutherford B. Hayes era to the attic, and the dusty quarto tomes that were the relics of twenty administrations to the Library of Congress, filling the awesome black-walnut closets that served as bookcases with the books that she and Theodore cherished and the children loved to listen to. When the job was completed, she dropped, went to bed and, for the better part of two days, slept "the heavy sleep of exhaustion." With her weariness went her fears. The "shadow" lifted; she was at last relaxed, even happy. Theodore was where he had always wanted to be, "and of course," she wrote her childhood friend, Fanny Parsons, "bears all this responsibility with the utmost ease."

The middle of October, Archie and Quentin joined them. "Theodore does long for them so," their mother had written Bamie.

Alice delayed her entrance upon the national stage. Theodore and Edith planned to send her to the Cathedral School in Washington for a final dose of education, since the social debut they had planned for her when her father was Vice-President might seem, under the circumstances, not in the best taste. But Alice, going on eighteen, had ideas of her own, as usual, and, in order to sustain her revolt, was keeping away from the family, staying with her beloved Auntie Bye in the attractive old Cowles homestead at Farmington. She had other reasons for absenting herself. None of the social eminences she admired did anything so public as office-holding and she was inclined to regard all the publicity about her father "rather vulgar," and wanted no part of it.

She could not dodge it even by her absence from Washington. The newspapers lost no opportunity to weave legends about the new "belle of the White House," who had both beauty and brains and, through her mother, they said, was an heiress to boot. Her father was quoted as having remarked jocosely that he always kept "on the right side of Alice, since she is the only one in the family who has any money," which—if one adds the comic falsetto —has an authentic ring.

Possibly, Edith was just as well off without Alice those first days in the White House. Painters, carpet-layers, curtain-hangers, decorators, filled the private rooms of the "Mansion," and she was forced to turn the care of Kermit and Ethel over to Henry Pinckney. Kermit, accustomed to Sagamore's eighty acres, was finding the White House grounds too confining in the clear September weather and was taking Ethel on bicycle spins over the asphalt pavements of Washington, with Henry in breathless pursuit. When they returned late for luncheon, their mother made the punishment fit the crime by one hour's confinement in the White House. That afternoon they went on a further tour of the city but were careful to return in time for the five o'clock supper which, according to the rules of the household their mother had established, they were to take with her. Whatever happened, she told herself, she was going to keep close to the children.

7

At Sagamore, sheets covered the furniture and grotesquely shrouded the game-heads. The clocks ran down and no one wound them. Dust settled on the desk in the library and on the bronzes on the bookcases, and no one disturbed it. The leaves on the trees around the house and down in the woods on the Cold Spring Harbor side, turned yellow and scarlet, and fell through the crisp October days; and no vigorous little bodies steamed through them like an engine through snowdrifts.

For a brief hour, in November, Theodore was back in Oyster Bay. The men and issues involved in the off-year election were bounded by the limits of Nassau County, but Theodore had said so much about both civic duty and the need of making performance tread on the heels of preaching that he could not afford not to be at his place of residence to vote. When he had cast his ballot he had his coachman drive him to Sagamore. Noah Seaman was at the porte-cochère to greet him, and Susie, the dog with the wrong kind of name, welcomed him with mad rapture. Theodore walked around the house, peered into the barn and the stable, stood for a moment on the piazza in the chill November air, looking over the Bay, and entered the house.

As he strode through the unheated rooms for a quick inspection, he would have been less than human if he had not been warmly conscious of all that the dear house had been to him since he and Edith had driven up the steep winding road together for the first time that blustery March day, fourteen and a half years before. Alice had grown to womanhood in this house. Ted had been born here, and Kermit and Ethel. He could almost hear their voices filling the empty rooms, and Archie's, and funny, bright little Quentin's. And through them all, steady, serene and wise, Edie's . . . Edie, so pretty, so slender, so young still, looking scarcely older than when he had married her!

Surely his heart was full, that November noon at Sagamore, full of gratitude for his family, full of wonder at all that had happened, since, a little more than two months back, he had left this house on a brief and not too important speaking tour to Chicago, Minneapolis and Isle La Motte, Vermont. Who could have imagined the events of the intervening weeks?—the shock of the attack on McKinley, the first trip to Buffalo, the reassuring, quiet, even happy days there, Tahawus, the climb up Mount Marcy, the relaxation of the picnic lunch beside the brook, the runner emerging from the woods with a paper in his hand, the wild ride to North Creek, the interminable journey again to Buffalo with the burden of a nation on his shoulders, the solemn hush in the Wilcox house when he had taken the oath.

How infinitely strange life was! For the moment it had lifted him to dizzy heights. He must be prepared to be dashed down to unexpected depths, and not to be too concerned if he were. He had been given work to do and he would do it with courage and a high heart . . . whatever happened.

Book II

SUMMER WHITE HOUSE

1901–1910

Chapter I

A CARTOONIST pictured Uncle Sam noting, with a dismayed "Gosh!" the departure, early in July, 1902, of the Executive branch of the government from Washington for the Long Island village that was for three years (or was it seven?) to be the summer capital of the United States. His dismay was not shared by the Eighty Million; emphatically not by the minute fraction immediately concerned.

WHITE HOUSE.
GONE TO
OYSTER BAY.
BACK IN THE FALL.
T.R.

A salvo of thunder appropriately greeted the arrival of the presidential special.

Four years before, when the Colonel of the Rough Riders had arrived home from Cuba, his fellow-townsmen had provided the artillery, a roaring bonfire or two, a band and a crowd of three or four thousand shouting enthusiasts. But no one had known the manner, the place or the hour of this return of the President for his first vacation. He would, presumably, be coming by the presidential dispatch-boat, the *Sylph*, the story had gone, possibly even by the repainted and refurbished presidential yacht *Mayflower*, landing at the private dock of one of the Roosevelt families inhabiting Cove Neck. But he had decided, after all, to come by train. So there were no cannon and no bands, only an engine's whistle that started screeching too early and ran out of steam before the President was near enough to hear it; and no more than a hundred or two villagers who had heard the news in time to dress up and run to the depot.

But the elements did what they could. As the train stopped and the crowd swept toward the forward steps of the second car, there was a crackle, almost directly overhead, followed by a thundering salute fit to greet Jupiter himself. Rain began to fall in drops that, one observer noted, made splashes "as big as saucers."

The President looked tired. He had had a long trip, having made a Fourth of July speech at Pittsburgh, the day before, but the famous teeth flashed their familiar light as he greeted his neighbors: "Delighted to see you!" "Well, old man, and how are you?" "Yes, I tell you, it seems good to be home again!"

His assistant secretary, Loeb, who had come ahead, pushed his way toward the President, holding ten-year-old Ethel, in a starched white frock, by one hand, and, by the other, twelve-year-old Kermit, in a golf cap of ancient vintage, torn corduroy trousers, a soiled shirt and canvas sneakers, having played too late to get "tidied up." The President stooped and kissed them both and with an arm around each pushed through the crowd toward the waiting carriages. Ted, fourteen, mounted and bareheaded, bent down to kiss his father as he reached the platform's edge.

The drops of rain became strings. Loeb, looking worried, urged the President to take the covered surrey in which he had brought Ethel and Kermit, instead of his own uncovered carriage.

"No, no," answered the President. "Just get me my overcoat,

134

please, and I'll get along well enough." His chief secretary, Cortelyou, brought the overcoat. An umbrella? No, indeed! When he reached the open vehicle he found Archie, aged eight, in a very limp white suit, in the front seat. "Why, Archie, you little rascal, what have you got to keep you from getting wet?"

The boy had nothing, but it did not worry him. He scrambled hastily over the seat to a place beside his father, refusing with Ethel the relative shelter of young Loeb's surrey. The President humored their devotion and wrapped his overcoat over both.

By this time the rain was a deluge, driving down in slanting files. The President tossed a carriage-cover forward to Kermit, which the boy promptly adjusted over his head and shoulders like a monk's cowl; whereupon the President pulled down the brim of his Panama hat and let the rain do what it would.

A deafening crash of thunder, close by, set the spirited bay rearing and plunging. Other vehicles stood near, too near, and a smash-up appeared imminent. Several men sprang to the horse's head.

"Give him room, please," said the President quietly.

The groom had the horse in hand and, as the other vehicles made way, let him have his head, and got free. At a gallop that sent the mud spattering wildly behind, the horse dashed off through the downpour. Ted and his cousin, George Roosevelt, who was with him, galloped after, the rain running down their faces and streaming from their hair. Another young cousin, who had come by bicycle, pushed manfully along through rivers of mud. Yet another cousin, a sister of George, looking very wet and disheveled, followed in a phaeton, driven by a groom. At a respectful distance followed the secretaries and Secret Service men.

Through the village at top-speed, then two miles down the muddy road, past farmhouses and patches of woods, through torrents of rain punctuated by rolling thunderclaps and flashes of lightning, the cavalcade splashed on. As it turned left at the old Revolutionary cemetery and up the Cove Neck Road, it emerged from the shelter of the trees and caught the full force of the storm blowing over the Bay. The cousins dropped out of line to make their wet way to their homes, but the Secret Service men stopped at the edge of the President's property to establish pickets, and the presidential family alone made its way up the steep, winding road that led to the familiar house on Sagamore Hill.

The mother of the family, and Quentin, her youngest, were on the porch to greet the bedraggled wayfarers, with the maids who had come with her and the children, three weeks before. The First Lady was quietly radiant—she was not given to exuberance—and very firm with her dripping but noisily happy family. It was "straight upstairs, everybody, and get into dry clothes." They obeyed, leaving a watery trail, and filling the house with their shouts.

"I have five boys now," the First Lady was heard to remark.

2

The storm was over next morning, but the sky was overcast. The day was Sunday and Sunday meant church for the Roosevelts; for all of them, excepting only Quentin, who, at four, could not be trusted yet to preserve, at least outwardly, the essential minimum of decorum. The boys had learned long ago that there was no use protesting; but this Sunday Archie protested, in tears. Bozzie, his pet Boston bull pup, had been taken sick the night before; Bozzie, presented to Archie's mother by his owner, a Chicago friend of the President's, in return for a collar he had sent its talented, performing sire. Archie had been up much of the night with the puppy and was plaintive at the thought of leaving him, even for an hour. But Sunday was Sunday, and church was church.

The surrey and the two-seated buckboard took the family to Christ Episcopal Church in Oyster Bay. The President, in the surrey with Archie, his Aunt Emily, on a visit from her home in Italy, and another guest, the family's beloved "Fergie," arrived early. The President, in a black cutaway with gray trousers, a white waistcoat and pearl-gray tie, was in high feather, waving his resuscitated Panama at the friends gathering on the lawn. The *Dee-lighteds* flowed freely as a group of villagers gathered about him.

"Teddy, how's your woman?" one old codger inquired.

The President grinned. It was the old boy's stock query, spoken, Roosevelt knew, with no disrespect either toward him or the First Lady, and he had come to expect it, and to delight in it. He had known the old fellow since his boyhood, and the query, startling to bystanders, had become a part of the ritual of his Oyster Bay homecomings.

A smart trap drove up, and the President ran down the steps to open the low carriage door for Mrs. John W. Weekes, one of the town's grand ladies. After a gay exchange of greetings, he escorted her into the church, returning just in time to help his wife out of the buckboard in which she had come with Ethel, Kermit and Ted.

The sermon by the Reverend Henry Washburn was theologically technical, dealing with the history and significance of the Holy Communion. The President gave the impression of absorbed interest, but Ethel's head drooped, and she slept. Her mother made no effort to wake her, rather drawing her close so she might sleep more comfortably. But Kermit, fidgeting, caught a reproving glance. The President had offered Archie a quarter for the plate as they entered the church but he had disdained it, saying, "I've got money of my own." At the critical moment, however, he dropped it, and there was a scramble in which the President joined, successfully, and just in time.

That afternoon was mournful for the children. Archie, returning from church, had rushed to the stable, to find Bozzie *in extremis*. After dinner there was a solemn procession to the family's pet-cemetery north of the house and a new grave beside the boulder guarding other faithful departed pets. The wires buzzed between Oyster Bay and Chicago and, before the day was over, Archie's grief was assuaged by the news that Bozzie's brother would be on the way to Sagamore Hill next day.

3

The Roosevelts were early about their business, next morning. Someone raised a shade. Young voices chirped and called. A maid opened the front door. There was a rush of children across the porch, down the steps and out on the sloping lawn. There were somersaults and impromptu wrestling matches on the dewy grass, in the cool morning air; and shouts and howls and wails; then the quick stride of the President on the wooden floor of the piazza, and more shouts, a general rough-and-tumble, followed by a united rush back into the house, and breakfast.

So the correspondent of the New York *Evening Sun* observed the scene.

The President had come to Sagamore Hill determined to have a holiday, just as any other American might go to his country home to enjoy an outing and rid himself, so far as possible, of the cares of business life. Cortelyou and Loeb, his exceptionally competent

137

right and left bowers, were eloquent in their declaration to the newspapermen, haunting Oyster Bay, that only essential business would be dealt with at the Summer White House, and even that would be handled, as far as possible, away from Sagamore Hill. Everything else would be shunted to the departments in Washington. The secretaries rented two rooms in a yellow brick building on Audrey Street, over the Oyster Bay Bank, pushing on into a third after protracted diplomatic negotiations with the local dentist, who was not at all sure that, under the Constitution, he need have his dental apparatus moved to provide space for the two stenographers who successively took the President's dictation in the library next to the front hall at Sagamore Hill.

For, say what he would about a vacation, the President was finding that there was a bulky minimum of mail which he could not shift to other shoulders. But he could keep uninvited visitors at a distance. A delegation of a thousand Negroes who telegraphed that they wanted to express to the President their gratitude for his cordial treatment of Booker T. Washington and his friendship for their race were told that the President would take the will for the deed. But all the visitors did not send advance warning of their intentions. The Secret Service men kept a close guard. It was simple enough to watch the two roads that led to the house, the main driveway winding steeply up through the woods, and the "farm-road," skirting the western edge of the property and climbing up the slope to the stable; but the unfenced reaches of the eighty-odd acres presented problems which might have proved baffling to an army of guards.

They stopped their first crank that Monday, a stout, muscular man who turned out to be an unfrocked priest with a grievance against some bishop for which he expected the President to secure redress. But the President remained happily unaware of him. He was playing tennis all morning with the children.

Tennis, at Sagamore, had peculiar complications. The court, in a hollow where the road started its sharp incline to the house, was of dirt, traversed liberally by moles and so heavily shaded that moss grew on it. No seventh son of a seventh son could ever have guessed how a ball would bounce. The branches of the trees were so low, moreover, that they had to be figured in the scoring: a ball that hit a branch when it might have struck within the lines was declared a "let" and the point was played over. There was a further jeopardy, represented by a chipmunk, living near the tennis-court and habitually crossing it while the game was in progress, apparently as unafraid as though the players were cattle.

But, for all such extraneous hazards, the President delighted in the game. His method of playing, Ted described, twenty years later, as "original to say the least. He gripped the racquet halfway up the handle with his index-finger pointed along the back. When he served he did not throw the ball into the air but held it in his left hand and hit it from between his fingers. In spite of this, and in spite of his great weight, he played a surprisingly good game."

Ted, even at fourteen, could be guaranteed to keep his father's weight down, managing to drop the ball just over the net when-ever his father was on the back line, encouraging fast and frequently unsuccessful leg-work on the part of his parent. At doubles, that day, Ethel, playing with her father, made a team, closely matched against Ted and eight-year-old Archie, who made up in guile what he lacked in delivery, lobbing the ball so that, if it escaped the branches overhead, his father would get the sun in his eyes when he reached up to smash it. Altogether, it was unorthodox tennis but a highly successful morning's exercise.

4

There had been lamentations among the children when they had found that their father would not be at Sagamore for the Fourth. He made a point of never failing the children that day if he could possibly avoid it, partly to watch over the operations of a baker's dozen of young Roosevelt cousins, not given to a "safe and sane" celebration, partly himself for a day to be a boy again. This year, Pittsburgh had claimed him, and he had had something to say which, he was convinced, should not wait. In his absence, sure enough, Kermit, exploding a firecracker in a bottle, had just missed blowing his head off. The President, reading about it in a Philadelphia paper on his way home, was unruffled. "I suppose," he commented, "that is to be expected of the family."

For the children, the Fourth was not the Fourth without their father, and there had been general agreement that the fireworks should await his return. The Monday evening, after his arrival, the Roosevelts opened Sagamore's wide, hospitable door to the branches and twigs of the Roosevelt clan, and the young and old of a half-dozen other neighboring families. At the foot of the hill, along the "farm-road," the uninvited but always welcome towns-people gathered.

One guest chose to crash the gate that led to the house itself. He was the portly and very black Negro who brought butter, eggs and milk to the Roosevelts. He came dressed in a long black frock coat, an old-fashioned collar reaching up his long neck to his ears, and a red, white and blue tie, and carried a huge umbrella.

The Secret Service men challenged him as a matter of course. He had known the President when he was a boy, he explained, and had told him, sickly as he was, that he would be President some day; he could "tell by the stars." And he had come a long way. His plea rang so true, the guards could not resist him.

Professionals set off the twenty-one saluting bombs that opened the celebration, the elaborate "set pieces" that followed and the fireworks sent the President by the Chinese and Japanese legations in Washington—balloons that sailed majestically away over the Sound, trailing red, white and blue stars, and skyrockets bursting in sprays of stars high overhead. But the Roosevelt cousins lighted the colored fires here and there among the trees, sent the Roman candles popping, and kept the firecrackers crackling like those "coffee-grinders"—the world's first machine-guns—that had helped save the day at San Juan Hill.

The President, with the First Lady and their friends, watched the spectacle from the piazza that looked westward over the Bay. From nearby came the strains of an orchestra, playing patriotic airs. Through the music and the noise of the fireworks, at intervals, sounded the President's hearty, happy laugh.

His wife, his children, his home, his friends, his neighbors, clear skies overhead and, behind the soaring and fading sparks, the eternal and unchanging stars shining on a people that had not forgotten the meaning of independence; all this, and he himself, President of the United States. This was life as he would not have dared imagine it.

Out of the darkness, like an echo, rang the big Negro's laughter He was happy, too, and proud.

Chapter II

THE TOWNSPEOPLE, making their way back to their buggies and buckboards waiting on the Cove Neck Road or getting into their stride for the long walk home, spoke of "Teddy" with accents of affection but without awe. As one villager remarked, "He ain't no better than the next man, he ain't," adding defiantly, "but he ain't no worse neither." They were proud of their fellow-townsman and glad to have him back among them.

But no true "Oyster" responded kindly to the idea that it was Theodore Roosevelt alone who gave their town distinction, or was inclined to forget that the town had a dignity of its own, established and maintained for two hundred and fifty years before a Rough Rider had come back from Cuba in triumph, and been elected governor. There had been an Oyster Bay, indeed, a dozen years before there had been a New York. As for Presidents, hadn't Washington once spent the night in the Youngs' house?

It was, it happened, a diminutive old lady of the Youngs clan who, one Sunday, not long after the President's arrival, took it upon herself to dramatize the independence of the local residents. As the first bell for the Sunday service at the Episcopal Church was tolling, the lady, tastefully gowned in the latest fashion and wearing a smart French bonnet of jetted gauze, marched up the aisle and entered the third pew on the right. There was a card at the entrance saying "Mrs. Theodore Roosevelt," but the old lady did not appear to notice.

Mrs. Washburn, wife of the rector, walked quietly over from her own place and spoke to a young girl who herself by mistake had strayed into the same pew. "Ask her to come into my pew."

The girl gave the intruder the message, but the old lady, who was known to be deaf, was even more deaf than usual. The sexton bustled forward to see what he could do. His emphatic and widely audible whispers brought no results.

The old lady sat unmoved and apparently immovable, gazing up at the bronze tablet exalting the virtues of a forebear, one of the founders of the church. There was a faint commotion as the President's wife, looking exceptionally young and pretty that morning in a white gown and wearing a straw hat with roses, entered with her children and advanced to her customary seat. Seeing the old lady, she looked down at the card to be sure she herself might not be wrong; then, with eyes sparkling with amusement, glanced at the sexton and Mrs. Washburn, still standing uncertainly at one side. Thereupon, marshaling her children, she swept them into the James Roosevelt pew nearby.

"But this isn't our pew," whispered Ethel and Kermit in a breath. "Miss Youngs has ours."

"Hush," said their mother softly, as she bent her head in prayer.

In the back of the church, one worshiper was heard to whisper excitedly, "Look, she won't give up even to the President's family!"

"She's sat right there ever since there's been a pew in the church," replied her neighbor.

The self-respect and independence of the local residents did not close their minds to the implications of the presidential visitation, or prevent their noting the flow of visitors filing out of the smoky Long Island Railroad coaches and flowing up Audrey Street into Main. If you kept the Octagon House, the only hotel in town, or a livery-stable or a restaurant, you revised your prices—upward— every time a train arrived. When the correspondent of the Washington *Post* complained that $3 a day seemed pretty steep for a dingy room which, a few days before, had cost $10 a week, the hotel-keeper explained, "I'm getting past middle life now, and it's time I made provision for my declining years."

The reporter paid fifty cents for a meal at the hotel one day and was charged seventy-five the next. When he protested, the pretty cashier said: "You're a newspaperman, aren't you? We charge newspapermen twenty-five cents more than we do other people." The livery-stable owner explained why, when a correspondent protested his charge of $3 for the drive to Sagamore Hill: "You newspaper fellers are down here making stacks of money, and I don't mind telling you that I propose to get my share of it."

It was one of the newspapermen, aggrieved by the thrift of some of the Oyster Bay residents, who etched the town in acid for the Boston *Herald*: "Its roads are muddy or sandy, according to the weather; its sidewalks are few and hard to find; it has but one public house, and that contains but nine rooms for the use of travellers; there is not a decent restaurant in the place. There are many one-horse towns on Long Island, but it is doubtful if there is another as uninteresting as Oyster Bay." That was a jaundiced view that missed the genuine rural charm of the place and the successful blending of an unspoiled old village and a summer resort of city people as anxious to have the community retain its flavor as the villagers themselves.

The thrift of Oyster Bay storekeepers did not keep back the curiosity seekers who swarmed about the stands of picture-postals, a new idea recently imported from Europe. There were cards of the President's house with "Teddy's" picture in an oval in the corner. But the visitors who asked for cards with pictures of Mrs. Roosevelt were told that the President had put his foot down on any commercialization of the First Lady.

On the whole, the Oyster Bay people rather liked that. They had a good deal of respect for Mrs. Roosevelt. She wasn't a "mixer" like "Teddy." No one ever dreamed of being familiar or "folksy" with her, but almost everyone knew of her work for the Needlework Guild and the cripples at the House of St. Giles the Cripple in Brooklyn; and could tell some instance of her kindness to people in trouble. Sitting at the meetings of the St. Hilda Society of the Episcopal Church, sewing, not saying much, but always friendly, she might be anybody in the town. When the Catholic priest in Oyster Bay, Father Belford, asked her for a gift to be raffled off at their church fair, she had sent a scarf with a card pinned to it, saying it was from her, and agreeing to let them raffle the card with the scarf. Now, of course, every church in town would be asking something from her and getting it. And those Christmas parties at the Cove Neck School! Everybody knew it was Mrs. Roosevelt who went to the trouble of finding out beforehand what each child wanted, and who did all the shopping. It wasn't as though she didn't have five children of her own, and a lively lot they were, too, besides Alice, her stepdaughter. And Alice, they did say, was quite a handful.

The "neighbors" cherished the warmth that lay behind Edith Roosevelt's reserve, and respected the thrift which made her somehow kin to them in their own efforts to make both ends meet. When a shrewd farmer, coming from Sagamore Hill with a load of hay, was asked if he had driven a sharp bargain with the President, he replied, "The President, my eye! I bought this hay from Mrs. Roosevelt, and gave her more than the market value because she's a mighty fine woman!"

The townspeople had a particularly warm spot in their hearts for the children. They had seen enough children of other "swells," or read about them in the papers, to appreciate the difference. The Roosevelt children were not dressed in Paris-made clothes, patent-leather slippers and white gloves, or accompanied by governesses and even armed guards like the children of potentates abroad or some of the rich, not so far away from Oyster Bay as you would think. These were just plain American kids who dressed sensibly, played sensibly, got their hands and faces dirty a dozen times a day; and didn't put on airs when they came to town.

Everybody knew them and loved them. When Archie, in Rough Rider costume, rode into the village, astride his diminutive piebald pony, Algonquin, he was greeted familiarly by old and young.

"Hello, Archie," the town's patriarchal baker would call. "How iss der datty?"

"Hello yourself!" the boy answered. "He's all right. Gimme five cents' worth of buns."

"Have you seen that Archie-boy ride his pony?" an old settler asked the correspondent of the New York *Evening World*. "Just like his father. Sticks to his back like he grew there. He don't bounce up and down like the riding-master teaches. He's part of the animal he's riding. Ethel, too," the old man went on, "she rides that pony just as good as her brother, boy-fashion, and makes the little fellow go over the ground with the best of them." There was a patter-patter of hoofs as he spoke. "Hello," the patriarch exclaimed, "here she comes now!"

Ethel was on Algonquin, accompanied by Ted, on one of the Sagamore horses, volunteering the news, as they passed, that they were on the way to the blacksmith's to get a shoe tightened.

"That there Teddy's a cute one," the old man mused, when they had gone. "Just as original as his dad, and will be heard from some day." He gave the reporter a picture of "a persistent, energetic little chap" who never "let up" on any work he had undertaken to do. "He works hard at his books and he works hard at his play, like his

144

father, and when he rides, he goes like a cowboy chasing a Comanche."

An odd friendship had grown up between this determined fourteen-year-old and the old man, and the boy had revealed to him uneasy depths which, possibly, he had not revealed to his father. "We've had many a talk," the old townsman remarked. "He said to me one day, 'Don't you think it handicaps a boy to be the son of a man like my father, and especially to have the same name?' I asked him what he meant and he went on, 'Why, don't you know, there can never be another Theodore Roosevelt? I will always be honest and upright, and I hope some day to be a great soldier, but I will always be spoken of as Theodore Roosevelt's son.' "

The old man replied with a cheery prediction of glories to come, unaware that he had been given a long glimpse down a cloudy vista.

Ted was, in fact, already suffering the penalty of being Theodore Roosevelt's son. It was some comfort, but not enough, to thrash the schoolmate who called him "the first boy in the land." "I wish my father would soon be done holding office," Ted said in deep disgust to his father's friend, Jake Riis. "I am sick and tired of it."

If a resident of Washington, corresponding to the Oyster Bay patriarch, had been placed in an easy chair and asked his ideas about the family in the house at 1600 Pennsylvania Avenue, grandiloquently known as the Executive Mansion, his reactions would in general have been the same, though his emphasis might have been different. Children in the White House were nothing new to the hardy perennials in the capital, but none since Tad and Willie Lincoln had projected themselves upon the public mind or imagination. If you thought about presidential children at all you thought of them as groups, intelligent on the whole and well-behaved, but not as individuals. You had heard their names, of course, but you had forgotten them. These Roosevelt children were different.

Before they had been in the White House a month, all Washington was aware of them. It might be only a fleeting glimpse of a little face pressed against a window-pane or a little figure flashing by on a bicycle; it might be a snapshot in the papers of Quentin on the White House steps with a little colored companion, or another picture of him driving his colored friend in harness; or a picture of Archie and Quentin at the end of a row of policemen at inspection in the White House grounds, with Archie's hand solemnly at the salute but Quentin quite casual, with both hands in his pockets; or it might be a story in the morning paper, of Kermit's engaging response to the school-teacher who asked him what his father did for a living. "Father? Oh, Father's *it*!" Or a grapevine story of Archie and Quentin at dusk following the lamp-lighter stealthily around the White House grounds and, as soon as he was out of sight, climbing like monkeys up the posts and turning off the lights, only to be caught at last by a happily friendly watchman. Or a report of Quentin's indignant reply when his father told him that the flower-beds in the White House grounds were not regarded as a proper practice ground for little boys on stilts: "I don't see what good it does me for you to be President. You can't do anything here! I wish I was back home!" Or it might be the episode of Kermit at the White House breakfast-table pulling a live kangaroo-rat out of his pocket to show Jake Riis; or a vision of four little figures in their "nighties" sitting halfway up the White House stairs, watching entranced the panorama of a presidential reception, defying the dazzling and bemedaled military aide and yielding scamperingly at last only to the gentle words of a First Lady who had slipped from her husband's side to ascend the stairs and say quietly, "Oh, yes, my dears, Mother says you must."

A new and exciting life was unfolding for three little boys and their sister; wholly different in its externals from the simple country life of Sagamore Hill, yet in its essential qualities unchanged. The father of the family, as President of the United States, was busier than he had been as governor of New York, but he still managed to have breakfast with the children and pillow-fights at night, or to read to them for a half-hour before they went to bed. The boys invaded his office, as they had invaded the gun-room, to show him a new pet or introduce a new friend, and he never seemed too busy to show appropriate enthusiasm. He dealt with the sob-sisters, as Edith had known that he would, with orders to "lay off" his family under penalty of being exiled from the White House as long as he were there. But stories began to be told in Washington about the engaging doings of the Roosevelt children, and a few got into the papers; and not even the President of the United States could do much about it.

The most striking of the episodes occurred early in the new régime and was itself so appealing that it fixed the children permanently in the imagination of the public. Archie was sick abed with measles, and Quentin conceived the idea that nothing would get him well so quickly as the sight of his calico pony. He appealed to Charlie Lee, the colored White House coachman. If they could take Algonquin to Archie's bedside . . . not by the stairs, of course, but by the elevator. Lee's devoted heart was captured by the idea. They led the pony into the basement, evading the ushers and the guards who swarmed about the foyer; Algonquin behaved like a gentleman; and Quentin's generous impulse was fulfilled. What Archie thought of it all is lost to history. What his father and Mother thought can only be surmised. What the public thought is indicated by the place the episode holds in the White House saga.

There was one unusual feature of the younger children's lives which escaped the observing eyes of the White House reporters: a part of each day they were under the absolute authority of a young colored man, barely more than a boy himself, named James Amos, a kind of assistant butler whose father was a policeman whom the President had frequently encountered on his rides through Rock Creek Park. The boys were proving too much for the French governess. "They had been reared in the wide grounds of Sagamore Hill," Amos wrote long after, "and were bursting with health, animal spirits and mischief. In fact, they had the very old Nick in them. So when they found themselves in the White House, where it was necessary to quiet down a little, they were slow in accommodating themselves to it. At one time or another, I paddled all of the younger children, and the President and Mrs. Roosevelt always backed me up."

One night the table in the state dining-room was set for an important dinner. Amos, looking in at the door to see if everything were all right, saw Ethel examining the brilliantly set table, going from place to place, occasionally reaching for a salted almond or a bonbon. Amos suggested that her place was elsewhere, but the little girl was so entranced that she was slow to obey. Amos took her by the arm and led her firmly toward the door.

"I'm a young lady," she cried indignantly, and the assistant butler had a hard time maintaining his stern mood. "I'm going to tell my father."

It was not long before Amos received a message to come to the President. Ethel was with him.

"Now, then," the President asked with mock severity, "what is it this scoundrel did to you?" Ethel told her story, and young Amos noted that she told it without embellishments. You could trust these Roosevelt children to tell the truth.

"James," said the President, "you did right."

If the three younger boys and Ethel intrigued the public, Alice fascinated it. Anyone reading the newspapers might assume that the nation had nothing to do but to watch "the belle of the White House" from the minute she got out of bed in the morning to the rather late hour she fell into bed at night. Her habit of life, her tastes, her clothes, her girl friends and her beaux, her extraordinary physical vitality, were the subject of news-stories, day in, day out, and occasionally of Sunday features, outrageous in their sensationalism.

Her debut at the White House, four months after her father became President, was played up in the press as an event of national significance. A month later she was the talk of two continents. The Kaiser, recognizing that his country had made a mess of its American relations during the Spanish War, had given orders to an American shipbuilding firm for the construction of a racing schooner, to be called the *Meteor*. Who more appropriate than the daughter of the President to christen his new yacht? Or who better to represent the Emperor at the ceremony than his only brother, Prince Henry of Prussia? Alice played her part with grace and decorum, acquiring a bracelet from the Emperor with a miniature of himself, surrounded with diamonds, and managing incidentally to have a very good time with the bearded prince. She sent a cablegram of congratulations and greetings to the Emperor, whose wholly gracious but informal phrasing, as between equals, and obviously her own, startled a monarch accustomed to subservience.

Not long after, Alice was agitating the British Foreign Office. Whitelaw Reid, the American ambassador to Great Britain, and his wife—old friends of the Roosevelts—invited Alice to be their guest that spring at the coronation of King Edward VII. Alice was thrilled, and her father and mother saw no objection until it appeared that Alice could be admitted to Westminster Abbey for the ceremony only if she were officially recognized as the daughter of a reigning sovereign. It took only a few rumblings in the American press to convince the President that the bestowal of royal honors on Alice would not sit well with the American public and might not be too good for Alice herself. The acceptance of the invitation

148

was withdrawn and, as a partial compensation for the loss, arrangements were made for her to go to Cuba as the guest of the American Governor General, Leonard Wood, and his wife. Fifty years later the Governor General's last surviving staff officer remembered the dizzy whirl that Alice led him and his fellow lieutenants.

A little breath-taking in her activity, like her father, she bore herself well. The photographs of the eighteen-year-old girl, suddenly thrust into the glare of international interest, reveal a young woman of intelligence and character, with a touch of sullenness in her lips, but poised, wary and mature beyond her years. "Look here, you, whoever you are," she seems to be saying, "I don't know what you're up to, but I can come back at you." In evening gowns, her graceful neck, the pompadour of light brown hair, her fine carriage and her proud blue eyes seemed brilliantly to justify the "Princess Alice" of the legend that the press was weaving about her. The Chicago *Tribune* etched her portrait: "straight and slender but supple and graceful; athletic, but not robust; likes to read, but is not studious; loves music, but dislikes the drudgery of practice; not domestic in her tastes but accepts gracefully the duties which of necessity fall to her lot"; altogether, "as Alice Roosevelt, the President's daughter," her friends declared, basically no different from "Alice Roosevelt, the romp of Oyster Bay."

"It has been an extraordinary change for the strenuous young Roosevelts, this transformation from the quiet country life of Oyster Bay to the dazzling, bewildering atmosphere of the national capital," wrote a feature-writer in the New York *Herald*. "But, according to all accounts, not a single head has been turned in the fierce light that beats upon the American throne."

Ted, whom Washington saw least of, since he was at Groton, came closest of all the children that winter to the American heart. In February, he was taken ill at school with pneumonia. For a week, the nation seemed to hold its breath and the business of the government seemed to hang suspended as the headlines unfolded from day to day the deepening gravity of the boy's condition. His mother hurried to Groton. Two days later, the President followed; then Alice. Archie could not go, so he sent a letter: "I hop you are beter." DOUBLE PNEUMONIA said the headline in the New York *Times*, ominously. The next day, the boy was improving, but still in danger; the day following his "chances" were "better"; the next day, the paper gave a jubilant shout that he was "safe," and once more, people felt they could breathe. The President returned to Washington and, a week later, the First Lady was back in the White House with Alice, and "bundled to his eyes with blankets," Ted.

He had long recovered from his illness and returned to school, when, in June, his mother, with the younger children, the maids, the coachman, the horses, the dogs and the guinea-pigs, fled from the Washington heat to the breezes that blew across Sagamore Hill.

Chapter III

IT DID NOT seem strange to the children to be back at Sagamore with the horses and ponies and dogs, the run of the eighty acres, with all Long Island beyond, the barns and the hay, the bathing-house and the long dock over the swamp on Cold Spring Harbor— all the familiar joys, all theirs, as in the past—and to have guards at the entrance and Secret Service men snooping around. They did not see the guards or the Secret Service men, really, not as what they were; as occasional, rather pleasant companions, yes; people to talk to and question and learn interesting things from, but as representatives of the majesty of the law, standing watch and ward over their father and mother and themselves, these burly keen-eyed men had no existence; they were not there.

To the children, Sagamore Hill meant freedom after the con-finement of the city and of school, freedom from ushers and guards with restricted ideas of what the White House was for. It meant renewed fellowship with Cove Neck's assemblage of cousins, the infinite variety of the days' activities, tennis or riding or swimming or fishing or clamming or crabbing or target-shooting, or jumping your horse over the hurdles on the lawn, or roaming the woods with your particular pick among the cousins, or playing perilous tag up and down the slopes of the many-gabled roof of the house, or, if you were old enough, camping with one of the cousins in the swamp on the Cold Spring Harbor side, waiting for daybreak and the snipe that might come tripping up the beach.

But Sagamore Hill meant something beyond all these things: it meant the companionship for hours at a stretch, sometimes for whole days, of a youthful and infinitely resourceful father who en-tered into your games with zest, and invented variations of his own that you yourself would never have dreamed of; a father, moreover, who did not make pets of his children but treated them as rational and responsible beings, his equals, having feelings that deserved the same consideration he might show any adult, great or obscure. The father was a busy man even at Sagamore. There were always tiresome people calling on him—senators and cabinet members and such—but four in the afternoon was generally their deadline and, if they didn't know it, the President enlightened them.

One afternoon, early that July, the President was in the library discussing Cuban reciprocity with a visiting statesman when a group of bareheaded boys, in old clothes and sneakers appeared at the doorway. "Cousin Theodore," said their lanky spokesman, respectfully, "it's after four."

"By Jove," the President exclaimed, "so it is! Why didn't you call me sooner? One of you boys get my rifle." A little figure detached itself from the group and ran upstairs. The President turned to his visitor. "I must ask you to excuse me. We'll finish this talk some other time. I promised the boys I'd go shooting with them at four o'clock, and I never keep boys waiting. It's a hard trial for a boy to wait." And he was off, with the boys around him, all talking at once, with "Cousin Theodore" this, or "Father" that, until they were out of hearing.

It was worth coming a long way, thought William E. Curtis, writing for the Chicago *Record Herald*, "to see the President of the United States at the head of this young band of savages on their way to the woods or to the target-grounds."

A newspaper poet, William J. Lampton, caught the flavor of it:

> "Down where the waters of the bay
> Break on the beach in a lazy way . . .
> The President runs at large and plays
> Like a boy let loose for the holidays.
> He is one of the kids and lets affairs
> Of state go soak with his other cares.
> They are not for him down there by the bay
> Where he gets his rest in a strenuous way."

If Sagamore meant to the children, above all, the companionship of a father who had a deathless boy dodging in and out of the poised and responsible adult that he was, it meant a companionship also with another guide, philosopher and friend, less uproarious but also imaginative and stimulating. The correspondent of a Ger-

152

man magazine, *Die Woche*, recorded a picture of the First Lady sitting under a spreading beech-tree at Sagamore, with the children around her on the grass, bringing her the day's "finds"—a butterfly, perhaps, or a beetle, a curious stone or an odd bit of moss or lichen, a strange flower or the feather of a rare bird. Around each "find," the correspondent noted, the President's wife wove some fascinating story, giving it an aura in the children's eyes.

There was nothing ever "set" about the day's program. It might be a ride today in the rain, through the woods, with five or six in the cavalcade and Archie on Algonquin, "following at top speed through the wild storm, as if the witches were after him, broomsticks and all," as the New York *Herald* had it. It might be a picnic tomorrow on some pleasant beach, or a run down the Sound in the dispatch-boat, *Sylph,* always ready for anything, in the Bay; with a clambake on some secluded beach and the President laying the stones in the holes the boys prepared, covering them with seaweed and making the fire; or happily, a long row in the skiff for the President and his wife alone with a picnic basket and two or three books. You seldom knew, long in advance, what it would be.

One morning, before breakfast, the President had an idea involving the presidential yacht, *Mayflower,* which had come into the harbor the evening before. Years after, Seaman P. A. Kersey, of Alexandria, Virginia, told what happened. On board the white, graceful, little vessel, preparations had been going on for twenty-four hours for the inspection by the President, expected later in the day. Fittings had been polished and repolished. The officers had gone below to have their breakfast and get into their dress-uniforms when a group of tars on the port deck observed a rowboat approaching with a stocky man in a sleeveless swimming shirt at the oars, and a woman in a light house-dress, holding a parasol and steering.

"The boat was such a commonplace affair and its occupants attired in such a negligée fashion, none of us thought of giving it another look. Anyway, we were too engrossed with the business of polishing up the brass for the President."

The rowboat proceeded to the starboard gangway, and the oarsman made it fast and ascended to the deck. The seamen nearly fell on their backs when they discovered whom they were receiving. "The President greeted us like we were kings and princes," Kersey remembered, "talked to us like we were buddies, thanked us for the look of the boat. 'Bully! Bully!' We had a party all to ourselves.

When the skipper and the other officers, their epaulettes, cocked hats and all, finally came on deck, they got the shock of their lives. The reception was over, the bloom was off the peach, and the band struck up *Down went McGinty!*"

Another day, shortly after, the wires hummed between Washington and Oyster Bay. The issue of the Pacific cable had just been settled, and the President's permission for the release of the report was urgently needed. But the President was not to be found. The secretaries were non-committal. The newspapermen, scenting a mystery, became importunate. If the President were not at Sagamore Hill, where was he? One of the reporters rowed out to the *Sylph*. No, the President was not there. The Secret Service men became anxious. Wherever the President was, who was guarding him? A general search was forestalled only by a friend of the President's staying at the house, with the reassuring statement that the President had not been shot or injured or even "kidnapped by Oyster Bay brigands."

The lost executive beamed on the reporters from the Sagamore piazza next morning, with a triumphant side-glance at the Secret Service men. He had, it appeared, been out camping on a lonely headland, several miles to the East, with Ted and Kermit and their cousin Philip Roosevelt. There had been steak, fried by the President in a pan with bacon; there had been a fox barking in the distance; there had been ghost stories and hunting stories around the fire—and the President's ghost-stories might have frozen the ghosts themselves—and, finally, four Navajo blankets spread out on the sand and the President of the United States asleep under the stars, guarded only by three boys, the eldest not yet fifteen.

An oysterman, encountering the party returning home, shortly after dawn, called over, "Good morning, Mr. President. Been out all night with the boys?" He gulped a little after he had said it. Er-er, he hadn't meant it just that way. He guessed he had forgot his manners.

The reporters made the most of the camping story, and it helped fix in the public mind the picture of a President who was not too preoccupied with affairs of state to be a father to his sons.

Occasionally, the boys staged a notable party on their own: once, a circus in the old barn, with admission by pins. The boys were secretive about it, so far as their elders were concerned, but uninhibited with their friends who transcended Cove Neck's customary standards of acceptability and took in most of the young fry in Oyster Bay.

Kermit opened the show with a wrestling match with Jimmie Dale, generally regarded as the best "scrapper" and wrestler his size in the village, ending in Kermit's triumph at the end of the fourth round. A tumbling bout by three of the village boys which followed drew such cheers that the Secret Service men came, threatening to "pull the show" unless more decorum were observed. But Archie, doing tricks on his calico pony, stirred even the Secret Service men to applause and, after that, all bars were down.

Event followed event, now with the Roosevelt boys, now with the villagers holding the center of the stage, and Ted providing the climax in an exhibition of marksmanship that reached the bull's eye in six out of ten shots.

"Altogether," wrote the *World* reporter, who "scooped" his colleagues on the story, "it was a rip-roaring event from the standpoint of this sedate place." It ended in lemonade and cake and exclamations of surprise and pride by the President of the United States, who, for once, had not had the slightest idea what was in the wind.

2

All the stories that the newspapermen and women, hopefully hovering at Sagamore Hill, sent over the country daily were not as charming as the accounts of the camping trip and the circus; or as true to the facts. In the yellow journals, the incidents recounted were frequently wild distortions when they were not unabashed fiction. "KERMIT THROWS THE PRESIDENT" was the headline of a two-column story in the New York *World* one morning, telling how Kermit, wrestling with his father, had "truly and cleanly thrown" him by a trick learned from his father's jiu jitsu wrestler. Like Queen Victoria on another occasion, the President was "not amused." His one conspicuous vanity was in the area of physical prowess. The picture of the apostle of the strenuous life being thrown in a wrestling-match by his twelve-year-old son made him look more than a little ridiculous.

The President respected and liked the newspapermen covering Sagamore Hill and talked to them with a candor which they seldom betrayed. Most of the men wrote factual accounts of the day's doings to which no one could object. The others the President bore with as long as he could. It was possibly the headline: PRESIDENT AND MRS. ROOSEVELT STROLL IN ARCADY. *Executive Realizes the Poet's Dream—"A loaf of bread, a jug of wine, and thou, singing in the wilderness"* that broke the camel's back. The President took action, sending for the worst of the offenders. The correspondent was in high feather as he entered the library, aglow at being singled out from among his fellows, and the President's first words appeared to confirm his expectations. The President had noted a good many stories about the children in the reporter's paper, the President remarked, good stories, too, except for certain slight inaccuracies. Hereafter, whenever any reporter wished exact information about the doings of members of his family, they could come straight to him. "I will give you a bully story right now if you wish it."

The reporter pulled out his note-book eagerly. This was wonderful.

"Mrs. Roosevelt and I are going riding. We shall ride 'cross country, jumping exactly twenty-seven fences and six ditches and when we return we shall go bathing in our riding habits." The reporter went a little cold. "My son Theodore," the President proceeded, "is hunting this morning, and I have just received a bulletin from the jungle informing me that he has already killed two elephants and a tiger. Isn't Ted a wonder?"

The reporter cast his eyes about for a possible exit, but the President was in the way, recounting gravely the exploits of Kermit, "fishing for tadpoles to be used as bait for whale," and Ethel, in the act of tearing down the windmill. "Step around the house and you can see her." As for Archie, aged eight, he had "just thrown a 200-pound Secret Service man two bouts out of three in a catch-as-catch-can wrestling match," and Quentin, the baby, was just setting fire to the back of the house. "There you have what I call a good story," the President declared, and he hoped the reporter would not exaggerate. "Dee-lighted to have seen you! Good morning!"

"I do not know that there is much harm in the stories," the President wrote Paul Dana, editor of the *Sun*, whose reporter was among the offenders, "but . . . they are not proper stories to be told about the President or the members of his family. . . . The plain truth, of course, is that I am living here with my wife and children just exactly as you are at your home; and there is no more material for a story in the one case as in the other!"

The President and his family are at Oyster Bay,
seeking rest and privacy

The American public could not accept so abstract a view of the presidential family. That family was the subject of discussion in countless homes across the country, in stately dining-rooms and lonely ranch-kitchens, beside camp-fires, in country stores where men sat around cracker barrels, and wherever women gathered. Archie and the pony that was brought up the White House elevator to see his sick master, the pillow fights in the White House corridors, the President sleeping under the stars with his boys, unguarded and unafraid. The stories were sifting down to the man on the street, not only in Washington but in remote villages.

It was inevitable that editors should seek to add to this new American legend and to deepen its colors; inevitable too that the unscrupulous should exploit it. Sensational editors were not above laying elaborate traps for the children, in one case ordering their Sagamore Hill man to arrange the arrest of Ted or Kermit on some trumped-up violation of the game laws. Lindsay Denison, of the

Sun, years later, in humility and shame, told of an effort of his own to dig a pit for Archie. He had ingratiated himself with the boy by praising his calico pony and, when he had quite won him, had proposed that they go clamming together. When they reached the beach the reporter had lost his interest in clams. Suppose they play photographer instead? He had a toy camera, he said, and would set it up and Archie would be the clam-digger who came with his pail and loved to have his picture taken.

Archie was dubious.

"By the way," Denison remarked innocently, "I bet you don't know what the tariff is."

"I have heard of it," the boy answered with dignity.

"How's that?" the man exclaimed eagerly, for tariff revision was a burning issue and the President's views on the tariff would be top news. "Did you ever hear your father say what he thought of it?"

"I think," the boy answered, "I heard a reporter ask my father about it. And Father said he'd rather not 'scuss it just then."

The reporter became engrossed in his camera. "Let's play that photographic game. You stand there with your pail and shovel. . . ."

" 'Scuse me for asking," Archie remarked. "I don't want to be too 'quisitive, but are you a reporter?"

Denison started to say, "No," but the boy's large gray eyes were too much for him. "Well, I suppose I am, old man," he said, adding airily, "What of it?"

"I'd rather not play photographer, please."

"Might as well," the reporter answered. "Because I can take your picture anyway, you know. You can't help it."

Archie walked up to him very quietly. "Of course," he said, "if you want to, you can. But if you're a gentleman, you won't."

The reporter, aware that any lie to his editor would rest more lightly on his conscience than the memory of those gray eyes, folded his camera. "Let's dig clams," he said.

"Thank you," said Archie.

Chapter IV

FOR KERMIT, life at Sagamore was not to be all fun that summer. He was to enter Groton that fall and had gaps in his primary education which had to be filled. So, the middle of July, a new element entered the life of Sagamore Hill, a tutor.

Walter Hinchman was a Harvard graduate in his early twenties, with an inquiring mind and a penetrating eye. He arrived at Sagamore, one evening in July, bearing a broken thumb. The President, who had guests, greeted him on the porch, under the porte-cochère, presenting, in his white shirt-front, the young tutor noted, a magnificent target for any would-be assassin. The tutor made a mental note that this President was, first of all, apparently not scary.

What was the matter with his thumb? the President asked. He had broken it at cricket, the young man explained. "Serves you right for playing such a game!" exclaimed the President, grinning as he said it.

Young Hinchman lived at a boarding-house in the village and spent the whole day at Sagamore, much of it, when he was not teaching Kermit, in the library by special invitation. The President dictated letters there in the morning, and the tutor shrank, at times, at hearing words spoken that should obviously be confidential. Loeb, the secretary, warned him that what he heard was, of course, not for publication, but the President felt no need of a warning. Whom he trusted, he trusted.

The tutor noted the President's freedom from the ordinary inhibitions of high office. "I'm sorry we can't have you to lunch today," the President remarked on one occasion. "We're having a Chink embassy. That fellow in the yellow jacket." The "fellow" happened to be Prince Liang Chen, and the "embassy" included the brilliant Chinese minister to the United States, Wu T'ing-fang.

The white shirt front, the dictation, the remark about the "Chink embassy" were, it appeared, all of one piece.

With eyes and ears wide open, no sense of awe but an ever deepening warmth that became admiration, then affection, the observant young tutor watched "the astonishing and lovable person" who was the President of the United States.

"I don't know when his morning began," Hinchman wrote, twenty years later, "but by nine o'clock he had ridden horseback or taken a long tramp, eaten breakfast, and read through a veritable pile of magazines and newspapers. The reading alone would have killed the morning for an ordinary mortal. If a few minutes still remained before Mr. Loeb arrived at Sagamore Hill, the President joined his family on the porch, rocked hard, and talked harder. Then till lunch he was closeted with Mr. Loeb or with visitors, but closeted with the door opened, so that one passing could see him, usually on his feet, dictating as strenuously as he talked in public. He seemed to have time for everybody. He might be dictating an important letter to Mr. Root. Just as likely he was dictating a letter of genuine gratitude to an old soul in Kansas who had sent him a trumpery gift with her compliments and the announcement that she had seven children; or perhaps he was answering, as if it really mattered, the letter of a little English boy who had written suggesting that the American President should have a bodyguard like King Edward's. They did really matter to Roosevelt, these letters; for he was always interested in human contacts.

"After such a morning, he talked his way through lunch, sometimes perhaps to keep the conversation where he wanted it if there were political guests, but more often, I suspect, for the same reason that Burke talked,—'not from a desire of distinction, but because his mind was full.' People representing all sorts of interests,—political, business, ecclesiastical, academic, diplomatic,—sat at his table nearly every day; yet, oftener than not, he knew more about their subject than they. I wondered at first if so much talk was not skilful bluffing; he might do it for a while, but surely he could not keep it up. It was fabulous, preposterous. But he stood the test day after day, routed us all, over and over again . . . but what made the conversation really memorable, was not its range, but its humor. He delighted in picturesque phrases. No phrase-maker, never 'precious' in his English, he had, rather, an Elizabethan exuberance of phrase. He rarely spoke of a person without adding a telling de-

160

scription; that was part of the 'fun of him.' I remember his speaking of one of the Secret Service men as 'Craig, that excellent fellow with the prize-fighting past.' Plain 'Craig' wouldn't do, not merely because he was 'excellent,' (as indeed he was), but because Roosevelt's imagination would not brook the mere colorless name. He nearly always had more than the bare name for his children,— sometimes a hilarious epithet when he was particularly affectionate."

Among the notables who came to Sagamore Hill that July was Senator "Tom" Platt, tall, lean and solemn. Like Mark Hanna, Platt liked his Presidents in frock-coat and top hat, and was disconcerted and knocked off balance by a President in riding clothes. The President was late for luncheon that day and, since even at Sagamore Hill a hungry family and its guests might not enter the dining room ahead of the President, Archie, who was conceded to have special powers over his father, was sent into the library to act as bait. It was not long before they appeared, Archie in the van, pursued by the President, shouting with melodramatic venom, "You abominable little rascal! You incorrigible scamp!"

The Senator was scandalized, casting a reproachful glance at the First Lady, as if to say, "You are smiling, madam? Do you approve of this strange behavior?"

The President took in the situation instantly and was ready with an encore. Rushing again at Archie, he repeated his lines: "You abominable little rascal! You incorrigible scamp!"

When the President finally caught and clutched his prey, the Senator clearly expected the boy to be eaten, then and there, and appeared relieved when he was merely hugged.

The Senator had a bad time of it that day. When the President asked him what he would have to drink—and Platt, the tutor noted, looked like a double whiskey—the Senator replied, "Whatever you take, Mr. President."

"I always take tea," the President answered with a malicious chuckle. "Give the Senator a cup of tea."

The President's chuckle might have expanded to a guffaw if he could have heard Platt's comment on his visit, that night. Admitting to a reporter of the New York *Journal* that he was tired out, he explained his condition by saying, "I have climbed Sagamore Hill." Wearily, he added, "I do not think I shall attempt it again. I am getting too old."

161

The public business brought other notables to Sagamore Hill that summer: John Hay, the Secretary of State, and Elihu Root, the Secretary of War, to discuss the thorny question of the Philippine friars, which the first civil governor of the Islands, William H. Taft, was trying to negotiate with the Vatican and which was upsetting American Catholics; Gifford Pinchot, to discuss reclamation of arid lands in the Southwest; Whitelaw Reid, "dressed," it seemed to young Hinchman, "as if he had just come out of Buckingham Palace," to report on the coronation of King Edward and the European grapevine, always especially audible on such occasions. It brought also a host of lesser lights, political leaders of various sorts and conditions who had grapevines of their own in this state or that section.

An Englishman, Frank T. Bullen, has left an attractive picture of the luncheons in the home of this President who looked like "a burly British farming squire of the old school" and, when he spoke, seemed "to bite off every word from a solid staff of truth." The Englishman told of going into lunch "quite informally, the President selecting our seats for us." The luncheon: a cup of bouillon, some lamb chops with new peas and potatoes, and watermelon for desert. "Not only the best but the brightest, jolliest meal I had in America. For the President would be the life and soul of any party. His vitality is so amazing, his fun so contagious, his earnestness so convincing. . . ."

Beside the friars and a dangerous strike in the anthracite coal mines in Pennsylvania, visitors that summer came to talk, in the main, of two things—the control of the trusts and the outlook for the President's nomination in 1904.

The two themes were actually intertwined. The public was demanding that something be done to curb the power of the great corporations, and Bryan was seizing the issue as the Democrats' most effective club to beat the Republicans with. The President's record as governor in dealing with corporate power, as well as his action in the Northern Securities case, the preceding winter, offered clear evidence of his own position. But, though that evidence might help him win the election, it would stand in his way when it came to the nomination. For the corporation leaders were convinced that, having brought prosperity to the nation, they had a kind of divine right to determine the course its government should take, and the Republican party chiefs, depending for their funds on the corporations, shared their sentiments. Mark Hanna was the 1904 nominee they were dreaming of.

But a fresh wind was blowing through the Party. The rank and file were shouting, "Teddy's our man!" Word came to Sagamore Hill that summer of Republican conventions in one state after another—eleven before the summer was over—endorsing the President for the nomination in 1904; and the Cincinnati *Commercial Tribune* was inclined to think that the President was "carried away a bit" by the enthusiasm of the endorsements. The fact was that the President wanted the nomination as he had never wanted anything in his life before; and was tempted to go after it too hard.

Meanwhile, he was doing considerable thinking on the issues, notably the problem of the trusts, in preparation for a series of speeches he expected to make in various cities of New England in the late summer. Prosperity, he recognized, was as sure as adversity to bring mutterings of discontent. At a time when most men prospered somewhat, some men always prospered greatly, and misused their power. How could you get the benefits of prosperity and check its evils? Obviously, there had to be some sort of regulation. Obviously, also, the necessary legislation must be drawn in a spirit not of envy, hatred or class feeling but of justice for all, the corporation as well as the public. The point was not to attack corporations, as such, but to get at the evil in them and correct that; and not to try to do everything at once. There wasn't any patent medicine that would heal all the ills of the body politic. Men and nations didn't progress by leaps and bounds. They moved forward a little here and a little there. There was no immediate or complete solution of the trust question. The only real answer was in the field of individual character. No action by the State could do more than secure for the individual the opportunity to show, under as favorable conditions as possible, the stuff that was in him.

Five top Republican senators, including Lodge and Mark Hanna, came to Sagamore Hill late that summer to discuss party policy. What about the control of the trusts? "Get at the evil in them and uphold the good," the President urged. That made sense even to the most conservative among them. Perhaps they felt it had better. "The President," the New York *Sun* quoted an "informant," "showed the utmost tenacity in holding to his theories." As for Cuban reciprocity, which was also dear to the President's heart,

163

the senators agreed, according to the *Sun*, "that it would be wise for the Party to adopt the President's view as a party view." Altogether, it was a good day for the President, though the senators, he wrote Hay, had not been much help.

| The President plays tennis. | He is also fond of riding. | And is a strong swimmer. |

A day at Oyster Bay

One thing, the New York *Sun* observed, was noticeable "in a general way" about the President's guests. After their return from Sagamore Hill "they were all in excellent spirits."

3

Not all.

Among the guests that summer was one who on his departure dragged his tail between his legs. He was the Russian Grand Duke Boris. He had been traveling across the United States, leaving a malodorous trail of chorus-girl slippers out of which he had quaffed his champagne. When the State Department, therefore, conveyed to the President the request of the Russian Ambassador, Count Cassini, to present the Grand Duke at Sagamore Hill, the President made a grinding noise with his teeth. The "creature" obviously deserved the snub direct or, better, the horsewhip; but he was a cousin of the Czar and to refuse to receive him might have ugly repercussions. That was one horn of his dilemma. The other was the strictly negative reaction of Mrs. Roosevelt. The First Lady was not given to ultimatums, but, in the set of her lips, the President recognized something he dared not disregard. The Grand Duke's presence in their house would be an insult, she pointed out. If he came, moreover, he would, of course, have to be asked to luncheon, and she would not have the man at her table, complications or no complications.

The wires hummed between Sagamore Hill and the State Department, and between the State Department and the Russian Embassy. Cassini was insistent on an audience, recognizing no doubt that the Czar might not look kindly on his ambassador's inability to get it; the State Department was firm on the exercise of the amenities. The First Lady remained unmoved.

The deadlock was resolved when "Edie" telephoned the President's beloved Aunt Lizzie, living at Yellowbanks, down the hill from Sagamore, and asked for an invitation to luncheon on the day that the Grand Duke was due to appear.

The pudgy, over-stuffed roué came on Ogden Mills' yacht, *Felicia,* landing with his host, four members of his suite, the ambassador, and a representative of the State Department at the Waldeck dock, from which the path led through the woods to Sagamore Hill.

The President received his guests courteously, if without enthusiasm.

The Ambassador was a massive creature with a tendency to shout when he wanted to make a point. "I regret," he said darkly, "not to find Mrs. Roosevelt at home."

The President ignored the remark, and the Ambassador repeated it. His host offered no explanations. "Mrs. Roosevelt has gone out to lunch, Mr. Ambassador. She is not in the house."

By no flutter of an eyelid did the President or his wife indicate to their friends, or to any representative of the press, the facts back of her luncheon engagement with Aunt Lizzie, and it was only eight years later, in response to a direct question by the Crown Princess of Sweden, that Roosevelt told the story.

The American public would have remained unaware of the incident but for the Grand Duke and the Ambassador themselves. Unable to conceal their chagrin, they spilled over to enough people to ensure the incident's getting into the newspapers.

"As the mistress of the ordinary American home would not have been at home when the Grand Duke called," commented the New York *Sun* editorially, "the mass of them will learn with extreme gratification of the President's wife's absence from her board when Duke Boris shared it with her husband."

Late in August the President began a tour of New England to make a series of addresses—actually a single address, delivered in parts, one in one city, another in another—presenting the trust problem as he saw it. On September 3rd, the thirteenth and last day of his tour, Edith Roosevelt, at Sagamore Hill, received word that he had met with an accident. Driving to a meeting near Pittsfield with W. Murray Crane, the Governor of Massachusetts, Cortelyou and the Secret Service man, Craig—"the excellent Craig"— his carriage had been run into by a trolley car and demolished. Craig had been killed. The President had been thrown thirty feet on to the pavement, but was going on with his tour, making his final speech that evening at Bridgeport.

Nearly frantic with apprehension, the First Lady, accompanied by Aunt Lizzie, Kermit, Ethel, and William Loeb, the President's junior secretary, hurried to Bridgeport on the *Sylph*, to meet the President. Late that night they returned together, the President cut and bruised but insisting that nothing mattered except the death of his faithful guard. They were vehemently welcomed at the Waldeck landing by Archie and Quentin, both shaken by their father's narrow escape and by Craig's death. The burly, blue-eyed Scot had become a cherished friend, particularly of Quentin, for whom he liked to interpret the comic cartoons in the newspapers. "How my children will feel!" had been the President's first words when he had been told of the Secret Service man's death.

Without much talk, by the light of a lantern in the hand of one of the hired men and with hearts deeply moved at the same time by grief for the dead and gratitude for the living, the President, his wife and the children walked through the dark woods and up the winding road to the house.

Such moments, too, had their part in the upbringing of the children on Sagamore Hill.

Chapter V

THERE WAS a neighborly relationship between the President and the people of Oyster Bay and the villages roundabout which was recognized and fostered on both sides. The President had a genuine regard for "plain folks," acquired during his ranching years in the Bad Lands, living under the same roof with two couples from Maine who ran his cattle or cooked his meals, and "visiting round" in bare but hospitable kitchens. What he had learned in Dakota interpreted and made valuable to him the men and women in Oyster Bay he had known since his boyhood. Remote as the currents of their lives were from his, these people sensed no barrier of caste between them because he himself tolerated none. This man might be President of the United States, they said, but, first of all, he was their friend.

That was definitely the conviction of the venerable hack driver, Jacob White, who had known "Theodore" as a boy and had a "pull" with the Administration, it was said, which statesmen envied. He was driving a group of sightseers one day when they met the President on horseback. "He slowed up when he came 'long side us,' " the old man said later, "and, salutin', calls out, Good mornin'. It set them people all a-flutter, and they began to figure out who he was bowin' to. One man began to give the impression that it was him. I stood this for about a minute, and then spoke up and says, 'The President was greetin' *me*. I'm about his best friend hereabouts.' This quieted 'em, and 'twasn't no lie, neither."

He never, if he could help it, refused any invitation to address these Nassau County neighbors of his. One year, it was Huntington's two hundred and fiftieth anniversary that they wanted him to lift to national significance, and he was there, with a speech that rang across the country; another year, it was Oyster Bay's Fourth of July celebration in Locust Grove, where he spoke in a deluge of rain, refusing with a laugh a proferred umbrella. He spoke on a favorite theme—the spirit of American citizenship—honesty, courage, common sense, love of country—and as was customary with him, brought it right down to the individual, in his own village, his own home. For all the downpour, not five persons in the drenched crowd left the grove while he was speaking. "They had come to hear what he wished to say to them," the New York *Tribune* reporter noted, "and were eager to stay there as long as he cared to speak."

The President appreciated his membership in the local Masonic Lodge because it afforded him an opportunity to meet some of his fellow townsmen at closer range. The master of Matinecock Lodge was the gardener on the estate of one of his cousins, Emlen, and he liked to maintain contact with him. As President, he could obviously not call upon this "most excellent, public-spirited citizen," as he once described him, without embarrassing him; nor could the gardener call upon the President without embarrassment. "But when I visit the lodge," Roosevelt said to the pastor of the local Presbyterian Church, Alexander G. Russell, "he is my boss, and I must stand up when he orders me, and sit down when he tells me, and not speak unless he allows me. That's good for him and good for me."

2

His sense of fellowship with his Nassau County neighbors impelled the President, at the end of his first summer as President, to arrange to receive as many as cared to come, at Sagamore Hill. He extended the invitation through the press; he asked the local clergy to announce it from their pulpits; and between eight and ten thousand of his neighbors came—"from the Sound shore and the other shore," noted the New York *Sun*, "and from the land between"; came "in special trains and in steamboats and behind their own farm horses," filling Oyster Bay early in the morning, "with a happy, jostling, county fair crowd" which, in the afternoon, moved like an invading army on Sagamore Hill and almost overwhelmed its capacity to provide ginger-snaps and raspberry shrub. There were flags everywhere in the village and along the Shore Road, and bunting festooned across the public buildings, mercifully concealing their architecture. The President's house was a bower of flags and bunting to the very peak. In two closely packed lines of vehicles—buckboards, buggies, surreys, victorias, farm-wagons, even antiquated stages—the procession moved up the Cove Neck Road and into the Sagamore Hill property. At a point opposite the tennis court, the guests alighted, trudging on foot up the road to the house.

On the surface, it was all informal, even casual; but actually every individual in the crowd was under observation, and bulging pockets were deftly touched by trained hands. The chief White House usher had come up from Washington to help direct the movement of the guests. Eight New York detectives—"Roosevelt cops" from the President's Police Commissioner days—re-enforced the men from the Secret Service. "No one," noted the Boston *Herald*, "kept a more careful watch on the President than his eldest son, Theodore, Jr. The fourteen-year-old boy had appointed himself a special guard over his father. Stationed at his left, and never once leaving his father while the reception lasted, young Theodore's keen eyes watched every person that approached, scrutinized his hands and every object he might be carrying."

For four hours the President shook his neighbors' hands. The First Lady, "in cream-colored voile with heavy embroidery of point appliqué, and a garden hat" (as the New York *Tribune* reporter described it), shook nobody's hand, true to the custom of letting her eyes and her smile say what she would not ask her hands to express. One wonders what emotions her apparently carefree courtesy concealed. It was at a public reception like this that the fatal shots that had killed President McKinley had been fired. These people were all neighbors, of course, many even friends. But suppose someone slipped in among them who was not a neighbor, not a friend?

The President clearly had no such thoughts. Dressed in a frock-coat and gray trousers, noted the Boston *Herald* correspondent, "he beamed with happiness as he chatted with his friends or exchanged hurried reminiscences with old acquaintances." In the line, the reporter noted "hundreds of serious-faced farmers, who tramped across the veranda with heavy boots and gripped the President's hand with considerable feeling, but rarely spoke." The women were inclined to talk. One boasted a grandson, named after the President; another, four Republican voters under her roof. Others told of large families. "Dee-lighted!" offered a safe response in every case.

The President gave no sense of rush but had a way of drawing the hand he was shaking inexorably past him as he shook it. An enterprising reporter clocked the presidential ordeal as sixty hands to the minute.

"Mr. President," exclaimed a woman, in sympathetic tones, after the procession had gone on for two hours, "how tired you must be!"

"Not a bit!" he answered quickly. "It takes more than a trolley-car to knock me out, and more than a crowd to tire me."

Everyone agreed that it was a great party, even those who arrived too late to get one of the souvenir punch glasses etched with the words *Theodore Roosevelt 1902.*

3

Six weeks later, the President's neighbors in Oyster Bay got back at him and gave him a reception of their own. The President was coming up from Washington to vote in the midterm elections, and the genial editor of the Oyster Bay *Pilot*, Albert L. Cheney, with his fellow-"Oyster," Frank C. Travers—described as a "Democrat in theory but a Republican in practice" when Roosevelt was on the ticket—conspired to make the welkin ring.

Lindsay Denison, who for years had covered Oyster Bay for the *Sun*, told New York about it next morning, with evident relish, and Cheney, to his dying day, vouched for its every detail. From Travers, on guard at Long Island City on the afternoon of the day preceding the election, Cheney received a wire: "President's baggage now here. Have fireworks arrived Oyster Bay?"

"Fireworks here," Cheney replied. "When does the President arrive here?"

"Don't know," came the answer from Travers, "but start salute at half past six."

"What about salute?" queried Cheney. "Have just enough to pay band. Who will pay battery?"

On the instant almost, the reply came: "I'll pay for battery and anything else you can think of. Have band for all night. Have you got bonfire? If not, get busy. Get busy anyhow."

At half past six came a final wire from Travers: "Train leaving. Let her go."

The local Republicans were about to hold their final campaign rally, and Cheney marched them down to the depot. Maurice Townsend, who, as a Democrat, differed from Travers only in so far as he actually voted the ticket, brought along the Democrats, explaining to his friends that the President was President of the whole United States, "and I guess the Townsends are prominent enough in the community to be broad-minded, even if it *is* the night before Election." The area about the station was already packed with men and women of both parties, or none.

"When the train rolled into the station," Denison noted, "it was indeed apparent that Mr. Cheney had let her go." The bonfire was roaring to the stars, lighting the great crowd and sending its red glow far out over the Bay. Rockets streaked heavenward, shedding their stars over the water. Roman candles popped their balls of fire, and the Oyster Bay band tried valiantly to make itself heard. Beside an anvil a blacksmith with a sledgehammer provided a presidential salute. "The anvil battery," the *Sun* reporter declared, "made the little railroad station jump six inches in the air once every two and a half minutes. Great was the racket," he added.

When the President stepped from the train, followed by Mrs. Roosevelt, the Secret Service men with him attempted to hold off the crowd, but they had no more luck than King Canute with the incoming tide. "The President pushed them aside and dove into the mass of people, shaking hands with both hands at once, laughing long and loud between greetings and handshakings."

The President and his wife climbed into the trap that had come over from Sagamore, the coachman called to the man at the restless horse's head, "Let go!" and in a flash they were out of sight up a side street.

"But the band and the fireworks," Denison reported, "went right on."

He first chops down
a few trees.

Then has a little canter
cross country.

After which he takes a brisk
stroll of twenty miles.

He then gives the children a
wheelbarrow ride.

And rests a
moment or two.

By which time he is ready
for breakfast.

The President is resting at his home at Oyster Bay

(By Courtesy of The Chicago *Tribune*)

Chapter VI

ONE SUMMER was like another at Sagamore, so far as the family life was concerned, even though the rambling house was the focus of eighty million pairs of eyes. You rowed, you played tennis, you wrestled, you hiked, you chopped fire-wood, you swam, you shot at a target, and it did not much matter that you were President of the United States so long as the politicians and the reporters left you reasonably alone.

The President's feeling about Sagamore was a good deal like his children's: he wanted to be free of the schoolmaster, Duty; free of the restrictions that hedged him round in a city and a city house—even the White House; particularly the White House. He wanted to get away from reporters and cameras, wear old clothes, old shoes, old hats, kick up his heels in the pasture; get a respite from the things he had been doing; for a few weeks, be a boy again. "Rest," to the President, meant something quite different from what it meant to most men after the winter's labor: the delicious stretching out of tired limbs in a comfortable hammock, on a shady lawn, or the dreamy contemplation of distant horizons by the vacationing, even the vacant mind. Most men might lounge and pipe-dream, in a comfortable half asleep way, but Roosevelt permitted himself no such moods. "He was either fully awake, at work or at recreation," his friend "Alec" Lambert once said, "or he was fully asleep."

It was characteristic of the President that, when Bleistein, his favorite mount, arrived from Washington, he should want to exercise him, though rain was pouring, and that he should ride him in the storm for two hours, returning, plastered with mud; characteristic, too, that, on a hot July day, when a clam-bake was arranged on a beach eight miles away, and the rest of the family prepared to board the *Sylph,* the President should choose to row Mrs. Roosevelt the eight miles there and back.

It was not inactivity that he craved. He was, in fact, in motion all day long, at one or another of his familiar pastimes, or, if Seaman needed an extra hand when a storm was threatening, helping to get the hay in.

Harry Graham, in the *Metropolitan Magazine,* gave the picture:

> "At 6 A.M. he shoots a bear,
>   At 8, he schools a restive horse,
> From 10 to 4 he takes the air—
>   (He doesn't take it all, of course.)
>
> At intervals throughout the day
>   He sprints around the house, or if
> His residence is Oyster Bay,
>   He races up and down the cliff;
> While seagulls scream about his legs,
> Or hasten home to hide their eggs."

If anyone had chosen to question his conception of rest, the President would, perhaps, have pointed out that one man's rest was another man's boredom; and what was a flabby body good for, anyway, even for a President?

As it was, he was inclined to feel that, in terms of physical prowess, he was slipping, getting both fat and stiff. Ted, at fifteen, was catching up with him in physical prowess, he recognized, outwalking and outrunning him, and matching him at riding and swimming. That was as it should be, and he would not have had it otherwise, but he was not going to let himself go softer than he could help.

2

It was the children who gave him his real rest, his truest recreation. "The children do have an ideal time out here," he wrote Emily Carow, "and it is an ideal place for them. The three sets of cousins are always together. I am rather disconcerted by the fact that they persist in regarding me as a playmate. This afternoon, for instance, was rainy, and all of them came to get me to play with them in the old barn. They pled so hard that I finally gave in. . . . The barn is filled with hay, and of course meets every requirement for the

174

most active species of hide-and-seek and the like. Quentin"—the baby of the lot—"enjoyed the game as much as anyone, and would jump down from one hay level to another, fifteen feet below, with complete abandonment. . . . I love all these children and have great fun with them; and I am touched by the way in which they feel that I am their special friend, champion and companion." He might have added, their "hero" and have still understated the children's awed admiration. "All young Roosevelts," wrote a reporter of the New York *Tribune,* "are convinced that the President can row a boat better, shoot a gun straighter, and set off fireworks louder than anyone else." He was the umpire, moreover, to settle all disputes that arose among the boys regarding the size of bait to catch snappers, the length of line between the sinker and the hook, or "the best way to hold a rifle when aiming at a grizzly that is coming in your direction."

Once more, the President gave his sister-in-law characteristic vignettes of his playmates: "Archie and Nick . . . after one of the picnics, walking solemnly up, jointly carrying a basket, and each with a captured turtle in his disengaged hand . . . Archie . . . a most warm-hearted, loving, cunning little goose . . . Quentin . . . a merry soul . . . now become entirely one of the children, joining heartily in all their games" . . . "Yesterday he not only ran down Cooper's Bluff quite alone," Quentin's mother wrote her sister, "but climbed it in the same way, much to Senator Cameron's delight. He watched him with interest, and exclaimed, 'he has the blood!' when the small blue object gradually neared the top."

The President wrote of amateur theatricals, got up by Ted and his cousin Lorraine, and given on the West Roosevelt tennis-court. "All the children . . . most cunning . . . especially Quentin as Cupid in the scantiest of pink muslin tights and bodice . . . Ted and Lorraine, respectively George Washington and Cleopatra," stealing the show. . . . Ethel, on her birthday, asking no entertainment but a romp in the barn under her father's leadership. "Of course, I had not the heart to refuse; but, really, it seems, to put it mildly, rather odd for a stout, elderly President to be bouncing over hay-ricks in a wild effort to get to goal before an active midget of a competitor, aged nine years."

The Fourth of July continued to be the year's high point of fellowship between the President and the sixteen growing cousins, but there were phases of it in which his part was mainly reticence and the discreetly averted eye. Kermit's Groton classmate, Barclay Farr, described by the President on one occasion as "the worst friend of the worst boy in the world," remembered, fifty years later, the expeditions which began shortly after one o'clock in the morning of the Fourth, when Kermit and Barclay and one or another of the Roosevelt cousins would make their way stealthily through the dark woods, laden with fire-crackers. Close to the front door of some neighboring house they would place a string of five hundred or so, from the harmless one-inch type to the six-inch terrifying "giant," light the small end of the chain and run for their lives.

The boys had a conviction that, since they were operating out of the President's home, "there was," as Farr put it, "some sort of aura about us. We were untouchable and could do these things," and no one would dare report them. Occasionally, however, there were reverberations of the nocturnal explosions which reached Sagamore Hill. The President would make what Farr called "little remarks, usually accompanied with a chuckle," indicating that he knew more than he was supposed to know. But there were no reprimands.

3

It was in Sagamore Hill's second season as the Summer White House that obstacle walks joined the headlong dash down Cooper's Bluff as the standard initiation for weekend visitors. The grafting of this new bud upon the strenuous life was the work of the United States Commissioner of Corporations, later Secretary of the Interior, James R. Garfield. The President's report of his first venture in a new field was eloquent. "I had six boys with me, including all my own, except Quentin," he wrote Garfield. "We swam the mill-pond (which proved to be very broad and covered with duckweed), in great shape, with our clothes on; executed an equally long but easier swim in the bay, with our clothes on; and between times had gone in a straight line through the woods, through the marshes, and up and down the bluffs. . . . I did not look exactly presidential when I got back from the walk!"

Ted occasionally suffered "obstacles" on these point-to-point walks that were not on the program. Once, he found himself on the bank of a pool covered with green slime. The little boy for whom he was responsible did not like the scum and, instead of

176

letting Ted tow him, insisted on wriggling high up on his shoulders. "No remonstrances on my part," Ted wrote long after, "had any effect." Under the boy's weight he sank lower and lower. "When we got to the other side I was almost under the surface and had taken a large gulp of the scum."

The President found that combining the point-to-point walks with the slide down Cooper's Bluff produced a maximum test of the intestinal fortitude of his guests. Cooper's Bluff always came first. The President would gather his children and the cousins and any unwary adult he could corral at the top of the Bluff. "There is a little path down the side," he would say to the novice with a tolerant twinkle, "but *I* always jump off the top." Then with a laugh he would leap off the bank, landing on the sandy incline and, sliding, leaping, falling, would somehow reach the bottom, with children of all ages tumbling around him. At the foot of the Bluff all sat around on rocks, pouring the sand out of shoes and stockings or socks. Then the "obstacle walk" would begin. There was one rule for the participants, and one only. You went "over or through" every obstacle, "never around." The President's sister, Corinne Robinson, noted one day an "especially unpleasant-looking little bathing-house with a very steep roof" on the line of march, and prayed that the leader might choose not to go over *that*. She had no such luck. "I can still see the sturdy body of the President of the United States," she wrote long after, "hurling itself at the obstruction and with singular agility chinning himself to the top and sliding down on the other side." The children followed with whoops of delight. By the aid of a large rusty nail, Mrs. Robinson scrambled up the roof, and over, to be greeted with such an ovation as she had never known before and would not know again, though, many years later, a national convention might do its best.

The wild sport was not as haphazard as it might look. There were rules not dissimilar to those that children played with cups and dice and discs which were "sent home" if they landed on a fatal spot. The children were expected, within reason, to protect themselves. If, because you had not used both hands, climbing a tree, you slipped, you went home. Hands were made to be used and a child must learn to use them. If you waded in a brook and fell in, again you went home. The rules were strictly enforced, but none of the children resented them since the leader played no favorites.

There were other rules, moreover, which seemed to the children

177

a clear indication that their mentor and friend had exceptionally sound judgment. Rents in clothes were not frowned upon. Rather were they regarded as honorable scars. Mothers at Waldeck or Yellowbanks were occasionally less understanding. When Lorraine Roosevelt, Cousin Laura's daughter, came home, soaked, one day with her dress torn and covered with mud, her mother took action. "Cousin Theodore took us," the girl protested. "I don't care," her mother replied. "*You* mustn't be a fool even if your Cousin Theodore sets you the example."

Romping with the children as though he were their own age, the President yet missed no opportunity to lift their spirits. "Today all, young and old, from the three houses"—the Emlen Roosevelts', the West Roosevelts' and Sagamore Hill—"went with us to service on the great battleship 'Kearsarge,'" the President wrote a friend, "for the fleet is in here to be inspected by me tomorrow. It was an impressive sight, one which, I think, the children will not soon forget."

4

As the years passed, more and more of the boys became eligible for the annual adventure of "camping out." The President himself established the eligibility rules which were two in number and strictly adhered to: a boy must, first, be able to dress himself and, second, as the President phrased it, have "sufficient discretion to understand that, when once off, all ills from mosquitoes to a downpour of rain must be borne not only uncomplainingly but cheerfully." The adventure became the high point of the summer's activities. Where there had been three boys to go, the first summer of Mr. Roosevelt's Presidency, there were ten or eleven in its fourth or fifth. When a schooner was wrecked on Lloyd's Neck, providing sleeping quarters, a new type of overnight camping expedition evolved, which was called a "squaw-picnic," since girls were included, the girls sleeping in the wreck, the boys and the President on the beach. But that was a later development.

The President generally managed to pick a day on which the omens were favorable for a clear night, though once the weather fooled him and the campers suffered an all-night drenching. But, as a rule, the day was cloudless and warm, with the Connecticut shore purple in the afternoon haze, and the night deep and magical with stars. In four or five boats, moored at the water's edge, the provender, blankets and axes, frying pans, cutlery and a kettle, would be stowed under the direction of the President. Wearing an old slouch hat, a flannel shirt, a rough tweed coat and old trousers, he would not look presidential. The boys, indeed, would have disowned him if he had.

It was generally a five- or six-mile row to the point that the President and the boys, between them, had selected for the camp. After the supplies had been landed, the camp prepared and the fire started, the boys would plunge into the water, while the President prepared the supper. The sun would be dipping below the westward ridges before the meal was spread, and the boys would fall to, with appetites whetted by memories of other such repasts. "The boys are sufficiently deluded," the President wrote a friend after one such meal, "to believe that the chicken or beef-steak I fry in bacon fat on these expeditions has a flavor impossible elsewhere to be obtained."

The gaiety of the supper would subside as twilight fell. The boys would pile fresh wood on the fire, and, as the sparks leapt upward, the high period of the adventure would begin—the stars, the deepening darkness, the mystery and menace of the night. The boys would draw closer to the fire.

One of them would ask for a story, and a chorus of voices would back his appeal. The President had plenty to tell—stories of the plains and the woods, the mountains and the desert, of hunting and desperate men, and cattle herding and charges through the Cuban jungle. Other adventurous spirits might have matched his tales of daring and adventure out of their own experience, and yet others might have recounted the "hero tales" of Stony Point and Kings Mountain, the Alamo and Pickett's charge, but none, surely, could have made them live as did he, in such a place, at such an hour, for such an audience. For these little boys, these gangling youths, were more than cherished sons or nephews or cousins, to whom he liked, periodically, as part of his conception of an elder's duty, to give a "wilderness" experience, synthetic though it might be, and whom he sought to entertain, perhaps to thrill. They were American boys in whom he was seeking to awaken the hunger to make themselves men who could be trusted to be resolute defenders of their heritage; boys in whom he was endeavoring to rouse or to feed a spirit such as had sustained the nation in crises in the past

179

and which the nation would need if it were to survive in the future.

He would give them the best he had and would not be concerned though he kept the younger boys up an hour or two or three beyond their customary bedtime. At last they would all roll up in their blankets under the stars, and sleep—and dream.

5

Once, the President took Ted and his cousins, George and Philip Roosevelt, on an all-night horseback ride to pay his respects to his uncle, Robert Barnwell Roosevelt, living at Sayville on the South Shore, thirty-five miles from Sagamore Hill. Through a heavy rain that made rivers of the roads, lit only by occasional, distant lightning, the party wound through the Sagamore woods, riding east to Huntington and then south. The sky was paling when they entered Smithtown, but no one was in the streets to notice the strange cavalcade or to realize that it was the President of the United States who rode at its head. The sun was well above the horizon when the party reached Lake Ronkonkoma. As they approached Sayville, passing farmers recognized the President and sent word to the village. Out of their houses, the residents came tumbling, lining the sidewalk and cheering, as the muddy and bedraggled company passed.

The party returned to Sagamore, next day, leaving Sayville at four in the morning, and reaching home just before luncheon, "somewhat fatigued," noted the reporter of the New York *Telegram,* but "enthusiastic over the trip."

The First Lady welcomed them under the porte-cochère. "I am glad to see you safely home, Mr. President," she said.

There was more than met the ear in her seemingly playful words. Her husband might forget that he was President of the United States and a magnet for the diseased or the criminal mind. She never could. And he had gone without guards. Torn between exasperation and relief, did she say to herself, Will he never grow up?

The New York *World,* for other reasons, was inclined to be sardonic over the episode. "Now that the President has proved by actual experience that the trip from Oyster Bay to Sayville and back can be made on horseback, with what new discovery will he next thrill a waiting nation?"

The writer might have shaken his head even harder if he had been told that the President had taken the trip for no reason except to make a kindly gesture toward an old man he was fond of, and to give three boys an adventure that would be one more golden thread in the weaving of manhood.

6

How valid Edith Roosevelt's apprehensions were was made evident a few weeks after the Sayville excursion. The President, one evening, was working in the library after the family had gone to bed when he heard angry voices outside. He hurried to the porch and stood for an instant in the light from the study, offering in his white shirt-front a perfect target for a man scarcely a hundred feet away with a loaded revolver in his hand.

The man was a young farmer, named Henry Weilbrenner, from the village of Syosset, some five miles away. He had had, therefore, the right to be in the procession filing past the President at Sagamore, the year before, but had happily not chosen to exercise it. A brother, out of a job, had passed on to him his grievance against the world and his zeal for the labor movement which the would-be assassin was convinced the President had neglected.

He had driven up the hill in a buggy and told the Secret Service man who intercepted him that he had an appointment with the President. The guard had been told of no such late appointment, and refused to let him pass. But fifteen minutes later the man was back. The President wanted him to marry Alice, he said.

The guard recognized that he had a "nut" on his hands and suggested that he see Loeb next morning at the presidential office in the village. The man appeared amenable, turned the buggy around, and drove down the hill. But a quarter-hour later he was back again.

"What do you want here?" the guard asked angrily, now fully aware that he was dealing with something more serious than the usual "nut." The intruder shouted, "None of your damned business!" At that moment, the house-door opened and the President appeared. "There he is now!" the man cried and, leaning over the dashboard, urged the horse forward.

The Secret Service man leapt at the lunatic and dragged him to the ground. "I wanted to kill him," the farmer admitted later. "I

181

had my shooting iron ready!" The pearl-handled, 32-caliber revolver was found on the buggy-floor.

While the President was standing on the porch, Seaman, his farm manager, ran up. Two men had crossed the porch of his own house, he said. "Come on," he had heard one of them say to the other. "It's all right."

The late evening shift of guards, driving up from town, arrived and found the men's footprints but nothing more. What connection, if any, there was between them and the man in the buggy, or what plot the commotion about the latter might have thwarted, no one could guess, or would ever know.

Meanwhile, the Sagamore household was in commotion. Mrs. Roosevelt, who had been wakened by the noise of the scuffle, ran downstairs. The President reassured her. The Secret Service men were having a "tussle" with a drunken man, that was all. But there was no sleep for her for the rest of the night.

Loeb next morning intimated that attempts on the President's life were nothing new. "This is one case that got into the newspapers," he said.

Jake Riis, who hurried out to Oyster Bay when he read the news of the attack, joined the First Lady in demanding of the President a promise never again to expose himself as he had exposed himself the evening before. Good-humoredly, the President gave in, though insisting he had been in no danger. "But what would you have had me do? The Secret Service man was fighting my fight, and he was alone. Would you have had me hide—with him, perhaps, one against two or three?"

"But you are not simply Theodore Roosevelt," Riis reminded him. "You are the President and have the whole country to answer to."

The object of his solicitude was not convinced. "There was nothing whatever in that crazy man incident," he wrote Hay. "He was a poor, demented creature with a revolver, who was wholly undecided whether to see me as a friend or to protest against my having done him some unknown wrong."

Exactly.

Chapter VII

ONE MEMBER of the Sagamore family had no significant part in the rough sports of the presidential summers. "Alice has been at home very little," the President wrote his sister Corinne that autumn of 1903, "spending most of her time in Newport and elsewhere, associating with the Four Hundred—individuals with whom the other members of her family have exceedingly few affiliations."

Alice was bored at Sagamore Hill. Its code oppressed her. When she wanted to smoke she had to blow the smoke up the chimney or wander off into the woods. The young men who came to the house were nice young polo-players or earnest youths about to save the world, and she was not interested in either. She had not yet discovered the excitement of politics, and the statesmen who sat at her father's table and monopolized the conversation—or would have monopolized it if her father had given them the chance—seemed to her stuffy and boring.

Alice liked "society," the sophistication, the gaiety, the easy manners, the relaxation of an atmosphere altogether free of high purpose, of any purpose, indeed, except the enjoyment of life. It was by no means a vapid society. There were plenty of brains in it and a good deal of sparkle of a sort, but it was doomed by its exclusive nature to function in a cramped little room with golden walls. Its world was as confining in its way as the world of any girl in a Fall River textile mill, year after year, going through the same motions, repeating the same words, though the background for the moment might be London, Paris, Rome, the Riviera, or New York, Newport, Pinehurst or Jekyll Island.

Alice's father had a sharp contempt for the "idle rich" and strong convictions on the duty of the leisure class to the community. He had, in fact, nearly died of ennui or exasperation when once, ten

183

years before, a stubborn chest affection had condemned him to spend three weeks among the "swells" in Pinehurst. Alice, conscious of no challenge, hearing no call such as had moved her father at her age, but young, exuberant and adventurous, was immensely intrigued by the life these handsome, wealthy, well-tailored and, on the whole, well-mannered and only occasionally fantastic people made for themselves. She was not particularly interested in any of the rich young play-boys or in those earls, counts and princes who were the charming and often cultivated hangers-on of society in Washington or Newport, on the look-out for an advantageous marriage, and, in a steady stream, offered to lay their hearts and coronets at her feet. But it was exciting to have them flutter around her candle and watch them singe their wings; exciting to be in the center of the competition, the fierce rivalries of a social group in which wealth and position were the great prizes. She had her father's consuming zest for life, and like him, periodically needed "the wine of life with brandy in it." She enjoyed danger and, like her father, ran to meet it. Like him, too, she might not seek a fight, but, if a fight came, she went into it with both fists.

The girl of nineteen, looking out on the world with smiling, parted lips, proud and assured in her quick intelligence and her physical well-being, was a very different person from the social fledgling who had made her debut in the East Room of the White House that January night four months after her father became President, or had stood demurely by her stepmother's side in the Blue Room, several afternoons a week, bowing to official Washington. She no longer had much to do with the official life of which her father was the guiding and directing force. She was of age, she had her own money, she chose her own friends, conscious of no obligation to sit through a long series of Cabinet dinners, diplomatic dinners, Supreme Court dinners, Senate and House dinners, or to receive an interminable line of army and navy officers or third-rate diplomats. She could not have evaded, if she had wanted to, the honors of high official position, but she saw no reason why she should carry its responsibilities.

The press reported her engagement to one young hopeful after another, a former Rough Rider or two, various rich young men of New York Society—some of whom she had never met—and countless noblemen. Alice affirmed nothing and denied nothing, being herself and nobody else, doing what she pleased, when she pleased, as she pleased, within the limits that she herself established and maintained. When a party at her Auntie Bye's (Mrs. Cowles) seemed to require enlivening, she brought out a toy-pistol with dynamite caps and started firing; and the party, from Alice's standpoint, was saved. She carried a little pet snake around with her which she called Emily Spinach—spinach for its color and Emily for her stepmother's sister, who was thin beyond belief. She did the unexpected, on principle, not so much because she wanted to attract attention but because she loved a good time and bridled at any kind of prohibition.

The press reported that, on the social side, she "puzzled" Newport; courteous as she was, and obviously wanting not to disappoint anyone, she had a way of not presenting herself when and where she was expected. But her independence enhanced rather than diminished her popularity, helping as it did to build the legend of a President's daughter who had wealth, beauty and the social graces, exceptional wit, daring, an untameable will and a gay, if ruthless, determination to be herself. The public took the legend to its heart. Babies were named after her. A special shade of blue was given her name, and every woman suddenly was wearing "Alice Blue." Her quips went the rounds. When she was told of an Italian cabman who had twenty children in twenty-five years of marriage, she exclaimed, to the delight of the country, "How father would love that man!"

During one of her visits to Newport she visited the "submarine boat" Moccasin, and persuaded its commander to submerge at its dock; and she took to the automobile with Rooseveltian enthusiasm. The press told lurid stories of a small runabout in which she drove about Washington at "reckless" speeds, until the police caught up with her; and of a "big red devil" which she acquired, able, in the words of the Washington correspondent of the Cleveland Plain Dealer, to "tear off thirty miles or more an hour"; and all of it was fiction. But it was true that she was in the Panhard racer which her friend Ella Drexel Paul drove from Newport to Boston in the record time of six hours. "The trip through the various towns," the Baltimore Herald reported, "was run at the required speed of eight miles an hour. But Miss Paul speeded the car to 25 miles an hour when they were in open country." The incident confirmed the public's impression of Alice as an exceptionally reckless daredevil.

The President was inclined to feel that Alice was overdoing the social whirl. A year or two was all right, but "upon my word," he wrote Ted, he didn't think it "healthy from the standpoint of permanence. I wish she had some pronounced serious taste. Perhaps she will develop one later." When Alice seemed to him to be getting too brash, he put his foot down, but, finding that the only effect was that Alice would absent herself from the White House for a few days until the storm had passed, he became philosophic. One day, when Owen Wister was with him in his office, Alice blew in and blew out, three times. Wister finally felt his hackles rise. "Theodore," he asked, mildly, "isn't there anything you can do to control Alice?"

"Dan," answered the President, using the nickname that went back to Wister's college days, "I can do one of two things. I can be President of the United States, or I can control Alice. I cannot possibly do both."

The fact was, he took pride in her. He cherished courage as the first of the virtues, and Alice had plenty of that. He cherished wit, and sympathized with her impatience of dullness. He enjoyed her well-stored mind and respected her political opinions. The press was nearer the truth than it frequently was in dealing with Alice when it called her "a chip of the old block."

Alice had a kind of enchantment for the public, indeed, that was not wholly different from the attraction her father had for men and women of every variety, high or low, brainy or dull. Wherever she was, she was the focus of all eyes, the magnet toward which everyone in the gathering seemed drawn. She might be witty, she might be rude, she might be worshiped, she might be hated; but the pull was there, and women as well as men found it irresistible. The attraction was as immediate in public places as in a drawing-room. The cartoonist McCutcheon went to a horse-show in Chicago and recorded, once for all, in a cartoon captioned, "Alice, where art thou?" the effect of a visitation by Alice Roosevelt.

She was cutting an enormous swathe, not only in her own country but also abroad. In Germany, she was one of the two leading characters—her father the other—in a dramatic sketch called "The Mad Year." In France, the Chamber of Deputies debated an appropriation to have the painter Chartran do her portrait. The *Journal des Débats* tabulated her activities over a fifteen-month period—407 dinners, 350 balls, 300 parties, 680 teas, 1706 calls, solemnly adding

"Alice, where art thou?"

(By courtesy of the Chicago *Tribune*)

a warning against "neurasthenia." "Bosh!" her father was reported as saying. "She often takes a tramp of several miles at the pace I set for her," which seemed as convincing an answer as any to the imagined menace.

Rumors that Alice was contemplating a trip abroad started a new wave of gossip and speculation on the general assumption that she was "on the prowl" for a title. The Parisian magazine *Femina* gave its front page to her photograph, surrounded by pictures of eligible princes, including Crown Prince Gustaf-Adolf of Sweden, Prince George of Greece and two sons of the German Emperor. "We know what she is coming for," ran the gossip of the Paris cafés. "Well, who is it going to be?" There was chatter about a dream that Alice was supposed to have had, in which the princes of Europe had knelt before her and offered her the insignia of their rank. "It would actually seem as though the whole of Paris were looking to Miss Roosevelt to do something notable," ran the syndicated story in the Hearst press, "something worthy of her career at the White House and worthy of their interest in her career in the future."

If Alice ever had any idea of going to Europe, she gave it up. She was not averse to marrying. There was a congressman from Ohio, in fact, who was delightfully entertaining and played the violin like an angel. . . .

Chapter VIII

THE FIRST LADY observed her stepdaughter's skyrocketings with compressed lips, wondering what would come of it all and wishing to goodness Alice would get married and settle down. She knew exactly how to handle Ted or Kermit or Ethel or the two little boys, but Alice, at nineteen, was a phenomenon beyond her Victorian horizon.

Frustration in any area of life was an unusual sensation to Edith Roosevelt. In her relations with her husband—the ever deepening mutual devotion, the comradeship in the outdoors, the intellectual give-and-take, their partnership in all the great decisions—as in her relations with her own children—their tender unfolding into physical and mental vigor, their affection for each other and for their father and herself: in these deep personal experiences she had known a fulfillment that came to few women. Her husband's Presidency, moreover, had brought unexpected fulfillment of herself as a personality which relaxed old tensions in her, obliterated feelings of inferiority, lingering from her girlhood, and filled her with a serene contentment that gave new substance and depth to her natural charm.

She had accepted the unwelcome fact that, as the President's wife, she was a legitimate object of public attention, and suffered the exactions of the press with patient endurance. She pasted in her scrapbook the clipping an admirer sent her, quoting the acid remark of the leader of New York's "Four Hundred," Mrs. Stuyvesant Fish: "The wife of the President, it is said, dresses on $300.00 a year, and she looks it"; and even when the local correspondent of the New York *Herald* showed her a telegram from his editor quoting a report that Mrs. Roosevelt had "discarded corsets," with orders to "ascertain whether true or not," she was able to turn aside the impertinent query with an amused comment.

But editors who bombarded her for articles or other signed contributions found her firmly negative, though she herself was invited to fix the length of the article and the price to be paid. When occasionally a check up to $500 was enclosed with the editorial plea, it was returned by the next mail with a courteous note. She would not exploit her husband's name.

The First Lady retained to a remarkable degree the "freedom" which had seemed to her husband's little secretary, Amy Cheney, five years before, so conspicuously hers. She continued, at Sagamore, summers, to be herself, dressing as she pleased, wearing her pink sunbonnet—and "very becoming" her husband thought it— seeing her neighbors as in the past, at their homes or at hers, listening to them, chatting with them, drawing them out, yet—Owen Wister, on his frequent visits, noted—never stepping "out of the magic circle of her discretion." She caused the neighbors, he observed, also to be discreet. "I doubt if anyone ever said to her more than once what they should not." In private, he added, she could express herself; and did, at times, pointedly, if briefly.

As in the happy, less burdened past, the First Lady kept herself free to accompany her husband, at the drop of the hat, for a day's picnic or a ride at a breakneck gallop with him through the countryside or, occasionally, even at his sessions with the axe, slashing the branches off a tree he had felled.

2

Yet she was not as she had been before the day she had entered the White House with her husband two years before. As a mother, she was, as ever, sympathetic, firm, courageous, imaginative, untiring, full of understanding and humor; and as watchful—more watchful, indeed, since the dangers facing the children were increasing—reserving a substantial part of every day for them, never failing to find time to read to them, or to hear their tales of the day's adventures. But, as mistress of the White House, she seemed a wholly different person from the attractive but self-effacing, almost shy, young wife of the Civil Service Commissioner or the president of the New York Police Board. As the Governor's lady she had learned to play a gracious part as head of the society of the state capital, but her part had still been merely that of the tactful helpmeet. As wife of the President, however, she had assumed responsibilities that were wholly her own, and risen to them no less dramatically than he had risen to his, both as administrator of the institution known as the "Executive Mansion" and as head of the society of the national capital.

Two weeks after she had installed her family in the gloomy house, still under the shadow of death, the President had written a friend how "dignified and wise" she seemed as mistress of the White House, and, with it, how happy. She had written her friend, Fanny Parsons, at the time, with what ease Theodore was carrying his new responsibilities, and he might have written the same of her. She seemed to flower under them, indeed, as one who, for the first time in her life, had work to do that brought into action all her latent gifts; not the least, an executive capacity which had been overshadowed by her husband's more powerful personality and his instinct for command.

She had found the White House in confusion, and had been appalled at the lack of businesslike care of public property that she found. No one had seemed to know what was in the house, or what was the property of the government and what the personal belongings of the out-going family. At the close of each administration there had been a public sale of household furnishings, with junk and priceless pieces distributed indiscriminately to the highest bidders. With no fuss or outcry, no publicity—not even a raised voice in a White House corridor—she set the establishment in order, organized an effective staff and saw to it that it functioned, keeping herself the strict oversight that was needed. White House officials, remembering other administrations, going back to Lincoln's, marveled how she managed to do it with all her personal and social responsibilities, and do it so thoroughly and apparently with so little effort.

There was a reason. Like the President she had her own rules for intelligent living, and followed them with a persistence comparable to his. She believed in sunlight and fresh air, and spent as many hours a day outdoors as she could, whether it were walking to school with Ethel or strolling in the White House gardens, riding with the President or merely having luncheon served on the south portico. For the rides and the walks, the weather did not much matter; rain or snow never daunted her and an occasional soaking failed to disturb her. She believed in simple food for her family and herself, moreover, as heartily as she believed in fresh

191

air and exercise. French caterers might prepare the formal White House dinners, but the Irish cook from Sagamore Hill prepared the meals of the presidential family and, though the White House steward might buy the supplies, he bought them from a list provided by Mrs. Roosevelt.

There was a third element in the First Lady's program to preserve her family's health and her own. She was determined to maintain her family's privacy; to be hospitable, indeed, but to be hospitable on her own initiative and her own terms; to make her contacts with the public a matter of *her* choice, not the public's. If her husband had to be President she was determined that, at least so far as she could control conditions, the power and the glory should not wreck his life or hers, or their children's.

It was this determination, no doubt, that played the decisive part in the remodeling of the White House, the first year of the new administration, not only to provide more bedrooms and restore its appearance to the spirit of its eighteenth century tradition, but to divide its private from its public aspects, make it a home as well as an office and a showcase. She herself took the direction of the restoration, guiding the architects, selecting the furnishings and taking as much care to see that every dollar of government funds was advantageously spent as if the money had been her own. Nothing but the best was good enough for the White House, the First Lady insisted, yet there must be no waste. Handsome hangings, which had been on the first floor but did not fit into the new scheme of decoration, were used to re-upholster furniture on the upper floors, and carpets that had been on the first floor were made over for upstairs. The total result, the President wrote a friend, was to transform the White House "from a shabby likeness to the ground floor of the Astor House into a simple and dignified dwelling for the head of a great republic."

3

Without ostentation or display, the new First Lady gave the social life of the White House a dignity it had not had since Federalist days. There were those who lamented the departure from the casual ways of the Cleveland era and the small-town stuffiness of the McKinley period; but others, who recognized the new position of the nation in world affairs, took pride in it and were grateful.

No one, seeing the poised and serene First Lady presiding over White House dinners and receptions, would have been able to imagine the qualms she had suffered at her first appearance in her new role at the time of Mr. McKinley's funeral. It was not long, indeed, before she was directing more varied and extensive social activities than the White House had ever known. The list of private entertainments in addition to the public functions might well have appalled any American woman. Yet she gave each its own character, moving in and out among the guests, "like a shuttle," Archie Butt, one of the President's aides, put it, "keeping everything in harmony." Like her husband, moreover, Edith Roosevelt never seemed to lose sight of the individual in the crowd. At a White House reception she became aware that a young woman, distinguished in appearance and beautifully gowned, was being cold-shouldered by the other guests. She recognized her as a saleswoman who had waited on her in a New York department store, in which, in prosperous days, the young woman had been a leading customer. The First Lady, noting that she seemed in the act of making as graceful an exit as she could, left the group about her and approached her guest with outstretched hand. "I think we need hardly be introduced," she said, "since we are such old friends. I am so glad to see you here." Then, placing her arm around the young woman's waist, she led her to a sofa and chatted with her for fifteen or twenty minutes.

Yet, in her role as social arbiter, she could be ruthless in defense of those moral standards by which she herself had been brought up. When an attractive officer, who had been an ornament of White House functions for two or three Administrations, married a woman who had been involved in a Washington scandal, twenty years before, he was cut off the White House invitation list for the duration of the Roosevelt Administration.

4

The First Lady was by her own insistence so little in the news that the public saw her only as a gracious but subordinate figure, moving without clear outlines in the shadow of the President's vivid personality. But acute observers of the Washington scene knew better.

"At the time the Roosevelts were in the White House," wrote

Mark Sullivan in the Washington *Star*, in the nineteen-thirties, "it was the judgment of many that Mrs. Roosevelt was greater among women than her husband among men." Part of her greatness, he pointed out, lay "in the quiet check of graciousness and humor she kept upon her husband's sometimes reckless exuberance." He recalled the smile, the twinkle in her eye, the affection in her voice on occasions at the White House table when her "Theodore!" would put "a gentle brake upon her husband's headlongness." The President's response on those occasions was "always to become meek" and was always expressed in the same words, "Why, Edie, I was only—"

The First Lady kept the President in touch with public opinion by carefully going over the abstracts of comments, favorable and otherwise, prepared for him by his secretaries, and herself reading three or four leading New York or Washington papers and calling his attention to items which she felt he should read. But she helped her husband most, Sullivan pointed out, through her "infinitely superior insight" into men, their motives and characters, saving him "many a slip." When the President lacked the benefit of her judgment about a man, Sullivan said, he was inclined to make mistakes. "Never, when he had his wife's judgment, did he go wrong or suffer disappointment."

She helped her husband, moreover, to keep in balance his relation to the cosmos. One evening at Sagamore Hill, between her husband's election as Vice-President and his inauguration, he was dictating in one of the second-story rooms to Amy Cheney, the little secretary who had fought the "battle of the letters" with him after his return from Cuba, when a peal of laughter came from Mrs. Roosevelt's boudoir, adjoining, followed by the appearance of Mrs. Roosevelt, convulsed, carrying a quarto tome. "Mr. Roosevelt *must* see this book," she explained to Amy.

It was a collection of Frederick Burr Opper's cartoons from the New York *American*. They dealt with the national campaign, recently concluded, with its principals presented in a hundred humiliating actions: Mark Hanna, depicted as Greed incarnate, dominating little "Willie" McKinley and a midget, drawn with huge teeth and a toy sword, marked "Teddy." Edith showed her husband the cartoon which had caused her outburst and, seeing he was busy, withdrew. Five minutes later she was back, shaking with merriment. "Theodore, you *must* see this one. It's the funniest thing I've ever seen." They laughed over it together (she more wholeheartedly than he) and she again withdrew, only to return with a third cartoon.

The Colonel's lady, Amy mused, was not one who was given to interrupting her busy husband. Here, then, was more than met the eye. Was Mrs. Roosevelt possibly saying to herself that, after six months' adulation and cheers, the Vice-President-elect could do with a little deflating?

The First Lady, who, in her earlier years, had been subject to moods which racked her and to have "good days and bad days," as her husband himself before their marriage had once intimated, gave an impression in the White House of astonishing poise and stability. Whether she were listening to a project of Quentin's or Archie's for camping out somewhere over night, or presiding at a dinner of fifty distinguished guests, or, later the same evening, receiving five hundred more people at a musicale—as was frequently the case—she seemed always the same—gentle, courteous, and mistress of herself; only occasionally, when she was confronted with someone of whom she disapproved, was she frigid, and the temperature in the room fell correspondingly. Her nerves were as steady in a gale on the Sound as in the occasionally troubled waters of the White House. Jake Riis was on the *Sylph* one autumn, going to New York with the President and his wife, when the tail of a West Indian hurricane struck the vessel. A tug was seen to sink nearby, and the question arose whether the little gunboat could make a harbor. The crew cleared the heaving deck, but the President and his friend, descending to the cabin, found the First Lady placidly winding yarn from the hands of the only other woman passenger. She had the less dramatic courage also to carry on when occasionally, though not often, her body—never over-strong—rebelled against the strain of her busy life. Standing beside the President at a state reception, she suddenly felt faint and left the line, only to return at the end of a half-hour and resume her place, remaining to serve as hostess at the supper that followed.

The President watched his wife, noted her happiness in her many activities, and glowed with pride and devotion. "I do not think my eyes are blinded by affection," he wrote a friend, "when I say that she has combined to a degree I have never seen in any other woman the power of being the best of wives and mothers, the wisest manager of the household, and at the same time the ideal great lady and mistress of the White House."

Francis E. Leupp, the President's Commissioner of Indian Affairs, was at Sagamore Hill at dinner, one evening, when the President was enthusiastically describing the delights of his life as a hunter and ranchman in the Bad Lands, and recalled later the comment of one of the other guests: "With your love of that free existence, Mr. President, I wonder how you ever settled down in the humdrum East. Honestly, now, don't you wish you had been born and reared on a ranch?"

An affirmative answer seemed on the tip of the President's tongue when he suddenly paused, casting a quick glance, clearly involuntary and almost embarrassed, toward the farther end of the table, with an expression, Leupp noted, "which could not be mistaken." Then he began hesitatingly, "No, because—"

"I know why," exclaimed one of the ladies.

"Why?" he asked with an air of challenge.

"Because you would not then have known Mrs. Roosevelt."

"That," he confessed, "was what I was going to say."

Chapter IX

THE PRESIDENT might talk about what he called "rest" at Sagamore Hill and, in his own fashion, achieve it, but there was no way of his evading the responsibilities of his authority, even if he had wanted to evade them, which was, in fact, the last thing that he wanted. He relished responsibility, welcomed it afar off and ran to meet it. There were no major crises hanging over Sagamore Hill during the seasons that it was the summer White House, but there were issues explosive enough to challenge the President's intelligence, moral sense and resolution; three of them in the summer of 1903. One involved American relations with Russia; another, the federal government and organized labor; a third, corruption in government.

Russia, which had been conceded a preferred position by the Powers in Manchuria, had agreed to observe the Open Door policy which John Hay, the American Secretary of State, had won for all China. Actually, however, the Russians were forcing the Chinese officials to keep the ports closed. "The mendacity of the Russians is something appalling," the President wrote Hay. Yet there was no way, short of war, of keeping the Manchurian ports open.

On top of Russia's double-dealing came news of a massacre of Jews in Kishineff. The American Jewish community was outraged and, backed by leading men and women of every faith, demanded diplomatic action against Russia. The President, sympathetic as he was with the humanitarian impulse behind the demand, refused it, unwilling to issue a protest which he knew he was not in a position to maintain by force.

A group of leading Jews approached the President with the query: Would he forward a citizens' petition to the Czar, stating the facts of the Kishineff massacre and its effect not only upon the

197

A chance for a real bear hunt

Jews in the United States but upon the whole American people? Yes, the President answered, that he would do.

The report of the proposed petition brought an immediate re-action from the Russian Embassy, not through diplomatic channels but in the press. "The Russian government must categorically refuse to receive from any Power any petition, representation or communication relative to its internal policy."

At Sagamore Hill, the President's blood boiled. The "imperti-nence" of the Russians in going to the American people over the head of the customary agencies charged with such matters! Perhaps it might be "just as wise," he wrote Hay, "to show our teeth." He gave the press a statement which said, in effect, that Russia was "unfriendly" and a breaker of promises.

In Washington, diplomatic circles declared darkly that the Russian government would not "allow this serious charge to go unnoticed," and predicted dire consequences. The anti-administration press lamented the boner the President was supposed to have pulled. But it became apparent, shortly, that the President's diplomacy might not be so bad as his opponents thought. His "square talk," noted the Washington correspondent of the Boston *Journal*, had "braced up" the British diplomats in Washington, St. Petersburg and elsewhere. The Russian Foreign Office, moreover, took none of the anticipated steps to make clear that Russia was not what the American President had said she was. From the Czar's official organ, on the contrary, came something close to a confession of guilt and the prediction that the Manchurian problem would be harmoniously worked out; and from the Russian Embassy in Washington the statement that the charge regarding Russia's "unfriendly attitude" would be "overlooked."

Meanwhile, the President was not losing sight of the Kishineff petition. Root and Hay, at Sagamore Hill, begged him to "go easy." "You've shown your willingness. Now let the incident be closed." In view of the still unsettled Manchurian situation, why risk a reaction from Russia which might put a further strain on Russo-American relations? The petition would never be received anyway.

But the President was not averse to letting Russia know what Americans thought of her barbarities. The middle of July he invited three leading Jews, among them, Oscar S. Straus, later Secretary of Commerce and Labor, with Albert Shaw, the genial, witty, hardheaded editor of the *Review of Reviews*, to luncheon at Sagamore Hill. As Shaw was sitting next to the First Lady at luncheon, absorbed in what he subsequently recalled as "an enjoyable conversation wholly unrelated to persecutions in Russia," he became conscious that the President was asking him to give his views about the sending of the petition. Quite off-hand and with no time for reflection (Shaw noted, forty years later), "I made a remark that I supposed would be taken whimsically." He admitted that the Czar's government could not entertain the petition. The State Department, in fact, he suggested, should take that view "rather ostentatiously," and send the petition to the American chargé in St. Petersburg with instructions to tell the Russian foreign minister "that our government absolutely declines to transmit it

officially unless the Russian authorities are willing to receive it."
By this procedure, Shaw pointed out, the petition would actually
be in the hands of the Russian authorities who would, in spite of
themselves, read it upon its merits. "They will, therefore, know
not only how representative American Jews feel but also that
American sentiment is informed and is opposed to mistreatment
of the Jews, since otherwise the petition would not have been passed
on from the State Department to our representative, and com-
municated by him to the Foreign Office."

Shaw uttered the proposal gravely and with a manner of much
deliberation, but with his tongue in his cheek. "I had no idea that
it would be regarded at the other end of the table as anything but
a journalist's jibe at the roundabout methods and manners of
diplomacy."

To Shaw's astonishment the President fairly leapt to meet his
idea, and his Jewish guests shared his enthusiasm. "Now let's finish
this thing up," the President exclaimed as the guests adjourned
with him to the library. He sat down at his desk, and, in longhand,
drafted a note to the chargé d'affaires and another for Straus to
give the Secretary of State, asking him to cable the petition at
once to the American embassy in St. Petersburg.

The Russian foreign minister declined to receive the petition.
But, actually, he had read it, and had been given a picture of the
American people's indignation and sense of outrage, which was
what the petitioners and the President wanted. Every newspaper of
any consequence in the world, outside Russia, published the petition, moreover, while statesmen and diplomats chuckled.

The Russians, shamed before the world, took action to stop any
further massacres. When, two years later, the Russian finance
minister, the great Sergei Witte, came to the United States, he went
out of his way to meet a group of leading Jews and to apologize to
them for the massacre.

2

The set-to with Russia had its comic aspects, and the President
thoroughly enjoyed it. There was no satisfaction for him at all,
however, in a domestic problem with which he had to deal that
summer.

In the Government Printing Office, an assistant foreman in the book-binding department, named Miller, was suspended by his union, the International Brotherhood of Bookbinders, for increasing and improving his department's output to a point where the labor force could be reduced; and, under pressure of the union, had been dismissed by the Public Printer. Miller protested to the President, who, after an investigation, ordered Miller reinstated. There was no objection, he said, to employees in government departments organizing a union, "but no rules or restrictions of that union can be permitted to over-ride the laws of the United States."

The union raised an outcry which was echoed by similar bodies over the country, condemning the President as "unfriendly," or lecturing him patronizingly as "honest and humane, but uninformed." The employees of the Government Printing Office threatened to walk out. "All right," the President declared, but "not a man jack" of them would get back into the government service while he was President. There was no strike.

With a presidential campaign only a year away, the tumult had obvious political implications. Roosevelt was sensitive to the fact that he was "President-by-accident." He wanted nothing so much as to be elected to the office. Some of his strongest supporters were in the ranks of organized labor. If they should turn against him. . . . The President was not above angling for votes, and he was angling for them so persistently that summer as to dismay some of his friends. But in this labor situation a principle was involved.

At a meeting with a group of labor leaders, headed by Samuel Gompers, president of the American Federation of Labor, the President pointed out that the laws were enacted for the benefit of the whole people, "and cannot be construed as permitting discrimination against some of the people. I am President of all the people of the United States, without regard to creed, color, birthplace, occupation, or social condition. My aim is to do equal and exact justice as among them all. In the employment and dismissal of men in the government service I can no more recognize the fact that a man does or does not belong to a union, as being for or against him, than I can recognize the fact that he is a Protestant or a Catholic, a Jew or a Gentile, as being for or against him."

The public liked that, and even the labor men appeared satisfied. Like the corporation leaders, they wanted special privilege if they could get it, but, if they couldn't, it was something to know that they had a President who was determined to keep an even balance.

"There was no alternative but to state our position unequivocally," the President wrote his Attorney General, Philander C. Knox, "without regard to what the political effect might be. We can no more afford to tolerate tyranny from a labor union than we can afford to tolerate it from a trust. These jacks in Wall Street, I suppose, never will understand that I am not against wealth because I make wealth obey the law. But they have had to take their medicine, and any labor man who goes the wrong way will have to take his medicine too."

3

The President was to have no rest, that year, from the temptation to let what he recognized as being right make way for what he knew to be expedient.

Frauds were discovered in the Post Office Department. The President appointed Joseph N. Bristow, a rangy Kansan with the eyes of a crusader, to make an investigation. "I want the truth," he declared, "the whole truth, and I don't care a rap who is hit."

Immediately, a group of Republican senators, whose own high principles could not be questioned, called on the President. They were glad, they declared, that he was getting after any corruption that might exist, but they hoped that he would avoid all scandal. "Make an example, Mr. President, of some one man and let the others quietly resign. But avoid any disturbance that will reflect on the Party."

If there was anything that the President himself wanted less at that moment than a war or a panic in the stock market, it was a public scandal in one of the executive departments. With the next presidential election just over the horizon scandal in the government was a bad break, playing straight into the hands of the newspapers fighting him on his chief issue, the regulation of corporations. The scandal would not be his fault; he would merely be exposing it. But try to make the press, or the public, make that distinction.

Yet here the scandal was, and here were honest men, leaders of his own party, wanting to have it hushed up. All his political impulses, which were many and deep, were with them, but a sharper

T. R.: "You must go clear to the bottom!"

POSTMASTER GENERAL: "There doesn't seem to be any bottom."

sense than theirs of the realities of public and private life prevailed.
"I intend to act with the utmost rigor against all the offenders," he
declared, "no matter what the effect on the Party. Moreover," he
added, "I do not believe it will hurt the Party."

Before the investigation was fairly started, the smelly brew in
the Department boiled over. One of the bureau chiefs resigned,
two others were arrested for receiving bribes, and the chief of the
legal division was dismissed when it was discovered that, during his
illness at home, his wife had entered his office and removed government papers. They were all appointees of previous administrations,
but the press was making no fine distinctions. Day after day, new

crimes were uncovered, from petty grafting on purchases and labor to bribery, blackmail and ingenious and elaborate conspiracies to defraud. Indictments multiplied, culminating in the arrest of a former congressman for acting as agent of a cash-register company while serving in the House.

The President appointed a leading Democrat and the Republican head of the Civil Service Association, neither allied in any way with him politically, as special counsel to expedite the cases. "There can be no greater offense against the government," he wrote the Attorney General, "than a breach of trust on the part of a public official, or the dishonest management of his office, and, of course, every effort must be executed to bring such offenders to punishment by the utmost rigor of the law."

The words, "of course," were directed at the eminent Republicans who were climbing Sagamore Hill to plead with him, "for the good of the Party," for God's sake, to call off the investigation. Their pleas became almost tearful as the summer advanced and conspiracies were revealed involving more and more friends or henchmen of Republican stalwarts. When, finally, a leading New York state senator and close friend of the Republican state chairman was caught in the net, Odell, the governor, indignantly sent the state controller to Sagamore Hill. Not only the governor, it appeared, but Platt, the "easy boss," was disturbed and angry. The controller brought the word that, if the senator were indicted, the Republicans would lose the state in the next election.

The President was painfully aware that the Party in the state was in a bad way, with Platt and the governor in a sharp struggle for control of the machinery, and neither too friendly to himself, Odell even hostile. "I am interested in carrying New York," he told the controller, "more interested than anyone else. But I am not going to let up on any grafter, no matter what the political effect may be. Besides, though we may, in my judgment, lose the state if we make it evident that we intend to prosecute every guilty man—may, I said, mind you!—we shall certainly lose it, if we don't."

Chapter X

BY THE TIME the Roosevelt family returned to Sagamore early in July, 1904, the head of it was, by acclamation, the Republican Party's nominee for the Presidency. The impending campaign, with Alton B. Parker, a heavy-footed and none too brilliant New York State judge, as the Democratic nominee, brought politicians in a flood to Sagamore Hill and, with them, a notable cartoonist, Homer Davenport, a recent convert to the Republican Party, who carried in his pocket a contract with the New York *Mail and Express* to wield his powerful pen in the good cause.

The President remembered Davenport's long association with Hearst and was skeptical. "You've thrown a good many snowballs at me with rocks in them," he recalled sharply. "I didn't duck them all, but it was a fair fight and I have no criticism." But was it really true that Davenport had cut his ties with the Democratic Party?

"I'm for *you*," Davenport answered. "That's as far as I am willing to go at present."

"We'll go together," the President replied warmly. "How are you with an axe? Loeb and I are getting into condition for the approaching campaign."

"I'm better with a hammer," said Davenport.

"We're not building anything this afternoon," the President said. "Something is coming down. It's bully exercise."

Shortly thereafter, the President and the cartoonist were felling a dead chestnut and stripping its limbs. After that, as Davenport told the story, with fanciful additions, to his managing editor, "Bob" Davis, they took a dip, ran a race, boxed a few rounds, walked five miles and dressed for dinner.

"It was a union of kindred souls," wrote Davis, twenty-odd years later, "at which Roosevelt revealed all his plans for the ap-

"He's good enough for me."

proaching battle of the ballots." Loeb told Davis that he had never seen the President throw his cards on the table so completely with a comparative stranger, and one who in the past had been an avowed and powerful enemy.

When Loeb drove Davenport to the Oyster Bay station that evening, the cartoonist admitted that he had been "knocked off his feet." Such sincerity, energy, and devotion to the best that was America! "I don't see how he can be beaten." He had been racking his brains, all afternoon, he went on, "trying to get an idea for an opening cartoon that will speak for the nation, a cartoon with a short caption that will fit the American tongue. Say, I wish he would talk to the people as he talked to me."

"He will," Loeb assured him, "and the people will listen. But, like all independent, self-reliant men, he has a full set of enemies. Don't forget that."

"Enemies? Of course," said Davenport. "But as far as I am concerned, he's good enough for me."

He lapsed into silence. When he spoke again it was to repeat musingly, "He's good enough for me. That's it!" he exclaimed suddenly. "I've got the idea for my cartoon."

The following evening, the Sagamore family saw, on the front page of the *Mail and Express,* what would be acclaimed, in Davis' words, "the greatest vote-making cartoon in all America's political history." It showed Uncle Sam behind Roosevelt, with his hand resting affectionately on the President's shoulder. Under the picture was the brief, significant phrase, "He's good enough for me."

2

Late in July, for the third and last time, Republican bigwigs climbed Sagamore Hill in buggies, buckboards, surreys and victorias, to inform Theodore Roosevelt, in accordance with American custom, that he had been nominated as a candidate for high office.

The day was cloudless and not too warm, in happy contrast to the day, four years before, when Roosevelt had been notified of his fateful nomination for the Vice-Presidency, and brows had dripped and collars wilted. Once more, the residents of Oyster Bay decked their houses with flags and, once more, its streets swarmed with the "neighbors" from the length and breadth of Nassau County. A farmer from Hicksville brought an old cannon hitched to his truck, and set it booming as the carriages with the committee members drove toward Sagamore Hill in a cloud of Long Island's friable soil.

The President who stood under the porte-cochère, awaiting the self-important political wheel-horses coming to tell him ceremoniously what everyone already knew, was, in the essentials of character and spirit, the same man who had stood in the same place, four years before, but he had matured beyond what the brief interval of time might have led an alert observer to expect. It was not only that—to his own dismay—he had put on weight which not even the strenuous life at Sagamore Hill seemed able to reduce. His face, in repose, had taken on the expression of a seafaring man, facing strong winds. Where there had been strength before, there was resolution now, and power; a sense of command; not over others but over himself.

His friends, in later years, would tell much of the dramatic actions of his first term, but none would tell, and perhaps none knew, of the persistent struggle he had been carrying on, those first three years of his Presidency, to discipline himself. Senators, members of Congress, diplomats, newspapermen, seeing the new President in his White House office the first year after his accession, had been painfully impressed by what seemed to them a lack of poise and repose, a nervous tendency to be aggressively strenuous and overdo everything he had to do. In his acts and conclusions he was the hardheaded, Dutch-cautious man he had been as Governor of New York; but in his manners and methods, the tones of his voice, all the little things which the limelight tends to exaggerate and blow up to larger-than-life proportions, "he seemed," wrote Walter Wellman in the Philadelphia *Press,* "like a man in a state of spiritual exaltation."

In the Capitol lobbies and the clubs men spoke of the President's erratic mannerisms, his quickness on the trigger, his loud talking. Elder statesmen cringed at the voice that rang out of the President's office with such forcefulness that everyone in the ante-room, was, willingly or unwillingly, taken into the presidential confidence, and callers on important state business found secrecy with the President possible only when elaborate precautions were made in advance. His effusiveness, moreover, gave an impression of emotional intemperance. He was "dee-lighted" to see every man who called; every other visitor was "just the very man I wanted to see." His adjectives were all superlatives, and visitors, less indiscriminately buoyant, decided he was either flighty or over-playing his hand.

The same tendency to excess had impaired the President's effectiveness as an executive. He had attempted too much, trying to run the whole government, as it were, single-handed, meddling in matters that belonged to his subordinates, going over their heads without too much regard for their feelings. The result had been that he had been unable to keep up with his work and tended to stew and fret because he was falling behind.

Those qualities, so painfully obvious in the President-by-accident during his first or even his second year in office, no longer cumbered the man waiting on the Sagamore Hill porch for the worthies who were to tell him that he had been nominated for President in his own right. He had retained his natural good fellowship, his fondness for his old friends, his boyish manner of greeting those whose devotion had been tested by the years, but he no longer exclaimed "dee-lighted" at every man he met; he no longer shouted in conversation. He had learned, moreover, to attend to the business that he, and he alone, could deal with, and to leave to others the burdens that were theirs; with the result that he was disposing of twice the work in half the time and his office was functioning with efficiency and without strain.

The President, it appeared, had acquired perspective; he had grown, gathered strength and poise, gained self-control and balance. "He has settled down to his job," a member of the Cabinet was heard to remark, in March, 1904, "and is moving as steadily and as safely as an old horse in the plowing."

What lay behind such sobering of a man, tempted daily, no doubt, by the chorus of his idolators to exaggerate rather than overcome his mannerisms and petty faults? Did his Secretary of State, John Hay, his father's cherished friend, and his own, tip him off? Did the Secretary of War, Elihu Root, who had sponsored the President's entrance into politics, twenty years before, skillfully inject in the presidential consciousness one of his brilliant, pitiless barbs? Perhaps. Or did Edith Roosevelt's quiet, "Now, Theodore!" uttered some evening in the family sitting room on the second floor of the White House, after the children were in bed, open vistas for her husband that he had not looked down before? If so, no one left a record of it.

There were no compelling external reasons challenging the President to change. He had suffered no chastening catastrophe, having, as one observer put it, had "all sorts of luck except bad luck"; suffered no personal grief or disappointment which might have driven him into some metaphorical desert for a season of soul-searching. Obviously, there was in this astonishing favorite of fortune, this triumphant, happy extrovert, a capacity for standing off and looking at himself, which no one who watched him at work or play in Washington or at Sagamore Hill—except, perhaps, his wife—imagined to be there.

Busy as he was, pressed by countless duties and responsibilities, he had sought to mold his manner to the dignity of his place, to adapt himself to his work, to rise to the full level of his station.

It was a chastened and changed President, then, who, in a frock-coat and white waistcoat, greeted the committee as they stepped from their hacks in the statesman's canonical regalia, generously covered with the dust of the Cove Road.

The chairman of the notification committee, Joseph G. Cannon, Speaker of the House, an astute Illinois politician, whom the President would subsequently characterize as "a strong, hard, narrow old Boeotian," dressed in a proper frock-coat, black string tie, and, in defiance of tradition, a Panama hat, arrived in a closed brougham with Benjamin B. Odell, the Governor of New York. Odell had successfully blocked Cannon's nomination for the Vice-Presidency, and the reporters were watchful for fireworks. But "Uncle Joe," noted the New York *Sun* reporter, "was trying to look pleasant and succeeding fairly well." Following these uneasy bedfellows came the representatives of the states and territories.

The First Lady, in a "white mull gown with lace insertion," the *Herald* reporter observed, received her husband's notifiers in the wide entrance hall just inside the front door, standing in the doorway to the library, under the watchful eyes of the huge buffalo-head above the fireplace, and of deer, antelope and mountain-goat close by. Among the guests mingled members of Cove Neck's three Roosevelt families, seeking to make the committee members feel at home and drawing them out to the piazza where again the notification ceremony was to take place. When the last committee member had descended from the antique vehicles which had brought him, Loeb looked up Speaker Cannon, who was deep in a homely story such as another Illinoisan had loved to tell in relaxed moments. He stretched, threw away his cigar and called for something to stand on.

Loeb provided a low stool. The committee and other guests, some hundred and fifty in all, took their places against the wall of the house or the low rail the President liked to sit on at dusk and watch the sunset over the Bay. The Speaker was about to begin when the President interposed, waving to a group of family servants and hired men and inviting them to come up on the piazza. The *Sun* reporter gratefully noted the brisk, refreshing breeze from the Sound, touching the hay-fields around the President's house into motion and keeping the flags on the piazza fluttering.

The Speaker's address was philosophic, urbane and confident, and carried a hint to the candidate not to stray from the true and tried Republican pathway. The President in his response, gave a review of his administration. Again Speaker Cannon stepped up on the stool. "The Committee on Notification," he said, "with the President, will now have their respective shadows secured before their substance fades."

The group assembled on the lawn below the piazza, the camera did its work, and the ceremony was over. Once more the Roosevelt children, with their cousins, passed around refreshments.

The reporters present agreed that it was all "most quiet and homelike"; no delegations with brass bands and buttons as there had been when McKinley had been notified of his nomination the second time; no hurrahing or demonstration of any sort, with the exception of "a little polite hand-clapping." If it had not been for the frock-coats and white waistcoats, you might almost have taken the crowd on the veranda "for a nicely behaved family house-party." Thanks to the breeze, the *Sun* man noted, Sagamore Hill was "a comfortable place for the guests and nobody got hot, not even Governor Odell when the President looked squarely at him during his speech and said that the value of a party to the people depended altogether on the efficiency and faithfulness of its officials in their public service."

3

"Mr. Dooley," noting less what the President had said than what he had not said, drew a picture of him at Sagamore Hill that summer which, in its hilarious nonsense, deserves a place on the wall not too far from the grave, earnest and eloquent cartoon of Homer Davenport:

"'It looks to me as though pollytical enthusyasm was dyin' out in this counthry,' said Mr. Hennessy.

"'Oh, I don't know,' said Mr. Dooley, 'Ye niver can tell. It's almost too early to begin throwin' bricks.' " Anyway, the candidates

211

were lying low, " 'thryin' to say nawthin' that will incriminate thim.'

" 'Tiddy Rosenfelt has put in an application to jine th' Quaker Church. He has burned his suit iv Khaky an' beaten his soord into a plowshare. Visitors who call on him at Oyster Bay find him re-readin' th' "Lives iv th' Saints." His fav'rite saint is wan iv th' arly martyrs who thanked a lion f'r bitin' him. He is thryin' to live down his past. . . . Whin th' hayro iv San Joon Hill wants to re-lieve his pint-up emotions he goes out on th' seashore far fr'm human habytation an' sings hymns f'r an hour. Sicrity Cortillyoo authorizes me to deny th' infamyous raport that th' Presidint was iver at San Joon Hill. At th' time if this gloryous an' lamintable performance th' good man was down with measles conthracted at th' Inter-naytional Peace Convintion.

" 'A day at Oysther Bay passes like a dhream. Th' Presidint arises early an', afther prayers, partakes iv a light breakfast iv Quaker Oats. He thin retires to his oratory an' spinds th' mornin' in midita-tion an' prayer. Afther lunchin' with his pastor he visits th' Dorcas Siciety, iv which he is hon'rary Presidint. Rayturnin' home he devotes a few hours to archery an' bean bag, at both iv which games he has become expert. His supper consists iv a bag iv popcorn an' a dish iv tea. Th' short avenin' is spint in readin' aloud th' wurraks iv Hinnery Wadsworth Longfellow, an' afther fam'ly prayers Thay-door Rosenfelt retires to a well-arned slumber. He is not well at prisint, th' smell iv gunpowdher on th' Foorth iv July havin' dis-agreeably affected him.' "

4

The President, who had a way of treating his elder boys as his intellectual equals, reported the course of the campaign to fifteen-year-old Kermit at Groton in letters such as he might have written to John Hay or Elihu Root. He wrote once a week, occasionally more often, reporting the ups and downs of the campaign, not at all sure that he would be elected and urging the boy repeatedly to "remember that we have had three years of great enjoyment out of the Presidency and that we are mighty lucky to have had them." Whatever happened, win or lose, he would feel "and I want you to feel, that I have been very, very fortunate. . . . I have enjoyed being President and we have all of us enjoyed the White House.

. . . It was a great thing for all of us to have had the experience here. So we are ahead of the game whatever comes."

The letter he wrote a few days after the election told of "the overwhelming victory . . . the greatest popular majority and the greatest electoral majority ever given to a candidate for President. . . . But, I tell you, Kermit," the President ended, "it was a great comfort to feel, all during the last days when affairs looked doubtful, that, no matter how things came out, the really important thing was the lovely life I have with Mother and with you children, and that, compared to this home-life, everything else was of very small importance from the standpoint of happiness."

Chapter XI

"Tis morning and King Theodore
  Upon his throne sits he,
As blithely as a king can sit
  Within a free countree.
And now he thinks of submarines,
  And now of peace and war,
His royal robe he handeth Loeb
  Then wireth to the Czar:

" 'Come off, come off, thou Great White Czar,
  Come off thy horse so high!
Send envoys straight and arbitrate
  Thy diplomatic pie.'
Then straightway to the Mik-a-doo
  This letter he doth limn,
'Come off thy perch, thou Morning Sun,
  And do the same as him!' "

Thus a popular American poet, Wallace Irwin, began "The Ballad of Sagamore Hill," recording, with some license, the historic events that made the green Long Island eminence, in the summer of 1905, the focus of the world's attention. Russia and Japan, involved in a costly war that neither could see the end of, in terms of their existing armed forces and bank balances, wanted to make peace, and decided that the only way to make it was to ask this astonishing President of the new world power across the seas to arrange it. The President shied away from the prospect. He despised the Russian government's corrupt despotism and its apparently congenital mendacity, and he was not at all sure that a peace based on Japan's overwhelming victories on sea and land might not pose serious new problems in the Pacific for his own country. The inter-

214

national politics involved, moreover, were tortuous beyond belief. But the President could not in decency decline the invitation which, through a hail of denials from both parties, came to him while he was hunting bear in Colorado. That was in April. By the time the President had reached Sagamore Hill, three months later, the ground-work had been laid for a peace conference at Portsmouth, New Hampshire.

2

Here let the minstrel resume the story:

> "Then straightway from the Rising Sun
>   Come envoys three times three,
> Komura neat and Sato sweet
>   (an Irish Japanee).
> Small men are they with domy brains,
>   And in their fingers gaunt
> A list of seven hundred things
>   They positively want.
>
> "Then straightway from St. Petersburg
>   Come envoys six times two,
> De Witty grand and Rosen bland
>   And Nebotoffkatoo—
> Volkyrieoffskygrandovitch—
>   (Here see the author's note:
> 'The balance of that noble name
>   Came on another boat') ."

There were, in fact, not nine envoys from each nation, or twelve, but two; for Russia, the president of the council of ministers, Sergei Witte, and Baron Rosen, the egregious Cassini's successor in Washington; for Japan, the minister of foreign affairs, Baron Komura, and the minister to the United States, Takahira. There was yet a third Japanese envoy, Baron Kentaro Kaneko, who had no official status but was destined to play a major role in the negotiations.

The President knew Kaneko for "a fox and a Japanese fox at that," who had been unobtrusively but persuasively presenting the Japanese case to the American people, but he liked him and, recognizing that he might prove useful, invited him to Sagamore Hill. They had a walk and a swim, followed by a family dinner *à quatre*, with Mrs. Roosevelt and seven-year-old Quentin the other

215

two; a very simple repast, their guest noted, with no ceremony or ostentation whatever. After dinner, the boy was sent to bed and the others sat in the library, talking. At half past nine, the First Lady folded her knitting. "I am going to bed," she said, "but I don't expect you to follow until you have straightened out the affairs of the world." She left the room but returned in a moment, bearing two tin candlesticks, a tallow dip and a box of matches in each. "Light yourselves to bed, gentlemen," she said, "and good night."

For another hour and a half the President and his guest talked of the forthcoming conference and a possible armistice, of Japan's terms, and of the Harvard they had both known in the late Seventies. "The memory of that visit will forever remain with me," the Baron told "Bob" Davis of the New York *Sun,* thirty years later, recalling the contrast between the power and personal greatness of the Chief Executive and the simplicity of his home life. The capitals of the world were humming with talk of what this man had said and done, of what he might be thinking and planning, but on Sagamore Hill he and his guest were just two Harvard men, "free from ceremony, expressing honest convictions without reserve and reliving old days."

At eleven o'clock, the President locked the windows, blew out the lamp and put the dog out, while the Baron lighted the candles that Mrs. Roosevelt had left. "Where else in the world," the Japanese was thinking, "could a similar situation have occurred: a President leading his foreign visitor upstairs by the light of a tallow dip?"

At the door of the room that had been assigned to his guest, the President had a thought. "The nights are cool at Sagamore," he said, "even in July. About three in the morning the temperature falls, with a breeze coming in from the Bay. Don't take risks. You must have extra covers."

He strode down the hall, returning a moment later with a blanket which he tossed across the end of his guest's bed. Then, with a final good-night, he closed the door.

For a long time the Japanese sat at the open window, wondering "what manner of country it was that produced such simple, genuine men as this soldier, traveler, statesman and citizen, whose creed was democracy in its finest form." He went to bed at last and, as the night wind came in from the Bay, "I pulled up the blanket thrown casually upon the footboard by the Chief Executive of the United States and kept thinking of his wife, knitting beside the coal oil lamp, the closing up of the house, the candles by which we found our way to bed, and—freedom. This, said I, is the ideal state toward which all men should strive, and that government should make possible in this life."

3

A very different type of man, with very different thoughts, heavily crossed the Sagamore Hill porch a month later and bowed stiffly over the hand of the President. A granite pillar of a man, over six feet tall and heavy-framed, Sergei Witte proved as dramatic a symbol of the bulk and power of Russia as the two wiry little Japanese whose ceremonial visit had preceded his by a week had seemed of the agility and adaptability of Japan. In his middle fifties, with a high, narrow forehead, emphasizing his disillusioned, penetrating eyes and the strong lines of his bearded face, he was Russia's greatest living statesman, the only one, indeed, who understood the forces seething under the surface of the Russian police state. The complex but integrated scheme of economic and social reform, which he was seeking to impose upon a blind and self-centered oligarchy was, in fact, a kind of "revolution from above." Like Roosevelt, he was a conservative with progressive leanings, but without Roosevelt's love for people, his faith in their sound judgment (at least "fifty-one per cent of the time") or his recognition that it was on them that the future rested.

An observer in the Sagamore study, seeing this heavy-browed and almost menacing Russian giant confronting Theodore Roosevelt, President of the United States, no less powerful in body, mind and spirit, but buoyant where the Russian was brooding, brimming with faith in life where the other was cynical, might have been excused for quoting Kipling concerning East and West, and "strong men" standing "face to face."

Witte presented a personal letter from the Czar which the President read with evident appreciation. Then, the amenities having been observed, they got down to business. They conversed in French; on the President's part, what Chaucer might have called "Frensshe-atte-Sagamore," but fluent and adequate to the purpose.

What the President was impelled to say, and presumably did say, is on record in a letter to Lodge, written six weeks earlier.

It was nonsense for Russia to stick at trifles. If the war went on, she would lose all her possessions in eastern Asia and the blow to her might be well-nigh irreparable. He had not sympathized with Russia at the outset of the war. His regard for the Russian people, however, and for the interests of the world in general would make him regret to see her driven out of territory which had been hers for a couple of centuries. But the Russian government might as well face the fact that their military position was hopeless, and accept, before it was too late, the concessions necessary to secure peace.

Witte, who had suffered under the humiliation of his country's defeats, was, by his own admission, "morbidly sensitive" to criticism. "We are defeated but not conquered," he said in a voice, inclined like Cassini's to the *fortissimo*. Russia was willing to negotiate on the basis of the successes the Japanese had won, but had no intention of negotiating on the basis of successes the Japanese expected to win if the war continued. "If the Japanese will not now adopt our point of view," Witte concluded, "we shall carry on a defensive war to the last extremity, and we shall see who will hold out the longest."

"It is in the interest of both belligerents to put an end to the war," the President declared. "If that can't be done without the payment of an indemnity, then the indemnity must be paid. Let me add, that, in view of the same considerations, I am strongly advising the Japanese to be moderate in their demands. The military party in Japan wants the war to continue. The moderate party wants peace, but with an indemnity."

The Russian shrugged his great shoulders. "Russia will not pay a kopeck."

His declaration was sheer bluff. "I was aware," Witte wrote in his memoirs, "that the conclusion of peace was imperative. Otherwise, I felt, we were threatened by a complete débâcle, involving the overthrow of the dynasty to which I was and am devoted with all my heart and soul."

The President saw through the bluff and was annoyed that Witte imagined that he could carry it off. The Russian military situation in the Far East was steadily deteriorating. Did reality mean nothing to this man? "If your decision is definite and unalterable," he said, "there will be no peace."

"He tried to scare me," Witte wrote afterward, "but he met with a firm determination on my part not to make concessions."

Luncheon was announced. Witte, writing his memoirs, long after, recalled unhappy details of the repast. "The luncheon was more than simple and, for a European, almost indigestible. There was no table-cloth, and there was ice-water instead of wine." Yet he could not escape the pleasant sense that he was being made to feel at home, and that what effort there was about it was sincere.

The talk, after the luncheon, was general, and brief. "If the views of the parties to the conference remain irreconcilable," the President said, "they will state their views, I assume, and the conference will dissolve. I trust, in that case, that arrangements will be made so that, in the future, if either party wishes to resume negotiations, it may be done without delay."

"We have instructions to that end," Witte replied stiffly, and there was tragedy in his eyes. But the warmth of the President's handshake, and the First Lady's, moved the proud, pertinacious, self-contained patriot. He mentioned it in his dispatch to his government that night.

4

" 'Twas on the royal yacht Mayflower
They met, that noble crew.
'De Witty grand, shake Sato's hand—
Komura, how-dee-do!'
While forty thousand gun-salutes
Concuss on Oyster Bay,
A proud man is King Theodore
Upon that trysting day!"

The President and the State Department had no precedents to guide them in the program for the official opening of the conference, so they followed their instincts, or more precisely, the President's. Witte himself had feared that the President, "as a typical American, inexperienced in and careless of formalities, would make a mess of the whole business," and had tipped off the Assistant Secretary of State, Robert H. D. Pierce, whom he had known in St. Petersburg. His precautions were unnecessary. Being a gentleman himself, the President knew what other gentlemen would want and, being a Chief Executive, with four years' experience of the peculiar sensitivities of diplomats, divined what might be expected to make high-mettled spirits buck and rear. The essential thing, he knew, was not to appear by the flutter of an eyelash to play favorites. Witte, continuously jumpy, had indeed, expressed to Baron Rosen, his fellow envoy, his dread that the Japanese might "be given some advantage" over the Russian envoys. "I will not suffer a toast to our Emperor offered after one to the Mikado!"

The harbor of Oyster Bay was the gayest body of water in any of the five continents on the morning of August 5th. It was Sunday and a cloudless day, with a light breeze ruffling the water and setting countless flags, American, Russian and Japanese, fluttering from mastheads and launches, flag-poles and residences. The harbor was alive with motor-boats of every description, darting hither and yon, laden with women in bright dresses and men in white flannels, all eager to see what was to be seen of the President of the United States and the envoys of two nations at war, trying to make peace.

Shortly after the noon hour, the *Mayflower*'s launch, with the President on board, approached the presidential yacht. The *Sylph*, anchored nearby, let loose the first of the twenty-one guns of the presidential salute. The *Mayflower* took up the deafening song, followed by the U.S.S. *Galveston* at the harbor-mouth and the U.S.S. *Tacoma*, which had arrived from New York, bearing the Japanese delegation. The private yachts and cutters in the harbor dipped their flags and sent cheers over the water.

As the President, in canonical regalia—frock coat, striped trousers, white waistcoat and high hat—ascended the gangway, the flag which in after-years visitors at Sagamore Hill would see hanging between the north windows of the Trophy Room rose to the after-peak of the *Mayflower*, and was greeted, on water and on land, by shouts that seemed to match the thunder of the guns.

At 12:40, the signal-flags of the *Tacoma* indicated that the Japanese envoys were ready to go over the side. Once more the guns of the warships made themselves heard, this time in the nine-teen-gun salute which was the tribute due ambassadors.

Pierce, round-faced, heavily moustached and urbane, received the Japanese and escorted them below to a large salon aft, furnished in dark oak and mahogany, where the President was waiting, surrounded by sundry generals and admirals.

Shortly after one o'clock, the *Chattanooga*, with the white, blue

220

and red flag of imperial Russia at its peak, reached the harbor, bearing the Russian delegation. Again a nineteen-gun salute from all the warships filled the placid sky with reverberations and blue smoke as a launch left the warship.

"Russian embassy is shoving off, sir," reported Lieutenant Phelps of the *Mayflower* to his commanding officer, Captain Winslow. Then, turning to the bandmaster at his side, "Stand by. Four ruffles and a march when I give the signal."

A deepening volume of cheers greeted the launch as it made its way down the lane of harbor-craft. "Witte! Witte!" came the cries. The Russian giant stood, bowing and smiling broadly. The tide of American opinion, which had been strongly pro-Japanese, was turning.

Once more, Pierce did the honors, escorting the delegation to a small ante-room and, one of the Russians noted, making hash of their names as he introduced them to the President. When the perfunctory greetings were over, the President led the Russians to the other salon to meet their Japanese opposite-numbers.

For a moment, the two groups gazed at each other blankly. This first meeting, face to face, with the Japanese, Witte wrote afterward, "was morally very painful to me, for, after all, I represented a country which, although the greatest empire on earth, had been defeated in war." The President quickly bridged the chasm. "Baron Komura," he said, "I have the honor to present you to Mr. Witte and Baron Rosen."

The frail little Japanese put out his thin hand and felt it engulfed in the huge hand of the Russian. Both men bowed ceremoniously, and, here and there, a faint smile came to the lips of spectators, seeing the Russian, towering over his chief antagonist, with an air of condescension, almost of protection.

The two chief envoys having shaken hands, general handshaking followed. Gorgeous uniforms, sparkling with decorations, gave the scene gaiety. Heels clicked, spurs jangled musically. The faces that, a moment before, had been blank, were animated and courteously alive. A low ripple of conversation indicated that a frozen stream was feeling the effects of a spring thaw.

The question of precedence in entering the dining salon for the luncheon that was to follow the meeting of the envoys, had been one of the President's toughest problems of protocol, with the seating question a close second. The President solved both to everybody's satisfaction. When the time for the luncheon came, he was in animated conversation with Witte and Komura, edging toward the dining salon. Talking all the while, the three entered the room simultaneously, neither of the envoys conscious of having crossed a threshold. No places were set, no banquet-table spread. A table in the center of the salon held the food, the plates and the cutlery. There could then be no question of precedence.

The President drew his four chief guests to a long upholstered seat in the corner of the salon and himself took the only chair in the room, facing them. He spoke in French of sports and outdoor life, in which the Russians were interested, of climate and Shakespeare, while they all balanced their plates on their knees in the accustomed fashion at receptions. A hush fell on the gathering as the President rose to his feet. Clearly, he was about to offer a toast. To the Czar? To the Mikado? With the defeated Russians sensitive as school-girls, the victorious Japanese proud and, inwardly, decidedly cocky, a false step now might wreck the conference before it started.

"Gentlemen," the President began, "I propose a toast to which there will be no answer and which I ask you to drink in silence, standing."

"Standing?" thought the clean-shaven, chubby foreign service man, Korostovetz, who was serving as Witte's secretary. "There are no chairs we could sit on." In his diary that night he noted that, "uttering each word distinctly, Roosevelt looked Witte straight in the eyes." All the envoys were regarding the President with serious and even reverent gaze.

"I drink," he went on, "to the welfare and prosperity of the sovereigns and peoples of the two great nations, whose representatives have met one another on this ship. It is my most earnest hope and prayer, in the interest of not only these great powers but of all mankind that a just and lasting peace may speedily be concluded among them."

So that final knot had been cut.

The conversation in the room began again, and was, if anything, more relaxed and friendly than before.

It was well after three o'clock when the presidential standard was lowered on the *Mayflower* and, to the reawakened thunders of twenty-one gun salutes, the President returned to Sagamore Hill. Shortly after, the Japanese delegation was taken to the *Dolphin*, which was to carry them to Portsmouth. The Russians remained on the *Mayflower*.

The opposing envoys shook hands warmly. "Until Monday, then," said Takahira to Rosen.

"Until Monday," echoed the Russian.

The New York *Sun* summed up the gathering next morning in five simple words: GO MAKE PEACE, SAYS ROOSEVELT.

Joseph Bucklin Bishop, secretary of the Isthmian Canal Commission, spent the night, following the ceremony, at Sagamore Hill. The President was tired but happy, and inclined to be pleased with himself. "I looked forward to this affair with a good deal of anxiety," he admitted, "knowing that a single slip on my part which could be construed as favoring one set of envoys over the others would be fatal. No such slip occurred, and I think we are off to a good start. I know perfectly well that the whole world is watching me," he added, "and the condemnation that will come down on me if the conference fails, will be world-wide too. But that's all right. I thought it my plain duty to make the effort."

5

"To Portsmouth town, to Portsmouth town,
    The sweating envoys puff,
To speak of tin and Saghalien
    And eke to bluff and bluff . . .
For many a day the Japanese
    Uphold their fingers gaunt,
And mention seven hundred things
    They positively want—
For many a day the Muscovites
    Down-plant their Russian shoes,
And mention seven hundred things
    They positive refuse."

Thus the poet, smiting the lyre. In general terms, his picture is accurate, except that the number of demands was actually twelve. They included spheres of influence in Korea and Manchuria, transfer of certain Russian leaseholds, railroads, fishing rights and other assets in the Far East and of her naval vessels in Pacific ports, the cession of the Island of Sakhalin and an indemnity covering the cost of the war to Japan. The Russians accepted eight of the clauses

223

The strenuous handmaiden of peace
"Now, boys, get together in peace and amity"

practically without debate; but rejected the other four, two of them not too emphatically. The final sticking-points were Sakhalin Island and the proposed indemnity.

Through trusted American agents the President kept in almost hourly touch with the Conference and through Kaneko with the Japanese government. Ten days after the conference began, it was deadlocked, with the Russians gloomily declaring that the negotiations had failed, and might as well be adjourned. From his friend, Speck von Sternberg, the German ambassador, the President received word, in fact, that Britain and France were planning to take the Conference out of his hands.

The President thought he would see about that. When Kaneko hurried to Sagamore Hill, confident that the President's inclination toward the cause of Japan would make him whip the Russians into line, he got a shock. Roosevelt was pulling nobody's chestnuts out of the fire. Japan's insistence on an indemnity, he told Kaneko, was having a bad effect on American public opinion, which was beginning anyway to veer toward Russia. Japan would continue to need American financial help and might have trouble getting it if she continued the war for the sake of money. Such action would be folly anyway. Japan might push the Russian armies back a thousand miles at a cost in blood and treasure which no indemnity would ever repay, lose American sympathy and be no nearer peace. Forget the indemnity, he advised, and let Russia buy back the northern half of Sakhalin for, say, what the United States had paid Russia for Alaska.

Kaneko was prepared to agree, and the President knew that a long cablegram would soon be dot-dot-dashing its way to the Mikado. So far, so good. When the Japanese had gone, the President wired Witte, asking him to send Rosen, "or some other gentleman who is in your confidence," immediately to Sagamore Hill.

The conference came to life.

The limited train carrying the Baron from Boston was stopped at Bridgeport, where the *Sylph* picked him up and bore him to Oyster Bay. The President was in white flannels on the tennis court at Sagamore, and held his conference with the ambassador during intervals of the game. The next day the proposal he had made regarding Sakhalin was rejected. Kaneko hurried again to Sagamore Hill, where the President urged him again to advise his government to give up all thought of an indemnity. With the Russians he felt baffled. Witte wrote him that they would not admit themselves vanquished, "making it all I can do," the President wrote his friend, Henry White, first secretary of the American embassy in London, "not to tell them some straightforward truths in uncomplimentary language." He was not at all sure, moreover, that Witte was submitting his proposals to the Russian foreign office or that the tricky foreign minister, Lamsdorf, was submitting them to his sovereign. "There were moments," the President wrote his English friend, Arthur Lee, after the conclusion of the conference, "when I wished I could get the entire Russian government to the top of Cooper's Bluff and run them violently down a steep place into the sea." Not being able to do that, he decided to ignore Witte and his foreign office and cable the Czar direct.

"I have not much hope of a favorable result," the President wrote White, "but I will do what I can." Actually, his patience was beginning to wear thin. "To be polite and sympathetic in explaining for the hundredth time something perfectly obvious," he wrote the French ambassador, Jusserand, who had become a cherished friend, "when what I really want to do is to give utterance to whoops of rage and jump up and knock their heads together—well, all I can hope is that the self-repression will be ultimately helpful for my character."

Thereupon he sent Kaneko—that is, the Japanese Emperor—a final appeal simply and eloquently phrased. As a matter of practical sense, Japan "would be wise now to close the war in triumph and take her seat as a leading member at the council table of the nations." Ethically, Japan owed a duty to the world. "The civilized world looks to her to make peace; the nations believe in her; let her show her leadership in matters ethical no less than in matters military. The appeal is made to her in the name of all that is lofty and noble; and to this appeal I hope she will not be deaf." He followed the message with another to the Czar, appealing in this case less to the ethical feelings of the Russian government—conspicuous mainly by their absence—than to such enlightened self-interest as an obtuse and corrupt oligarchy might be able to muster.

6

The Associated Press reported the next day that the Czar's answer to the President's second appeal was "partially responsive," though Witte denied it. Anything might happen that day: a move toward peace, perhaps; more likely a break-off of negotiations.

> "But Theodore at Oyster Bay
> Doth while the times between
> By taking trips and dives and dips
> Within his submarine."

So sang the minstrel, with more truth than poetry.

The day was wet, with a northeast wind of gale-velocity whipping up the waters of the Sound. All morning the President was in his study, negotiating by cable with the Czar, the Mikado and the German Kaiser. Regarding his plans for the afternoon, he was non-committal. But shortly before three o'clock, wearing a long raincoat over his customary knickerbockers and soft shirt, he slipped out of the house. A carriage drove him to the Waldeck pier where oilskins and the *Sylph*'s launch were awaiting him. Even in the bay the water was running high, and the launch bucked as she made her way across the harbor.

It was not to the *Sylph* that the launch bore the President, but

226

to the tug *Apache*, at whose side lay a rounded steel shell, some sixty feet long, called *The Plunger*, one of the Navy's six submarines. The President had ordered her to Oyster Bay from her Newport station. He wanted to see what she could do, he said: see it from the deck of the *Sylph*, its commander, Lieutenant Charles F. Nelson, known in the Navy as "Dare-devil Nelson," had assumed. Not at all. When the young commander reported at Sagamore Hill the President told him: "I'm going down in your boat, but please don't say anything about it. When it's all over, it'll be time to talk about it."

No idle curiosity possessed the President, no adolescent's hunger for danger, though the danger would tend to deepen his determination rather than deter him. He had been a student of naval warfare since his college days and, as Assistant Secretary of the Navy and as President, had kept abreast of the latest developments in naval construction, techniques and weapons. The submarine was an old idea that had only recently and rather hesitantly been received in the domain of the practical. As commander-in-chief of the Navy it was important for him to know how practical it was, how manœuvreable, how capable of swift attack and swift escape. How much of a menace was it, actually, to the battleship? Were the enthusiasts right about it? He was always eager, moreover, to encourage officers of the Navy undertaking original and daring work. Young Nelson had attracted his attention as one of the ablest and most fearless officers in the service. Such a man deserved support.

In a whirl of rain, the President squeezed his bulk down the 18-inch opening of the conning-tower, and clambered down the little ladder inside. The commander followed, closing the hatch.

With the *Apache* standing by, the submarine made for the open waters of the Sound. The President stared at the maze of wheels, valves, batteries, switches, tubes, tanks, and shafts around him, asking more questions than any thirteen-year-old. The commander explained their functions and took the President forward to examine the torpedo-tubes. "If you hit once, I suppose that's all you want?" observed the President.

"Yes, sir," the commander answered. "That sinks a battleship."

They went aft to examine the two motors, whereupon the commander took the helm in the conning-tower. They were in open water by this time, exceptionally stormy water, for the Sound. In response to the commander's signal, one of the crew of seven turned a valve and the submarine quickly dropped to the Sound floor, and after a minute, as quickly rose again.

Then came the great "stunt" of the submarines: "porpoise diving," for the purpose of quick observation and as quick disappearance. *The Plunger* submerged at a 45-degree angle; then, with the shift of a lever, rose again at the same angle, and, a minute later, dove once more.

"Wonderful!" the President exclaimed, and at the commander's suggestion, took the controls himself. With the delight of a boy he put the craft through her paces, sinking her thirty feet so she hung like a hawk in a windless sky, motionless, unaffected by the angry sea overhead. Oddly, as the submarine hung thus suspended, a small school of porpoises swam past the portholes, and the naturalist in the President studied their movements eagerly from his unusual vantage-point. Then again he was sending the ship forward and backward, to the surface, bow foremost, back again into the depths and again to the surface, this time stern foremost.

The commander again took the controls to demonstrate the submarine's ability at top speed to stop abruptly, reverse, turn within the space of three lengths, remain completely still. Then, without warning, while the ship was moving at full speed, he turned off the lights, carrying out with the crew in darkness all the former movements, and doing it with a celerity and an accuracy which delighted the President.

Altogether, he was on the submarine for three hours; almost one-third of the time submerged. "I've had many a splendid day's fun in my life," he remarked, beaming, as he climbed out of the hatch, "but I can't remember ever having crowded so much of it into such a few hours."

The news was out that night, unofficially on the lips of the crew, on leave in the village, officially by direct communication from Sagamore Hill. The incident brought lifted eyebrows next morning and, the day after, an editorial in the New York *Times*, scolding "Our Submerged President" for his recklessness. The President would do well to recognize that "his life is not his own; that eighty millions of people . . . have an interest in its prolongation," and were seriously concerned when he entrusted himself and all he represented to "some newfangled, submersible, collapsible or otherwise dangerous device."

Amen! said the Washington *Star*, which, being Democratic like the *Times*, was inclined to be schoolmasterish with the President.

"I was immensely amused at the fuss made about my going down in the 'Plunger,'" the President wrote Grant La Farge. His own explanation of his escapade was as boyish as everything else touching the incident: he had gone down in the submarine, he wrote Speck von Sternberg, "because I did not like to have the officers and enlisted men think I wanted them to try things I was reluctant to try myself." No doubt. To the press correspondents at Oyster Bay, he gave a different reason, which was unquestionably as true as the other: "I went down in 'The Plunger' because it would have broken the boys' hearts if I hadn't." But there was, probably, a reason that went deeper. With the peace negotiations approaching a dead center and his last trump played, did his intuition tell him that he needed nothing so much to clear his mind as a totally irrelevant adventure?

7

While the President of the United States was happily cruising under the stormy waters of Long Island Sound, the envoys at Portsmouth, Russian and Japanese both, were telling the world that the conference was on the point of breaking up. On the day that Kaneko told reporters that Japan must get no less than $600,000,000, the Czar replied to the President's appeal, saying in effect, "Not a kopeck of indemnity, not a *verst* of territory."

In the library at Sagamore Hill, the President, unwilling even yet to admit defeat, drafted a new message to the Kaiser urging him to bring pressure to bear on the Czar; characteristically tipping off the German chargé d'affaires in Washington—von Sternberg was on vacation—that, if the Kaiser could persuade the Czar to accept the terms he had stated, the President would at once give him credit in the most public and emphatic manner for what had been accomplished. The message was to be his supreme and final effort to resolve the differences between the warring nations, and he threw into it all he had. Quite apart from his eagerness to bring the hostilities to an end, he recognized the ignominy that would be his if the conference failed, his, and because of him, his country's. How these emperors and kings and their gold-plated and bemedaled foreign ministers would gloat as they took over, and, perhaps, succeeded where he had failed! He did not let the prospect depress him. That was a part of the toughness of life, and you took it as you took the triumphs, with a steady heart.

As the President was writing, the telephone on his desk rang. Loeb picked up the receiver. There was a moment's pause. "What?" he exclaimed excitedly. The message was repeated.

His excitement and incredulity startled the President. "What is it?"

"The Associated Press has announced, in an official bulletin from Portsmouth," Loeb said breathlessly, "that the plenipotentiaries have agreed on all points of difference, and will proceed at once to draft a treaty of peace."

The President ran upstairs to tell Mrs. Roosevelt and the children. Herbert Parsons, member of Congress from the "silk-stocking district" in New York, was at Sagamore Hill for luncheon that day and saw the President come down, a few minutes later, his face wreathed in smiles. "It's a mighty good thing for Russia," he said, "and a mighty good thing for Japan. And," he added, thumping his chest, "a mighty good thing for *me* too!"

It was a joyful family party that gathered around the table in the dining-room a few minutes later. After luncheon a cipher dispatch from Portsmouth gave the President the details of the settlement. Over the heads of their so-called plenipotentiaries, the Czar, it appeared, had agreed to the cession of the southern half of Sakhalin and the Mikado had renounced not only an indemnity, but even a payment for the Island's northern half. The President's appeal to Japan "to show her leadership in matters ethical as well as in matters military" had not been wasted. Facing the dilemma of making peace, at a sacrifice, or continuing the war for the sake of what had been called "blood-money," "we have made peace," said Takahira, "for the sake of humanity and civilization, in the interest of both countries and the world."

All that afternoon and evening and through the days following, telegrams and cablegrams rained on Sagamore Hill from emperors, kings, presidents and many of the world's lesser notables. Among them was a wire from the Russian envoys: "To you history will award the glory . . . of . . . the generous initiative . . . in establishing a peace generous to both sides." The press of the world, indeed, rang with praise of the President; the general consensus, as expressed by the Berlin correspondent of the New York *World*, being that, while Japan, in the Conference, had "won a great moral victory" and Russia "a great diplomatic one," President Roosevelt had emerged from it as "the most important figure in international statesmanship." The President was inclined to be a little sardonic about the laudations, and about success in general, and to wonder what these seemingly so devoted admirers of his would have said if he had failed.

There was a suggestion current in Washington that, because of the scene of the determining action in the great drama, the treaty should be signed there and should be known as the "Treaty of Sagamore Hill."

The last word is rightly the poet's:

> "And now when ancient grandsires sit
>   Within the evening gray,
> And oysters frolic noisilee
>   All over Oyster Bay,
> The graybeard tells his little niece
>   How Theodore did trek
> To drag the gentle Bird of Peace
>   To Portsmouth—by the neck."

Chapter XII

THE STATESMEN and politicians, the diplomats, generals and admirals, the foreign notables, the newspapermen, the old friends, the sisters, the cousins and the aunts who, during the President's second term, and thereafter, climbed the winding road to Sagamore Hill in the village hacks or, if they were so up-to-the-minute as to possess motor-cars, wheezed and puffed around the first and the second of the narrow bends and invariably got stuck on the third —the comers-and-goers, welcome or unwelcome, entertaining or dull—found themselves sooner or later standing on a broad mezzanine, rejoicing in an experience which earlier visitors to Sagamore had not known—the gratifying apprehension of unexpected architectural harmonies.

Recognizing that he required a room, more spacious and dignified than the library and more formal than Mrs. Roosevelt's "parlor," in which to receive distinguished individuals or delegations, the President had commissioned his old friend, C. Grant La Farge, to design a structure to be attached to the house at the northern end of the main hall. La Farge had produced an annex whose brick walls were in keeping with the rest of the house, and whose interior, triumphantly different from anything the original architects could have imagined, miraculously harmonized with their heavy-handed Philistine creation and somehow shed beauty on it.

The room—with wooden walls and ceiling a monochrome of luminous, soft red-brown—was some thirty feet wide by forty deep and set two steps below the general level of the first floor. A square alcove, on the west, with book-shelves on two sides and great windows looking out on the sunset, gave the room added breadth; a high ceiling, flat in the center and following the slanting roof-lines, east and west, gave it spaciousness. Substantial columns with Ionic

capitals, set in pairs against all four walls, heightened its dignity without making it seem a place apart from the daily life of the household. Between tall windows on the north wall, carved in wood and gilded, was the American eagle with outspread wings circled by a wreath of laurel. Above and to either side of the impressive fireplace, opposite the alcove, were small panels with the initials TR and EKR, similarly carved and decorated. Theodore had built the rest of the house by himself, Edith might have said. This room they had built together. The architect, who cherished them both, had succeeded in making it a monument to the noble qualities they had in common.

"You cannot imagine how delighted I am with the new room," the President wrote La Farge, the day that he arrived from Washington. "The most attractive feature" of the house, he called it—a notable understatement—"in comfort, in beauty and in dignity, all that could be wished. Really I like it better than any room in the White House which, as you know, is my standard of splendor!"

He took delight in shifting the best of his hunting trophies into the new room, bringing the buffalo-head from the gun-room to join the buffalo-head in the front hall, at either side of the new fireplace. Across the wide antlers of an elk on the opposite wall he laid his Rough Rider sword and hat and revolver. Day by day he and Mrs. Roosevelt moved more trophies into the room—the First Lady, one suspects, not too sorry to get the antelope and deer out of the dining-room!—experimented with furniture, hung pictures, installed books.

A writer from England telling in the *Pall Mall Magazine* of a visit to Sagamore Hill, fills in the background after they were done: "books . . . companionable books, often used and well taken care of . . . small books to fit the pocket . . . a cluster of flags— battle-flags that have figured in the Americo-Spanish war . . . pictures . . . two oil paintings . . . one, a lonely calvary, high up above the middle arch of a brown stone bridge, beneath which speed the dark waters of a mountain torrent . . . a touch of loveliness and grandeur, of Christian hope in adversity. . . . The other . . . a great tower uplifted against a dark background . . . the glories of the sunset and the bold outlines of architecture . . . beauty of conception . . . greatness of execution."

The room grew on the President from week to week. "What delights my American soul," he wrote the architect, "it is not an imitation of anything." It was "a joy just to sit in it," he added, "and will be a joy to me as long as I live."

2

The family lived in the new room as they lived in every other room in the house. With its high ceiling and its high, wide windows on three sides, the great hall was cool on the hottest day of midsummer and, on chilly evenings, the tall fireplace sent its heat happily to the center where, when the family was alone, they would gather around the kerosene lamp while the President read aloud and the First Lady embroidered, mended socks or sewed for the Needlework Guild.

It was not often that they were alone. There were guests for luncheon, almost invariably, and overnight guests every week end and often throughout the week: people who opened new vistas into art or literature or social reform or international understanding or the habits of some obscure feathered friend, and were a delight; other people whose little lives were bounded by an election district and were merely suffered as you suffer ants at a picnic.

MONDAY—He entertains the champion tennis player.

TUESDAY—He entertains some old Rough Rider comrades.

WEDNESDAY—He entertains some fellow LL.Ds.

THURSDAY—He entertains a couple of old-time hunter friends.

FRIDAY—He entertains a few fellow politicians.

SATURDAY—He entertains some brother historians and authors.

Our versatile President and his summer friends

(By Courtesy of the Chicago *Tribune*)

The Englishman who, while he was waiting for the President to dispose of a previous caller, had so perceptively taken in the details of what the family called the North Room and visitors would forever insist on calling the Trophy Room, left a revealing picture of the man whom visitors came from far and near to see: "the khaki riding-suit, terminating in brown gaiters and brown boots. . . . The priceless gift of putting you immediately at your ease—indeed, more . . . the gift of making you feel that your friendship and regard, as well as your personal opinion, are of moment to him. . . . The activity, the impetuosity, the enormous vitality. . . . A staccato kind of speech by which words are curiously, but not unpleasantly, underlined. . . . The utmost geniality" with which the President plunged into one topic after another, discussing them "not only with the ability and relish of a man of wide interests and splendid energies, but as a man of culture with deep intellectual grasp of the problems, as well as the literature, of the world."

Visitors with a single idea—most often, politics—were given courteous reception and, if the particular aspect of the idea was important, concentrated, if brief, attention; if it was not important, a veritable waterfall of words drowned the idea and swept its luckless bearer toward the door. Men with fertile minds, on the other hand, were likely to find that the subjects discussed covered a wide range: in the Englishman's case, Dickens, "Martin Chuzzlewit," international criticism . . . Tammany . . . the blameless, austere reformer, the politician lacking perhaps some of the moral virtues "yet with kindness and overflowing charity" . . . Chesterton, Shaw, Ruskin. . . . The President, "pleading for today at the bar of yesterday . . . the train in the mountain gorge, the modern battleship . . . moving majestically over the water . . . are these not beautiful things. . . . ?"

Visitors found the range of his knowledge perennially astounding. "In one afternoon," said Archie, a dozen years later, "I have heard him speak to the foremost Bible student of the world, a prominent ornithologist, a diplomat and a French general, all of whom agreed that Father knew more about the subjects on which they had specialized than they did."

The President seemed always the same, yet each visitor, in a sense, saw a different man. To one he was the Big Stick, the man of swift decision; another thought the Big Stick manner a pose—at heart, the President was a scholar. A third saw an extrovert, predominantly interested in outdoor life; a fourth saw the moralist, making ancient truths sound radical, almost revolutionary. One man who came to Sagamore to speak his farewells before returning to his native land, saw, one suspects, mainly the exalted ruler of a great nation, to which his own owed much. He was Baron Komura, and he brought the gift of an ancient Japanese sword. The Baron was of the order of the Samurai, the chivalric order of Japan, and the sword he brought was a Samurai sword. The First Lady, who stood at the President's side in the North Room for the presentation, noted that the fragile little Baron would not let his companion and fellow-envoy, Takahira, touch the sword, since he was of "inferior" birth.

The impression which another Oriental visitor carried away from Sagamore Hill, embraced the house, the lawns and trees that framed it, and the relation of it all to the unseen world. The Empress Dowager's emissary, a charming old Chinese mandarin, in yellow jacket and peacock feather, stood with his host on the piazza, looking over to the Connecticut shore, and appraised his surroundings with alert eyes. Finally, in the manner of one who has solved an interesting problem in quadratics, he remarked gravely that the President's home had an excellent *feng shuey*, "a better *feng shuey* indeed, than any other house I have seen in America, except Mount Vernon."

The President replied, in effect, "That's nice, but what, if you don't mind enlightening me, is a *feng shuey*?"

Feng shuey, the mandarin replied, signified the capacity of a house to be hospitable to the good spirits, resistant to the evil spirits. No one built a house in China, he explained, without careful thought for its *feng shuey*. When a young couple married, the family went into a huddle, consulted the Buddhist priest and, with nodding heads, pondered solemnly the details of the location and design of the house they were to live in, with an eye to its *feng shuey*. The evil spirits, it appeared, came from the north. So there must be no door on that side, or, if there were a door, there must be screening walls before it to guard the entrance.

"We know a lot in China about the good and bad spirits," the mandarin declared. "You didn't know, did you, that a bad spirit can't turn a corner in a hurry? And he doesn't like hill-tops where the soul looks far out and is at peace. The good spirits do, and they like spreading trees without brush, and green grass all around.

So when we find the spot where everything is best for the good spirits and most inconvenient for the bad spirits, then that is good *feng shuey*, such as you have here."

3

The groups that came to luncheon or dinner at Sagamore were seldom homogeneous. The President, indeed, appeared to take a mischievous delight in harmonizing incompatibles. When politicians predominated there was bound to be "a literary damn cuss," to borrow a phrase the President occasionally applied to himself, or the editor of a magazine devoted to sports; and, when literary folks were the chief guests—Owen Wister, perhaps, Finley Peter Dunne, Dr. Lyman Abbott or Lincoln Steffens—there was, like as not, a prize-fighter, or some gnarled plainsman or mountaineer to give the talk a dash of tobasco. Socially, they always got along— the President, drawing out the special contribution of each, saw to that—but, after the meal, the diverse elements occasionally seemed to tear asunder the President himself.

The ornithologist, Frank M. Chapman, was at Sagamore for luncheon one day with Senator Lodge as the other guest, Lodge to talk legislation and Chapman to confer about a monograph on the protective coloration of animals that the President was at work on in such intervals as his crowded schedule gave him. After luncheon, the President drew Chapman outdoors to point out certain experiments he was making. They talked, and talked. An hour passed, and a second hour.

Finally, Mrs. Roosevelt appeared at the door. "Theodore, have you forgotten that Cabot is waiting for you?"

The President, sitting in one of the high-backed rockers on the porch, jumped to his feet. "By Godfrey!" he exclaimed, "I had. Excuse me for a moment," he said to Chapman, "while I go in and settle the affairs of state. Then I will return to the infinitely more important subject, the protective coloring of animals."

The President was happily capable of going from one to the other without getting his wires tangled. During the final stages of the Russo-Japanese negotiations a party of naturalists was spending the night at Sagamore Hill. Among them was C. Hart Merriam, the leading scientist in the field of the American bear. "With characteristic thirst for authoritative information," Chapman, who was

238

present, said, twenty years later, "Mr. Roosevelt was taking deep draughts at the fountain-head," when he was called to the telephone. The instrument, it happened, was in the pantry, adjoining the dining-room. "From his side of the conversation, which we could not avoid over-hearing, we realized the seriousness of the situation to which he was being urged to give his immediate and entire attention."

After about ten minutes, the President was back at the table and, turning to the bear expert, resumed the conversation at exactly the point at which it had been interrupted. "Where did you say, Dr. Merriam, the Hudsonian form integrated with the Alaskan?"

The President's multiplicity of interests kept his mind fresh for the problems of domestic and international statesmanship that daily confronted him, even at Sagamore Hill. He was having breakfast one morning with his friends, "Alec" Lambert and Speck von Sternberg, so different from each other, the one robust and hearty, the other, slender, cultivated, urbane; both deeply cherished. Sternberg having told of his hunts in the Ural Mountains, the President referred to the "glorious hunting" that the kings of Babylon and Assyria had known, drifting into an account of the ancient forms of life in North and South America before the isthmus had linked the continents, in the northern the carnivorous, in the southern the grass-eating. When the land-bridge had risen, how the sabre-toothed tiger and the huge cave bear had licked their chops as they swept south to feast on the slow-moving, tree-browsing creatures, while the land-bridge sank again and again rose! "We listened, charmed and amazed," Lambert wrote, long after.

"Where in the world did you pick up all that?" asked the ambassador.

The President smiled whimsically. "It's all the fault of the fourth-class postmasters," he explained. When problems of state, including the pestiferous questions of patronage, interfered with his sleep, he read "how the empire of Alexander broke to pieces or how the strange creatures of former days developed and seem to have lived. The change of thought gets me ready for sleep."

4

Lambert was at Sagamore on another occasion when the discussion again dealt with the "land-bridge" between North and South

America. This time, however, the subject of the talk was not the sabre-toothed tiger but the humble *Stegomyia* mosquito and its relation to the construction of the Panama Canal. This time, moreover, the President, for once, was not the speaker but the listener: and his listening made history.

The effort to dig the Canal had bogged down. The Isthmian Canal Commission, which had been set up by Congress to direct the work, had proved ineffective, and the President had overhauled it, appointing a veteran railroad-builder, Theodore P. Shonts, chairman, with absolute authority. Shonts had come to Sagamore Hill asking, as the first point in his program, the dismissal of the chief sanitation officer on the Isthmus, Major William C. Gorgas. Gorgas was following the Walter Reed theories of yellow fever and doing nothing, Shonts said, to clean up Colón and Panama City. Gorgas must go. The Secretary of War had agreed.

The President was in a quandary. He had followed Reed's experiments in Cuba with absorbed interest, and, in spite of a vocal faction in the Medical Corps which insisted that the general clean-up of Havana and not the destruction of the mosquitoes was responsible for the conquest of yellow fever, was inclined to believe that Reed's theory had proved itself. But here, the President recognized, was his promise to Shonts to give him a free hand. Shonts was a big man who would not be trifled with. To keep your promises, moreover, was a basic moral issue with the President, and to stick to decisions, a part of his philosophy of sound executive action. How then could he disapprove his new Commission's first major recommendation, and incidentally override his Secretary of War? But, on the other hand, how could he assume responsibility for dismissing a man of Gorgas' eminence and undeniable achievements?

He did what he was always inclined to do when he was in doubt. He sent for a personal friend who had no ax to grind. A week after the President's interview with the engineers, "Alec" Lambert was in the study at Sagamore Hill. The two men had, for years, been on a first-name basis, but Lambert was fully conscious that he was talking, not to the hunting-companion with whom he had eaten and slept and joked and ridden and pursued bears, day after day, in Colorado, two months before, but the President of the United States.

The President was aware of it too and got quickly to the point.

"Shonts tells me that Gorgas is a failure, spending all his time oiling pools, trying to kill mosquitoes and doing nothing about the filth and smells of Colón and Panama City."

"Smells and filth, Mr. President," Lambert declared, "have nothing to do with either the malaria or the yellow fever." Mosquitoes were the imps of destruction, and they must be exterminated if the disease were to be eradicated. "It is for you, Mr. President, to choose between the old methods and the new. You can back the old idea and clean out the smells and see your workmen die of malaria and yellow fever; or you can clean up your puddles and kill the mosquitoes and, after you've done that, clean up the Canal Zone by the ordinary sanitary methods. If you do this, you will have a healthy personnel with which to build your canal."

The bearded physician, so deeply respected in his profession, so genial, so boyish and direct in his relationships, spoke with the earnestness and self-forgetfulness of a man conscious of enormous issues at stake. Men had dreamed of a canal across the Isthmus of Panama for four hundred years. The commerce of the world needed it; the security of the United States demanded it. Would anyone, remembering the torturingly slow voyage of the battleship *Oregon* around Cape Horn in the early months of the Spanish War, ever forget the lesson it had rubbed into the American consciousness?

These memories, these emotions, were in Lambert's mind as he spoke. He recalled the failure of the French company under de Lesseps and the experience of his own uncle, seeing five hundred young French engineers come to work in the Panama swamp and die to the last man before their first pay-day. Napoleon had sold Louisiana, he pointed out, because his army in Santo Domingo had been annihilated by yellow fever. Gorgas was right. There was only one way of controlling yellow fever and malaria, and that was by eradicating the mosquitoes.

With Lambert's concern for the issue mingled concern for the man he loved with all the devotion of his warm and honest heart. "I am sorry for you tonight, Mr. President," he went on, in a voice whose low-pitched eloquence was overpowering in its impressiveness. "You are facing one of the greatest decisions of your career. You must choose between Shonts and Gorgas. If you fall back upon the old methods of sanitation, you will fail, just as the French failed. If you back up Gorgas and his ideas and let him pursue his campaign against the mosquitoes, you will get your canal. It is your

241

canal, Mr. President, and you must choose tonight whether or not you are going to build it."

The President was sitting quietly, absorbing his friend's eloquent plea. When he spoke his eyes were dark with thought. "It's queer," he said shortly. "I never appreciated before how essential it was. But I do now. By George," he added, suddenly his natural, brisk self again, "I'll back up Gorgas and we'll see it through."

5

The premonitory rumblings of world conflict were heard those years at Sagamore Hill, faintly but disturbingly. A newspaperman on the staff of the New York *Times*, Oscar King Davis, whom the President greatly respected, brought the notes of an interview which the German Emperor had given another *Times* man, William Bayard Hale. The President, sitting at his desk in the library, read a page or two and jumped from his chair. "You must not print this!" he exclaimed, almost savagely.

The *Times* had no intention of printing it, King declared, but the editor had thought that the President should know about it.

Greatly relieved, Roosevelt returned to his chair and resumed reading. The interview bristled with rancor, hate and psychopathic incitement to war. Germany was expecting to fight England, the Kaiser said, and intimated that he did not care how soon. "That jack of an Emperor!" the President exclaimed. The Kaiser's jumpiness, his sudden and irresponsible eruptions, had, throughout his administration, been one of the President's minor annoyances. He had learned how to handle "the jack": by helping to save the Kaiser's face when he had been off the beam and was ready to get back on it, and, when the Emperor was internationally helpful, by giving him whatever credit might decently be given him; never forgetting that basically the Emperor respected only force—personal and national. There had been that incident in Venezuela in 1902. "He backed up then," the President told Davis, "and the trouble was settled. Ever since, he has been profuse in his expressions toward me."

In the interview the Kaiser had declared that, within a year or two, the United States would be fighting Japan, and was glad that America seemed to be preparing for it. The relations between the United States and Japan were, in fact, on a very precarious balance. The people of California were indignant at the invasion

242

of cheap Japanese labor and were excluding Japanese children from their schools. There were anti-American riots in Japan and growing agitation in the United States, fostered by the Hearst press. The President did not expect war but was worried, and sent indignant appeals to the Californians to mend their manners, but without success. From the European chancelleries came ominous rumors of Japanese purposes. The President decided that a sight of the American battleship fleet in the Pacific might prove salutary, and made arrangements in Congress for its dispatch.

It was against this background of thunderheads on the horizon that a former navy minister of Japan, Admiral Yamamoto, came to Sagamore Hill with blood in his eye. Defying the midsummer heat, he came in Prince Albert and high hat, looking, the New York *Herald* correspondent noted, "disturbed," and making no effort to hide it.

The party at luncheon was as mixed as such parties had a way of being at Sagamore Hill, including the handsome Acting Secretary of State, Robert Bacon, and his vivacious wife, another charming and interesting couple and the New York politician and Congressman, Herbert Parsons, who had no special interest in Japan at all but was concerned at the moment about the appointment of a new postmaster in New York City.

The President had his own way of preparing for a conference, and there was possibly more method than his foreign visitor might have assumed in the odd assortment of guests at the luncheon-table, the gay and wholly irrelevant talk, the President's stories, and his direction of the conversation—not unlike an orchestra-conductor's —as he beckoned one guest after the other into the improvised and refreshing harmony. Neither the grim intent of the Admiral to speak his mind, nor the fact that he could say nothing at all except through an interpreter, or in fact, understand anything that was said by anyone else, seemed to cloud the social prelude to the international argument in the library, afterward.

"Why cannot the Japanese be treated by the United States on the same basis as European immigrants?" the Admiral burst out, when, in the library, after lunch, he and his host got down to business at last. The President reminded his guest that there were facts in the American situation which the Japanese government would have to face; economic facts. If American laboring men entered

Japan and cut the wages of Japanese working men, "they would be instantly shut out."

As the afternoon wore on, the Admiral's indignation softened noticeably. Was it possibly the lingering influence of the engaging spirit of the luncheon? Whatever it was, the Japanese statesman became almost apologetic for his previous indignation. Any feeling which Japan might have had because of occurrences on the West Coast, he assured the President, was "directed solely against the people of that section." The President in turn spoke with warm admiration of the Japanese people, but casually referred to the proposed voyage of the battleship fleet to the Pacific, announced in the press, the week before. It was his familiar method: "Speak softly, but carry a big stick."

"How much impression I made upon him I cannot say," the President wrote his Secretary of State, Elihu Root, when the Admiral had gone. Perhaps he had done better than he thought. The *Herald* reporter who had noted that the Japanese statesman had seemed "disturbed" on his arrival, depicted him on his departure as in "high good humor." The President did his part in the cause of good feeling by issuing a statement to the press stressing "the thoroughly good understanding between the two governments and the fundamental friendliness between the two nations."

The *Herald*, in large headlines, greeted the innocuous words as a "Peace Manifesto," which was something less than realistic, but hurt nobody. Meanwhile, the President, under no illusions, went on with his preparations to send the fleet to the Pacific.

6

Some who came to Sagamore were drawn there by the President on urgent national business; others, like Lambert in the Gorgas controversy, because they had special knowledge or a quality of disinterested judgment that the President needed; or, like Lodge, because they were trusted friends with the intricacies of congressional politics at their finger-tips; or, like Lyman Abbott or Albert Shaw, because the President could depend on them for a clear vision of the moral issues in public affairs, or use the magazines they edited when the President wanted to send up a trial balloon. Others, like Owen Wister, Hamlin Garland, or Brander Matthews, came because the President, under the pressure of public affairs, liked nothing better than to talk books for an evening—books and ideas and other matters wholly unprofitable to the utilitarian mind.

There were people who were not beckoned to come to Sagamore but found a compelling excuse to ask for an appointment for no reason except to be touched and revitalized by the fire of the President's spirit. Two such were sea-faring men who felt, perhaps—each in his own way—that they could not comfortably face their nightly companions, the stars, if they missed the opportunity, which a pause in their journeys gave them, to share their dreams not with the President so much as with the man, Theodore Roosevelt.

The two were as different as cocoanut milk and whale oil; the one a pursuer of aimless adventure; the other, incarnate purpose to the point of fanaticism. Daring was the quality they had in common, the *open sesame* that swung the door wide at Sagamore. The intrepid water-tramp, Captain Joshua Slocum, had all his adult life sailed the seven seas in his forty-foot sloop, alone, with no crew, surviving by a succession of miracles which in themselves gave him a kind of oblique significance. When, after his visit with the President, he descended the hill to return to his boat, he took Archie with him for a week's cruise, to the boy's ecstatic delight.

The other mariner who anchored his vessel in Oyster Bay harbor and climbed the hill was Captain Robert E. Peary. He had named his ship *Roosevelt*, to remind the members of his expedition, in this final effort of his to reach the North Pole, "of strength and insistence and persistence and unvarying victory over all obstacles." The explorer, who regarded the President as "the most intensely vital man and the biggest man" that the nation had produced, had come, in fact, like a son to get his father's blessing on his all-but-hopeless venture. "Mr. President," he assured his host with boyish sincerity, as he was speaking his farewell, "I shall put into this effort everything there is in me—physical, mental, and moral."

The President's blessing was simple and deeply felt. "I believe in you, Peary," he said, "and I believe in your success—if it is within the possibility of man."

7

The hackdriver who remarked that visitors to Sagamore Hill were generally in a happy frame of mind on their return to the Oyster Bay "depot," said more than he imagined. The President had an exhilarating gift of pushing out men's horizons. To be with Theodore Roosevelt, as William Hard was to write, a dozen years later, was not only to live "more strivingly but to live more abundantly." It was not only that he was, as Julian Street was to point out, "the most interesting American." The quality that put the light into man's eyes and the lift into their frames came from a deeper source. Beneath the President's vivacity, the flow of eager, evocative talk, the droll stories out of his own experience, the forthrightness, the earnest, sometimes angry, sometimes comical, often eloquent, occasionally thunderous expression of his convictions on life, literature, ethics, government, politics, reform, reformers, and the idealism that is helpful only if it has one foot at least on the solid earth; beneath all these was a fire that—like the burning bush that Moses turned aside to look at and see why, burning, it was not consumed—affected all who came into the circle of its radiance.

Men talked of an "electric quality" in him because, perhaps, he made them tingle, and not knowing how else to describe his effect on them. The truth went deeper. There was in him a seemingly inexhaustible ardor that expressed itself in his love of life, love of action, love of people, love of the natural world, love of heroic deeds, love of family, love of country. He deprecated any suggestion that he had genius. But his ardor was beyond the ardor of other men; the intensity, the glow, of his living, the fervor of his caring, were, indeed, a form of genius, and one that was rare in his country's history. Men felt it in him as they felt first love, or the birth of a first child or the first challenge of death, and went from his presence with a sense that their lips had been touched with the burning coal and they had become capable of doing what they had not dreamed they could do. Under his leadership, indeed, men rose to heights of vision and service which few could maintain when the leadership terminated and they were, as it were, on their own.

"I don't know what you would call him," mused his friend, W. Sturgis Bigelow, the Boston Brahmin—Orientalist, thinker, physician—after Roosevelt's death. "A man? A creature? An entity, perhaps? Call him what you want, he was more than man. If one could imagine the impulse and force of a divinity inhabiting a human body, with the divinity's overpowering energy and only a human mind, one might begin to get his measure."

A person very different from this contemplative convert to Buddhism, an extraordinary, if unlettered Irishman, Mike Murphy, the great Yale athletic trainer, was groping toward the same conception when he expressed, in terms of his own lifework, the effect that Theodore Roosevelt had on the men and women who went to talk to him—or hear him talk—in the library or the new North Room. Murphy was returning from Sagamore Hill with members of the triumphant 1908 American Olympic team. The President had welcomed the young victors, referring with enthusiasm, in each case, to the man's individual achievement. He had not "brushed up" in advance, Loeb declared; he had merely read the newspaper accounts of the games from day to day and, because he had cared about these boys and what they had done, had stored the records in his memory.

On the chartered excursion boat taking the team back to New York, a friend, Gustavus Kirby, came upon Murphy, sitting in the cabin in deep thought.

"I suppose," Murphy mused, "you think that I am the greatest athletic trainer in the world?" Kirby assented. "Well, you're all wrong. Until we went to Oyster Bay, I thought I might be, but now I know I'm not."

"Mike, that's nonsense!" exclaimed his friend.

"No," said the other, quietly. "Give me sixty men, every one a champion, and let that man at Oyster Bay have sixty other men, and every one of 'em a dub, and his team would lick mine every time. You see it's this way," he went on, when his friend's renewed protests had subsided. "That man down there would tell a miler that he could reel a mile off in four minutes." ("As you know," Kirby explained, telling the story to the President's sister, Corinne Robinson, "no one has run or ever will run a mile in four minutes.") "And," Murphy went on, "not only would that man *think* he could run a mile in four minutes, but, by God, he'd go and do it!"

Chapter XIII

THE YEARS of the Theodore Roosevelt administration were more easy-going than any that the next succeeding generations would know. That was due less, perhaps, to the whim of a fickle Destiny, happening to smile upon the first ten years of the twentieth century, than to a President of the United States who could spot the small, apparently inconsequential threat when it first raised its infant face and knew how to deal with it before it grew whiskers and a tail. All the elements of the World War that broke out in Europe five years after Roosevelt left the White House, were in the atmosphere during the years of his administration, but he used the power and prestige of the United States to keep them in hand. The world's statesmen noted an American President who kept the American Navy strong and ready for action, and the sabre-rattlers abroad kept the sabres sheathed.

In the broad reaches between the Atlantic and Pacific, the Canadian border and the Gulf of Mexico, the picture was less peaceful. The President knew that before he could make the regulation of corporations a reality, he must prove to their owners and managers that, like all other Americans, they were subject to the law of the land. To some, that was news; bad news. They fought against so "radical," so "socialistic" an idea, fought through the press and the legislators they controlled. The air on Capitol Hill became agitated and very hot.

But no searing winds reached Sagamore Hill or invaded the house at 1600 Pennsylvania Avenue where the presidential family lived its happy, noisy and eventful life. With Alice here, there and everywhere, except at home, Ted and Kermit at Groton, and Ethel, except for week ends, at the Cathedral School in Washington, the family, winters, was reduced to Archie and Quentin, who made up in energy and resourcefulness what they lacked in numbers and size.

The boys were as free of the White House as they were of Sagamore. Visitors might come upon them roller-skating or even riding a bicycle in the corridors. Once a guide, after a rotund oration on the historical importance of the East Room, opened the door and hastily shut it again when he discovered a little tow-headed boy, stumping around the very historical furniture on very high stilts, declaring to an appreciative audience of his contemporaries that, even though it was a rainy day, there were always ways of getting exercise in the White House. That was Quentin. Hide-and-seek took the boys and their friends into every closet and corner in the house, with the President occasionally hiding-and-seeking with the best of them, and now and again there were obstacle races up and down the halls, with the President a lively participant.

> "The White House knew untrammelled joys
>   That shamed its customs prim and starchy,
> When cataracts of little boys
>   Came storming down the stairs with Archie."

So sang the poet, Arthur Guiterman.

> "And there were puppies, little cats,
>   And lots of other pets and cronies,
> Like pink-eyed rabbits, piebald rats,
>   And lizards, guinea-pigs and ponies."

A favorite among the cats was Tom Quartz, who found Senator Mark Hanna a sympathetic playmate, but Speaker Cannon superior and unapproachable. Another cat, gray, six-toed Slippers, acquired fame by stretching lazily in the middle of a corridor one evening after a diplomatic dinner and forcing the President of the United States and all his glittering guests to make a careful detour around her. Numberless dogs, Jack, Bozzie, and others, were integral parts of the family.

2

There was an inviolate Children's Hour in the White House as at Sagamore. "If Mother has a headache, I generally read to them or tell them a story," the President wrote Ted. "They always clamor for the latter and I always try to compromise on the former, as I feel as though my powers of invention had completely given out." When Quentin took to his bed with bronchitis, the President was "driven nearly wild," he wrote, "by the effort to invent stories. Why they should both prefer to have me invent a poor story on my own account rather than read them an excellent one which some master of the profession has already invented, I don't know; but such is the fact." He finally took to reading them "what the absurd little geese call 'I' stories . . . hunting stories told in the first person, which the little boys imagine to represent the deeds of the same individual. My reading for the last two evenings has been a most satisfactory man-eating lion story."

Sooner or later the reading ended in a romp. One evening, after the reading, the prayers that followed and his inspection of the sixteen china animals which shared Archie's bed, the President read some of the nonsense rhymes of Laura E. Richards, including, "How the President takes his tea." The boys christened themselves "Punkydoodle" and "Jollapin," and then the roughhouse began. "First I would toss Punkydoodle (Quentin) on Jollapin (Archie)," the father wrote Kermit, "and tickle Jollapin while Punkydoodle sprawled and wriggled on top of him, and then reverse them and keep Punkydoodle down by heaving Jollapin on him, while they both kicked and struggled until my shirt front looked very much the worse for wear."

The President was always getting his starched shirt fronts messed up. Before a diplomatic reception, finding that he had fifteen minutes to spare, the President, in "white tie and tails," went into the nursery where, he wrote Kermit, "the two small persons in pink tommies instantly raced for the bed and threw themselves on it with ecstatic conviction that a romp was going to begin. I did not have the heart to disappoint them, and the result was that my shirt got so mussed that I had to change it."

The President never did learn his lesson; or perhaps, putting first things first, he was convinced that a change of shirts was a small price to pay for two boys' squeals and sparkling eyes.

The "romps" were nothing to the pillow-fights. "Quentin's idea is to get as many pillows as possible in a heap and then lie on them apparently on the theory that he is protecting them from me. This enrages Archie, who addresses him with lofty contempt as 'kid' and adjures him to stand up manfully and 'fight the bear.' "

250

"Quentin is a roly-poly, happy-go-lucky personage," the President wrote the wife of his old friend Lodge, "the brightest of any of the children but with a strong tendency to pass a very happy life in doing absolutely nothing except swim or loaf about with other little boys." He had an original turn of mind which, in the judgment of his elders (including his brothers and sisters), demanded stern suppression at meal times when guests were present. Quentin might say anything, and say it so everybody heard. So it became a habit with the family on those occasions, when Quentin spoke for any purpose, to hiss with one accord, "Quentin, keep quiet!" For Quentin's remarks had a way of precipitating trouble. There was the time that Mrs. Roosevelt was away and, after what his father called "a riot in candy and ice cream with chocolate sauce," Quentin was in bed—"a very sad bunny." The faithful Mame, too, was ill. "I think Archie escaped with a minimum of washing for the three days," the President wrote Kermit. "One day I asked him before Quentin how often he washed his face, whereupon Quentin interpolated, 'Very seldom, I fear'—which naturally produced from Archie violent recriminations of a strongly personal type."

When Quentin was "going on" nine, his father noted that he was "the same cheerful pagan philosopher as ever." He developed the philosophic mind at an early age. A friend of the family, visiting at Sagamore, came on him at Snouder's drugstore in Oyster Bay, grasping a nickel firmly in his grimy hand and looking longingly at the soda fountain. The friend, knowing that the boy was supposed to be on a diet, remarked: "Quentin, I wouldn't take a soda. It might make you sick."

Quentin looked at the lady with round, solemn eyes. "How sick?" he asked.

"Perhaps sick enough to be sent to bed."

He let her words sink in for a long minute while he weighed profit and loss. Then he deliberately walked forward and deposited his nickel on the counter. "Chocolate sundae, please."

The boy was inclined, indeed, to face the realities without fear, resentment or repining. "Last night I had to spank Quentin for having taken something that did not belong to him and then not telling the truth about it," his father wrote Kermit, when his youngest was six. "Ethel and Mother acted respectively as accuser and court of first resort, and then brought him solemnly to me for sentence and punishment—both retiring much agitated when the final catastrophe became imminent. Today Quentin has been as cunning as possible. He perfectly understood that he had brought his fate on himself."

His philosophic reach widened with the years. Toward the end of his father's administration, at breakfast one morning, he remarked, "I just saw a picture of you whacking the trusts, and the motto 'We're for Teddy because Teddy protects the poor man.' But I expect next year all the enthusiasm will be for Mr. Taft."

He recognized comically his father's tendency to extreme partisanship. One morning at breakfast the President took the paper and exclaimed, "Oh, Lord! It's too bad, Pennsy won."

"I suppose," Quentin remarked meditatively, " 'Pennsy' is a Democrat."

The newspapermen who tried to trap the boy into giving them information about his father got nowhere. "I see him occasionally," the boy admitted to one persistent reporter, "but I know nothing of his family life." Yet, with all his uncanny perspicuity, he had a child's fancy, gathering flowers at Sagamore one morning and putting them beside his father's and mother's plates, with a note around each bunch saying it was a gift from the King of the Fairies.

He was an independent soul, and at Sagamore inclined to be a "social butterfly," his mother wrote Mrs. Cowles, spending much of his time on Algonquin, making calls on his friends. In Washington he picked up friends where he found them, the younger son of the Secretary of War, one day, and the next, an odd character who lived by hunting rabbits and fishes. The President commented in a letter to Ted on the philosophy with which Quentin seemed to take "alternations of grandeur and the life of a street-mucker." One day he went to school in a carriage and pair; the next he rode with a Negro in a brick-wagon, to find a pig for Thanksgiving dinner, and was as much at ease in the one case as in the other. "He found his pig all right," his father wrote, "and brought it home in triumph. The rest of the day he passed with various small boy friends, doing everything imaginable, and was so dirty by nightfall that, when his head was washed, Ethel said it yielded a thick stream of muddy water." Quentin, like Archie, was all boy. "His towhead was always mussed," Earle Looker, a Washington playmate, wrote long after, "his tie coming untied, his clothes being torn, his stockings refusing to stay up. He was as irrepressible mentally as he was physically and, either way, there was no holding him down or back."

Quentin had a second pig-adventure which his father recounted to Kermit: "He heard that Schmid, the animal man, wanted a small pig, and decided that he would turn an honest penny by supplying the want." He called on an aged colored man who he knew "possessed little pigs; bought one; popped it into a bag; astutely dodged the school—having a well-founded distrust of how the boys would feel toward his passage with the pig—and took the car for home. By that time the pig had freed itself from the bag, and, as he explained, he journeyed in with a 'small squealish pig' under his arm; but, as the conductor was a friend of his, he was not put off. He bought it for a dollar and sold it to Schmid for a dollar and a quarter, and feels as if he had found a permanent line of business. Schmid then festooned it in red ribbons and sent it to parade the streets. I gather that Quentin led it around for part of the parade, but he was somewhat vague on this point, evidently being a little uncertain as to our approval of the move."

Quentin hurt his mother's feelings desperately at Sagamore, the summer before he was nine, by pleading to be allowed to go to boarding-school. "This is the first time," she mused, sadly, "that one of the little birds has been willing to leave the nest even before it can fly. All the other little birds have hated to go even when it was time." When one of his brothers reminded him sagely that it was not well for boys to go to boarding-school too young, Quentin remarked, "It won't make any difference in my case because I'm naturally of a bubbling-over nature."

He did not go to boarding-school at that time and was entirely content. For in Washington he acquired a "gang"—"the White House gang," they called themselves—including Charlie Taft, and a half dozen other youngsters with boundless energy and inventive minds.

One night he had three of the "gang" with him in the White House—"an evening and night of delirious rapture," Quentin's father wrote Archie, "it being a continuous rough-house, save when they would fall asleep for an hour or two from sheer exhaustion. I interfered but once and that was to stop an exquisite jest of Quentin's which consisted in procuring sulphurated hydrogen to be used on the other boys when they got into bed."

The story of the "White House Gang," so engagingly told by one of them, Earle Looker, is an immortal part of White House history: the fellowship, among the boys and with the watchful and wise First Lady; the adventures, in the basement, the garret, the elevator, the corridors, the garden, or the city streets; the genial camaraderie between the boys and the President, based on mutual understanding and happily lighted by the President's unfailing sense of humor.

There was the occasion when the boys were riding on the back seat of a trolley-car making faces at everybody who went by in carriages, and especially the bearded dignitaries. Up from the White House came the President's open carriage, with the President in the rear seat. The boys made their worst faces, and the President responded with incredible grimaces of his own. As the car halted in a tangle of traffic and the presidential carriage stood for a moment next the rear of the car, the President leaned forward and, in a voice clearly audible to everyone in the car, said "Quentin Roosevelt and you other little rascals, I think you have very nearly succeeded in making a fool of me in public. I had the idea of asking you to hop in, and ride the rest of the way with me. On second thought I have concluded that it is entirely too dangerous for me to be seen with you."

The colored coachman and footman lost their decorum and grinned as the carriage swept forward and away.

It was a priceless relationship.

Quentin became leader of the gang not at all because he was his father's son but because he had his father's qualities—the boldness, the initiative, the courage, the bubbling vitality—had them not imitatively but in his own individual forms. Quentin was original, as his father was original. He imitated nobody, he was himself; and, in his astonishing vitality, his ardor for living, gave the same breath-taking impression that his father gave of that unaccountable, unpredictable freshness of vision and response that men call genius.

Whether in Washington or at Sagamore, "active, alert, eager, bubbling over with ideas, strange words, humor and deeply seated sentiment"—as Looker saw him—the boy was full of surprises.

"Quentin is really too funny for anything," the President wrote Alice. "He got his legs fearfully sunburned the other day, and they blistered, became inflamed, and ever-faithful Mother had to hold a clinic on them. Eyeing his blistered and scarlet legs, he remarked, 'They look like a Turner sunset, don't they?' And then, after a pause, 'I won't be caught again this way! "quoth the raven, 'Never-more!' " ' I was not surprised at his quoting Poe, but I would like to know where the ten-year-old scamp picked up any knowledge of Turner's sunsets."

Quentin had a high regard for snakes which occasionally brought terror to those who thought of reptiles as enemies of humankind. From Sagamore, one summer's end, he brought a snake he had made a pet of, and, on his return to Washington, left it at his favorite haunt, Schmid's animal store, receiving, in return, the loan of a very friendly king-snake, some three or four feet long, and two small snakes. He bore them home to the White House, and rushed unannounced into the semi-circular presidential office to show his father his treasures.

The President was in conference with the Attorney General, and was mildly disconcerted to have three snakes literally dumped in his lap. The king-snake, though friendly with human beings, had other feelings toward its own kind and was resolutely trying to swallow one of the smaller reptiles. Since industrial mergers were not the topic of discussion, the effort was clearly irrelevant to the conference. "Hadn't you better go into the next room?" the President suggested. "Some congressmen are waiting there and the snakes might enliven their tedium."

Quentin was caught by the idea and departed, rushing up to the congressmen, "with the assurance," as the President wrote Archie, "that he would there find kindred spirits." The congressmen—among them the eminent "Pete" Hepburn, author of the highly controversial railroad rate bill—were politely interested, thinking the snakes were of wood, but recoiled actively when they discovered they were alive. The President, taking his Attorney General to the door, noted their dismay as the king-snake went up Quentin's sleeve; and set out to lend a hand. But the snake would not be dragged back against the natural flow of his scales. "The last I saw of Quentin, one congressman was gingerly helping him off with his jacket so as to let the snake crawl out of the upper end of the sleeve."

The press got hold of the story, and even the staid New York *Times* gave it a column.

The President never minded the interruptions in the day's work that the children provided. They were always reasonable in recognizing that brevity might be the essence of devotion, and he knew they came only because he was important to them in every aspect of their daily existence. He relished, moreover, the sunlight they brought into the day's work. The house seemed "big and lonely and full of echoes," as he wrote Quentin once, when he was alone in it, "and I do not hear any small scamps running up and down the hall just as hard as they can; or hear their voices while I am dressing; or suddenly look out through the windows of the office at the tennis ground and see them racing over it or playing in the sand box."

Whenever the children were away, or, if they were home, and he were away, speech-making or hunting, or both, he sent them what they called "picture-letters," recounting in text and drawing some adventure which he knew would appeal to them. It was an old habit of his, going back to the Spanish War days; and he would keep it up, sporadically, long after the children were grown.

Father and Mr. Burroughs galloping up on some elk — bulls and cows. The elk are tired and have begun to open their mouths and pant. You can tell Mr. Burroughs by the beard. There are a great many rocks on the ground. The pine tree is small and scraggly.

4

Archie, three years Quentin's senior, was less robust than the other children, looking "very delicate and frail," his mother wrote her sister-in-law, Anna Cowles. "I only keep myself from being very anxious by remembering what midget skeletons Ted and Kermit were at his age." Archie had, from the first, endeared himself to the ushers, policemen, tradespeople, politicians and statesmen who went in and out of the White House as he had already endeared himself to the Sagamore neighbors and the townspeople of Oyster Bay. The public had a particular affection for Archie. Throughout the early years of the Administration, before Quentin's emergence

256

from the nursery, the boy whom visitors from afar talked about when they went home was the towhead they had seen or heard of —hatless, even barefoot, occasionally, happily regardless of dirt, conventionalities or even life and limb—doing hair-raising stunts on his roller-skates or charging down the asphalt on his Shetland pony with his cowboy chaps tight on his legs and his cowboy hat flapping in the breeze. Whenever there was a new story of the Roosevelt children going the rounds it was generally Archie who was the hero of it. It was Archie who slid down the banisters at a state function, Archie who enticed Quentin into the White House fountain, after the Commissioner of Corporations, "Jim" Garfield, had recounted his own plunge in it, while his father was President. It was Archie again who gave Charles Wagner the answer that went from coast to coast when the apostle of the simple life asked him whether he slept with his hand open or shut, and he responded that he didn't know because he was asleep!

In the White House, as at Sagamore Hill, Archie was Tom Sawyer, he was Huckleberry Finn, he was the American boy incarnate. Baron Rosen, the Russian ambassador and Witte's fellow envoy to the Portsmouth peace conference, tells in his memoirs of his first glimpse of the Sagamore Hill family when he landed at the Waldeck dock and saw a son of the President of the United States, a fishing-pole in his hand, dangling his bare feet over the edge of the dock, totally unconcerned by the arrival of this foreign personage. That was Archie. When a few weeks later, the Japanese envoys—Baron Komura and the Japanese minister, Takahira— drove up from the "depot" in the President's surrey to make their initial call they were startled when two grimy and disheveled boys hailed the colored driver and climbed up beside him. That again was Archie, accompanied this time by his beloved cousin Nick. They had filled up on sodas at Snouder's, the day was hot and the way home was long. And why should two Oriental gentlemen in high hats keep Lee from giving them a hitch? Why, indeed? Lee agreed.

A month before he turned thirteen, Archie was taken seriously ill, and, as at the time of Ted's illness five years before, millions, in mansions and cottages, farm-houses, ranch-houses and dingy city flats, held their breath, as it were, and, if they were praying people, prayed for the light-hearted boy who, as one newspaperwoman put it, had "his father's genius for making and keeping friends."

257

"Poor little Archie has diphtheria," the President wrote Kermit, "and we have had a wearing time of it."

Washingtonians, passing the White House in the small hours and remembering how completely dark the building generally was after midnight, noted with a pang the light in an upper room where they knew the President and his wife were watching at Archie's bedside. "This dreadful time," Archie's mother wrote her sister Emily, "has been a terrible strain on Theodore."

At the end of ten days, the boy had what his father, in a letter to his cousin Emlen Roosevelt, called "a bad turn," and there were a few minutes when it seemed to the stricken parents "unlikely that he would pull through." But he did pull through by a hair, though for days the cloud of anxiety did not lift.

"A friend to everybody!" a woman wrote in the New York *Times*. "That is the reason why the yellow square of light from the White House window has had many anxious watchers in the night, and also why all Washington, on getting up these mornings, eagerly scans the newspaper with the query, 'How's Archie? Progressing favorably? Isn't that fine!' "

Archie had difficulties with his studies, but he could be counted on in emergencies. One day, during the recess, at school in Washington, a boy was hit square in the eye by a baseball. His frightened playmates stood around helpless, sneaking off when the principal appeared; but not Archie. He suggested that the boy be taken to his father's friend, the great Dr. Wilmer, the oculist, and, jumping on his bicycle, "scorched" to the doctor's office. Might he bring the boy at once? Of course, of course. So Archie "scorched" back, returning shortly after, leading the injured boy. "Dr. Wilmer told me about it," the President wrote Kermit proudly, "and said, if Archie had not acted with such promptness, the boy (who was four or five years older than Archie, by the way) would have lost his sight."

"Archie, in an emergency, has a good deal of wisdom in his funny little head," the President wrote Kermit a year and a half later. Sailing his dory in a heavy wind in the Sound, the boy saw a boat in trouble and was the first to reach it, keeping beside the sinking craft with a life preserver tied to a rope, ready to throw, in case the boat foundered before a rescuing launch could arrive.

Archie's dory, which he called the *Why,* looked, the President thought, "like a black wooden shoe with a sail on it," but Archie loved it and fairly lived on the water, taking as his crew one of the Sagamore hired men or a sailor from the *Sylph,* winning successive races and bringing home sundry cups. He delighted in anything connected with the water, the pet of the crews of the *Sylph,* the *Dolphin* and the *Mayflower,* and stumped all but two or three of the *Sylph*'s sailors when he dove from the deck, twenty-two feet, to the bottom of the Bay.

Archie's life on the water was shared by Skip, a mongrel who had attached himself to the President during his Colorado bear-hunt and, returning to Sagamore Hill with him, had adopted Archie as his lord and master, never letting him out of his sight. One day as the President was rowing into the harbor with Mrs. Roosevelt, they passed Archie in the *Why,* and the President wrote Kermit about its crew—"Archie, one of his beloved playmates, a seaman from the '*Sylph*', and Skip, very alert and knowing."

A day later came tragedy. Skip was run over by an automobile. "You can imagine Archie's grief," the President wrote Mrs. Lodge, "and, indeed, for the matter of that, the grief of the rest of us. So poor little black Skip was buried under the stone that bears the names of the dogs for which we have cared the most."

The next day Archie went to boarding-school for the first time, carrying with a stiff upper lip the double grief of separation from home and the death of his playmate. But he passed through his ordeal as his brothers had passed through theirs, aided by a copy of "The Lunatic at Large" which Kermit thoughtfully provided.

Chapter XIV

"*ETHEL IS* as good as gold with both little boys," the President wrote Kermit, when Archie was ten, Quentin seven, and Ethel thirteen, capable, motherly, and infinitely companionable both with her mother and father. Three years later, "sixteen now and wellgrown," as her father described her to Mrs. Lodge, she was having house-parties with Ted at Sagamore and going off very occasionally to other house-parties. But the "homing instinct" was strong, he noted, and Ethel generally came back earlier than she had planned. He chuckled over a letter she wrote her mother on one of her trips, complaining of "the old bores" who talked about her father's career until "she earnestly wished her father had never had a career."

With all her gaiety, her love of fun, Ethel, even at sixteen, had exceptional depth of feeling, sensitivity, and capacity for suffering, but, with it, an inner citadel of faith which gave her security. She was not beautiful, except for her eyes, which were deep and blue and alert, and were clouded when her emotions were momentarily stirred. Her figure was straight but not impressive; yet she made the sensitive observer, now and again, think of a caryatid.

She had long outgrown the tomboy, who had followed her brothers at a mad gallop through the woods, riding astride, her bloomers frequently bumpy with apples, falling off occasionally and climbing back, cheerful and unafraid. At fifteen she was as fearless a driver as she was a rider, prevented from driving a runaway horse home after an accident only because the carriage would no longer hold together. But the tomboy was in the past. Five years of hard work in the Cathedral School, with highly educational week ends in the White House, had made her an exceptionally cultivated young woman who knew her way among the arts, and consumed

260

books as her father and mother consumed them, but looked demure and altogether proper when she was seen in the theater or at symphony concerts. She was no bluestocking, remaining the independent, emphatic, capable person she had been at the age of five, and relishing as much as her father a game of hide-and-seek with the "White House gang," or a good roughhouse with anybody. But she was inclined to be serious-minded. Observers commented on her deepening intimacy with her mother, who guided her reading, taught her embroidery and, when she was sixteen or seventeen, put her in charge of the White House linen. At St. Mary's chapel for colored children, she taught the Bible, Sundays, teaching football also, in a vacant lot, Saturdays, umpiring the game, and afterward serving lunch from a White House hamper.

Ethel "came out," socially, at the end of her father's last full year as President. She was young to be introduced to society, being only seventeen, but the First Lady, who had given her step-daughter a brilliant debut at the White House, seven years before, was determined that her own daughter should have the same dazzling experience.

> "Wend you with the world tonight!
>   Brown and fair, and wise and witty—
> Eyes that float in seas of light,
>   Laughing mouths and dimples pretty,
> Belles and matrons, maids and madams
>   All are gone to Mrs. Adams."

So a poet of an earlier time had celebrated another presidential ball. From various cities, the young people came, flowing through the Red Room, the Blue Room and the East Room; the Marine Band played; and, as the Washington *Post* put it, "in the dignity of her first ball gown, simply fashioned of soft white satin, with a trimming of crystals," Ethel Roosevelt entered the social whirl in which Alice had preceded her.

2

Kermit, at Groton, had his ups-and-downs with his studies. "Not at all a showy little fellow," as his father described him, he was, like the other members of the family, an inveterate reader and was finding treasure-trove in the library of his house-master, a son of

261

that Laura E. Richards whose nonsense rhymes so delighted all the Roosevelts. Among the books that he unearthed was one by an obscure poet, whom the master had known in his home town of Gardiner, Maine, and no one else that Kermit could find had ever heard of. His name was Edwin Arlington Robinson, and the book was called "The Children of the Night." Its freshness and originality caught his imagination and he sent a copy to his father. The President was as impressed as Kermit, though he admitted that he wasn't at all sure that he knew what all the poems meant— no one ever would be altogether sure—but he recognized that "he has the real spirit of poetry in him." Kermit found that Robinson was working as time-keeper in the construction of the New York subway. That was no place for a poet, he told his father. Couldn't he do something about it? Couldn't he give Robinson a job in which he could make a living and still have time and the heart to write poetry?

The President had strict views about the civil service; but he saw the point. After all, other Presidents had helped American poets, and Kermit was insistent. A place was found for Robinson in the New York Custom House. "Tell it not in civil-service reform Gath," the President wrote a correspondent, "nor whisper it in the streets of merit-system Askelon." Under the proddings of his son, he went farther. He bludgeoned the Scribner firm in New York to take over the publication of the book, and he and Kermit collaborated in a review of it for the *Outlook,* finally published under the name of the President alone, to give it more carrying power. The review made a sensation in the American literary world. The President was patronized by the critics, derided, scolded, put in his place; but Robinson was talked about wherever poetry was written, published, read or criticized.

So Kermit, at fifteen, started a major American poet on his climb to fame.

3

Meanwhile, Ted and Kermit had been seeking adventures outside the world of books. Both had demonstrated their capacity to take care of themselves in the open on Long Island or in Maine, and their father and mother were glad to have them try their wings in more distant flights. In order that the boys might know something of the life that he himself had known and loved in his youth, the President sent, first one and then the other, each with a cousin, to his cherished friend, Seth Bullock, in Deadwood, South Dakota, for a taste of the hardy life of the plains and the mountains, camping under Western stars, following a round-up, "feeding" at a chuckwagon, riding herd at night. The President hoped, he wrote Bullock that, in the preliminary stages of the trip, the boys would be treated like any two boys who go off on a spree, "just as if I was not President." As soon as they were among the cowboys, he knew, there would be no danger of anyone treating them "as if there were such a being as a president in existence."

Bullock, tall and rangy, a Westerner out of the story-books, was himself an experience for the boys which any boy might have envied them. He had been marshal in the Black Hills in their wild frontier days, and had numerous notches on his gun, but in his social contacts he was the gentlest of men. Direct, daring, cool, rich in humor and drawling in speech, he seemed, to the President, Owen Wister's Virginian to the life. The engaging plainsman gave Ted and Kermit a priceless interpretation of the "idyl" of their father's youth and a fresh link to their father that was all the closer because of what the honest, warm-hearted frontiersman wrote the President of their sportsmanship, their hardihood and their courage.

Ted entered Harvard the autumn after his father ended the Russo-Japanese War, the President watching him go with the feelings that a bear might have, seeing his cub disappear into the depths of the forest. Ever since the boys had been tots, hardly able to walk, he had, in fact, been the Big Bear to them, and they the Little Bears. So it was natural that the letter that he wrote Ted, even before the term had got under way, should begin, "How is the little bear getting on with his troubles?"

The troubles came mainly from reporters and photographers from the Boston newspapers, who waylaid him on his way to lectures, outside his lodgings or on the football field; doing their best to set him apart from his classmates in vicarious notoriety. Those who thought him a snob as he crossed the Yard on the way to his lectures, intent, looking not to right or left, did not guess with what care a President's gay-hearted son had to go about the supposedly care-free business of being an undergraduate. Was there nothing that could be done about it? the President asked the president of Harvard, the stately Dr. Eliot, in a letter revealing a mood approaching desperation. The reporters were on the way to ruining Ted's chances of a happy and profitable college life. To Ted himself the agitated father admitted that this was "just one of the occasions when the big bear cannot help the small bear at all." The only thing for Ted to do was to go on as he was going, attracting as little attention as possible and making no fuss about the newspapermen, "camera creatures, and idiots generally." They would soon drop him. Meanwhile, it was a great comfort to know that "though these creatures can cause you a little trouble and make you feel downcast, they cannot drive you one way or the other, or make you alter the course you have set out for yourself." A characteristic hint.

Ted, in fact, kept his head and his temper, "very modest, very manly," observers thought, and going his way, regardless. He "made" the Freshman football team, and could generally be discovered where the play was hottest, running with the ball, or prone, "with half the team criss-cross above him," always good-tempered and working "like a demon" for victory, "a chip of the old block, a slice of the old fruitcake," as the New York *World* correspondent called him. He played in the game against the Yale Freshmen and won his numerals, together with a broken nose. There was a rumor current in the press that the Yale team had deliberately "ganged up" on him. That was "a lie," Ted wrote his father. "They played a clean, straight game and played no favorites. They beat us by simply and plainly out-playing us."

Ted overcame the handicap of being the President's son, doing so well socially and in athletics that he began to throw his chest out, reminding the President of his own cockiness after his first success in the New York Assembly. During one of his absences from the White House, the amused father wrote Ethel, asking whether "the lordly Ted" had turned up and whether "his loving sister" were able, unassisted, "to reduce the size of his head, or does she need any assistance from her male parent?"

Life itself shortly deflated Ted, with the aid of the Harvard College dean. Having worked with admirable concentration and persistence to get into college, Ted had been inclined to relax, after he got there, so far as his studies were concerned. His father worried over the "gentleman's grades" he received—C or worse—and was fairly appalled when 38 lecture-cuts in ten weeks brought probation. The President's long minatory letter ended characteristically: "Good luck, old boy! You'll come out all right. I know you have the stuff in you and I trust you entirely. Anyone might come a cropper like this; now get up and retrieve it."

Ted, humbled and resolved, did so vigorous a job at "retrieving" that his father was shortly writing him not to overdo it.

4

The autumn that Ted entered Harvard, Alice was riding high, half a world away. She had joined a party, headed by the Secretary of War, William Howard Taft, and including a commission of forty-odd senators and representatives, and their wives, to visit the Philippines and other points East. The press was agog. The Ohio congressman, Nicholas Longworth, with whom Alice's name had been romantically linked in Washington, was in the party. Longworth, a Harvard graduate and a member of Harvard's most exclusive club, the Porcellian (of which the President, too, was a member)—and incidentally one of the best amateur violinists in the country—belonged to one of Ohio's "best families," linked by marriage to the Lafayette family in France. Did the presence of this eligible bachelor in the Taft junket mean an engagement, the press asked hopefully?

The spell which Alice exercised on the imagination of the public was undiminished. A sob-sister, writing about her in the San Francisco *Call* on the eve of her sailing, pulled out all the stops, describing her "mobile face . . . the frank, fearless eyes, the firm, round chin, the full lines of the mouth, the saucy little nose . . ." the "slender, supple, lissome figure expressing youth and life in every line." With what "talent" she wore her clothes! How she managed to get "just the right swing to her skirts, the right "set" to her bodice, the right tilt to her hat! How the crowds gathered, how they stared, and how they queued up to be introduced!

"You must be tired to death shaking hands with so many people!" exclaimed a pretty girl at her side at one of the San Francisco receptions.

Alice seemed less to smile, as she replied, than to radiate. "Tired?" she cried. "Why, I could throw my arms around their necks and kiss them! Everyone has been so *nice* to me!"

It was this inherited quality of ebullient warmth that kept her the darling of the public and muted the jibes of the envious and even the criticism of her well-wishers, who noted an independence of spirit that had charm but could be ruthless, a wit that sent quips flying from mouth to mouth but could give pain, and a daring that occasionally set teeth on edge not only in the White House or on Sagamore Hill.

Before she even reached the Philippines, Alice made news that literally went around the world. On the forward deck of the *Manchuria,* just below the bridge, a large canvas bathing tank had been set up. One hot morning, Alice, attractively attired in a linen skirt and shirtwaist, was standing at the rail of the deck above the pool with Bourke Cockran, one of the congressmen in the party, and an old family friend. "That water looks so refreshing," Cockran remarked. "I'm tempted to go in, just as I am."

"Come along," cried Alice. Kicking off her shoes, she handed her watch to a bystander and jumped. The congressman followed. The Secretary of War, who had a way of laughing all over when he laughed, agreed with the rest of his party in regarding the episode as a harmless joke on Cockran and a typical Alice Roosevelt prank; but, at the *Manchuria*'s next port the press clutched the story to its bosom, sending it out on all the cables available, and added another shock to the Alice Roosevelt saga.

Alice was in the news a good deal during the months that followed. The party made its first stop in Japan, where the government exhausted its resources of courtesy to show honor to the daughter of the President who, that week, was receiving Baron Komura and Minister Takahira at Sagamore Hill and, the week following, would introduce them to their Russian opponents. One of the smaller royal palaces, the Shiba Rikyu, was placed at Miss Roosevelt's disposal by the Japanese government, but the handsome young American minister, Lloyd C. Griscom, demurred. The Secretary of War would, of course, be glad to dwell under the royal roof and it was fitting that he should. But Alice? Royal honors for the President's daughter would not sit well with the American public. Alice would stay at the American Legation.

The *Manchuria* steamed into Yokohama harbor to the popping of fireworks and the fluttering of American and Japanese flags. The journey to Tokio was a triumph. The locomotive of the train was draped with bunting and, as it passed, peasants in the fields lifted their arms in salute, shouting *banzais.* The Japanese were convinced that Alice was the Princess Royal of America and, as the carriage in which she was riding passed through the Tokio streets, the men shouted *Bei-ko-ku-banzai*—"America for a thousand years!"—while the women bowed from the waist again and again.

Alice clutched Griscom's arm. He was an old friend. "Lloyd, I love it!" she exclaimed. "I love it!"

Griscom, writing his memoirs, thirty years later, recalled how Alice, standing beside him at one of the festivities given for the Taft party, had tapped him on the shoulder.

"Do you see that old, bald-headed man scratching his ear over there?"

"Do you mean Nick Longworth?" Longworth was actually thirty-six, and fifteen years her senior.

"Yes. Can you imagine any young girl marrying a fellow like that?"

"Why, Alice, you couldn't find anybody nicer."

For once Alice seemed a little lost. "I know, I know," she said. "But this is a question of marriage."

The Secretary of War had a fatherly concern for the state of her heart. "Alice, I think I ought to know if you are engaged to Nick," he had a way of saying at intervals, a little plaintively.

Her reply was always the same and always elusive. "More-or-less, Mr. Secretary, more-or-less." And that was all the satisfaction he got.

According to the American press, Longworth's was not the only proposal Alice achieved on that memorable journey. The Sultan of Sulu, Hadji Mohammed Kiram of Jolo, a four-foot, very dusky Moslem chieftain whom the American humorist, George Ade, had already immortalized in the text of a comic opera, welcomed the Taft party with pomp and ceremony on their inspection of the Moro Province and, as a climax to the festivities—so the story ran— invited the "American princess" to join his harem as wife number seven.

The story was pure fiction, but the newspapers had a high time with "the proffer of the hand (or part of the hand) of His Imperial Highness." Alice would do well not to reject the proffer too lightly, thought the editor of the New York *Press*. "Here she has only meta-phorical slaves; there a whole regiment of the real article would be at her feet," and, at least for a few years, she would be the "jewel of one of the nicest little harems in the far Pacific." "Lots of nice little Sulu girls," thought the Des Moines *Register and Leader*, "would jump at the chance." But American girls were choosy.

"Probably, with the perverseness and the independence of her American sisters, she will promise her little brown brother, the Sultan, to be a sister to him."

Oriental potentates, male and female, gave Alice such a whirl as no American girl had ever received in the Far East. The Empress Dowager of China, Tz'u Hsi, an exceptionally able and sinister old lady, frequently bracketed by historians with Catherine II of Russia and Elizabeth I of England and notoriously hostile to foreigners, invited her and two other women of the Taft party for the night to the summer palace at Peking. Alice never forgot the "small, brilliant, black eyes, alert and piercing," that the Empress fixed on her, as she approached the throne with successive curtsies, or the "cruel, thin mouth, turned up at one corner, drooping a little at the other." There was an emperor, a man in his middle thirties, who sat, limp and huddled, on the lowest step of the throne, looking about with vacant eyes; but he clearly did not count, and she was not presented to him.

It was this dismal young man who ought to marry Alice, an American reporter suggested, in the hope that "under the vitalizing inspiration of her American genius and energy," he might awaken from "the humiliating stupor of his manhood's years and retire his managerial mother to a nunnery, or the bowstring, as the case may require." The old Dowager might twist all of China's great men under her thumb, but "she has never yet met the irresistible onslaught of an American girl!"

The soul-sister to the Borgias, however, was holding her own very well, that morning in the Summer Palace. After the formal presentation she moved among her guests as casually as any Occidental hostess, chatting with them through an interpreter. As she was speaking with Alice, however, she revealed her ingrained mediaevalism in a fashion that would have made any other American girl's blood run cold, but merely made Alice's tingle with the delight of a new experience. The interpreter was the Chinese minister in Washington, Wu T'ing-fang, a brilliant and popular figure in the diplomatic corps, whom Alice had met at countless dinners in the White House and elsewhere. As he was translating the perfunctory inquiries of the Empress about the health of the President and whether she were enjoying her visit, the old lady, Alice recalled twenty years later, uttered an "aside" in a small, savage voice. The distinguished diplomat turned suddenly gray, dropped on his hands and knees and bowed his head to the ground. "The Empress would speak"; Alice wrote in her memoirs: "he would lift his head and say it in English to me; back would go his forehead to the ground while I spoke; up would come his head again while he said it in Chinese to the Empress; then back to the ground would go his forehead again."

Alice never knew why the Empress had chosen so to humiliate one of her ablest public servants. When she got home to Sagamore Hill she asked her father if he could interpret the dreadful scene. "It may have been intended to convey to you—and to me," the President answered, "that this man, whom we accept as an equal, is to her no more than something to put her foot on, and that none of us amount to much more than that in her opinion."

Alice saw the episode's proper setting that afternoon when she was being carried in a chair, tasseled and cushioned, through the palace gardens, accompanied by chattering court officials, past ponds and pavilions and yellow- and green-tiled roofs of palaces and temples showing brightly among the trees. Her eight bearers were swifter on their feet than the members of the party not in chairs and, for brief periods, she was the only Occidental amid the ancient splendor, the exotic, irresistible beauty. She was Marco Polo, back in the thirteenth century. "It was fantastic, incredible Cathay of the old tales." No wonder, that night, she got drunk on rose wine, reaching her bedroom, without revealing her condition, only by the closest attention to that straight line which, in the East as in the West, is still the shortest distance between two points.

At Seoul, capital of Korea, Alice made a triumphal progress from the railroad station to the American Legation, through masses of Korean and hastily hand-painted American flags, riding in an imperial yellow chair (hitherto used only by royalty) and heralded by trumpeters. The Korean, like the Japanese and Chinese sovereigns, loaded her with presents she could not in courtesy refuse, and, in fact, never dreamed of refusing. "I was filled with greedy delight at getting them, a frankly unashamed pig," she wrote. "I did so love my 'loot,' as it was called by the family."

The American press looked upon the reception accorded the delightful, unpredictable Alice not only by the rulers but by the statesmen and peoples of the Far East, as a tribute to the American girl, as such, took pride in it, and turned its fancy loose on the details. But the thoughtful here and there found themselves wondering whether the restless young lady, in love with life as she was, were not assuming an importance that was out of keeping with the Constitution? Democrats, who were seeing imperial specters in every White House closet, saw their worst fears confirmed.

The New York *World*, which did not love Alice's father, made much of a report from Rome that the Vatican had actually held up the Pope's congratulatory message to the President on the happy ending of the Russo-Japanese peace conference, pending an investigation of reports from Manila that Alice had "made too much" of a personal call by a certain Filipino archbishop who was at outs with the Church.

European observers, indeed, were inclined to take Alice's junket more seriously than Americans took it, assuming that it represented some new American implement of diplomacy. The Paris correspondent of the *Mattino* of Naples purported to reflect French opinion of the "quasi-imperial journey" of the American President's daughter. After all, who was this girl that she should be received with royal honors in the Oriental capitals and should give the impression that she represented the American people? "Even among the oldest and most glorious royal families of Europe no female member would assume to go to a foreign country and speak in the name of the people." How did it happen that "an American young lady who will tomorrow become a simple bourgeoise, is allowed to assume an attitude which is never taken even by the descendants of great kings?" There is no evidence that Alice ever did "assume" such an attitude; but there were clearly those who thought she had assumed it. The writer concluded that it was all a part of the glorification of the American girl, to use the phrase a later beauty-specialist would exploit, and the tendency of "every reception-room queen" in America to regard herself "a sovereign."

The London *Chronicle* quoted "one of the ablest writers in the French press" as observing that this "heiress presumptive of the United States crown," had reduced the American Secretary of War to a "subaltern." Did Mr. Roosevelt, "whose fondness for instructing his countrymen is as great as the Kaiser's, offer the royal progress of this dangerous young woman (why, at one place, she was actually presented with a gold cup!) as an example to the *jeunes filles* of France?" Let the French people take care "to elect no President who has a daughter!"

The lively and engaging object of all this sardonic comment

270

knew nothing of it and would not have given it a second thought if she had. The world—its Eastern Hemisphere, at least—was at her feet; golden trinkets and precious stones were raining into her lap; she was experiencing the splendor, the beauty and a little of the terror of the Orient from inside its mysterious palaces; she was in love, and her lover was with her, seeing her triumph. What American girl before her had ever sat enthroned in such a dazzling quadrilateral of bliss?

Alice and "Nick" Longworth were married in the White House the following February. The event created enormous excitement in the public and the press from the first rumors of the engagement to the young couple's departure on their honeymoon. There had been no presidential daughter marrying in the White House since Nellie Grant's wedding to Algernon Sartoris, thirty-two years before, and this time it was no other than "Princess" Alice! Every move that Alice made was recorded in the press, and for once, even the husband-elect was considered important. The "national bride-groom," as the Washington *Times* dubbed him, was in fact given the Speaker's chair for a minute, the day before the wedding, in the presence of a cheering House. The reports of the gifts that poured in from emperors, kings, presidents and parliaments—"fantastically exaggerated," Alice wrote in her memoirs—thrilled the public, which pored over the accounts of the colorful, even dazzling, ceremony in the East Room like a kitchen-maid over a penny-thriller. Alice lived up to her reputation to the last, claiming the sword of one of the President's aides to cut the wedding-cake; and herself reported later her stepmother's exclamation of relief, as Alice changed to her beige-colored "going-away dress" and, with her husband, slipped out of a side door of the White House.

Chapter XV

TIME IS SWIFTER in its flight in the White House than in other houses; and it was swifter at Sagamore than in the neighboring habitations on Cove Neck. The year that saw the President of the United States achieve a position among the chiefs of governments of the world that none of his predecessors had attained, and saw the nation he represented accepted among world powers as second to none, was buried under the snows that covered the silent house and the woods and meadows round about. The young year that rose from the old year's grave had on its lips a question which the man questioned had sincerely believed would never thrust itself across his quiet assurance of what was proper and right: "Theodore Roosevelt, will you give up the power you have won? Will you keep the word you gave on Election night after such a triumph as no American President had ever known, your word not to be a candidate to succeed yourself?" The answer which had seemed easy in 1905 was not so easy in 1906. "Will you, can you, keep that word?" He answered first with quiet certitude, then with emphasis; finally, with vehemence, as 1906 gave way to 1907, and his own doubts deepened. "Can you, will you, *dare* you? Issues are involved, bigger than you, Theodore Roosevelt, your philosophy of government, even your word, however solemnly given. You have remolded a great party, serving industrial and financial power, into a party serving the interests of all Americans. Can you trust your successor to maintain it in the new course? Think well, Theodore Roosevelt."

The First Lady was convinced that he should never in the first place have given his word on the matter of a re-election. If she had known that he was thinking of giving it, she told Owen Wister, she would never have suffered it, though for herself she wanted nothing so much as a return to private life and an end to the perpetual dread of assassination. There were moments, no doubt, when the President himself regretted his declaration of self-abnegation. But he would have undergone the same inner struggle in the later years of his second term, if no words of his had stood between him and his continuance in office. He had a definite philosophy of the Presidency: It was good for the nation that it should be an office of great power, but there must be a safeguard against abuse of the power. The best safeguard he knew was the recognition, in the heart of the people, established as a sacred tradition, that no man should hold the executive power for more than two successive terms.

The pressure on him to run again in 1908 began early in his second term. It was a pressure not from office-holders or high-ranking officials, whom self-interest might motivate. It came from the grass-roots, from little people in little towns who saw a President in Washington who was doing the things they had hoped for decades to see done, a President who thought about the little fellow and was doing what he could to give him a square deal, a President who wasn't afraid of the tough capitalist or the tough labor leader, but was trying to be fair to all, putting the big fellows in their place and keeping their hands off the rudder; a President who talked turkey to emperors and kings and made them respect his country and accept it as one of the great world powers. Now that they had that kind of President, the people were saying, why couldn't they keep him? He was doing a good job, and he was having a good time doing it. Why shouldn't he go right on for another term? Why should he himself insist on giving it up? It didn't make sense.

There was something, the President recognized, in what they were saying. He was, as he wrote his friend, John C. Rose, United States attorney for the Baltimore district, moving toward "a revolution in the relations of the Government to the big corporate interests of the country." The only "safe and proper" way of doing it, he was sure, was "by the aid of the moderate people." Was it right then to leave the field to the Bryans, the Hearsts and the La Follettes, appealing to the radicals and splitting both parties down the middle?

The more successful the President proved, the stronger became the pressure on him to accept a renomination. Men who were doing important and constructive work, and whose effectiveness depended to a great degree on the public recognition that they had the President's backing—sitting in the library with him at Sagamore Hill or striding across the fields—expressed their uneasiness and chagrin at his decision to relinquish power. Why, just as they were getting things in hand, moving to a point where real and permanent achievement was possible, should they lose their leader, not through the tragedy of defeat or death, but needlessly, by his own quixotic choice?

The President admitted to these faithful lieutenants that their arguments made him "acutely uncomfortable." He hated "for personal reasons," he wrote a British friend, to "get out of the fight" and he wasn't at all sure he wasn't shirking a duty. And yet. . . . there was the precedent set by Washington, and it was a good precedent. "I believe in power," he added. "But I believe that responsibility should go with power, and that it is not well that the strong executive should be a perpetual executive."

He did not convince his friends or, perhaps, wholly himself. The cheers of his political enemies at his announcement that he would hold to his determination gave him some bad moments. If his foes wanted him so much to go, there must be more weight in the arguments for his staying than he had imagined. The pressure on him from the outside was supported by pressure from within his own heart and mind. He had no illusions about being indispensable. There were plenty of able men who, he was sure, could effectively carry on his domestic policies—"*my* policies," as he had a way of calling them. But he could have no such assurance about foreign affairs. Who was there, he might have asked himself, who had the knowledge and experience that he had acquired to deal with the international complications boiling up on the horizon—the menace of Japan, the possibilities of disaster in Europe? He had intervened by diplomacy twice, effectively, to keep the European powers from each others' throats—once, at the outbreak of the Russo-Japanese War when France and Britain were preparing to take sides and a world war was an immediate possibility; and, again, in the struggle between France and Germany over the "open door" in Morocco.

He knew something about the subterranean currents in Europe—the political and dynastic intrigues, ambitions, stratagems; not enough, for they were unbelievably devious, but more, certainly, than any other American; and he had enjoyed considerable instruction in the Japanese mentality. Did he have the right to withdraw from the American people the knowledge he had acquired in their service, the skills he had developed, the prestige he had won? The European governments knew him, knew he was no intriguer and no plunger, knew that, in Western terms, he would not draw unless he meant to shoot, but would be ready to draw if he had to; knew that, with all his persistence in building up the navy, he was a man of peace, and that the most dangerous man in Europe, because the most unstable and backed by the biggest battalions, the German Emperor, was his, the President's, admiring, almost fulsome, devotee.

Had he, Theodore Roosevelt, the right to disregard all that as though it were of no account?

2

The President, bringing his horse down to a walk in the dappled sun-and-shadow of the Long Island woods, thought about another term. Were the people who were pressing him to run again possibly right? Was he abandoning great work on a fantastic point of honor, evading a great duty, a great opportunity? Like that mediaeval pope whom Dante consigned to hell because he had slipped from under the prospect of a heavy responsibility, was he making "the great refusal?" The thought gave him "ugly qualms," he admitted. There was something to be said—a great deal, perhaps—for the theory that the public had a right to demand as long service as it thought useful from any man who was doing a good job.

Yet . . . he had given his word. Whatever service he might yet render the American people depended on their continued trust in his sincerity and disinterestedness. He was convinced, as he wrote his friend, the British historian, George Otto Trevelyan, that "a great many honest people in this country who lead hard lives are helped in their efforts to keep straight, and to avoid envy and hatred and despair, by their faith in me and in the principles I preach, and in my practice of those principles. I would not for anything do the moral damage to those people that might come from shattering their faith in my personal disinterestedness." Yet, by not permitting himself to be renominated, was he possibly leaving these very people in the lurch?

A cartoonist suggested that the people most conscious of being left in the lurch were certain citizens of Oyster Bay.

A friend who visited the President in the White House got the impression that he had been "tempted almost to the point of yielding." But he had asked himself, "What is right in this matter?" and acted accordingly.

The visitor over-simplified the situation. The President's real trouble was not the choice between right and wrong, but the effort to see what was right.

He was not given to brooding, but he brooded a good deal—though he would never have called it that—over this business of another term. He recognized that it was a moral issue; he liked moral issues, and could, as a rule, deal with them. But he liked them black and white and could generally make them appear black and white, at least to himself. But this one stayed gray for all that he could do; and it tormented him. For the issue boiled down to this: the public will and (perhaps) his duty, against his given word and his philosophy of presidential power. What alternatives to put up to a man who wanted to be honest with himself and his countrymen! He would be wrong, whichever way he acted. It was small comfort to know that, whatever road he finally took, he would also be right.

3

Possibly, the issue went even deeper than the President's capacity to choose between right and wrong. Other men, facing that choice, have chosen what the strictest moralist would have admitted to be right, and brought confusion on themselves and others. Perhaps the ultimate quality in statesmanship, as in personal life, is the capacity to recognize the point at which reason and conviction must pause and let another force take over: the unaccountable perceptiveness, perhaps, of the subconscious, or the Intelligence which the wisest of men have recognized and only "the fool in his heart" denies; or perhaps Intelligence speaking through the subconscious. To the President, God was a clear reality, but there were moments when, like the sorcerer's apprentice, he thought that he could go it alone.

4

The President's inner debate might shake, but did not change, his initial resolution. It brought him the recognition, however, that, if he expected to maintain his decision, he would have to take aggressive action. The old political maxim that "you can't lick somebody with nobody," held good, he realized, in his own case. He must have a candidate himself, and fight for him. He looked over the field, dangled the prize before Root, who refused it; before Hughes, who was so proud of his independence that he would not reach for the nomination because it was the President who offered it; played—not too seriously—with the thought of Cannon—"You, Mr. Speaker, will be the next President"—and finally picked Taft as the most likely to win the nomination and the election, and, if elected, to carry on his policies.

The announcement of his choice did not stop the movement to renominate the President himself. To settle the issue once for all, he gave the press again the text of his 1904 renunciation and forbade government employees working for his nomination. But the new evidence that the President had meant what he had said, four years before, merely sharpened the protests of his friends and the innuendoes of his enemies, neither the devotees nor the doubters dreaming with what deliberate certitude the President was making his plans for the following year, not for Washington but for Africa. In order that there might be no last-minute swing in his behalf, the President arranged to have Lodge made permanent chairman of the Republican National Convention, and gave him a definitive letter of renunciation to produce if he had to.

Taft was nominated on the first ballot.

The President, supposed by his enemies to be biting his nails, listening for the first rumble of a stampede in his favor, noted in a letter to Kermit that he thought that the spring that year in Washington had been lovelier than any others he had known. "The iris flowers have, curiously enough, flowered again around the north fountain, and now the lindens are heavy with fragrance. . . . A yellow-throated vireo is nesting and singing finely, in the grounds; and I wish you could see our cardinal bird, which is also nesting, and singing among the white blossoms of the catalpa; he glows like a live coal." "I do not believe anyone else has ever enjoyed the White House as we have enjoyed it," the President wrote Lodge, the day the convention adjourned, "and now we are ready to leave it without a pang, with plenty of pleasure and interest ahead of us."

Not so, his youngest son. "That cheerful small pagan, Quentin," the President wrote Kermit, "remarked thoughtfully today, 'There is a little hole in my stomach when I think of leaving the White House.'"

There was, for all the President might say, no doubt, "a little hole" in the "stomach" of every member of the Sagamore Hill family.

5

"When I am through with a thing I am through with it," the President wrote Mrs. Cowles, from Sagamore Hill, shortly after, "and so long as I have power to work I want to turn, heart and soul, to the next bit of work to be done."

He plunged into plans for his African hunting-trip, invited to Sagamore Hill anyone he could find who had ever hunted in Africa, consulted scientists and an expert on hunting-rifles. He was, in fact, looking forward to his hunt like a school-boy to the summer holidays. He was taking Kermit with him. Ted's friends were urging him to go too. Why not? He had graduated from Harvard and was a free man. Ted hooted at the idea. He was taking a job in a carpet-factory. Besides, there was Eleanor Alexander. He wasn't taking any chances of losing Eleanor if there was any possibility of winning her. Eleanor was a very exceptional young lady, a flower with a brain, a beauty with a backbone. It was different with Kermit, who was heart- and fancy-free. Africa, his father knew, would be a glorious experience for Kermit. Might it, possibly, be too glorious, unsettling him, unfitting him for the routine of college and later of business? It was a gamble, he recognized, but, knowing Kermit as he did, he was willing to take it.

Meanwhile, it was good to be back at Sagamore. Two or three years earlier, one day in Washington, the President and Mrs. Roosevelt had said to each other how much they had enjoyed the White House; yet they had agreed that, year by year, they would find it not harder but easier to leave. "Sagamore is our own home," the President had written Kermit. "It is Sagamore that we love; and while we enjoy to the full the White House, and appreciate immensely what a privilege it is to be here, we shall have no regrets when we leave."

To be under his own roof-tree, surrounded by his own things; to live the life of a gentleman of moderate means and quiet, literary tastes; to be free to do as he pleased; to write, to read, to travel, to see his friends; to fight for some public cause worth fighting for when that cause might need his help . . . that was the President's dream.

It was a good dream, he thought, but there was something wrong with it; or with himself. He felt deflated. He enjoyed power, and it was passing from him, or, if not yet the power, the prestige. He was still President and still head of the Party, but it was Taft whom the state and congressional leaders were consulting. That was natural, of course; that was inevitable; that was right. But it had a discomforting *Sic transit gloria mundi* flavor which made him feel a little hollow inside.

A friend, staying overnight at Sagamore Hill, noted (for the first time in his experience) that the President seemed tired. "Well, I'm through now," he said several times. "I've done my work."

His friend wasn't so sure. "You may think you are through," he said, "but the people may not think so. Four years hence they may be clamoring for you even more insistently than today."

"No," the President said with what seemed to his friend a curious finality, a note of sadness which he had never heard him strike. "Revolutions don't go backwards. New issues are coming up. People are going to discuss economic questions more and more; the tariff, currency, banks. They are hard questions and I am not deeply interested in them. My problems are moral problems, and my teaching has been plain morality."

279

His friend was conscious of a "humanness" he had never noted, in that degree, even in this very human man; a breadth, a bigness, he had not recognized. Surely this was an extraordinary character, this man with his curious flashes of genius in which he saw himself truly, more truly than anyone else saw him; perhaps the greatest man of his time.

The President talked of Africa, the need of getting out of Taft's way, the prospect of getting close to Kermit and seeing "east of Suez" through a boy's eyes. "We'll have a great time!" But for all the President's assurance, his visitor noted, there was still that sadness in his voice, that sense of great days ended.

The Roosevelts returned to the White House late in September; returned for the last time. The townspeople in Oyster Bay were sharing the President's feeling of sadness, not wholly for selfish reasons. They had had seven great years together—he and they— what years!—packed with color and noise; with banners and bands and election campaigns, receptions, speeches and fireworks, actual and metaphorical; with battleships and the thunder of guns saluting; with ambassadors making peace, and politicians making politics; with Secret Service men and sob-sisters and submarines, and reporters like deer-hunters on the first day of the season. They had been great years not only for the President; they had been great years for them, too, his neighbors and fellow-townsmen; years they would never forget and their children would never forget. And now they were over. You couldn't help being a little sad; and when you heard that the President was leaving Oyster Bay to return to Washington you just naturally went to the station and sang with the others, "God be with you till we meet again." And it wasn't only in the President's eyes that there were tears.

6

The President was back at Sagamore Hill on the evening of March 4th. "Good Ethel had the house as comfortable as possible for us," he wrote Mrs. Cowles, "and really it is a lovely house. I am dictating this in the North Room with the big logs blazing on the hearth. So lovely it is that I am utterly unable to miss the White House. . . ."

Three weeks later, he sailed with Kermit for Africa.

The scene at the Hoboken pier had the quality of an election campaign. Archie Butt, bringing greetings and farewells from President Taft, noted that people seemed "more frenzied" in their anxiety to get a glimpse of Roosevelt than ever before, literally fighting their way to the steamer's side, though they knew there was no chance of seeing him.

Edith Roosevelt was not in the crowd. She did not like this African adventure. Africa, in the closing year of the Roosevelt administration, was still the "dark continent" where unimaginable dangers were supposed to lurk, and, in fact, did lurk, beyond the circle of any camp-fire's light. Besides, Theodore was fifty; too old, she thought, for the exertion of big-game hunting. She was not one, however, to protest against a project on which her husband's mind and will were fixed, or to cast a shadow on his anticipation by revealing her own dread.

Archie Butt, running into Kermit on the deck, asked him how his mother was bearing up.

"She was perfectly calm and self-possessed when we left home," Kermit answered, "but I had the feeling that her heart was broken."

She spent the day walking in the woods with Alice and Ethel and the younger boys, trying with them to follow in imagination the minute-by-minute doings of the hunters, as they set out on their journey. "It was a dreadful day," she admitted to Butt when he called at Sagamore Hill to pay his respects, four or five months later. "I have never known but one like it; that day when Archie's fate was in doubt and we didn't know if he would live or not." But neither she nor the children were the sort to let apprehension possess them. "We all crawled into bed about eight that night," she went on—and there was no need for her to tell the story of the night watches—"and, since then," she added characteristically, "we have been very happy and content."

7

A cartoonist pictured the Oyster Bay railroad station, after the ex-President's departure, with a sign upon it, "Trains every other Friday," four bearded ancients asleep on the platform, and grass growing between the rails.

There was no question about the quiet that settled over Oyster Bay, and over Sagamore Hill. Mrs. Roosevelt and Ethel went to Europe together to let new sights and sounds make the months a

little quicker in their passing and help them forget the dangers from wild beasts and jungle fever that the husband and father, the son and brother, might at any moment be encountering. The letters that came at long intervals brought satisfying news. The two hunters were in perfect health, and having a "bully time," Kermit, growing into manhood, the admiration of the other hunters in the party, the idol of the native gun-bearers, "as hardy as a moose," the proud father wrote the Lodges, able to "outrun, when after a wounded beast, or outlast, in a day's or week's tramp, any man, black or white, in the outfit." The timid boy of four years before, he wrote Ted, had turned out "cool and daring." Indeed, he was "a little too reckless and keeps my heart in my throat, for I worry about him all the time."

At last, the long, long winter was over and Edith Roosevelt and her daughter were again on a steamer sailing eastward, a long way eastward, to Egypt; and then they were on the Egyptian state railway speeding southward along the Nile through Luxor, through Assuan, through Wadi Halfa to the Sudan. On the dock at Khartoum they watched with beating hearts the river-steamer coming from the depths of Africa bearing the ex-President and his party. . . .

Two months later—rich months, with emperors and kings, presidents and cheering thousands—there was another steamer that had the ex-President on board, and with him Mrs. Roosevelt and Ethel and Kermit, who had made the royal rounds with him, and Alice who had joined the family in London. The steamer—a huge ocean-liner this time, the *Kaiserin Auguste Viktoria*—hung with flags from stem to stern, was entering New York harbor.

Not New York only, all America seemed to stand waiting for it. Fort Wadsworth, at the Narrows, hailed the returning traveler with a twenty-one-gun salute, generally reserved only for Presidents in office. The battleship *South Carolina* and a flotilla of destroyers, yachts and harbor-craft escorted his ship up the harbor. Every vessel on either shore, from ocean-liners to ferryboats and tugs, opened its whistles, and blew. A revenue-cutter, the *Manhattan*, drew alongside the liner. On the deck were Archie and Quentin, Ted and the vivacious and altogether charming young lady he was to marry two days later.

Mrs. Roosevelt glowed and appeared ready to jump on to the deck of the smaller craft. "Think!" she exclaimed to Archie Butt, who had again come as President Taft's emissary. "For the first time in two years I have them all within reach!" She ran to the cabin where the ex-President was talking to Loeb, now collector of the Port of New York, and to Lodge and Nick Longworth, who had come aboard at quarantine. "Come here, Theodore, and see your children," she called. "They are of far greater importance than politics or anything else."

He agreed. A roar came from the shore as he descended the gangway to the *Manhattan*, a roar that lasted five minutes. There was a happy family reunion and then a shift to another cutter, the *Androscoggin*, on which the reception committee was waiting to escort the returning hero to shore. As the cutter approached the

"Hurrah for Teddy!"

(Drawn by Charles Dana Gibson. Copyright, 1910,
by P. F. Collier & Son)

Battery, such a shout went up from the tens of thousands that
filled the park, the streets that flowed into it, and the roofs of the
ferry houses and buildings nearby, as New York or, indeed, the
country itself had not known; a roar that was all America speaking its mind. Not America, looking backward and paying tribute
to the past; America looking forward; America, troubled and bewildered by inept leadership, welcoming home a leader it loved
and knew it could trust to set a course clearly and steer it intelligently. It was America welcoming the man whom Europe had
acclaimed as not only "the foremost citizen" of the United States
but "the most famous of living men"; the America that had begged
Roosevelt to stay in the White House four more years; the America
that had seen him go and had been watching a lesser man in his
post. It was that America that roared its devotion and its plea.

Only a poet could adequately do justice to the scene and, happily,
a poet was on hand, the minstrel of the Russo-Japanese peace
negotiations, Wallace Irwin:

"Muses, lend me an earthquake
  To rattle the big blue dome.
Or a dynamite bomb
Or a fierce tom-tom,
Or a bugle-call,
Or Niagara's fall—
Full justice to do
To the hullabaloo
Which roared New York and the Country through
  When Teddy came sailing home.
Thunder and smoke, how the Patriots woke
  From Kalamazoo to Nome!
Your Uncle Sam fell off o' the porch
And the Statue of Liberty swallowed her torch
  When Teddy came sailing home."

As the ex-President stepped ashore, hundreds of personal friends pressed close to grasp his hand, former Cabinet-members, Rough Riders, policemen, army and navy officers, politicians, wolf-hunters who had come on horseback from Oklahoma, editors, naturalists, reporters, welcoming him as the "Colonel," the title he had borne with pride in the pre-presidential days.

His response had all the old heartiness. "I'm so glad to see you!" But it wasn't said, the *Times* reporter noted, the way it looked in type. "The *so* went off like a firecracker. The smile backed it up in a radiation of energy, and the hearty grip of the hand that came down on the respondent with a bang emphasized again the exact meaning of the words." If the crowd was happy, so was the ex-President.

There was a Court of Honor in Battery Park and a speakers' stand, hung with flags. The bearded mayor, William J. Gaynor, made a speech of welcome. The ex-President replied, offering to serve the people in any good cause to which they might call him. Then began the procession up Broadway, with a troop of Rough Riders in new uniforms as a guard of honor and the ex-President standing in his carriage, moving slowly northward to 59th Street, through solid walls of cheering humanity.

"Through the Ready-Money Town
  They paraded up and down,
    Teddy bowing right and left like Julius Caesar;
  And the Nation, which had slumbered

285

As the empty months were numbered,
  Thrilled again to greet its Corporation Squeezer.

"When the tumult and the spouting
  Died away amidst the shouting,
    And the Captains and the Colonels had departed,
  Sat a Grafter in his clover
  Chuckling: 'Gee! I'm glad it's over!'
    Echo answered: 'Over, man! He's scarcely started!' "

When the crowds had dispersed, and the ex-President was on his way to Oyster Bay, a policeman was seen holding his right glove in his left hand, looking at it in so rapt a fashion that the man at his side asked him what was in his mind.

"Why, I was at the Battery when the procession was starting," the policeman replied, "and Mr. Roosevelt saw me and shook hands with me. 'Why, Jim,' he said, 'is that you?' This is the glove he shook, and I'm taking it home to put it in my library and all my descendants will be proud of it."

Apotheosis . . .

Book III

BEACON ON SAGAMORE

"High on a bleak, black headland, a beacon flares to the sky;
  And its flames like banners clap and like bugles in battle cry;

And its sparks roar to the stars with a roaring louder than fame,
  And the hearts that they strike as they fall kindle and burst into
    flame."

Book III

BEACON ON SEASHORE

Chapter I

THE COLONEL was grateful for the welcome and, when he was back in the city for Ted's and Eleanor's wedding, two days later, appreciated the devotion of the people in the streets who recognized him and crowded round him and wanted to shake his hand. But it all made him a little uneasy. He knew history, the "roses, roses, all the way," followed by the tumbrel and the executioner; he remembered Dewey, the adulation, the avalanche of scorn. In his personal life, he had had a watchful eye on the cycle of destiny ever since his youthful triumph in the New York Assembly had, at its height, met the catastrophe of his wife's death and his mother's on the same day; and, ever afterward, when life had looked a little rosier than any man had a right to expect, he had kept his fingers crossed.

Yet, actually, the conviction that he was in for trouble was based on no uneasy hunch or superstition. While he was in Africa, he had been urged by many of his friends to go on to India or the Far East, go anywhere, so he did not return until after the midterm elections in the fall. Taft was proving a disappointment; the Republicans would lose the House; and there would be a unanimous call for Roosevelt to pull victory out of otherwise inevitable defeat in 1912. Obviously, he recognized, the "shrewd" thing for him to do was to stay out of the midterm fight; but he would not consider another year of "exile." He was homesick for his country, his wife, his children; homesick for Sagamore Hill.

The evening after his return he and Mrs. Roosevelt sat in rockers on the west piazza, he recalled, when he was writing his Autobiography, "looking across the Sound toward the glory of the sunset." From the belt of forest at the base of the long grassy slope rose "the golden, leisurely chiming of the wood thrushes, chanting their vespers. Through the still air came the warble of vireo and tanager and, after nightfall, we heard the flight-song of an ovenbird from the same belt of timber. Overhead an oriole sang in the weeping elm, now and then breaking his song to scold like an overgrown wren. Song-sparrows and catbirds sang in the shrubbery. . . ."

What if this return to his beloved Sagamore, this reunion with his family, *did* spell trouble? As he gazed over the burnished golden bay, was he recalling that, long before he had touched his native shore, he had known that, sooner or later, he would be called upon to make political decisions which would antagonize one group or the other of his followers? He might, of course, as some of his friends had suggested, retire into a kind of golden sunset and, as the Sage of Sagamore Hill, utter eloquent platitudes that would make everybody happy and would solder no single, leaking tin-can; but, at fifty-one, he was too young for such lime-lighted futility. He was no longer President, but he was still a citizen! He would keep out of a fight as long as he could, but, if the time came when he had to fight, well, he would be there.

The "insurgent" Republicans, as the men in Congress who had rejected Taft's leadership were called, came singly and in groups

All roads lead to Oyster Bay

to the Long Island mecca to tell their side of the story, followed by the "standpatters" who agreed with their opponents at least on the fact that the Party was headed for trouble in the midterm elections. Roosevelt leaned—inevitably—toward the "insurgents." They were the men who had stood by him while he was President, supported his policies, fought for the legislation he asked for: the men around whom he had striven to build a progressive Republican Party. Yet, disappointed in Taft as he was, the Colonel shrank from committing himself publicly against the President or in favor of the men who were fighting him. He had everything to gain by keeping out of the factional wrangle, everything to lose by getting in. But his progressive friends were determined not to let him preserve his position "above the battle." He was amazed by the tide of feeling he saw rising against him among the men who had been his closest followers and supporters. Was he afraid to take sides? they asked in tones of mingled astonishment and anger. They were prepared, Roosevelt recognized, to have him go wrong, from their point of view, and support Taft, but they were not prepared to have him dodge the issue. He tried, in vain, to make them see the implications of the action they were urging: an open split in the Party, with himself leading a faction against the President he had put in the White House, the probable loss of the midterm elections, the inevitable loss of the Presidency in 1912.

The "insurgents" would not listen. "Are you going back on your principles?" they asked. "Are you going back on your friends? Are you a quitter? Are you yellow?"

The bitter queries caught the Colonel on his pride as a fighter and a straight-shooter. "Poor Theodore is so harassed and worried that I could almost wish him back in Africa," Mrs. Roosevelt wrote Mrs. Cowles, "and the worst of it is that he sees no way out of his present position."

As the summer advanced, the pressure on him from the extremists at both ends of the Party grew from week to week in force and bitterness. The Old Guard leaders were imploring him to come out for Taft in what Roosevelt described as a "general flaming endorsement" which, he recognized, would not only be insincere but would alienate all his supporters, and in the end be no service to Taft since it would deprive him, Roosevelt, of all power to be of any use to him at all. On his other side were the "lunatic insurgents," as the Colonel described them, "who have no conception

"I've got to see him!"

of the difference in difficulty between tearing down and building up." Whatever he did, the Colonel knew that the Party would be beaten and he would get the blame.

"But, Colonel, under those circumstances," a veteran newspaperman asked him, "why don't you stay out?"

"Because I couldn't live with myself if I didn't go in," he answered.

2

The Colonel took his unhappy dilemma into the Sagamore woods and along the roads he galloped over, day after day, or out on the smooth waters of the Sound, rowing Mrs. Roosevelt to one or the other of their old haunts on Lloyd's Neck or beyond. But such excursions were less frequent than during his Presidency. He wrote his sister, Mrs. Cowles, of the "intolerable burden" of his correspondence, the "multitude of good people" who wrote him and expected replies, his inability to protect himself from such kindly attentions, as he had been protected as President. There was no noisy host of children, moreover, to give him the relaxation their very presence had always provided. Kermit and Ethel were visiting friends, Archie was in South Dakota with Seth Bullock; Quentin was alone, and lonely, since the cousins on the neighboring estates were scattered too. "This summer," the Colonel wrote Ted, "has marked the definite end of the old Oyster Bay life that all of you children used to lead."

3

The Colonel took the active direction of the progressive effort to take over the New York State Republican organization, and on successive campaign trips across the country fought for a continuation and development of his Square Deal policies as President. What he preached was traditional American progressivism, in terms that, forty years later, would seem conservative. But the Old Guard in the press and the Party made it their excuse to whip up the fears of the timid against this "dangerous radical," this "socialist," this "revolutionary," who was "undermining the foundations of the Republic."

In New York, Wall Street's "organized crusade," as the Colonel called it, went to extremes of virulence that persuaded the "best citizens" to flee to the open maw of Tammany Hall from the menace of "the man who would be king." There was not a club in the neighborhood of Fifth Avenue, the Colonel was certain, where he was not regarded "as well-nigh a bomb-thrower." He took it all philosophically. "It matters little," he wrote Ted. "I have nothing to ask, for I desire nothing personally, and attacks pass just as praise passes."

4

The men who were calling the Colonel a "megalomaniac," obsessed with his own importance, might—if reason had played any part in their feverish conclusions—have found difficulty in reconciling their view of him with an episode of one of his campaign trips that summer.

In St. Louis, the Colonel ran into the aviator, Arch Hoxsey, who had just completed a record flight from Springfield, Illinois. Seeing the Colonel on the Aviation Field with Missouri's Governor Hadley, Hoxsey invited him to take a "hop."

"A broad grin of delight spread over the Colonel's face," a New York *Times* correspondent noted, but the Governor looked grave. "You're not going up, are you?" he asked, anxiously.

The Colonel pondered a moment. "By George!" he exclaimed, "I believe I will."

He took Hoxsey by the arm and strode with him toward his plane, a flimsy crate that, to a later generation, would look like a box kite, all match-sticks, paper and wire.

The Colonel climbed into the seat next to the aviator. There was no cockpit, and nothing but air under his feet. The Colonel's face was grim with determination, the *Times* man noted, but his eyes were sparkling. "Let her go!" he cried.

The propeller started to whirl and the plane moved forward. Roosevelt's two hundred pounds had their effect on its capacity to detach itself from the ground, but, fifty yards from the starting-point, it labored upward. The word had been passed that the great "Teddy" was going up with Hoxsey, and a cheer rose from the field that became a roar. The plane rose to a height of about fifty feet and flew around the field. The Governor and Roosevelt's other friends on the field held their breath. As the plane passed the grandstand, there was a quick cheer, then abruptly, silence. "Every man and woman in that vast crowd," noted the *Times* correspondent, "seemed suddenly to be overcome with the same sensation of wonderment and sudden fear that something might go wrong."

Happily, nothing did. The plane circled the field twice; then, after some four minutes in the air, made an easy landing near the Colonel's car. The crowd yelled with relief and pent-up emotion, rushing forward to greet the former President as he climbed out of the machine.

"It was great," the Colonel exclaimed. "I only wish I could have stayed up an hour!"

"Wasn't it a bit scary?" someone asked.

"Not a bit. I enjoyed every minute. By George, it was great!"

One of the Colonel's friends, commenting on the episode in St. Louis that night, remarked, "There's nothing left for him to try now. He's been down in a submarine and up in an airplane, That's about the limit."

Arch Hoxsey crashed to his death a year later.

5

The defeat the Colonel had anticipated came with the colorless Democratic candidate for governor overwhelming the Republican candidate, Henry L. Stimson, and doing it mainly because Stimson had Roosevelt's support. Even the candidate for Congress from the Oyster Bay district was defeated for a similar reason.

The newspapermen, crowding the porch at Sagamore Hill to get a statement from the Colonel, encountered Archie at the door. "Father has nothing to say," he reported. "What *could* he say?"

Yet there was something, and the ex-President said it in a letter to Ted: "Every dog has his day, but the nights belong to the cats."

A gloomy prediction he had made, forty-eight hours after his return to the United States, that, within six months, the public would be "throwing rotten apples" at him, had come true, almost to the letter. Four and a half months after his triumphant welcome, millions were calling him a "discredited and broken politician," who, the New York *World* exultantly declared, was definitely on his way to St. Helena.

6

"I have never had a more unpleasant summer," the Colonel wrote Elihu Root, after the election. It was not so that he had dreamed in Africa that that summer, back at Sagamore, would be.

The winter made up for it. "Mother and I are having the most enjoyable time possible here at Sagamore," the Colonel wrote Ted early in December. "It is really ideal. Twenty years ago, or even ten years ago, I should not have been contented, simply because I would have felt I had not any business not to be doing work. But I have not that feeling at all now. I am fifty-two, I have worked very hard for thirty years, and, while I am perfectly willing to do more work if it comes in the line of a duty, I don't in the least feel that I must at all hazards find it to do; and I am perfectly willing to acquiesce in the view that it may be much the wisest thing not to try to do it, but to let duty jump with inclination, and stay home." He added a postscript. "Mother and I had a three hours ride yesterday; in the evening we sat in the North Room before the blazing log fire, while a snow storm outside gradually turned into a blizzard."

"All our children," the Colonel wrote his classmate "Bob" Bacon, now American ambassador to France, "are each in his or her particular sphere doing what they ought to, and seem to be happy and yet behaving themselves. Ted is perfectly absorbed in California politics, and writes me long letters on the subject; and yet he talks in the most sensible way and understands thoroughly that for the next fifteen or twenty years his work must be in business, and politics must be merely an avocation." Ted's business experience was widening. He had started in with the Hartford Carpet Company in Connecticut at seven dollars a week for a twelve-hour day, five and a half days a week, and had lived on his salary refusing an allowance. He had now been moved to the San Francisco branch where he was working effectively in the sales office. Eleanor was proving the kind of wife Ted's father himself had chosen. "Somehow, I always felt, right from the beginning," the Colonel wrote Ted, "that Eleanor was one of those very, very rare girls who are like Mother." Indeed, he added, "she is just as sweet as Mother, and more than that cannot be said."

Kermit was back at Harvard, trying to be a sophomore when, after his year in Africa and Europe, he felt like a graduate, ten years out of college. Ethel was at home, and Archie building up his uncertain health at the Mesa School in Arizona. Quentin, who could always be trusted to do the unexpected, had, after a dismal record for scholarship at Groton which had worried his father and mother, suddenly bobbed up near the head of his class. "Heavens! To think of one of our family standing as high as that!" his father wrote him. "It's almost paralyzing."

The happiness of Sagamore reached a new pitch, the middle of January, with news from San Francisco that Ted and Eleanor were expecting a baby in August. "Mother and I are almost as delighted as darling Eleanor and you," the grandfather-to-be wrote his son. "Both of you are now even more in our thoughts than ever; and our hearts well over with tenderness for Eleanor. . . . Home, wife, children—they are what really count in life. I have heartily enjoyed many things; the Presidency, my success as a soldier, a writer, a big game hunter and explorer; but all of them put together are not for one moment to be weighed in the balance when compared with the joy I have known with your mother and all of you; and, as a merely secondary thing, this house and the life here yield me constant pleasure. Really, the prospect of grandchildren was all that was lacking to make perfect mother's happiness and mine. . . ."

Chapter II

RIDING OVER the snow, or sitting before the fire in the library —the North Room, much as he loved it, was with its wide spaces and high ceiling, impractical for winter use—the ex-President recalled, perhaps, a cartoon that had appeared in *Harper's Weekly* at the time of his return. It showed him sitting thoughtfully in his study with a lion beside him marked "personal popularity" saying, "I wish I knew what you are going to do with me." What *had* he done with it? If he dwelt on the query at all, he did not dwell on it long. What was done was done. He had seen the dangers from the start, had known that he would get hurt; but, good Lord, did a general avoid a battle because he thought he might get shot?

The point was, what should he do now? His mail was heavy with appeals to come out for the nomination in 1912. They gave him no satisfaction. He did not want the Presidency again. He had had it, and gone out in a blaze of public approbation. If he returned to the White House, the circumstances might be such that he could not accomplish what was expected of him. The pomp and glory no longer had any lure for him. The power? That was different. He liked power. When you saw things that needed doing, it was a great satisfaction to be where you could see that they were done. But he told his friends he was getting old. There came a time when just sitting by the fire had its charms, in the home that you loved, with your wife at your side and your children making their way in the great world and coming back from time to time to report on their adventures.

He knew, moreover, what his nomination would entail—a bitter factional fight, the charge of treachery to Taft, old friendships broken, and, even if he were nominated and elected, only lukewarm support, if that, from Taft's friends in Congress. No, no, no!

"As things are now," he wrote William Allen White, "it would be a serious mistake from the public standpoint, and a cruel wrong to me, to nominate me." To Joseph Bucklin Bishop, he was even more direct. "They have no business to expect me to take command of a ship simply because the ship is sinking."

2

Even while he was begging his friends not to impose on him the labors and the pain of leadership, he was writing articles in the *Outlook* and making speeches in the West that gave the progressive cause the most penetrating definition and direction it was getting anywhere. What he was trying to do was to bring the Republican Party back on the path on which he had led it, as President, the path of orderly change, orderly progress. The speaking-tour he embarked on in the spring of 1911 was ostensibly "non-political," but it brought him back on the front pages of the newspapers and obviously had political overtones. He had told himself, and his friends, that the only thing that might persuade him to accept the nomination would be the recognition on his part that the people demanded it. Being human, and ever intrigued by the challenge of battle, was he possibly not averse to stimulating such a demand, gently, unobtrusively, on moral and spiritual levels? The Colonel would, no doubt, have rejected with indignation the suggestion that talks on "Realizable Ideals," "The Bible and the Life of the People" and "The Adventure of Living" might have political implications. But, at a time when the public appeared to crave nothing so much as the vigorous moral leadership that Roosevelt as President had given them—and Taft, with all his integrity and personal warmth, had failed to give—anything that Roosevelt might say even on the Ten Commandments—and he discussed two of them at length—had political overtones.

There was about this tour of his none of the organized "hoopla," the shouting, the competing bands, the surging crowds, of his campaign trips or his presidential "swings around the circle." The significant thing about them, moreover, was not the numbers who greeted the Colonel at railroad stations or flocked to his addresses —so colorful a personality would naturally draw crowds anywhere, at any time—but their temper, the peculiar feeling of warmth and personal devotion that the men and women clearly had for him, their obvious hunger for leadership, his type of leadership, that presented political issues in a frame of moral purpose. They were not thinking of him as a politician or even as a former President, but as a friend. This man, they said to themselves, understood them. Other politicians, they knew, thought of them as masses without individual identities. Even so good a man as Taft saw them that way, and was afraid of them, talking of the dangers of mob rule, of the "tyranny of the majority." Not "TR," they said. TR thought of them as people, as fathers and mothers with names and homes and children, and troubles.

TR knew the things that were bothering them, the difficulty of making both ends meet, the strangle-hold of the railroads and other corporations on the communities in which they were raising their families, and its relation to their own lives, the crookedness of boss rule and its cynical disregard of common decency. TR wasn't afraid of the "tyranny of the majority." He knew that the "tyranny of the minority," the corporation lawyers, working in the dark with the crooked political bosses, was the real danger. TR, as President, had dealt with that danger. That was why they had wanted to keep him in the White House. He had refused, and see what had happened! Now they wanted to get him back. Perhaps he would listen this time.

The "plain people" had a feeling for TR, indeed, that they had had for no other public man since Lincoln. He saw qualities in them, they knew, which they themselves had not known they possessed—heights of idealism, depths of feeling, capacity to sacrifice, the longing to be better and bigger. They felt self-respecting when they thought of him, important to themselves, their community and their country. In the tumult of many voices, the dust and smoke of political controversy, they looked to TR as to a beacon blazing upward through the dark.

3

The Colonel was back at Sagamore in May. It was good to be home, to stride across the fields with an axe on his shoulder, pitch hay with the farm-hands, play tennis or climb to the gun-room and look far out over the woods and water; or, evenings, to sit in the high-backed rockers on the piazza with Edie, and watch the lights of the Fall River boats as they steamed up the Sound. "The Spring

is late and we are enjoying every minute of it," Mrs. Roosevelt
wrote Mrs. Cowles. Ethel, after what her mother described to her
sister-in-law as "a fine winter, working hard at her classes, intellectual and philosophic, and diverting herself by dancing untiringly,"
was on the Maine coast for a part of that summer, visiting friends
—"quite a staid young lady," her father wrote Spring-Rice, "within
moderate and reasonable limits."

Ethel was twenty, and in the valley of decision. Richard Derby,
an able and attractive young surgeon, member of an old Boston
family and ten years her senior, wanted her to marry him, and she
could not make up her mind. Derby belonged to the Porcellian
Club at Harvard of which her father, Ted and Nick Longworth
were all members, and which Kermit also would subsequently
be invited to join. Ethel and the young doctor were friends of
long standing. As a sophomore at Harvard, Derby had, indeed,
rounded up the Harvard contingent for the session on politics and
social work which her father, then Vice-President, had held, all
one long June day, on the Sagamore piazza. There was no one, the
Colonel and his lady thought, they would more happily trust Ethel

to. The family, in fact, was unanimous about it, except for Ethel, who, being the most concerned, was suffering the agonies that, for highly intelligent and responsible young women, were customary under the circumstances.

Archie was home that summer, working for his Harvard entrance examinations, his mother tutoring him in French, his father in history and civics. Archie had delighted his father by an Arizona experience of his. Visiting a cowcamp, he had won ten dollars from a cowpuncher who had bet that Archie could not sit a certain horse for ten successive buckings. "Apparently on the strength of this performance," the Colonel wrote Arthur Lee, "he then went off with the cowpuncher outfit as cook for a week. Think of the stomachs they must have had!" Quentin, his father wrote Mrs. Cowles, was "an affectionate, soft-hearted over-grown puppy of a boy," absorbed in his wireless "and anything mechanical."

Quentin was melancholy when the time came to return to Groton.

"It is not necessary to say," remarked his mother in parting, "that I hope you will be a good boy."

"No," answered Quentin, with a gloomy shake of the head, "that would be a bromide." A "bromide," in the lingo of the time, was the crassest of clichés.

The Colonel was not one to play favorites among his children, but Kermit's periodic returns home were a particular delight. "The African trip," Mrs. Roosevelt noted, "is a great bond!" Kermit was doing well at Harvard, winning golden opinions. "Copey," the famous teacher of English composition, Charles T. Copeland, was reported to have said that Kermit wrote better than any boy he had ever had under him. Yet, the Colonel wrote Arthur Lee, "it has been a hard year for him and he has needed to call on all his sense of duty to make him stay, because it is like going to school after having been out in the great world; and naturally his experiences made him older in all essentials than his classmates, and therefore put him out of touch with them, although he has very earnestly and with genuine humble-mindedness sought to efface every trace of these past experiences and to be just like any other college boy." At the moment he was in the Mexican desert south of Arizona, "hunting highly problematical sheep, and, as the temperature is higher than in Africa under the equator, and as there is no water and a reasonable chance of being killed or kidnapped by Mexican insurrectos, I think Kermit is probably enjoying himself." His mother was uneasy about the "insurrectos," but his father was inclined to be philosophical. Kermit, he said, could take care of himself. Besides, the boy had to take risks, and there was no use worrying about it.

The Colonel thought of himself as unconscionably idle. Actually, he was deep in the writing of his monograph on "Revealing and Concealing Coloration in Birds and Mammals." Once or twice a week he went to New York for an editorial conference at the *Outlook,* on whose staff he had agreed to serve. He was fond of the venerable but alert Lyman Abbott, its editor, and his two attractive sons—Lawrence, gracious and urbane, and Ernest, conscientious, industrious and able. The magazine they edited was gospel to thousands, influential far beyond the narrow limits of its circulation, since its subscribers were largely molders of opinion in their communities. The weekly staff luncheons were stimulating occasions, with the talk wide-ranging, and neither the ex-President nor the Abbotts feeling any hesitancy in expressing divergent opinions; at the luncheon-table or, indeed, in print.

The Colonel's friends from all over the country dropped in at the office—cowboys, hunters, politicians, prize-fighters, bishops, ambassadors, writers, talking of old times in the Bad Lands or Cuba or Washington, and giving him their views of the changing political scene. Now and then the Colonel brought one or another of them to Sagamore overnight. This was, at last, his life as a private citizen as he had dreamed it might be. "I am almost ashamed," he wrote Eleanor, "to be living so easy and happy and contented a life."

When, in August, Eleanor's baby came and was a girl—Grace was the name Eleanor and Ted gave her—the cup was full for the grandfather and grandmother.

4

In his happiness, the Colonel had forgotten the jealousy of that "destiny" on which, like the neo-Stoic that he was, he habitually kept a weather-eye when the sun was shining with particular brightness. That autumn, Mrs. Roosevelt was riding with him along the Oyster Bay Cove Road, when, passing the Cove schoolhouse, her horse suddenly swerved and threw her violently on the hard macadam. She was knocked senseless, and, for a fortnight after the accident, "she was never conscious," the Colonel wrote the novelist,

Edith Wharton, "unless so far as to be conscious of a well-nigh intolerable agony."

For weeks the outcome was doubtful. "Ethel," the Colonel wrote Ted, "has been a tower of strength, and has just done everything. Archie also has been as good as gold." As for the Colonel himself, "Sometimes I just sat quietly and held her hand and at other times she wants me to repeat poetry, which I do conscientiously but not as successfully as Ethel, for the poetry I know by heart is apt to be of a grandiose and warlike character, not especially fitted for soothing purposes in the sickroom."

Through the weeks of excruciating pain, heroically borne, the mistress of Sagamore slowly recovered her strength. "We had an old-style Christmas," the Colonel wrote Ted, "but we felt it was not really Christmas as long as Gracie was not present. Christmas loses some of its fine edge when the youngest child is a boy half an inch taller than his father!"

5

As summer gave way at Sagamore Hill to the bronze magic of autumn and fires blazed again in the North Room and the library and icy winds blew over, and through, the house, the thought of the 1912 political campaign occasionally cast its shadow across the Colonel's sunlit heart; but never for long. Taft was doing better; he would be renominated, the Colonel was writing his friends, and probably elected, though Woodrow Wilson—if he were the Democratic nominee—might give him a stiff run. All this Roosevelt talk would fade out by the time the convention came round. The American people were tired of him, he thought, and he rather sympathized with them in that. So all was well and was going to be well.

But the political leaders who came to Sagamore Hill to ask the Colonel to declare himself on the question of the nomination got no satisfaction. If he said *Yes,* he knew he would be regarded as seeking the nomination, which was not true; if he said *No,* he would put himself in a position where he could not respond to what might prove a patriotic duty. No doubt, the fact that he had once issued such a self-abnegating statement, with disastrous effects, impelled him to hesitate before he did it again.

"Father," remarked Mrs. Roosevelt to Ted's wife, "has tied so many knots with his tongue that he can't undo with his teeth."

The Colonel admitted in a letter to Ted that, in case the movement for his nomination became "sweeping," he might not be able honorably to decline the nomination. "But I feel as Nick Longworth strongly feels, and as most of my best friends feel, that for me personally the nomination would be a veritable calamity, and I do not want to take it if it can possibly be avoided."

William Loeb, his former secretary, adjured him not to let himself be persuaded to be a candidate. Let Taft be nominated and take the defeat that was coming to him. "The only course for you to take is to stay quietly at Sagamore Hill and mind your own business. By the time 1916 comes around the whole Republican Party will be yelling their heads off wanting you to be their candidate."

Roosevelt agreed. He must not, and he would not, get into the fight. He was undoubtedly sincere when he said it, for all the political realities supported it. But in giving Loeb this assurance, he had not reckoned with the determination of the "insurgents" to defeat the reactionary leadership in the Party which had taken Taft captive, or with the propaganda that they unleashed. From different parts of the country came reports that the people wanted Roosevelt, and would take no other Republican, reports that the primaries, the following spring, would confirm. His silence on the question of the nomination, moreover, he was told, was being misinterpreted. Men he respected were beginning to wonder whether he were not playing a devious game, using his reluctance to announce his candidacy as a screen to hide possible under-cover machinations.

That argument, touching his honor, weighed heavily with him. The idealism of the young progressive leaders, moreover, their enthusiasm, their determination that the Republican Party should represent the will not of crooked political bosses and corporation lawyers but of the rank and file of the people, called to the idealism and the enthusiasm in the Colonel and to his determination that the Party should represent the spirit not of Mark Hanna but of Abraham Lincoln. Between the arguments of the progressives, supported by his own best purposes, and the pleas of the friends, no less disinterested, supporting his own judgment of the realities, the ex-President was, he admitted to Nick Longworth, in a "dreadful quandary." "As far as I know my own soul," he wrote Herbert S. Hadley, "I am telling you the exact truth when I say that I do not wish and will not take this nomination unless it comes to me as a public duty." The anger of his followers at what they regarded as Taft's betrayal of the policies on which he had been elected, an anger that the Colonel shared, and Roosevelt's own impatience to get his hands on the wheel again, finally overwhelmed his judgment of the political facts of life, including his recognition that, if he could only wait, the nomination would, in 1916, be his for the taking. He would not—he thought he should not—wait.

The storm in the Party and the press that followed the announcement of his candidacy was so bitter and violent that Alice, who seemed indifferent to the family when skies were blue and was always on hand when days were dark, ran up from Washington, feeling she had to face the gales at his side. "I think she felt she just had to see me," the Colonel wrote Kermit, "because of course all respectable society is now apoplectic with rage over me. Literally, I have no supporter of prominence in the East—a fact," he added, "which weighs with the utmost lightness on my soul."

One wonders. The Colonel's childhood friend, Fanny Parsons, spending Sunday at Sagamore a few weeks after he had made his decision, noted with a pang that the man who strode across the fields with her seemed to have lost the "buoyant lightheartedness" that had always been one of the most charming facets of his personality. "On that long, rapid, for me almost breathless walk through the bleak March woods," she wrote, almost forty years later, "I realized that he was starting out on a strange, untravelled road, the end of which he could not see—a road where he would be unaccompanied by the able, devoted colleagues whose loyalty and gifts had enabled him to transform the old road into a continuous march of triumph."

Chapter III

THE MONTHS that followed were a nightmare of feverish organization, successive conferences at the *Outlook* office and at Sagamore Hill, of speaking tours such as the Colonel had confidently hoped he would never have to engage in again, and of personal recriminations between Taft and himself that grieved the friends of both. "Theodore bears all these worries and hurts marvellously," Mrs. Roosevelt wrote her sister-in-law. Baby Gracie was in part responsible. "He runs in half a dozen times a day and picks her up in his arms."

Week by week the popular enthusiasm for Roosevelt mounted. There could be no question whom the rank and file of Republicans wanted as their standard-bearer. But the convention machinery was in the hands of the Taft forces. When the national convention met in Chicago, they used that machinery ruthlessly for their own ends, disqualifying sufficient Roosevelt delegates to control the nomination.

"The great bulk of my wealthy and educated friends regard me as a dangerous crank," the Colonel, on his return from the convention, wrote the British novelist, H. Rider Haggard, "because I am trying to find a remedy for evils which, if left unremedied, will in the end do away not only with wealth and education, but with pretty much all of our civilization. . . . It is a fight that must be made, and is worth making; and the event lies on the knees of the gods."

The course of the Democratic convention in Baltimore, early in July, gave Roosevelt brief encouragement. If the conservative Champ Clark were nominated, the issue between the old parties and the party that was about to be formed would be sharply drawn, and there was a chance for victory. "Pop's praying for

Clark," Kermit was heard to remark. The Democrats refused to oblige, nominating Woodrow Wilson instead.

That evening there was a family conference at Sagamore Hill. No irrevocable decision regarding a new party had been made in Chicago, but letters and telegrams were pouring in, urging that such a party be formed with Roosevelt as the candidate. Every impulse of statesmanship and politics (and, indeed, of personal rancor, as well) made the Colonel want to say *Yes*. This was a fight for the things he had fought for since he had become governor of New York: the control of arbitrary power, the right of every American to equal opportunity. Thirty years later, William Allen White would see the Roosevelt of those July days in a new perspective, "the first American statesman of major proportions who saw and dramatized a new phase of the truth about freedom, its economic implications." Here, said White, was "a new turn in the path to freedom."

Roosevelt was determined to follow that "new turn," and yet . . . He had been unable to make up his mind to jump into a fight that would be costly to others beside himself. He drew the family into council—Mrs. Roosevelt, Ethel, Kermit, Archie, Quentin. All would suffer if the fight were made, old friendships would be strained, the boys' careers would be affected, their opportunities restricted. If he kept out of the fight, on the other hand, the picture would be rosy. Wilson would beat Taft, "hands down." Then, in 1916, if he, Roosevelt, should want the nomination, he could have it without lifting a finger.

There was no argument in the family, no division. All agreed that the Colonel must make the fight. Even though there were no chance of his winning, he must make it.

"My public career will probably come to a close on Election Day," the Colonel said, next day, to E. A. Van Valkenberg, the genial but redoubtable publisher of the Philadelphia *North American*, "but I've got to make the fight. Only by so doing will I get a satisfying sense that I have answered a clear call of duty. Actually, I have no choice. If I don't run, everything I've stood for, and tried to advance politically, will be lost."

"Mrs. Roosevelt, standing beside the Colonel, her hand in his, was radiant with trust and affection," Van Valkenberg later recalled, "as she expressed her faith that the path through honor to defeat was the one to take."

So the die was cast. The reports that came in from the country indicated that the progressive leaders had heard from the grass-roots in no uncertain tones. Progressive Party headquarters were opened in New York. Roosevelt's remark in reply to a newspaperman that he felt "like a bull moose" gave the new party a nickname.

There were conferences at all hours at Sagamore Hill, with the Colonel's capacity to listen, take advice and separate the wheat from the chaff, a constant surprise to newcomers. Mrs. Roosevelt, emotionally as deeply involved in the campaign as her husband, kept out of the formal gatherings, but, in the informal aftermath, quietly "filled in," as Frederick M. Davenport put it, "in those matters in which she thought the Colonel might be wrong."

"Now, Theodore," she would say, after some indiscreet or over-emphatic word of his, "you know that is just one of those remarks that make it so difficult sometimes for your friends to defend you."

His response, as in the White House days, was always the same, spoken with an air of injured innocence, "Why Edie, I was only—" but he sobered down instantly.

"As a team," Davenport pointed out, "they produced a judgment that was not infallible, of course, but dangerously near it, humanly and politically."

The Colonel was in his element at such conferences, but harbored other interests in life than politics and occasionally found that he was being forced to swallow more politics than even his stomach could take. One day, that summer, O. K. Davis, whom he cherished, came to Sagamore Hill to consult the Colonel about the Progressive campaign in which Davis was a key figure. After talking with him in the library for a half-hour, the Colonel strode to the North Room, where Mrs. Roosevelt was sitting with Eleanor, Ted's wife, and, slipping quietly, almost furtively, into a chair, started to read.

Mrs. Roosevelt looked up from her needlework. "Has Mr. Davis gone?" she asked.

"No," he answered. "He's in the library. I just got tired of talking politics."

"Theodore," his wife protested, "you can't treat a guest like that! You go right back!"

He laid the book down with a sigh and went back.

But the Colonel relished people as people too much not to return each day with apparently undiminished zest to the round of interviews and conferences. Each caller was a person to get to know in the least possible period of time, to appraise, to reject as too light or too unstable, or, when the soundings showed depth, to fit into the great design.

Among those who came that midsummer was Medill McCormick, one of the Bull Moose leaders in Illinois, tall, cadaverous and enthusiastic. He brought his wife Ruth, daughter of Mark Hanna, who had inherited her father's astuteness and force and had come to offer them to the service of the new Party. McCormick, the Colonel recognized, had the political facts but his wife had the judgment. After luncheon, standing on the piazza with another midwestern leader, Raymond Robins, he watched the pair descend the western slope to the path through the woods that led to the yacht landing and clicked his teeth, noisily. "Raymond," he remarked—*click, click, click*—"my money's on the ma-r-re."

The convention was held early in August. Its high, emotional moments did not affect the Colonel's judgment of the probable outcome. "But I am perfectly happy," he wrote Arthur Lee, on his return to Sagamore, "for I have never in my life been in a movement into which I could enter as heartily as into this; and, although I expect to lose, I believe that we . . . may be able to give the right trend to our democracy, a trend which will take it away from mere shortsighted, greedy materialism."

2

At Sagamore Hill, politicians and reporters came and went, conventions loomed and were past, headlines screamed and were forgotten; but the family life went on.

"I have been taking Mother out to row instead of having her ride," the Colonel wrote Ethel, who was away, visiting. "She is as charming and pretty (in my eyes, and I think anyhow!) as when she was the slender girl I made love to—and I can't help making love to her now. Archie is a perfect trump. He has me much on his mind." Kermit, who had received his degree at Harvard about the time that his father was graduating from the Republican Party in Chicago, had taken a job with the Brazil Railroad Company, and was packed up and given a family send-off. Quentin, not yet fifteen, "tranquil, efficient, moon-faced and entirely merry," as his father described him in a letter to Ethel, was growing up, "a most

311

amusing and companionable young man," of whom James Amos, the houseman, remarked to Mrs. Roosevelt one day, "Indeed, madam, Master Quentin is more of a man than Miss Ethel is of a lady!"

Like Kermit, Quentin had depths of feeling which only his mother was aware of. When his great-aunt Lizzie died, he mourned for the matriarchal old lady on the neighboring estate who had played so large a part in all their lives. "He has not the blessed faculty which Ted inherits from Theodore," his mother wrote Mrs. Cowles, "of a wild blaze which settles into peaceful ashes. Quentin's troubles smoulder away inside, eating into that big, tender heart which your Father gave him."

Alice, on her occasional visits that summer, was torn and unhappy. The young woman who, before her marriage, had found "society" and its pleasures wholly satisfying, and was still, Archie Butt noted, the "drawing-card of Washington society" for whom people would "forsake palaces and feasts," had experienced the excitement of politics, its conflicts, stratagems and intrigues, its passing eclipses, its exhilarating victories; and was proving a resourceful supporter of her able husband. She had no strong convictions herself about progressivism in or out of the Republican Party or the basic issue of privilege, but she adored her father, and had been known to refuse an invitation to one of Washington's great houses because its master had criticized him—"the one unpardonable sin in her eyes," Archie Butt recognized. If her father, moreover, believed that "social justice" and "popular rule" were worth fighting for, she was for them, lock, stock and barrel, and ready to annihilate with a quip anyone who thought otherwise.

"Poor Alice is here," her father wrote Ethel during a midsummer separation. "It is all horrid for her; she would feel better if Nick were strong for Taft." Her husband, a leading congressman from Taft's own state—his own city, in fact—was obligated to support him, though his natural sympathies were with his father-in-law. Alice felt no obligation whatsoever even to pretend that she was for Taft and had been disconsolate when her father had pointed out that, in loyalty to her husband, she must stay away from the Progressive national convention. Much of the distress that the Colonel noted was due to the canny political sense that told her that her father was spending his energy and ardor on a hopeless cause. When, at Sagamore, the stream of politicians and newspapermen got too much for her, she carried her perturbed spirit to the arbor, north of the house, known as the Nest, where in earlier, brighter days her stepmother had found refuge from her and the other children.

3

Eleanor, Ted's wife, came to Sagamore for the summer, bringing her baby. For the Colonel and his wife, having their first grandchild in the house for months on end was an experience that made a presidential candidacy seem so secondary as to be in the nature of an impertinent periodic interruption.

For the lovely little Dresden-china person, sensitive and demure, who was Gracie's mother, that summer was an education on an heroic scale. Eleanor Alexander had been an only child; in no way spoiled, but fluttered around by adoring relatives and servants who were accustomed to tiptoe about the house and talk in whispers until she woke in the morning. People were always inquiring whether she were not "doing too much" and urging her to lie down and rest if she looked tired. She did not know why they did it but they had always done it, and she assumed they always would.

She had not been at Sagamore twenty-four hours before she recognized that nothing in her bringing-up had remotely prepared her for the furious activity into which she was plunged.

"Something was going on every minute of the day," she wrote some fifteen years later. "The house was always full of people. They came by ones, by twos, and by tens. All day long, conferences were held in every room downstairs. The telephone never stopped ringing. A car full of newspapermen was always in the offing."

Her first day at Sagamore she panted for the night as the hart panteth for the water-brooks. Surely, after all this activity everyone would be glad to go to bed early. Nothing could have been farther from the reality. "The Roosevelt family enjoyed life far too much to be willing to waste time sleeping. Every night they stayed downstairs until midnight; then, talking at the tops of their voices, they trooped up the wide, uncarpeted oak staircase and went to their rooms. For a brief ten minutes all was still; and, just as I was dropping off to sleep for the second time, they remembered things they had forgotten to tell each other and rushed shouting through the halls. I used to go to bed with cotton in my ears, but it never did any good."

The first night she found consolation in the assurance that no one was likely to wake up before eight at the earliest. "That won't be so bad." Eight? By six, the younger ones were up, and by seven, "I was the only one who was not joyously beginning the day."

Eleanor learned things that summer beside what Kipling calls "the true Oriental indifference to mere noise"; among others, the Sagamore conception of a picnic. In his "Autobiography," the Colonel paints an idyllic picture of excursions in the rowboat and landings for lunch "under windbeaten oaks on the edge of a low bluff while the sails of the coasting schooners gleam in the sunlight, and the tolling of the bell-buoy comes landward across the waters." But that was not like anything that Eleanor recalled, in after years, of that first summer of hers at Sagamore.

One morning—"a boiling hot day," she described it—her father-in-law at breakfast proposed a picnic. Everyone was enthusiastic, including Eleanor. She liked picnics—the cold chicken, the lemonade, the lettuce sandwiches and other delectables, wrapped in waxed paper. It would be pleasant on so blisteringly hot a day to have lunch outdoors in the cool shade of some big tree, not too far away, and easily reached.

She found shortly, however, that the Roosevelts had ideas about picnics which bore no relation to hers. The provisions were plentiful but consisted of a large basket of clams, another of thick ham sandwiches and a demijohn of water.

By ten o'clock a dozen friends and cousins had gathered at the house. Carrying the supplies, they walked the half-mile through the woods to the beach at a pace that seemed to Eleanor uncalled for, until the mosquitoes started operations. The mosquitoes in those woods were "as big as bats," she remembered.

On the beach were five rowboats, two of them more desirable than the rest, since, in the stern, they had comfortable back supports. Eleanor waited for someone to suggest that her place was in one of those, but no one spoke. Subsequently, she learned that she should have run ahead, leapt into one of the boats with back supports, and held it against all comers. At Sagamore picnics it was everyone for himself and the Devil take the hindmost. Eleanor finally found a place, squeezed between the basket of clams and the demijohn.

"Under the blazing sun, we rowed and rowed. There was not a vestige of breeze; the Sound was as calm as glass. By and by I began pointing out places where we might stop, but they were all declared quite unsuitable and far less attractive than the spot to which we were going. Some two hours later, we landed on a beach precisely like the one from which we had started, except that it was farther from home. There was not the least shade. Because of the poison ivy we could not go near the trees."

A roaring fire raised the temperature to heights that no one dared measure. "When the clams were judged ready, my father-in-law selected one, opened it, sprinkled it with pepper and salt and handed it to me. It was very large and had a long neck." By a valiant effort she managed to get all of it in her mouth. "At first, although gritty with sand, it was delicious; but that soon wore off and it became like a piece of old rubber hose."

Eleanor looked around. Everybody else was consuming large quantities of the clams. How did they do it? The more she chewed, the larger the clam seemed to get. This was dreadful; this might go on forever. Surreptitiously, she slipped the clam under a log.

"You're not as persistent as Archie was when he was small," remarked her father-in-law, who had observed her desperate stratagem. "The first time he ate a clam on a picnic, he chewed for a time, then ate three sandwiches, half a dozen cookies and an orange. About half an hour later he came to me and asked me what he should do with the poor little dead clam. It was still in his mouth!"

As the party was packing up to go home a head wind sprang up. The two-hour row of the morning was a five-hour row back. "Faces and necks were burned to a crisp; hands were blistered. My father-in-law had a difficult time reaching shore at all as the boat in which he was rowing my mother-in-law began to leak badly. In spite of it all, everybody considered that the picnic had been a great and glorious success."

What with the eighteen-hour-a-day schedule, picnics, not to speak of the slide down Cooper's Bluff and the inevitable point-to-point walks, Eleanor told herself, by the end of the summer, that she had "gained immeasurably in valuable experience," including the capacity to sleep under any and all conditions. "It was splendid training, but, while it was going on, I lost twenty-six pounds."

Chapter IV

A GOOD PART of that summer of 1912, Edith Roosevelt sat on the Sagamore piazza, or, evenings, in the North Room, and, in the daily papers, followed her husband's course, hither and yon, over the country, speaking in packed auditoriums and from the rear of his special train. Once more, as a dozen years before when the vice-presidential candidate had carried the ball for the national ticket, the press told the wife at home the story of cheering crowds and a triumphant progress. "Politics are booming along," she wrote her sister, "and Theodore is whacking at Wilson, who deserves all he gets." Her heart was with her husband in this campaign as it had not been wholly with him in 1900 when she had resented what seemed to her the exploitation of his enthusiasm by the Republican managers. She believed in the cause for which he was spending himself and being spent, this fight for national unity and a Square Deal against privilege, recognizing that it was the climax toward which the past dozen years had pointed. In this campaign, moreover, Theodore was touching new heights of personal power. Here was leadership, in its essence, stripped of all the supports he had known in the past—office, powerful party organization and unlimited financial backing; leadership, rising hot from the fire in his own heart and sending up sparks that set others on fire.

Reading between the lines of the matter-of-fact reports in the papers, Edith Roosevelt felt the impact of her husband's ardor and the response of the crowds surging about him. Yet it gave her no lasting elation. Victory was not in the cards, as it had been, those rich, crowded days, twelve years before, when they had all still been so young, with the great days all ahead. The rushing music now had a dying fall.

Edith Roosevelt decided, the middle of October, that she needed an evening's distraction in New York, and invited Theodore's cherished Cousin Laura, their Cove Neck neighbor, Mrs. J. West Roosevelt, her son Oliver and his cousin George to see a popular musical comedy, "The Merry Countess," at the Casino Theater. Oliver had been detained at the Progressive headquarters where he was working, and when Mrs. Roosevelt became aware of him making his way past her and dropping into the seat at her side, she laid her hand on his knee in welcome. She noted that it was trembling; and, recognizing that something was wrong, gripped his hand firmly. His voice was steady as he whispered that a report had come to the headquarters that there had been an attempt on the Colonel's life at Milwaukee. Happily, the bullet had passed harmlessly through his overcoat.

Mrs. Roosevelt gasped, then asked quietly: "You say he wasn't hurt, Oliver?" Hadn't he better go back to headquarters to make sure? As the young man hurried away, she sat, silent and composed. Here it was, a reality at last, this menace of assassination that had hung over her since that fateful day when, at the Tahawus Club in the Adirondacks, she had received word of the shooting of Mr. McKinley.

Oliver returned, reporting that the Colonel had been scratched but had made his scheduled speech. Oliver's mother suggested that they leave the theater. No, Mrs. Roosevelt said quietly, she preferred to stay. If he had made his speech he could not be really hurt, and if they went to the headquarters they might be caught up in the emotionalism inevitably attending any fearful happening.

When the play was over—and one wonders how much of the final act Edith Roosevelt heard—George hurried the ladies out of the side entrance of the theater on 39th Street into a waiting cab. In the suite in the Hotel Manhattan, occupied by George W. Perkins, the chief financial backer of the Progressive Party, there was disquieting news: the Colonel had definitely been wounded. Should she go to Milwaukee at once, Mrs. Roosevelt, calm and self-possessed, debated with herself, or wait till the next afternoon? The issue was decided for her, shortly after midnight, by a telegram from the Colonel himself: he was "in excellent shape," and had made an hour and a half's speech. The wound was "trivial." The bullet had "merely glanced on a rib" and had certainly not touched the lung. It wasn't "a particle more serious than one of the injuries the boys used continually to be having." He was at the Emergency Hospital at the moment and anticipated "going right on" with his engagements.

Mrs. Roosevelt read the message with skeptical eyes. "That's just the sort of thing," she recalled, "that was said when Mr. McKinley was shot."

Gradually, as the night wore on and successive bulletins arrived, Mrs. Roosevelt got the outline of what had happened. The Colonel was leaving the Hotel Gilpatrick and getting into the automobile that was to take him to the Auditorium where he was to speak, when a man on the farther side of the street had rushed forward and shot him at close range. A stenographer in the Colonel's party, a former football player, Elbert Martin, who had been standing by the automobile, had caught the glint of steel, catapulted himself over the hood of the car and brought the assailant to the pavement. The Colonel had insisted on proceeding to the Auditorium, before permitting even a cursory examination of the wound.

"We stayed at the headquarters," Mrs. Roosevelt wrote her sister, "until we heard that Theodore's wound had been dressed at the Emergency Hospital in Milwaukee, and he was sleeping quietly in his car on the way to Chicago."

She spent the night in New York with Cousin Laura, restless with anxiety that was not relieved next morning by the dramatic details of the shooting that the New York papers gave her: the wild shouts in the street, "Kill the brute! Get a rope!" and the Colonel's voice, rising above them, "Don't hurt him. Bring him to me!" the blood-stained shirt-front as the Colonel walked on the stage at the Auditorium, the shudder passing through the audience, the angry cries of the men, the sobbing "Oh's!" of the women, the tense silence as the Colonel began: "I'm going to ask you to be very quiet. You see there is a bullet in my body"—the unfolding of his manuscript and his evident shock at the discovery of the bullet-holes in it; the long, earnest, occasionally repetitious, not always coherent speech, the efforts of his friends to make him desist, his repeated response, "I will make this speech or die, one or the other!"

The morning papers—and all but one, the *Press*, were politically opposed to the Colonel, and opposed with a virulence such as

New York had not known since the Bryan campaign, sixteen years before—gave their first three or four pages to the shooting, with headlines and text in the best American tradition of good sportsmanship. The reader might have thought the Colonel was their own candidate, their own cherished hero. INSISTS ON SPEAKING. NO THOUGHT OF SELF. PLEADS FOR THE TRUTH, URGES THAT MISREPRESENTATION BY HIS OPPONENTS SHALL CEASE. SMILES THROUGH IT ALL. *That* was the *Sun*, whose misrepresentations and distortions during the campaign had enraged the Colonel. The *Times*, which had been only a little less bitter, reserved its eloquence for the editorial page: "Only the exceptional man, the extraordinary man, can offer to the world such an exhibition of fortitude as Theodore Roosevelt gave, when, suffering a serious hurt . . . and against the protests of his physicians and the entreaties of his friends, he insisted upon making his speech. Mr. Roosevelt showed the indomitable courage that is ingrained in his being. It was rash . . . an act of hardihood . . . even an act of folly, but it was characteristic, and the judgment of the country will be that it was magnificent." Under the caption, "We are against his politics, but we like his grit," the New York *Herald* published a cartoon of the Colonel, addressing the nation, with the bullet-pierced manuscript in his upraised hand.

White-faced but composed, Edith Roosevelt was back at the Progressive Headquarters early in the forenoon, to find, as she wrote her sister, "that Theodore had reached the Roman Catholic Mercy Hospital in Chicago. They had put him to bed and hoped to avoid blood-poisoning by rest, etc. The bullet entered half way up the right side and went upwards to the left for about four inches where it is still lodged."

There was a report that the Colonel had been wakeful during the night, suffering from the reaction to the shock, followed by numerous bulletins indicating that the surgeons were worried because they had been unable to keep him from conducting political conferences and seeing newspapermen. "These men are my friends. You let me handle them."

Mrs. Roosevelt, reading the reports, pressed her lips together. She was going to Chicago at once, she said. "I am the only one who can manage him, and make him obey the doctor's orders."

At four that afternoon, with Ethel and Ted and the beloved "Alec" Lambert, she boarded the Twentieth Century Limited.

The reporters thought Lambert's presence suspicious. If the Colonel's wound was not serious, as the bulletins appeared to indicate, "Why, Doctor," they asked, "are you going out?"

Lambert was forthright as always. "Because Mrs. Roosevelt is worried, and wants me to go."

Would Mrs. Roosevelt be strong enough to make the trip? an *Evening Mail* reporter asked Dr. Lambert.

"A woman," he answered, "is always able to do anything she wants to do at any time"; a happily married man's generalization which failed to receive the editorial attention it deserved.

Alice, as her way was when trouble hit the family, was on hand when they arrived in Chicago. "We found Theodore looking really well, and rested," Mrs. Roosevelt wrote Emily Carow, "for his whole condition is good, owing to his general health." She installed herself in a room adjoining the Colonel's and, in her customary way, with a glance, a gesture or an occasional smiling yet firm ukase, took command of the situation—and of the Colonel. Before the day was over, noted the reporter of the Chicago *Tribune*, "she was practically managing the hospital, as far as the Colonel was concerned."

Her husband characteristically made the best of what he couldn't do anything about, read Macaulay's essays and called it a vacation. He was really a good patient, Mrs. Roosevelt pointed out, when he had to be.

Yet for days her heart was bleak with anxiety. "That frightful week in Chicago," she called it, writing her sister again, ten days later. But there was balm. "The feeling of the hundreds of thousands who were thinking of him and loving him seemed to strengthen and help."

As for the patient himself, "I did not care a rap for being shot," the Colonel wrote Spring-Rice. "It is a trade risk, which every prominent public man ought to accept as a matter of course. For eleven years I have been prepared any day to be shot"; adding, to the Lodges, that he "felt a little like the old maid who, when she at last discovered a man under the bed, seized him and said 'You're the burglar I have been looking for these last twenty years.'" As for all the commotion about his making his speech after he was shot, why, at San Juan he had expected every officer to "fight as long as he could stand; and what I expect lieutenants to do I expect, *a fortieri,* a leader to do."

320

The Colonel and his lady returned to Sagamore Hill a week after the shooting. "Getting home seems like a tonic to him," noted the New York *Times* reporter, but the Colonel admitted he was tired and, when he dropped off shortly after, he slept as though he never intended to wake again. He found his beloved colored house-man, James Amos, standing guard over him when he awoke, and a cordon of sturdy farm-boys from the environs keeping visitors from approaching the house.

But, after a night's rest, the Colonel was in revolt against such "mollycoddling." He was going to see George Perkins that day and O. K. Davis, not to speak of Dr. Abbott, and anyone and every-one might as well know that he was going to make his scheduled speech at Madison Square Garden on October 30th, a week away. Mrs. Roosevelt, it was noted, smiled graciously and said nothing, eloquently. The physician in attendance looked encouragingly at the Colonel and timidly at Mrs. Roosevelt. "Maybe," said the *Times* man, "the Colonel will speak at Madison Square on October 30th. If he does, Mrs. Roosevelt will be intensely mistaken." One wonders how the reporter got the picture, but it sounds authentic.

The Colonel stood his confinement to the house for three days; then he thrust on his black campaign hat and made for the open. He looked around for Mrs. Roosevelt and couldn't find her. Where was she? In the garden, he was told, picking flowers for the table. He went to look for her. She was not too happy to see him, not approving of his revolt, but let him walk north as far as the stable and south as far as the tennis-court. The Colonel's birthday, next day, was "a day of Thanksgiving for us all," Mrs. Roosevelt wrote her sister. "But the horror of the deed still overshadows all who love him."

The day after, for the first time, the Colonel's vigilant lady let him see the newspapermen who had been hovering about the door since his return. They were in the drawing-room when, as the *Times* had it, next morning, "the Colonel came breezing in as if he had never been shot in his life."

"By George!" he cried, shaking hands all round—which was the one thing the doctors had told him he must not do—"It's good to be back in the old channels!"

"How does it feel, Colonel?" one of the men asked. "The bullet, I mean."

"It feels like rheumatism," he answered ruefully. "Only a lot worse."

The newsmen begged him for his own account of the shooting, and he gave it to them, including items of drama which the on-the-spot-reporters had missed. As for his plans, besides the Garden speech there was one he must make in "the village." The "village" was Oyster Bay.

"What do you want to spend your strength in Oyster Bay for," asked one of the reporters, "when you could make more votes by talking in some of the other places that are trying to get you?"

"Why, Great Scott!" the Colonel exclaimed, as though he regarded the query as quite beyond the bounds of reason. "I couldn't pass up the village!"

The *Times* man had no answer for that, but what he was thinking and would write in his next morning's story was that the Colonel was "pretty fond of his home town, for a fact. Still, as the town is sure for him, it seems like a waste of energy. But you can't argue with the Colonel on a question of that kind."

4

People began arriving at Madison Square Garden in the middle of the afternoon. When the doors were opened at seven o'clock the gilded Diana at the peak of the house was, in fact, looking out over 30,000 of them, milling around the entrances. Some 16,000 jostled and pushed through the doors and stampeded for seats; the rest waited around in hopes of seeing the hero when he arrived.

Only a few actually saw him, but those few made the most of it. When a troop of automobiles came dashing down Madison Avenue, a yellow taxi leading, with a limousine following, they broke the police-lines and, as the *Sun* told the story next morning, "came down with the limousine, yelling their immortal souls out. They went through a battery of photographers, tried to sweep the cops off their feet, tangled, jammed and shoved into the throng." Two younger Roosevelts got out first, with Lambert, as physician in charge, and Cecil Lyon, a Texas stalwart, as bodyguard. "Then the last man of the party appeared, and then they let it all out again in shouts, yells and screams."

322

"Here he comes again!"

The police made a lane for the Colonel, walking a little slowly,
a little stiffly, toward a fire-escape. The crowds tried "to climb over
and under the guards back of him," but the police held them. Then
"suddenly the big walls seemed to bulge. The Colonel had arrived
inside."

What made the walls seem to bulge were sixteen thousand people
trying to tell the Colonel what they thought of him.

Mrs. Roosevelt was in a box with Ethel, Ted, Eleanor and Quentin, listening to warming-up speeches by Oscar S. Straus, Progressive
candidate for governor of New York and Governor Hiram W. Johnson of California, the vice-presidential candidate, when a sound
of distant cheering, growing ever louder, began to be heard. A sud-

den rush of men filled the entrance beneath the speaker's tribunal. The next moment the stocky, energetic figure, so familiar and so dear to American audiences, appeared, striding to the front of the platform, and bedlam was loose.

It lasted forty-one minutes. "Such demonstrations," noted the *Times* reporter, "are commonplace in national conventions where they are carefully worked up by cheer-leaders and kept going by megaphones and other mechanical means. This thing, however, was spontaneous. The crowd kept on yelling because it wanted to yell." How much of the enthusiasm was due to sympathy with a man who had dramatically demonstrated his courage, and how much was due to enthusiasm for his politics the writer could not guess. But it was "astounding" that 16,000 persons "should go so absolutely crazy for forty-one minutes as these 16,000 men and women in the Garden did. A moment before the Colonel appeared in his somber black suit, they appeared to be perfectly orderly and respectable persons. But the moment his ruddy face, gray moustache and eye-glasses showed up on the platform they lost all semblance of order. Perfectly respectable, gray-haired matrons climbed on chairs with flags and handkerchiefs in their hands and forgot themselves for three quarters of an hour. After about half an hour, persons who, in the ordinary course of life, may be deacons or assistant bank cashiers were dancing around the floor in a frenzy. Occasionally, the band would try to intervene with the 'Battle Hymn of the Republic' or 'Onward, Christian Soldiers,' but it could not even make a dent in the uproar."

Roosevelt stood looking over this sea of emotional human beings with a gaze that was "quite different from that of the ordinary stump speaker. He knew that he had to stand there and take it as long as it lasted, but really it annoyed and disturbed him, great as the tribute was." He had, in fact, not felt well when he had left Sagamore Hill that morning, and had counted on the inspiration of the crowd to invigorate and sustain his spirit. But this was more than he had expected. He clearly enjoyed the reception, but the *Sun* reporter noted that at the end of a half-hour "his face was gleaming with perspiration and his jaws were snapping nervously as though he were bent upon keeping himself in trim for the speech." He wanted to get his message to the American people, not knowing if or when he might get another chance. Observers noted that, though he smiled happily, now and again, he seemed troubled

324

at the homage these followers of his were showing him; and his acceptance of their devotion was less smiling, more stern, than in other days. Finally, when, after forty minutes, the uproar showed no signs of subsiding—and the *Times* man was sure it would have gone on for twenty or thirty minutes more but for the former President's "perfectly obvious refusal to permit a longer demonstration"—the Colonel strode to the desk and pounded it with such "commanding sincerity" that the crowd fell silent at last.

"My friends, once in a generation . . ." he began. His words were drowned out by a new wave of cheering near the platform. The Colonel pointed his arm at the disturbers. "Quiet, down there!" he cried sharply.

"The tumult and the shouting dies," quoted the New York *Press* editorially, next morning, "and now the hushed multitude hears the low, impressive tones of a servitor of mankind breathing a pledge of brotherhood, a reproach without a tinge of malice, a plea for human rights, a supplication for equal justice and liberty—a demand for the survival of the American form of government." Listeners remarked on the complete absence in the speech not only of bitterness but of the first-person singular. He who customarily moved to the attack at the drop of the hat, moreover, attacked nobody; and never once did he let his voice rise into the falsetto that frequently heralded some comical sally and never failed to delight the crowd.

Surely, the editor of the *Press* was not alone in that audience in asking himself, "Is this the Roosevelt we have seen reviled as a firebrand in the national powderhouse, as a vindictive egoist, bent on revenge?"

With passionate ardor, that night, the Colonel was stating the fundamentals of his political faith, and stating them as though he were conscious that he was still under the shadow of death.

5

A little before midnight following the election, the reporters, covering Sagamore Hill, "rather more subdued than usual," the *Times* man thought, crowded into the library to which, in other years, they or their predecessors had come for the Colonel's reaction to happier election returns. How, they wondered, had the Progressive candidate taken the Democratic landslide? They found the Colonel sitting under his study lamp with a book in his hand and a log-wood blaze shining softly from the broad fireplace. "So far as anyone could read him," ran the *Times* story, next morning, "he was all-buoyant and good-humored," chatting with the newspapermen "in the most cheerful manner imaginable."

"I accept the result with entire good humor and contentment," he said in a formal statement, which was all he would give the men for publication. "I can only repeat what I have already so many times declared. The fate of the leader for the time being is of little consequence, but the cause itself must in the end triumph, for its triumph is essential to the well-being of the American people."

Chapter V

ROOSEVELT had expected defeat, and it brought him neither disappointment nor bitterness; only pride at having fought a hard fight in a high cause. "We have posed the vital questions that are now before the nation," he wrote Charles D. Willard, "and the parties will have to deal with them." He did not share the illusion sustaining many of his followers that the heavy vote that the Progressives had polled established them as a permanent factor in American political life. "Theodore," his wife admitted to Mrs. Cowles, was "rather blue. Many things," she added, "that he had no time to think of during the campaign come to him now."

Was he asking himself, as he suggested in a long autobiographical letter to Kermit, two years later, whether it might have been well if, after he left the Presidency, he had taken no part whatever in politics? But how could he have held back against the appeals of men he believed in, men who had fought for the policies he had been fighting for when he was President? After all, there was no use his talking about virtue in the abstract unless he applied it in concrete cases; and he had either had to act as he had acted or abandon all effort to say anything on any public question whatever. Perhaps he should have done just that. But, if he had, might he not now be feeling that he had ignobly played safe?

Winter closed in on Sagamore, and something sharper than winter. This hilltop that for almost fifteen years had been a chief focus of national interest, with visitors coming and going at all hours, and newspapermen clamoring for stories, was deserted except for the master of the house and his lady, their daughter, and the Roosevelt cousins roundabout. The telephone, which had rung like sleigh-bells all day and half the night, was silent. The North Shore neighbors who, in the old days, had flocked to Sagamore at every opportunity, on horseback or in their high fancy traps, did not drive their new shining motor-cars up the new, hard-surfaced road the Roosevelts had put in the year before. The Colonel was outside the pale. He had done the unforgivable thing—he had "turned against his class." For them, as for the Progressives, the campaign had had a religious quality as they rose in defense of things-as-they-were and of their injured patron saint in the White House. Most of them were not too sure about the details of the doctrines with which their old neighbor and friend was assailing the citadels of their security, but everyone agreed that they were "wild" and "revolutionary." With such a "destroyer" you couldn't pick up the threads, the day after election, and pretend that nothing really had happened. Casual encounters on the roads or in church were correct but cold.

"Alec" Lambert, sensing, with his intuitive tenderness, that all might not be well at Sagamore, tossed a toothbrush and a night-gown in a satchel and received a welcome whose hungry warmth he never forgot. The Colonel was alone; even Mrs. Roosevelt and Ethel happened to be away.

"You cannot imagine," the Colonel exclaimed, "how glad I am to see you! I have been unspeakably lonely. You don't know how lonely it is for a man to be rejected by his own kind. I have just come from Boston, where I attended a meeting of the Harvard overseers. They all bunched at one end of the room away from me, and I stood all alone there except for one man, nice General Hallowell, who acted like a perfect trump, standing by me through it all, gnashing his teeth in rage at those other fellows. By George!" he added, his voice rising suddenly into the familiar comic falsetto, "we were like a pair of Airedale pups in a convention of tomcats!"

The role of pariah was new to him and he didn't like it. "I wish he could see Gracie oftener," his wife wrote his sister, "for she distracts him and amuses him more than his own children can!" Fortunately, the weather had been so mild that her husband could ride. "He has made a pet of the horse he has now, and finds him companionable."

If he was not to have people at Sagamore, a horse was not too bad a substitute.

But he had something even better than a horse to restore his bruised spirit: the blessing of a multi-track mind. He had agreed to collaborate with Edmund Heller, one of the Smithsonian scientists who had accompanied him on his African trip, on a series of "Life Histories of African Game Animals"; more immediately he had a presidential address to prepare for a meeting of the American Historical Association in Boston, the end of December. He was calling it "History as Literature," but the dry title gave no warning of the surging rhythms, the arresting images to which he would rise in its concluding passages. There was a poet among the various beings who lived harmoniously together in the capacious frame of Theodore Roosevelt but, in the tumult of action, he had only rarely made himself heard—once, in "The Wilderness Hunter," when he had sung of the mocking-bird; again, in the preface to "African Game Trails"; finally, and most compellingly, in the peroration of this address to the historians, seeing "the kings of Nineveh where they drink from ivory and gold," "Queen Maeve in her sun-parlor where she watched the nearing chariots of the champions," and a dozen other flashing moments in the world's colorful past.

Boston, it happened, forgot politics and redeemed itself, so far as the Colonel was concerned, turning out in appropriate numbers and distinguished personalities, listening with absorbed attention and crowding round him afterward.

The experience did him good. With his crop filled to bursting with politics and politicians, it was something to have made the stuffy Bostonians dream dreams of "the terrible horsemen of Timur the Lame" riding "over the roof of the world," as their latterday descendants might conceivably some day ride over even Boston.

But it was not enough. The Progressive Party lay like a mountain on the Colonel's mind. The leaders came to Sagamore to discuss the future of the Party, and at conferences in New York and Chicago he worked with them to do what he knew was hopeless —build an organization that should be permanent. At gatherings, and in the intervals between them, his chief occupations became a seemingly never-ending effort to keep the extremists in both wings of the Party from tearing each other's eyes out. The Colonel was forced to spend hours and occasionally days arguing with some cherished but erratic friend or dictating ten-page letters, pleading for realism. "I think I shall be able to keep both sides together," he wrote Kermit. "But it is very weary work, and it is

329

irritating now because I ought not to be required to do such work.
. . . This whole business of leading a new party," he added, "should
be for an ambitious young colonel, not for a retired major general."

"Theodore works like a dog," Mrs. Roosevelt wrote her sister-in-
law. "He is not having an easy time, poor dear."

The Colonel, returning to Sagamore from the party conferences,
feeling old and doubly defeated, sought forgetfulness in a new
purpose. Convinced that he had reached the end of his public life,
he did what plenty of other men, similarly facing the inevitable,
had done before him; he began to look backward and to set down
what he saw. It was escape, and something better, to lose himself
in his boyhood's distant past, to recapture the strength and charm
of his father, his mother's beauty and Southern grace, his Aunt
Annie's devotion and her evocation of plantation life and Negro
fancy, the heroism of his mother's Confederate brothers, the Victorian solidity of the East Twentieth Street house.

Politics, defeat, the loss of power, prestige, friends—the gnawing
question, "Had it all had to come as it had?"—the shock of the
attempted assassination, faded from his experience and he was in
the New York legislature again, climbing the first rungs of the ladder that had led to the Presidency; in the Bad Lands again, on the
round-up and the hunting trail, making his mark among daring
stalwart men and being accounted their equal. What matter if his
active life were over, if he were that most pathetic symbol of eva-
nescence, a popular hero who had outlived the cheers? He had been
a man among men; he had cut a swathe.

As the months passed, the work to which he had run for refuge
took possession of him and gave him new life.

"Theodore is the same old darling," the Colonel's old friend,
"Winty" Chanler, wrote Cecil Spring-Rice, lamenting the effect of
time on their friends. "He too is older. His egotism has grown on
him, but so has his fat. These are trifles, the warty growths on a
magnificent oak tree. A man cannot be at the top—the real top—
for six or seven years—the leader of the world—and not show the
effects. And no man who went through such a phase in the world's
history, perhaps, has come out of it so little harmed and changed.
That he will ever be President or even candidate again is open to
every doubt, political turn or popular fancy. Look at his victory,
and look at his defeat. He remains through it all the man we know
and have known."

The children came and went. Ted had returned East to become a bond salesman for a New York firm and was doing well, in spite of his being thrown out of Wall Street offices occasionally because he was his father's son. From time to time he came to Sagamore with Eleanor, "too pretty and darling for anything," the Colonel wrote Kermit, bringing Gracie, "full of little tricks and very blooming in her white bonnet with its wreath of rosebuds," as Mrs. Roosevelt described her. "Graciekins is the very dearest baby you ever saw," her devoted grandfather wrote Kermit. "She loves me now, and calls me Grandpa, and runs up with her arms out to be taken in my arms and allowed to pet the animal heads." Archie came from Andover, where he was entering his final year of school— none of the Roosevelt boys thought much of school—and Quentin from Groton, with a broken nose from a blow with a hockey-stick. "They are very different from one another," their father wrote Emily Carow, "but they are dear boys, each in his own way; and they give hope for believing that they will turn out all right and do their work in the world honestly and fairly." Quentin might be mentally quicker, but Archie's "steady commonsense and resolution" kept the balance even.

"Christmas was great fun," the Colonel wrote Emily Carow. "All the children acted as if it were fifteen years ago. They hung up their stockings, and came in and opened them on the bed next morning, and after breakfast trooped in to see their presents in Edith's drawing room." The "fun" was not confined to Christmas. There were house-parties for Ethel and fancy-dress parties among the buffalo-heads, antlers, elephant-tusks and African spears of the North Room in which the father and mother gaily participated, the father a schoolmaster in cap and gown and the mother a sedate Puritan matron.

Into his chapter, "Outdoors and Indoors," the Colonel packed his love for his family and for the home that had been the focus of his life for a quarter-century. "At Sagamore Hill," he wrote, "we love a great many things—birds and trees and books, and all things beautiful, and horses and rifles and children and hard work and the joy of life." That joy returned to him as he wrote. "We have great fireplaces and in them the logs roar and crackle during the long winter evenings"; and they roared and crackled at his back as he sat at his desk in the library and the snow beat against the window.

3

Across the panorama of the past, unfolding under his pen, fell a bright shaft of light into the future. Mrs. Roosevelt was sitting reading one afternoon in February—the year was 1913—when Ethel came into the room with "Dick" Derby, who was visiting at Sagamore.

"Mother," Ethel said, "I am going to marry Dick."

"I could scarcely believe my ears," Mrs. Roosevelt wrote her sister. Ethel's decision had hung fire so long that most of the family had lost hope. The two months that followed, Mrs. Roosevelt wrote Mrs. Cowles, were among "the happiest times" of her life, with Ethel, "the dear child, so sweet and unselfish, but living in a rose-colored cloud quite alone with Dick."

The young people were married early in April in Christ Church in Oyster Bay, the little Episcopal church that had been the background of the family worship for twenty-five years. Even before the invited guests arrived at the church, citizens of Oyster Bay—neighbors all—had gathered outside—a thousand or more finally—with a band that played "My Sweetheart" for the bride and "Pride of America" for her father. Inside the church, Ted and Eleanor's Gracie, not yet two, made the hit of the day when she greeted with a shrill chuckle Dr. Endicott Peabody's query whether anyone knew of any reason why this marriage should not be performed.

"The day was beautiful and warm with the air of Spring and the approach of Summer," wrote Owen Wister in "Roosevelt—the Story of a Friendship." "Its brightness came in through the open windows among the flowers and the friends that filled the little church. As one looked about, familiar faces were smiling everywhere. After the quiet, solemn services, in whose sweetness the whole congregation shared, the same feeling went with us all to Sagamore Hill. That concourse of men and women, so many of whom knew each other so well, had a quality that was like the flowers and the day. Most of us had been at the White House when Alice was married in the East Room. In that stately atmosphere, beneath the inevitable spell, we could not be quite as we were in that country house. The cordiality, the welcome, were alike under

332

either roof—but here at Sagamore Hill the host was not our President. Mrs. Roosevelt and he were free from every obligation but their own natural hospitality and the pleasure they always took in showing it."

The wedding breakfast was served in the dining room, the North Room and on the piazza, with a table in the drawing-room where the Colonel and Mrs. Roosevelt had gathered particular friends. At last, in a shower of rice, the young couple ran out the wide front door to take a steamer, next day, for Europe; the guests departed; and only the family remained amid the disorder, the melted ice cream, the crumpled napkins and the scattered punch-glasses. "We had a nice quiet hour, all of us together," Mrs. Roosevelt wrote Mrs. Cowles, who had gone home earlier, "with Gracie as center. Then Quentin read me to sleep with a fairy tale, and when we came together for dinner the house was all in order."

4

Sagamore seemed empty with the last of the young birds out of the nest. "Mother and I have dear evenings together," the Colonel wrote Ethel, honeymooning with Dick in Italy, "but I wish I played cards and was more of a companion to her." He told of rides together through the dogwood, "lovely" as never before, of rows to their favorite haunt, Lloyd's Neck, "among the blooming beach plum bushes." It was a satisfaction to note the way Ted naturally gravitated to Sagamore whenever he had a holiday, bringing Eleanor and the "grandbaby," and "relapsed," as his father put it, into the small boy.

Harried by importunate Progressive Party leaders, the Colonel snatched whatever free time they left him to push the Autobiography forward. He was "working like a steam engine," Mrs. Roosevelt wrote Mrs. Cowles, and was "tired and jaded—having far too much to do, and the least interruption upsets him." He had agreed to give a series of addresses in the South American capitals and was planning an exploration into the Brazilian wilderness; but he must finish the Autobiography and the "Life Histories" before he went, in early October, he said, and take Archie and Quentin into the Indian country north of the Grand Canyon, in July. There was a lawsuit, moreover, against an editor who had brought up that hoary libel of his drinking, that was coming to trial in May. "The

Japan imbroglio," Mrs. Roosevelt wrote Mrs. Cowles, "worries him dreadfully too."

The California legislature was debating a bill to forbid the lease or sale of land to individuals ineligible for American citizenship. The Japanese ambassador protested; in Japan there were riots. Roosevelt as President had dealt with a similar situation by his customary combination of soft speaking and the Big Stick. Wilson, the new President, however, announced that he would take no action until the California legislature had passed the law and the courts had "examined" it.

"There is such a lack of the real grasp of things at the White House, to all appearance," Mrs. Roosevelt wrote her sister-in-law, adding significantly, that, "for the first time," Theodore was beginning "to wish that his hand was on the helm."

For this Japanese business came close home. He knew the psychology of the men at the Japanese end of it. There must be instant contact with them before they got out of hand. Wilson was just drifting, and you could not afford to drift in foreign affairs; there were too many rocks and shoals. Quietly, as a private citizen, and as friend to friend, he poured oil on the troubled waters, writing both the governor of California, his 1912 running-mate, Hiram Johnson, on the one hand, and his Japanese friend, Baron Kaneko, on the other, to keep their shirts on.

Eleanor, forty years later, remembered the flurry the Japanese incident caused at Sagamore. She was spending a week end there with Ted and was appalled by the zest with which her husband and her father-in-law discussed the possibility of war. Neither thought that war with Japan would come, but, if it did, they were going to be in it. The Colonel spoke of the division he would raise and Ted eagerly claimed a place in it.

Eleanor, heartsick, appealed to her mother-in-law. What did it all mean? Was there really going to be war? Mrs. Roosevelt was unruffled. "You mustn't take this too seriously," she said. "We women are like that occasionally when we talk about some day owning a string of matched pearls. It doesn't mean a thing."

The incident illustrates the curious dualism of Roosevelt's mental processes in relation to the question of war. As a statesman who during his Presidency had missed no opportunity to maintain and strengthen world peace, or to re-establish it when it was broken, the Colonel was appalled at Wilson's complacent inaction in an explosive international situation; but as a private citizen he was day-dreaming of a major-general's stars on his shoulder and heroic service on a desperate field. His frame of reference was the war he had fought vicariously, day after day, as a boy, and the war he had himself actually been in. The battles in which he saw himself participating were, in fact, nearer in nature and technique to Roncesvalles and Agincourt than to the Marnes, the Ypres and the Verduns just under the eastern horizon.

5

The Colonel finished his Autobiography and the "Life Histories," took Archie and Quentin to the Arizona Indian country, as he had promised, attended a farewell dinner that the Progressives gave him in New York and, early in October, with a sigh of relief, set off with Mrs. Roosevelt for South America. "I think he feels like Christian in 'Pilgrim's Progress' when the bundle fell from his back," Mrs. Roosevelt wrote her sister from the steamer. "In this case it was not made of sins but of the Progressive Party."

They made the rounds of the South American capitals together, but when the Colonel plunged into the wilderness with Kermit and a group of American naturalists, accompanied by three or four adventurous officers from the Brazilian Army, Mrs. Roosevelt returned home. That was in December. During the four months that followed no word from the jungle came to tell her whether her husband were dead or alive. At last, in April, came a message: he had reached civilization, having discovered and explored a new river, nearly a thousand miles long.

The Colonel reached New York, the middle of May, pallid, hollow-cheeked, leaning on a cane and lighter in weight by fifty-five pounds. "I was pretty well laid up in Brazil," he admitted in a letter to Arthur Lee. Infection and fever had, in fact, brought him to the verge of death and failed to claim him only because he had known that Kermit would not leave him behind, living or dead; and he had battled his way through to survival, not for his own sake so much as for Kermit's.

At Sagamore Hill the Colonel was instantly caught up in a whirl of Progressive Party politics. Once again, the midterm elections were looming, candidates were to be nominated in every state; rumors of reunion with the Republicans were rife and some were promising; he himself was being pressed to run for governor of New York. There were successive conferences, followed by a hurried trip to Washington, for a lecture on his South American expedition before the National Geographic Society, and then he was once more on the wing, bound for Madrid, where Kermit was marrying Belle Willard, daughter of the American ambassador to Spain.

The jungle fever laid hold on him on the way home, and he was groggy with it when he returned to Sagamore the end of June. Again the Progressive leaders came flocking from all over the country, each with some problem he wanted the Colonel to solve, some tangle he wanted the Colonel to unsnarl, and all hectoring him to get into the fall campaign. "The trouble with Father's situation," Quentin, now sixteen, was heard to remark, "is that he is expected to pull everybody's chestnuts out of the fire." And he was in no condition, an anonymous friend told the New York *Times* reporter, even to pull out his own. "They can roast a little longer with no harm to himself."

"Alec" Lambert, pointing out that the Colonel's larynx was in dangerous shape, issued orders, supported by the authority of Mrs. Roosevelt: the Colonel must rest for three or four months. Lambert's decree got into the papers. Progressives hung their heads; Republican and Democratic politicians and editors threw metaphorical hats skyward: the Colonel was "done for" as a factor in public life; the Colonel was "through."

If the Colonel thought that the rejoicing was premature, he did not say so; perhaps he did not greatly care. He agreed to lie low, except for one speech in Pittsburgh. He had made a promise there, and he would keep it. After that, he would stay home and rest.

He made the speech and gave his opponents the shock of their lives. For it was not the pallid invalid, returning, broken in health, from the exertions of his South American exploration, who presented once more the principles of the Progressive cause. Perhaps the cheering crowds, lining the Pittsburgh streets, revitalized him; perhaps the very hopelessness of the campaign, that this speech of his was opening, recharged his fighting energies. What the crowd saw, the Philadelphia *North American* reported next day, was "the vigorous, fighting Roosevelt who so long had led the people's battles." The New York *World*, which generally looked on Roosevelt with a droopy eye, gave a picture of "the Colonel" enjoying every minute. "Malaria was forgotten and all physical weakness along with it as he stood at the vortex of the night's enthusiasm."

The Colonel's larynx proved to be not worse but better after his two-hours speech. "There is a spirit in man . . ."

Chapter VI

SUMMER LAY warm and peaceful over Sagamore Hill. In the woods at the bottom of the western slope the wood-thrushes sang, as usual, joined by the tanager and the vireo, and, at dusk, the oven-bird. In the weeping elm, near the house, the orioles perched, and, in the shrubbery, the song-sparrows. In the pasture back of the barn, an eager ear could catch the bubbling melody of the bobolinks and, as July advanced and the hot weather came, the bright-hued indigo buntings and thistle-finches added their voices to the Sagamore chorus.

The Colonel was resting; at least, he called it rest. A stream of visitors, a deluge of mail. The children, growing up, yet eager always to run back to Sagamore: Ted and Eleanor with a second baby, a boy—TR III—and Gracie, "the dearest small soul you ever saw," the Colonel writes Emily Carow, "and my heart is like water before her." . . . Kermit home with Belle from their honeymoon ("Belle is a perfect trump") . . . Ethel and Dick and their baby, a boy, Richard . . . Archie and Quentin ("really such fine fellows!"). On the Fourth, a typical Sagamore picnic on Lloyd's Neck with most of the effete younger generation going in cars, but the Colonel, as usual, rowing Mrs. Roosevelt in the skiff, eight miles there, eight miles back. Then again politicians from everywhere . . . Progressive candidates for governor or senator, in this state or that . . . New York politicians in a flood . . . What about the governorship? You can save the Progressive Party all over the nation if you will run. . . . No, no, no . . . and yet . . . public office—to be active again, not to talk only but to act—the thought allures him.

The Colonel sends for Victor Murdoch of Kansas, Albert J. Beveridge, of Indiana, and one or two others. After dinner they are together with Mrs. Roosevelt in the Trophy Room. What about the governorship?

"I don't know, Colonel," Murdoch answers. "After a man has been President of the United States, it lowers his dignity, it seems to me, to run for anything like the governorship of a state."

"That is exactly what I feel," cries Mrs. Roosevelt. There is a chorus of assent in which the Colonel himself joins.

Beveridge is silent. Then, as the chorus subsides, he unfolds the handsome slender length of him and rises to his feet, talking quietly but with fire. He is, in fact, not talking in the conversational sense at all, Murdoch recalls, a quarter-century later. He is making a speech, saying what he thinks of a general who has trained and led an army to a certain point and then refuses to take part in a fight because in the course of it his personal dignity may suffer injury.

His speech carries the group away, in spite of their better judgment. "By George!" the Colonel cries, "I'll do it, I'll run."

2

He did not run. For a third time in his life, the bullet of a crazed fanatic cut across his purposes. The shot at Sarajevo had thundered around the world but, in the relaxation of midsummer, of baseball, yacht races, swimming marathons and local murders and divorces, America had all but forgotten what looked to the average newspaper-reader as just another typical Balkan bloodletting. Even the Colonel, to judge by the letters he wrote that July of 1914, had apparently never thought of it again. His letters were all domestic politics, the midterm elections ahead, the doomed Progressive Party, his own unhappy dilemma.

But in Vienna, a bemedaled foreign minister and his senile emperor were not forgetting Sarajevo. On July 25th, their ultimatum burst over Europe. Within forty-eight hours, Austria and Serbia were at war; within a week, Russia, Germany and France were furiously mobilizing. The German army invaded Belgium. Britain, plagued by militant suffragettes, torn over the issue of Irish Home Rule, confused by pacifist doctrinaires and wanting nothing so much as to retain the comfortable ways that it had always cherished, was hesitating, wondering whether she could not maintain her neutrality. The decision was to be made at a cabinet meeting on August 4th.

The Colonel had four men for luncheon at Sagamore Hill that

day. One was Herbert Croly, founder and editor of the *New Republic* and author of "The Promise of American Life." The Colonel had a kind of reciprocal relationship to Croly's *magnum opus*, since his actions as President had stimulated Croly's thinking and he himself had drawn much of his "New Nationalism" from the Croly book. With Croly had come one of his associate editors, Walter Weyl, and a brilliant young lawyer, Felix Frankfurter, who had just been called to the faculty of the Harvard Law School. The fourth guest was an elderly and exceptionally handsome Englishman, Charles Booth, who combined, as only a cultivated Englishman could, the presidency of the Cunard Steamship Company with the sensitivity and compassion that had enabled him to write the first comprehensive, detailed and scientific study of the poor of London.

The Colonel had invited these four men to talk about industrial relations in Britain and the United States. But they did not talk about industrial relations that day; they talked about the war.

Critics of Roosevelt, biographers and historians, would, for the next forty years, say that Roosevelt had, at the beginning of the war, been "confused" on the basic issues, had sat on the fence until he had caught the trend of popular opinion, had even, for a while, been pro-German. His guests on that historic August 4th were under no such illusions, as Frankfurter testified, unequivocally, for the historic record, thirty-nine years later. "I remember very vividly what TR said and will even go to the stake for it."

Frankfurter paints the two central figures in the Colonel's library with a portrait painter's skill: the Englishman, "an exquisite-looking creature, delicate, with a beautiful Van Dyck beard" and "refined reticence and hesitation of thought"; Roosevelt, "so boisterous a creature . . . so much animal zest, so much horsepower. The contrast between them in physical appearance was enormous, but also in attitude."

They all knew that, as they were conversing in the midsummer calm, in a comfortable American home, three thousand miles from the thunder of the guns, the British cabinet was meeting at Whitehall. Would Britain support Belgium, whose neutrality she had agreed to defend? Would she throw the power of the world's greatest navy in the scales against the world's greatest army?

Frankfurter recalled the drama in the Sagamore Hill library, with the Colonel, doing a "tomahawk war-dance" around "this beautiful creature, this exquisite old gentleman, seventy-four at the time"—seeing, Frankfurter might have added, all the might and glory of the British Empire in the slender old gentleman before him—"shaking his fist and saying, 'You've got to go in! You've got to go in!'" and Booth, "head of the Cunard Line, with God knows how many ships on the water, just sitting quietly, shaking his head, like one of those china mandarins, and saying slowly, 'I suppose we've got to go in.'"

The issue to Roosevelt was crystal-clear. Germany was an aggressor and you had to stop her. "I say all this," the Colonel went on, "though probably in a few years Germany will be an ally of ours in our fight against Japan."

They talked of the future, the immediate future and the far future. "We all of us sympathized with Belgium, and therefore with England and France," the Colonel wrote Hugo Münsterberg, three months later, speaking of the August 4th meeting, "but I was interested to find that we all of us felt that the smashing of Germany would be a great calamity, and would result in the entire western world being speedily forced into a contest against Russia."

All five men agreed, Frankfurter recalled, that the war had "implications that nobody could have any confidence wouldn't sweep us into the swirl."

They talked all afternoon. "While we were talking," Frankfurter recalled, "the English Cabinet was sitting." Before they finished luncheon—it was seven o'clock, Greenwich time—Britain entered the war.

3

For the two months that followed, the Colonel made no public statement regarding the war except for one article in the *Outlook* which was so meticulously balanced in its judgment of the rights and wrongs of the participating nations that it returned to plague him, the rest of his life. He would say nothing, he told himself, that might embarrass the President. The Colonel had no confidence in Wilson—"a scholarly, acrid pacifist of much ability and few scruples," he described him in a letter to Rudyard Kipling—and less in Bryan, his Secretary of State. But the President was carrying the burden of responsibility, and a President, he well knew, had sources of information not open to his would-be critics.

Wilson must be permitted to develop his policy without advice from the side-lines. "I am an ex-President," he pointed out to Arthur Lee, "and my public attitude must be one of caution and impartiality."

But Belgium was continuously on his mind, the violation of its neutrality, the devastation of its cities, the oppression by the German occupying forces. "It seems to me that if I were President," he wrote Lee on August 22nd, three weeks after the outbreak of the war, "I should register a very emphatic protest, a protest that would mean something, against the levy of the huge war contributions on Belgium." You might see Germany or Britain or France or Russia as right or wrong in the war, and make out a case; but with Belgium there was no room for argument. "The Germans, to suit their own purpose, trampled on their solemn obligations to Belgium and on Belgium's rights. The Belgians have fought for their hearthstones and homes and for the elemental rights without which it is not worth while to exist. To visit them with grinding punishment because of such action is proof positive that any power which now or hereafter may be put at the mercy of Germany will suffer in similar shape—and this whether the power were the United States, or England, or France, or Russia."

Let America beware, he was thinking, and prepare to defend herself. The war might not always stay three thousand miles away.

4

When the Colonel returned, early in October, from a campaign trip for his Progressive friends—"an utterly hopeless fight," he wrote Belle, Kermit's wife, "but it was my clear duty to go down with the rest of my associates"—he was startled to find that the war had ceased suddenly to be merely a public concern for him and had become a direct personal menace. Dick Derby was one of seven American surgeons who had gone to Paris in late September to serve in the American Ambulance Hospital in Paris, and Ethel had gone with him, to work as a nurse. Apprehension and pride mingled in her father's heart—any day, Paris might again be under bombardment—but, in the letters he wrote her, pride predominated; pride that two of his family "should have worthily met the call of high privilege to do their part in this great world tragedy . . . their part, and a portion of this nation's part."

343

But her mother's anxiety and his own, he added, were great. Ethel must come back soon to her baby whose "cunning, cooing little 'hymn to the sun,'" in the morning, in the room adjoining his own, was shedding a tender ray of light for him across the darkness of the times. "I have completely succumbed to him," the proud grandfather added, "and am immensely flattered because, when I go into his room before breakfast, he smiles and coos to be taken up and waves his little arms and legs. . . . Thank Heaven he's not a prophylactic baby! When he's on his back and I can only amuse him with my watch, he promptly stuffs it into his mouth, microbes and all."

5

Roosevelt waited in carefully guarded silence for the President to declare the national policy, but when, after three months, no policy emerged, beyond a formal declaration of neutrality and an appeal to the public to be neutral "in thought" as well as in act, Roosevelt tore off the self-imposed gag, and spoke out.

"I am utterly sick of the spiritless 'neutrality' of the Administration," he wrote Ethel, "and I have at last said so, in emphatic language." "I got out of patience," he explained to his Cove Neck neighbor, Frederic R. Coudert, "with having the public representatives of America deal in diluted mush." "It has been very hard," he admitted to Spring-Rice, "to keep myself in."

Earlier in the fall, in a series of articles written for the Wheeler Syndicate, and published weekly in the New York *Times* and other leading newspapers across the country, he had said what he thought of "the Belgian tragedy," called attention to "the duty of self-defense," spoken his mind about universal arbitration and pointed out ways of doing something for world peace that might really mean something. He bent over backward to be fair to Germany, but made no pretense that, in regard to Belgium, Germany had not committed a brutal wrong.

The German-language newspapers in the United States went after him in fury; the German-American organizations, the *Sängerbunde*, the *Turnvereine*, the German cultural societies which, in most cases, were—many unwittingly, perhaps—effective agencies of German propaganda, directed from the German embassy in Washington, denounced him in indignant resolutions.

The Colonel was amazed by the heat of their attacks. He was not criticizing Germany from the standpoint of Germany's enemies, but from the standpoint of the United States. He had, moreover, always got along well with the German-Americans. He liked the German people and had, again and again, as President, gone out of his way to say so; he admired German thrift and integrity. He had acclaimed, moreover, the contributions that men of German stock had made to American public life, from Carl Schurz and Franz Sigel down. So the bitterness of the German-American antagonism disturbed him. He had always assumed that the American melting-pot was, in the main, doing a thorough job of Americanizing the immigrant. But here were these people, most of them, no doubt, American citizens, taking the direction of their thinking obviously neither from their President, who was pleading for suspension of judgment, or from their American neighbors, who were not taking sides as yet to any notable degree, but from across the seas. The Irish, too, he noted, were, in general, flamingly anti-British. The homelands retained a stronger hold on the hearts and minds of citizens of foreign stock than he had dreamed.

Sitting in one of the comfortable rocking-chairs on the piazza at Sagamore, with the rocker traveling over the piazza floor as it had a way of doing when he rocked, he thought about these people who were Americans and were something else also. After all, was America a nation or was it just a "polyglot boarding-house"? This was a pretty grave question; it went to the foundations; yet no one was saying anything about it. All right! Then he himself would have to get after these "hyphenated" citizens, these "fifty-fifty Americans!"

On chill autumn evenings, sitting before the Trophy Room fire, he counted the cost. These German-Americans had in the past been among his most loyal political supporters. He could talk all he wanted about never running for public office again; yet conditions might arise when he might have to. But with these German-Americans against him—millions of them—what chance would he have?

He carried the issue into the autumn woods and let his axe bite into it and send the chips flying. He found nothing admirable or romantic in committing political suicide. But, for the sake of the national unity, some hard truths had to be said.

The Colonel was making other enemies, that fall of 1914. The professional pacifists had always been critical of him, but they had

never altogether lost hope of winning him at least partially to their cause. A delegation of them from Britain and the United States, had, in fact, that summer, spent an afternoon with him at Sagamore Hill. But his reaction to the war in Europe set their teeth on edge. Their leaders were, in the main, earnest, wholly sincere, high-minded men of culture and education, many of them university presidents, recognizing the folly and waste of war and groping for ways and means of doing something about it. Exceptionally articulate and experienced in leadership, they were accepted by millions of similarly high-minded people as men who could be trusted to guide their thinking in a national crisis.

They had every quality for such leadership, indeed, except one, and, unhappily, the most vital: they did not understand the world in which they were living. They assumed that, because they themselves carried on their personal lives and their institutions on a basis of reason and persuasion, all men everywhere could be trusted to carry on theirs similarly. To them, living in a free society, insulated by three thousand miles of ocean from close contact with the venomous snake-pit of mutually hostile peoples that was Europe, violence, and defense against it, were as unreal as unicorns. Force itself was an anachronism that they thought no intelligent human being could bring himself to make the basis of public policy. All the European nations, of course, had great armies or navies, or both—even the United States had a big navy—but that was a concession to the Stone Age mentality of the average politician who didn't know any better, and no twentieth century statesman would use them.

The fact that quite a number of statesmen were, that summer and fall of 1914, using these armies and navies to attain certain very practical ends appeared to have no effect on the thinking of the pacifist leaders. The use of force—at least, by Americans—was unthinkable. There was a better answer to international disputes, the answer not of the brute beast but of the thinking animal, man. Arbitration! That was the thing! Thank God there was a man in the White House who had been a college president also and knew the potency of the human intelligence!

The bland insouciance of the academic mind in the face of the realities of life raised the Colonel's blood pressure to dangerous levels. Farmers, mechanics and railroad men might make "frightful blunders," politically, he wrote James Bryce, but how much more dependable they were than these "educated incompetents!" "I know a good many different kinds of prize jacks," he wrote Arthur Lee, "but the most flamboyant of all is the American peace-at-any-price universal arbitrationist." Had these people no conception of the ugly forces seething under the thin crust of civilized society?

Roosevelt himself had started his political career among the tough, bare-knuckle bruisers of the New York Assembly and had come to his maturity in what had been the last unregenerate sector of the American frontier. In the Bad Lands of Dakota Territory, he had lived and worked with men from every stratum of society, rich and poor, educated and ignorant. There had been good men there, honest, decent and law-abiding; others, who had been confederates of thieves and murderers, and, a few, thieves and murderers themselves. He had ridden on the round-up with them, served among them as deputy sheriff, represented them at cattle-growers' meetings. He had, finally, led them—the evil with the good—in their first steps toward law and order. Among the many experiences that had contributed to his maturing, incidentally, had been an instance of pacifism in action in a neighboring community, where he had observed the catastrophic effect of good men, reasonable men, prematurely surrendering their guns.

The pacifists knew in their own lives nothing of the rough-and-tumble of physical competition, the lusts and hates of violent, determined men, or the depths of potential ruthlessness in cold, ambitious men. Their philosophy of sweet reasonableness—projected internationally in Hague courts and arbitration treaties—worked admirably in Quaker meetings, but occasionally broke down even there. Yet they were proposing that attitude and procedure as the means of settling the life-and-death disputes of a generation in which Lenin, Trotzky, Stalin, Mussolini, Hitler and the thousands of little replicas who would operate their purge-trials, their concentration-camps and their gas-chambers, were alive and moving toward their destiny!

The Colonel could not speak of the pacifists without getting red in the face, writing his friend Lee of "preposterous little fools" who have "thought this a happy time to pass idiotic treaties with Paraguay and similar world powers. . . . The apostles of the utterly inane scream joyfully that this shows that the United States does not need battleships, and that, if Europe had only had these treaties, there never would have been any war!" He counted Wilson among these "apostles." "In international affairs," he wrote his friend, "Wilson is as much of a prize jackass as Bryan."

Roosevelt's demands for the strengthening of the national defenses in the light of what was happening in Europe brought on him, metaphorically speaking, eggs, tomatoes and dead cats. Americans were inclined to be idealistic. They acted realistically enough in their personal affairs but, in public matters, hankered at intervals "to hitch their wagon to a star" and sweep through the empyrean, singing "Onward, Christian Soldiers." The pacifist gospel had made deep inroads among the "best people." What kind of antediluvian creature was Roosevelt, anyway, rose the cry, talking of armies and navies and criticizing the "noble idealist" in the White House? Didn't he know that military preparedness inevitably brought war? Couldn't this perpetual adolescent, waving his toy sword, ever learn that he was living in the twentieth century? Was there no vision in him? Couldn't he see that force belonged to the past and that the mind of man was on the march? This war in Europe was definitely the last; and thereafter, what a new, wonderful world opening! Even Arthur Lee, hardheaded as he was, was inclined to think of the conflict as "the last war for civilization."

The grim realist at Sagamore Hill demurred. "I see no reason for believing that Russia is more advanced than Germany as regards international ethics, and Japan, with all her politeness and her veneer of western civilization, is at heart delighted to attack any and every western nation whenever the chance comes and there is an opportunity for Japan to gain what she desires with reasonable safety. If Germany is smashed, it is perfectly possible that later she will have to be supported as a bulwark against the Slav by the nations of Western Europe."

There was no embrace of the lion and the lamb in the crystal ball at Sagamore Hill.

6

The Colonel was a lone and very lonely voice in America, that fall of 1914; and he didn't like it. It had been a principle of leadership with him never, never to undertake a reform in which he would be so far ahead of the people as to be out of touch with them. Cynics, indeed, had spoken of him as habitually "twenty years behind the leaders and twenty minutes ahead of the procession." "I am a strong believer in being practical and working with your fellows," he wrote Wayne MacVeagh, "but now and then the time comes when it is quite impossible to compromise and do your duty to the nation . . ." the time when a man must "hoist the black flag and sink or swim, without regard to what his fellows think, for the cause in which he with all his heart believes. . . . No other public man has ventured to tell the truth of Germany, of the pacifists, of the German-Americans, of Wilson. I have told it and I shall tell it as strongly as I know how and without regard to its effect upon me."

The Colonel's own friends and followers, in and out of the Progressive Party, besought him not to attack the President's "noble and humanitarian peace policy." The Republicans took the same ground, criticizing Wilson on the tariff but praising him fulsomely for his position in regard to the European War. The Colonel, convinced that that position was neither "noble" nor "humanitarian," and was more likely to lead to war than to peace, was, in effect, standing almost alone against the hundred million.

His isolation from his countrymen appeared complete and final when, in November, the election returns showed the Progressive candidates everywhere snowed under. The Colonel no longer had a party to give his judgments carrying power, and what remained of his personal following was obviously diminishing to the vanishing point.

A cartoonist for the New York *World* pictured the Colonel tossed in the political scrapbasket. Everybody who knew anything about American politics agreed that this time the former President was through, forever and ever. Amen.

Chapter VII

THE COLONEL accepted his fate cheerfully. "I am fifty-six years old," he wrote, a day or two after the election, to his new daughter-in-law, Belle, with Kermit in Brazil. "I have led a very active life; I am no longer fit, physically or in any other way to continue to lead an active life." He was really glad, he added, that it had become his duty to "stay quietly at Sagamore Hill and loaf and invite my soul."

Meanwhile, the children—children no longer—were a great comfort: Archie, returning from a hunt in New Brunswick with "a really magnificent moose," and two or three deer as the spoils of his rifle; not caring too much about college, impatient to get out into the big world and demonstrating his descent from the Puritan moralist, Jonathan Edwards, by his forthright individualism and his stubborn defense of the moral standards he had acquired at Sagamore Hill . . . Quentin, recovering too slowly from his "tumble down the mountainside with the pack-horse last summer out in Arizona" (a mere incident of travel for the Roosevelts) . . . Ted, doing extraordinarily well in business, making a lot of money . . . Ethel, "under a great strain in Paris, but I am glad that she and Dick are over there"; a few months later, back from France, having, as her father wrote Belle, "a lovely time" with Dick and the baby, and keeping open house in New York for her brothers and the Cove Neck cousins, having "all the hospitable inclinations of her Auntie Bye and Auntie Corinne, and able to entertain and make everyone love being with her"; yet, home at Sagamore for a week end, going "straight back to being a little girl again . . . working industriously at the bonfires with Archie and one of his classmates. . . ."

"I *never* want to leave Sagamore again!" the Colonel had written Ethel at the conclusion of his final campaign trip before the election.

Vernon Howe Bailey
Open Days – 1936

"Most of the time we two old people pass out here alone," he wrote Belle, "with walks in the winter woods, and books, and blazing log fires, and for me an occasional ride or afternoon's chopping; and we are very happy; I doubt if I have ever passed, not merely a more contented, but a happier two and a half months. My dear, I hope you and Kermit may have the like privilege of growing old peacefully together, after having faced your life work without flinching."

2

The Colonel clutched his family happiness all the more closely to his heart because he recognized that he had become estranged from the American people. Ever since his ranching days he had felt that he knew "that good fellow," the average American citizen, and "that even better fellow," as he liked to put it, the citizen's wife. He had understood their thoughts and their feelings, and they had seemed to understand his, and, because of this reciprocal relationship, he had felt secure, during his Presidency, in appealing to them occasionally over the heads of the men they elected to represent them. His contacts with the public on his speaking-tours in the years following his return from Africa had seemed to re-affirm the validity of this mutual trust.

That relationship, the Colonel recognized, with dismay, apparently no longer existed. He had not changed; what he was fighting for was merely an extension of what he had fought for as President, but the currents of thought had changed. What had come over this people that he had loved and led, that they should accept, even acclaim, the pacifism, the backing and filling, the irresponsible short-sightedness and "spineless neutrality" of the Administration in power? He felt he no longer knew his countrymen. Yet in his heart he knew them; better, indeed, than they seemed to know themselves. "The majority," he wrote Lee, "know very little about international matters. . . . Deep in their hearts they have a high and fine purpose, which can be aroused by the right kind of appeal. But . . . absorbed in their own affairs . . . horror-struck by the thought of the hideous slaughter and of all that war would bring . . . they do not want to face risk . . . leave their business, or break into the easy routine of their lives if it can be avoided. . . . They get angry with me, just because they have an uncomfortable

feeling that maybe I am right, and that action should be taken."
When President Wilson assured them that no action was required,
they were happy to sink back into the pleasant cushions of self-
concern.

But they could be roused, the Colonel knew. Well, he was going
to rouse them.

3

The two and a half years that followed the outbreak of the Great
War were, for the Colonel, as an American and as a citizen, the most
anguished of his life. To know, in the light of history and personal
experience, what ought to be said, and to see it left unsaid, or said
bravely, and then withdrawn or watered down in words used not
to clarify but to confuse; to know what ought to be done and see
it left undone, or half done, or, being done, reversed; to see threats
made with no recognition that they might have to be backed by
force, and no means of backing them and no sense of responsibility
for providing such means; to seek to negotiate from weakness with
a nation that glorified strength, and to imply to the American
people that that weakness was a kind of superior virtue; to see the
word confused with the act, and the word itself regarded as the
act; these things, to a man of Roosevelt's impassioned love of country, his realistic mind and executive force, his knowledge of history
and of the motives and passions of men, were not only infuriating;
they were heart-breaking. "It has been criminal for us not to have
been preparing during the last seven months," the Colonel wrote
Belle in February, 1915. "But Wilson . . . has refused to allow any
preparations to be made. In consequence we are just as helpless as
we were last July."

In cold anger, the Colonel at Sagamore Hill watched the epistolary
duel between the ruffians of Berlin, pursuing their unrestricted submarine warfare, and the cultivated rhetorician in the White
House—the "Byzantine logothete," Roosevelt called him—seeking
to catch a shark in a silken net of words. The President was not
preventing war; he was inviting it, the Colonel wrote Senator
George W. Norris. "It is not the first time that an incompetent
and incapable administration, from sheer vacillating indecision,
has brought a country into the very war which in theory it desired
to avert."

"If I had been President," he had written Arthur Lee, three weeks after the outbreak of the war, "I would, from the beginning, have taken a stand which would have made the Germans absolutely alter all their conduct or else put them into war with us." "I do not believe that there would have been war if I had been President," he wrote Lodge, a year later, "but if, in order to stop the murder of American women and children on the high seas or in Mexico it had been necessary to go to war, I would have gone to war."

4

When the Colonel had written Belle that he intended to "loaf" and "invite his soul," he had proposed what to him would have been as unnatural as flying to a fish or swimming to a bird. He required action in order to live, and the only action open to him, a "private of the privatest kind," as he described himself, exiled from power at Sagamore Hill, was writing. Day after day, he sat at his desk in the library, inditing what were in effect Epistles to the American People, wandering in the darkness of pacifism and doubt. Day by day, he hammered into the national consciousness the need of "preparedness" to defend the national existence. Look at Belgium! There, if ever, was a peace-loving people. But it had stood in the way of a strong and unscrupulous neighbor. America must be strong if it wanted to be secure.

"Militarism!" shouted his critics.

No, he answered, you can have national defense without militarism. It isn't the arms that make militarism. It's the way you use the arms.

Why prepare? asked Bryan. If the nation were attacked, "a million men would spring to arms between sunrise and sunset."

Perhaps, replied Roosevelt. But to what arms? You can't improvise camps, equipment, rifles, artillery. You have to think ahead, you have to prepare. And, if you prepare, you probably won't have to fight. Preparedness for war is preparedness against war.

At the Sagamore Hill dinner-table, Edith Roosevelt made her own contribution to the debate, commenting on a sentimental ballad, "I Didn't Raise My Boy to Be a Soldier," which was entrancing the public. "I didn't raise my boy," she remarked, "to be the *only* soldier."

The articles that took shape under the Colonel's hand became a book, "America and the World War." Day after day, more articles, laboriously written in longhand in the Sagamore library, leapt to vigorous life in magazines and in the headlines of thousands of newspapers across the country. If you wanted to preserve the values of a free society you had to be prepared to defend them. "Where there is a sword for offense, there must be a sword for defense." With a strong, ruthless, ambitious, militaristic nation like Germany on the loose in the world, you had to be prepared to defend yourself, or go under. He pleaded for universal military service and was reviled, and saw his phrase adapted and devitalized by the President in an appeal for "universal *voluntary* service," which stripped the idea of all its meaning.

Month after month, in his articles for the *Metropolitan Magazine*, that finally became another book, "Fear God and Take Your Own Part," in his occasional addresses, and his public statements in response to this or that word or act of the President, the Colonel hammered at international duty and the obligation of the strong to aid the weak. Explaining to a bewildered people the facts of international life and the principles underlying national security, he missed no opportunity to hit at the President for what seemed to him Wilson's incapacity to face the realities of the world in which he was doomed, for good or ill, to exercise enormous influence.

The Colonel hit; he did not thrust. He was no fencer, flashing a rapier according to ancient courtly tradition, with seconds alert to see that nobody got really hurt. He was a knight-at-arms, swinging a battle-axe. He hacked and he hewed with a kind of merciless fury that shocked the timid and made even his friends and supporters wince, and wonder at times whether a little moderation might not better serve his cause. Wasn't he inclined, perhaps, to overstate his case? You had to be "emphatic" to make people listen, he explained in a letter to Willard Straight. "We are not in a rose-parlor, pink-tea crisis at present, and what I am trying to do is to get the American people to think about its position and to face its responsibilities."

Here and there people began to take the cotton out of their ears and listen; but the response was scattered and uncertain. "Our people lack imagination," the Colonel wrote Arthur Lee. "They do not understand the conditions abroad; and above all they have been misled by the screaming and shrieking and bleating of the peace people until really good men and women have gotten so puzzle-headed that they advocate a course of national infamy. I have spoken out as strongly and as clearly as possible; and I do not think it has had any effect beyond making people think that I am a truculent and bloodthirsty person, endeavoring futilely to thwart able, dignified, humane Mr. Wilson in his noble plan to bring peace everywhere by excellently written letters sent to persons who care nothing whatever for any letter that is not backed up by force!"

The sinking of the *Lusitania* by a German submarine, with the loss of a thousand American lives, roused the public at last. When, however, the President pointed out, with philosophic insight that took no account of possible national or international implications, that there were occasions when a nation might be "too proud to fight," much of the anger at home and the apprehensions of the guilty in Berlin subsided in bewildered relief. But across the nation an uneasy minority began to wonder whether the Colonel might not be closer to the realities than the President. Once more, the eyes of men and women who loved their country and wanted it to play an honorable and effective part in the world, turned in hope to Sagamore Hill.

"People always used to say of me that I was an astonishingly good politician and divined what the people were going to think," the Colonel wrote his cherubic friend, Van Valkenberg. "I did not divine how the people were going to think; I simply made up my mind what they ought to think, and then did my best to get them to think it. Sometimes I failed, and then my critics said my 'ambition o'erleaped itself.' Sometimes I succeeded, and then they said that I was an uncommonly astute creature to have detected what the people were going to think and to pose as their leader in thinking it."

The Colonel made a series of addresses on the Pacific Coast that summer and was struck by the "substantial assent" he met, the flood of letters he received. The directness and vigor of his statement of the issues gave cheer to millions who were as sick at heart as the Colonel himself at the President's naïve trust in the power of words to bring cut-throats to reason, and his reluctance to do anything about the national defense. Month by month the Colonel's following grew. As the effectiveness of his furious, occasionally intemperate onslaughts became evident, the President's supporters struck back: Roosevelt's campaign for Americanism and prepared-

357

ness was nothing but a frantic effort to return to power. "Inasmuch as what I am doing has forever alienated the entire German-American vote and inflamed with hatred of me the entire pacificist and mollycoddle vote," the Colonel wrote Lee, "and inasmuch as there is no politician in this country who does not shudder at the mere thought of ever following me, this particular argument contains an element of sheer delight."

The summer of 1915 saw the barely perceptible turning of the tide to Roosevelt's conceptions of national and international policy. The Colonel did not take the turn too seriously. The Administration, he wrote Archie, was "cordially supported by all the hyphenated Americans, by the solid flubdub and pacifist vote," by "every soft creature, every coward and weakling, every man who can't look more than six inches ahead, every man whose god is money, or pleasure, or ease, and every man who has not got in him both the sterner virtues and the power of seeking after an ideal." The good citizens, on the other hand, were puzzled, "and so a majority of them also tend to be with him." It was easy to mislead people, he wrote Kermit, "if one chooses to give them high-sounding names to excuse ignoble deeds."

5

As the year 1915 advanced, a new element entered into the American psychology. The Allies were buying most of their munitions in the United States, their trucks, their planes and their ships, and business was booming. Everybody was making money, and money was talking, naturally, in support of the agreeable *status quo*. The President's policy was bringing prosperity. "For God's sake, don't upset it!" The pacifists took a new lease of life, finding contributions easy to come by.

Roosevelt was thinking in other terms. Quietly, and supported by some of the ablest officers in the Army and Navy, friends who had been with him in Cuba, and other "outdoor men," he was planning the organization of a division of mounted riflemen—the Rough Riders, once again, on the scale of a division. There were successive conferences in the library at Sagamore Hill that the newspapermen covering the Colonel learned nothing about. "I have the whole skeleton of my Division worked out," he wrote Lee, "and I would guarantee to bring it over in ninety days if I were given the chance; and I would guarantee that it would do its duty when brought over." But, he added, "this Administration cannot be kicked into war." Within a month of the *Lusitania*'s sinking, Roosevelt had his brigade and regimental commanders picked. "I only wish I and my boys," he wrote Lee, "were beside you in the trenches . . ."

Three of the boys, it happened, were preparing themselves for just such an eventuality, at the officers' training camp at Plattsburg, New York. Archie was given a second lieutenancy toward the close of the camp with a final citation that he was fit to be a captain in a volunteer regiment, and Ted was recommended for a major's commission. Quentin returned with a certificate saying that "with more age and experience," he would make an "excellent" second lieutenant. Once more, the "little bears" were following in the way of the "Big Bear."

As another presidential campaign approached, the issue was sharpened between the realists, on the one hand, who were supporting Roosevelt in his fight for a workable foreign policy, based on national strength, and the pacifists, the profiteers, the doctrinaire liberals and the rank and file of the Democratic Party who were supporting the President. *Safety First!* was the slogan that flew over the country and blossomed in the buttonholes of the President's supporters. *Duty Frst!* boomed Roosevelt. "You can't have the millennium for the scratch of a pen on parchment. You can't have security without strength. You can't have peace without sacrifice. You can't retain rights without fulfilling obligations." It was a hard doctrine, but increasing numbers across the country were accepting it: a thousand letters a week were being dumped on the Sagamore Hill porch.

But a movement to make Roosevelt the presidential candidate on the Republican ticket found the Colonel himself skeptical. There was a growing sentiment "for the things for which—pretty nearly alone as regards the public leaders—I have been standing for the past year and a quarter," he wrote his former associate of the Bull Moose days, Frank Knox. "But the very men who are reluctantly coming to the conclusion that I am right will wish to relieve their feelings by being against me personally. It is a very old experience that when men finally have to pay heed to a prophecy they relieve their feelings by stoning the prophet. This is of importance only from the prophet's standpoint, and in this particular case the prophet does not give a hang!" Moreover, if the country were not determined to put honor and duty ahead of safety, he wrote Lodge, "then the people most emphatically do not wish me for President and the party cannot afford to run me for President; for I will not take back by one finger's breadth anything I have said during the last eighteen months about national and international duty." Unless the country were "somewhere near a mood of at least half-heroism" it would be useless to nominate him.

The Republicans proved less than "half-heroic." The effort in Roosevelt's behalf foundered before the reluctance of the Republican politicians to take any position which might suggest that they were less peace-loving than the Democrats or more likely to make the German-Americans toe the line. Charles Evans Hughes was nominated as the "safer" man. "They thought it wise," the Colonel wrote Lee, "to dodge the issue I thought it vital to raise."

6

In Oyster Bay, the crotchety editor of the Oyster Bay *Guardian* sang happy hallelujahs. He was both a Democrat and a devoted "Oyster"; and he was sick and tired of seeing Oyster Bay and Theodore Roosevelt regarded as synonymous in the nation's press. He was going to get Oyster Bay into the headlines on its own account, with no reference to the "dead duck" on Sagamore Hill. The Fourth of July was just ahead, and he organized a parade with floats, accompanied by the Oyster Bay band, civic organizations of all sorts, and a contingent of sailors from the U.S.S. *Baltimore,* at anchor in the harbor. The parade was to be followed by a meeting at which, for once, not Roosevelt but another Cove Neck resident, Frederic R. Coudert, the New York lawyer, was to be the speaker. Coudert would make the welkin ring. Roosevelt would be invited to sit on the platform, and no more.

So the meeting was arranged, with a third citizen of Cove Neck, Howard C. Smith, as master of ceremonies. Coudert made his speech, and it was a good one. Then Smith turned to the Colonel. Would he not speak a word of greeting to his fellow-townsmen?

"The spectators nearly went wild," the New York *Times* reported next morning, "as they saw the well-known figure rise and step forward to the edge of the platform."

The headlines next morning were all Roosevelt's with his militant speech printed in full, and Oyster Bay and its parade barely mentioned.

One of the town's leading citizens, Maurice E. Townsend, himself a Democrat, was asked next morning what he thought of the way the editor's little stratagem had worked out. "What did you expect?" he grunted. "First thing, some people we know will be scheming to keep squirrels on the ground."

Chapter VIII

THE PRESIDENT was re-elected on the implied promise that he would keep the nation out of war. The Colonel was convinced that the promise had been political eye-wash, but the impartial observer, seeing the President's efforts to keep peace after the German government, late in January, 1917, forced the United States to break off diplomatic relations, could scarcely doubt the sincerity of the promise. What that observer was forced to doubt—and millions once more did doubt—was the President's capacity to understand the realities of life, chief among them, the contempt that the ruthless men directing the German government felt for weakness and fine phrases, the probability that war would come, in spite of his promise, and the need of getting ready for it. "There is no question about 'going to war,' " Roosevelt declared, the middle of March, 1917, in a speech at the Union League Club in New York. "Germany is already at war with us. The only question for us to decide is whether we shall make war nobly or ignobly."

Two weeks later, the President addressed a joint session of Congress and asked for the recognition of a state of war. The Colonel at Sagamore Hill purred as he read the address. It was not only that the President had decided at last to call the nation to the defense of its heritage. "His message," the Colonel wrote John Callan O'Laughlin, "bears out all I have said for the past two and a half years, and condemns all he has said and done for those two and a half years."

The Colonel had for weeks been in correspondence with the Secretary of War, Newton D. Baker, regarding the proposed Division. Between two and three hundred thousand able-bodied men, over draft age, had volunteered for service under him. He was prepared, indeed, to raise not one division but four, and to have them trained and in the trenches months before the draft army would be ready. The Secretary was courteous but discouraging. The Colonel went to Washington to present his case in person, to confer with his friends in Congress, in support of the President's draft bill, and to call upon the man in the White House whom, for almost three years, he had excoriated.

"I put before the President my proposals and the reasons therefor," he wrote O'Laughlin. The President had evidently felt pleased that Roosevelt was planning to support the draft bill and to ask for "action supplementary to it, and not contradictory to it." Thereupon, the Colonel went on, the President had "suddenly entered into a defense of his past conduct," saying that he had for a long time felt what he now said in his speech to Congress, but that the American people were not awake to the need, and that he had to bide his time; and he added that many people had misunderstood him (hastily interpolating, with obvious insincerity, that he did not mean me).

"I answered in substance, and almost in words, as follows: 'Mr. President, what I have said and thought, and what others have said and thought, is all dust in a windy street, if now we can make your message good. Of course, it amounts to nothing, if we cannot make it good. But, if we can translate it into fact, then it will rank as a great state paper, with the great state papers of Washington and Lincoln. Now, all that I ask is that I be allowed to do all that is in me to help make good this speech of yours—to help get the nation to act, so as to justify and live up to the speech, and the declaration of war that followed.' "

"I had a plain talk with the President," the Colonel, returning from Washington, said to Bill Hoster, one of the "newspaper cabinet," covering Sagamore Hill, "and if it were anyone but Mr. Wilson, I'd say that it is all fixed up."

It was, it happened, not at all fixed up, though Roosevelt and his friends fought hard. An amendment to the draft bill was introduced in Congress, authorizing the President, at his discretion, to raise four divisions of volunteers. In the course of the debate in the Senate, Roosevelt was bitterly attacked as a "self-seeker" and "political opportunist"; and as bitterly defended. "Today, *you* have adopted *his* preparedness plan!" cried Senator Hiram Johnson. "Today, *his* undiluted Americanism that he preached to many, but to which but few listened, has become the slogan of the nation.

My God! when was it that a nation denied to its sons the right to fight in its behalf?"

Across the nation rang the cry, "Send Roosevelt to France!" and from the nations fighting Germany came impassioned appeals, "Send us Roosevelt!" In an open letter to the President, Clemenceau, the leader of the opposition in France, pointed out that no other American had such a hold on the French imagination, no other American name had such legendary force. Give the war-worn French soldiers the "promise of reward for their years of service and sacrifice. Send them Roosevelt." What would the magic name of Roosevelt not mean to hard-pressed Britain and bleeding France! exclaimed Van Valkenberg in the Philadelphia *North American*. "The appearance of an ex-President of the United States leading American soldiers to the battle front," wrote Henry Watterson, a Democratic stalwart and fighting editor of the Louisville *Courier-Journal*, would "electrify the world."

"I ask only that I be given a chance to render service which I know I can render," Roosevelt said in a speech to a Brooklyn audience, "and nine out of ten of those who oppose me do so because they believe I will render it too well."

"The President need not fear me politically," he said at tea at his sister's, Mrs. Robinson's, in New York, with his old friend, Jusserand, still France's ambassador, as the other guest. "If I am allowed to go I would not last. I am too old. I should crack. But"—and his teeth gleamed whitely—"I *could* arouse the belief that America was coming; I *could* show the Allies what was on the way." He knew, indeed, that, to a greater degree than any other living man, he had the capacity to inspire youth. He would assemble and train ten thousand, twenty thousand men and take them to France, on fire for their country and for the cause, prepared to set on fire anew the drooping spirits of the British, French and Belgian veterans in the trenches. He hoped that he might live to "face the foe" in the trenches; if that could not be—if he "cracked"—"the President could use me to come back and rouse more enthusiasm here and take some more men over. That is what I am good for now, and what difference would it make if I cracked or not?"

The amendment authorizing the enlistment of volunteers over draft age was adopted. Roosevelt immediately wired the President for permission to raise two divisions or, if the President desired, four. The President curtly refused the offer, giving his reasons in a statement to the press, in words chosen to reduce the patriot to the romantic adventurer.

"I wanted to go to the war," the Colonel said to a group of friends, "and the people wanted me to go. I keep my good health by having a very bad temper, kept under good control."

"Of course, I was disappointed . . ." he wrote Belle, "but I have not the slightest feeling of rebellion against fate."

One wonders.

There was consolation, indeed, in the fact that the President had yielded to Roosevelt in the larger issue he had, since the President's April 2nd address, been hammering at, day in, day out: the war must be fought not with munitions or money or food, as the Administration had seemed to be planning, but with men; the American flag must, without delay, be planted on the battlefront. On the day that the President rejected Roosevelt's offer, he announced that he was sending an expeditionary force of regulars to France under General Pershing.

2

Two days after the President's rejection of the Division, some twenty of the men who had been most active, recruiting kindred spirits all over the country, gathered in the Trophy Room at Sagamore Hill to witness the act of disbanding. Jack Greenway, who had been a Rough Rider and was now a mining engineer in Arizona, was there, with Henry L. Stimson, who had been Secretary of War under Taft, and James R. Garfield, former Secretary of the Interior. Seth Bullock, of Deadwood, was with them, and Colonel John C. Groome, head of the Pennsylvania State Constabulary; a former governor of Wyoming, Robert D. Carey, and a former governor of Louisiana, John W. Parker; the hunter and scout, Frederick R. Burnham, and other men of the great outdoors who had hoped to join the Colonel on this last and possibly greatest of his adventures.

The New York *Sun* correspondent noted the sunshine, the serene beauty outside, and the gloom in the Trophy Room, where, among "the priceless souvenirs of world venturing," the elephant tusks, the gongs, the skins of wild beasts, "a company of gentlemen all forlorn, gentlemen of the Colonel's own Old Guard," sat "dismally" in a circle, with the Colonel himself in the center. "Through the open window came the haunting chorus of the robins," the reporter noted, "the liquid calls of the little birds whose names the Colonel might have called offhand, the bright chatter of children. But these evidences of nature, awake and gay, fell blunted against the gloomy company. Only the Colonel spoke—rapid, emphatic sentences that beat hard upon every ear and still held silent every tongue."

It was an occasion, the reporter noted, that called for no comment, "a sort of funeral service, a kind of requiem," with the Colonel "outwardly the most cheerful of the company," though all the men knew well enough that he had suffered the bitterest disappointment of his life. He made no complaint beyond pointing out that "if the Administration had deemed it wise to grant the request I made, three and a half months ago," he, Roosevelt, could have placed in the front line, not one division but two, fully equipped and trained, on the date the Secretary of War had set for the beginning of the assembling of the draft army in September. As for the President's statement that the Army could not spare the trained officers that Roosevelt had asked for, the contingent of regulars which the President had ordered to France would take ten times the number that the President had said could not be spared for the Division.

The reporter noted the "unquenchable energy" in the Colonel's reading of the mustering-out order. "There was more of indignation than anger in the Colonel's choice of words and in his manner of reading them."

But the anger was there, bitter and burning. "Of course, the President, in turning down my Division," he wrote Ted who was again at Plattsburg, "was actuated by the basest and most contemptible political reasons. Dick was immensely impressed by the fine character of the leaders who had come on here. They were heartbroken, of course. Well, I am out of it! But I need not grumble about fate; I had my day, and it was a good day."

The scene he pictured for Belle the next day showed how resilient his spirit was. Ethel and Dick were at Sagamore with Richard. "Late this afternoon I found them in the North Room; the victrola was playing 'Garry Owen,' while Ethel, Richard and Dick, hand in hand, executed a dance-step march to the tune; whereupon I joined in and executed pigeon-wings in time, opposite them, while the enthralled Richard gazed at my feet."

3

The evening after the farewell in the Trophy Room, the Colonel dipped his pen into the rhinoceros-foot that was his inkwell and wrote to Pershing. They had met in the Santiago campaign. As President, Roosevelt, impatient of seniority rules and on the lookout for able young men, had jumped Pershing from captain to brigadier-general. There was nothing he could, or would, have asked of Pershing for himself. But for his boys—that was different.

It was in the family blood—as Ethel had demonstrated at the outset of the Great War—to claim what Roosevelt had called the "high privilege" of standing at the point of duty and of danger. Ted and Archie had their Officers' Training Camp commissions. Kermit was at Plattsburg that spring. Quentin, now a sophomore at Harvard, was planning to join a flying squadron. Three of the boys were married—Archie, only a month before, to Grace Lockwood, of Boston. Quentin was engaged to Flora Payne Whitney, granddaughter of the wealthy traction magnate who had been in Cleveland's cabinet. But neither the boys nor the young women involved seemed to regard the fact that they were married or engaged as in any way affecting their obligation to enter the service.

None of the boys, indeed, had had any decision to make as to entering it or not entering it. Quentin gave the picture with his customary directness. "We boys thought it was up to us to practice what Father preached." Ted and Archie were, in fact, sending their father impassioned appeals by letter and telephone to help them get over where the fighting was. The Colonel transmitted their pleas to Pershing. The boys had asked to go as enlisted men, but, the General replied, that would be a waste, with the training they had had. He would be glad to have them with him as officers.

"The big bear was looking out for the little bears, wasn't he?" Ted, signing himself "Little Bear," commented in his reply, recalling the game that the boys and their father had loved to play in the gun-room through a chorus of grunts and growls and shrieks of sham-panic.

"The big bear," the father replied, "was not, down at the bottom of his heart, any too happy at striving to get the two little bears where the danger is; elderly bears whose teeth and claws are blunted by age can far better be spared; but (to change from allegory to the first person!) I do not sympathize with the proverb: 'God keep you from the werewolf and from your heart's desire!' It is best to satisfy the heart's desire, and then abide the fall of the dree of destiny."

4

"Eleanor and the children are out here," Roosevelt wrote Ted the end of May, "and I fairly revel in them."

It would be much, he was thinking, to have Ted's family keeping vigil with Edie and himself through the months, perhaps years, ahead. Emphatic as he was about the men of the family (including himself) getting to the front, if they could, he was equally emphatic about the women of the family staying home and looking after things there. "No women of mine are going to France if I know it." He was reckoning without a spirit that was as innate in Ethel and in Eleanor as it was in the boys. The fact that Ethel had just had a second baby constrained her to give up her determination to do war-work of one sort or another in France. But for Eleanor there were no responsibilities which her capable mother could not carry.

One evening, in June, sitting with the Colonel on the piazza, she decided to take her courage in her hands—and, knowing how he felt, it took courage. "Father," she said, "there's something I want to tell you. I'm going to France as soon as I can, after Ted goes."

The air over the western lawn was very still. "My dear," the Colonel said, after a moment of pregnant silence, "I don't know of anything I can do to help you get off. But if you can think of anything, tell me and I will do it."

Eleanor recognized that he had not changed his position. He still disapproved, but he respected her determination and would not argue with it.

At Sagamore Hill, children and grandchildren came and went and, when they went, the grandfather was desolate.

"I miss the little family *very* much!" he wrote Eleanor, "most of all the dainty, pretty, exceedingly efficient and exceedingly companionable little mother, but also the three blesséd small people; Gracie and Teddy and Cornelius of the white head and the black heart. I can just see Gracie marshalling Teddy for the extraordinary effort to frighten at least one pig; and breakfast is a distinctly tame affair when I no longer have to guard against an affectionate, busy and officious Ted doctoring 'Grandfather's soup,' with salt."

The middle of June, Ted and Archie left Plattsburg "on confidential orders." While they were waiting in New York for the transport *Chicago* to sail, they used a brief leave to run out to Sagamore Hill. Alice had come up from Washington and Quentin had come over from Mineola where he was in training. Alice noted her father's "grim elation" at the thought that the boys would soon all be in the war.

At a Red Cross rally, at Oyster Bay, a week later, the Colonel proudly announced that Ted and Archie had sailed for France. Quentin had his commission and was about to sail. Kermit, owing to his absence in South America, had had no opportunity of taking the Plattsburg training his brothers had experienced. With two Roosevelts already in France, holding commissions, he knew he might have difficulty persuading a hostile Secretary of War to let him have an early place in the American Expeditionary Force. By a triple play, involving his father, Arthur Lee and Lord Derby, head of the British War Office, he secured a commission in the British forces in Mesopotamia.

Kermit sailed for Madrid, where his wife's father was still the American ambassador, taking his wife and baby son with him. Then came Quentin's turn. He went to communion with his mother at Christ Church, the last Sunday before he was to sail. The last night, his mother went to his bedroom, as she had gone a thousand times in the past, and tucked him in bed. He was still the "baby." The day of his sailing was scorching hot. Alice, who came up from Washington to see all her brothers off, noted how bitter it was for her father to see the last of his sons go, and not go himself. "The old lion perisheth for lack of prey," she quoted to herself, "and the stout lion's whelps are scattered abroad."

"It was hard when Quentin went," his mother admitted to a visitor at Sagamore Hill. "But you can't bring up boys to be eagles, and expect them to turn out sparrows."

"I fairly eat my heart out at not being with you," her husband wrote Archie. "Or rather I wish I could replace you, and have you home. But I am *very* proud of you."

Chapter IX

"*MY INTEREST*, of course, now lies entirely in the work of you four boys," the Colonel wrote Ted, "for my work is of no real consequence—what I did was done in the Spanish War and the decade following; and now I am overjoyed that you four have your chance, whatever the cost." "Slacker-in-spite-of-Himself," he signed the letter.

Actually, that first summer of the war, he was one of the most active and effective men in the country in behalf of the war effort, pleading for practical action in Washington rather than boasts and what he called "magniloquent" promises. "I almost break my heart over the slowness in preparation," he wrote Archie, "and of course I am powerless."

The contrast of his four boys, in the war, and himself, safe at home, was wormwood to the head of the clan at Sagamore. "Everybody works but father!" he wrote Archie (adding, in a post-script, "This shall be my motto hereafter!"). "All I can do is to wade into the pacifists, pro-Germans and rioters here—which is a pretty poor substitute for work at the front! . . . But the Administration does not intend that I shall have any share in the excessively leisurely preparation for us to exert our strength seriously. . . . Of course I am doing everything I can to make our people put the fight through until overwhelming victory comes. But I am not at all sure that my voice carries any distance, under existing conditions."

He went to the Middle West—which was supposed to be pro-German and still inclined to follow the arguments of Wilson's election campaign—to preach the gospel of Americanism and all-out war at the semi-centennial of Nebraska statehood, paying his compliments to the "professional pacifist," whose motto, *Safety*

First! had kept the country in a state of weakness that invited disaster. "They"—and of course he meant Wilson—"cared nothing for righteousness. They cared nothing for humanity. They cared nothing for our national honor or interest. All they asked was a 'peace' that would permit us to get all four feet in the trough."

He returned East to paint "the instant need" at a huge Fourth of July meeting at Forest Hills, New York. He could not guess that, that day, the first American contingent, including Ted and Archie, marching through the streets of Paris, was greeted by cries of "Teddy! Teddy! Long Live the Teddies!" Not the Sammies, the New York *Times* pointed out, the *Teddies*. Clemenceau had known his people, when he had begged that the champion of American intervention be sent to them.

Roosevelt spoke as his sons would have had him speak. At the outbreak of the war in Europe, the American people had been "stunned, blinded, terrified by the extent of the world disaster. . . . But at last we stand with our faces to the light. At last we have faced our duty. Now it behooves us to do this duty with masterful efficiency."

He struck at the isolationism which would not see "that the oceans and even the air have become highways for military aggression"; at the blindness, the sentimentalism, which had kept the country unprepared, on the ground that preparedness invited war. The "moral sense of our people has been drugged into stupor by the men in high places." He did not name Woodrow Wilson, but no one could doubt whom he meant. Was the country really at war "to make the world safe for democracy"? Roosevelt brought the issue down to earth. "We went to war because for two years the Germans had been murdering our unarmed men, women and children, and had definitely announced their intention to continue the practice." The nations which Germany had over-run and oppressed must be liberated, but let no one forget that the future of America was at stake, "and it is this for which our concern is deepest."

In speech after speech he stressed the need of "single-minded Americanism"; on the one hand, undivided loyalty; on the other, the equality of all loyal citizens, regardless of race or creed or place of birth; and pleaded again and yet again for that social and economic justice which he had fought for as President. You could not keep the struggle for justice in Europe and the struggle for justice

371

at home in air-tight compartments. There must be steadfast endurance "to win the peace of overwhelming victory," but military victory by itself was not enough. "Industrial democracy" must come after, "to consecrate the war."

2

To Ted's wife he wrote of the "unimportant work" that was engaging him and of the delights which were his solace: "Ethel's baby is here and in my capacity as natural-born grandfather I take immense satisfaction in the wee thing."

The "unimportant work" to which he referred included a speech in Pittsburgh in which he pointed to the nation's desperate unpreparedness for action four months after America had been dragged "sternforemost" into the war: no "single airplane fit to send over the German lines," no heavy artillery, only "a tiny fraction of the submarine chasers needed"; no cargo ships to speak of; few rifles and little other equipment; altogether, "a miracle of inefficiency." And here the government was saying that the emergency measures, being taken at last, would be terminated when the emergency was over. It was this "blind," this "criminal" refusal to provide for the future that forced "every honest and far-sighted lover of America" to speak. This time the nation had been saved by Britain and France. But what of the next time? "We cannot afford to count for our safety on anything but our own armed strength."

His basic message was two-fold, and he expressed it in the first of the editorials he had contracted to write two or three times weekly for the Kansas City *Star*: "the Prussianized Germany of the Hohenzollerns" must be defeated. That was its first aspect. The other was his impassioned insistence that never, never, *never* must the nation again be caught unprepared to defend herself.

He threw all his legendary vigor of spirit and speech into the fight. At Rockford, Illinois, he spoke to 20,000 men of the 86th Division of the national army. Referring to the lack of equipment in most of the camps, he quoted the pre-war expectation of "an eminent statesman" that, in case of war, "a million men would spring to arms between sunrise and sunset."

"Bryan!" yelled a dozen voices, "Old Doc Bryan!"

"They are still springing," Roosevelt went on. "To broomsticks."

372

Let his hearers, when they had finished the task they were about to begin in Europe, become apostles of universal military service.

In successive speeches Roosevelt flayed "the Hun within our gates . . . the tool and ally of the Hun without," the "foolish agitator," the I.W.W. leader, "who is against all government and all civilization and all orderly liberty," the German Socialist, "who in this country has helped turn the Socialist Party machine into the tool of the German autocracy," the German-American "bundist" working for Germany against America, and the editors of German-language newspapers, directly or indirectly preaching disloyalty to the country's cause. Would that all the "new copperheads" could be "bundled straight out of the country to any other country willing to receive them."

There had been some doubt in the public mind whether the Middle West might not be lukewarm about the war. "In St. Paul and Minneapolis the crowds were enormous," the Colonel wrote Quentin, "and the men of Scandinavian and most of the men of German blood were as loyal and enthusiastic as the rest. The maddening part of our shufflings and delays and inefficiencies has been that they were all quite needless. If the President had dared to lead, our people would have followed with eagerness and resolution; the long hesitation and the backing and filling merely confused them and made them less unanimous when the time came."

3

Back at Sagamore, the Colonel was overwhelmed once more by the sense of his "uselessness." In France, the boys recognized how fantastic his conception of himself was, and sent comforting words. "Though you call yourself useless," Archie wrote, "don't forget that it is through you entirely that we got to the front so early, and, through yours and Mother's training, I really believe, that each of us has certain gifts which enable him to handle his own job fairly well. . . . I cannot say what a comfort you are to both Ted and myself over here, and we talk about you continually. You have taken on the powers of a seer and a prophet, and we have seen really everything you have predicted come to pass."

But the father at home was not comforted. "I spend my time refusing innumerable requests from tom-fools who think speeches *would* count, and making a very few speeches which, as a matter of fact, *don't* count. Large masses of men still vaguely feel that some-how I can say something which will avoid all criticism of the Government and yet make the Government instantly remedy every-thing that is wrong; whereas in reality nothing now counts except the actual doing of the work; and that I am allowed to have no part in."

"I cannot overstate how I loathe speech-making now," he wrote Quentin, "partly because I am tired of making speeches anyhow and very earnestly wish I was not to make another as long as I live, and partly because I have grown thoroughly to distrust and dislike the whole professional orator class. This is not a time for talk; it is a time for action. I talk merely because I am not permitted to take any action. However, I suppose it is necessary that I should, now and then, speak and write, because somebody has to say the neces-sary things, and if I don't say them they remain unsaid." But all he was doing, he wrote Ted, was all so "trivial," compared "to the real work, the work of all of you at the front. I am so emphatically out of kilter with the Administration that I can do little except . . . try to spur our people forward to constantly speedier and more effective action." "I am steadily preaching our duty to see this war through, at no matter what cost," he wrote Archie, "no matter how long it takes; and this although selfishly I should rejoice beyond measure at anything that sent you four home. But as you say, there are prices too dear to pay for safety!"

Chafing at his inability to be at the point of danger himself, the Colonel, indeed, was missing no chance to put in a blow for the things that seemed to him important to the winning of a war: most of all the necessity for efficiency in providing the arms and equipment that should, for the past two years, have been in the making. He demanded speed, and ever more speed, paying his compliments to "broomstick apologists," the "policy of dawdle," and specifically the Chief of Ordnance, who, sharing the General Staff's contempt for the calendar, had accepted six months as a "perfectly endurable delay" in providing the new army with rifles. Endurable? Certainly, warned Roosevelt, "if we are content to accept the speed standards of Tiglath-Pileser and Pharaoh Necho." But, if America expected to win the war, it had better "adopt the speed standards of the Twentieth Century A.D. instead of those of the Seventh Century B.C."

The Colonel's denunciations and adjurations brought hot shot from the Administration's defenders. He was not "standing by the President," he was using the emergency to make political capital, he was "intemperate." He replied with the familiar vigor: It was the duty of every American citizen "to criticize not only his government, but his own people, for wrong-doing, or for failure to do what is right," citing, a little maliciously, Wilson's earlier demand for "pitiless publicity" for evildoers. Criticism was "absolutely indispensable" if the war were to be won, and "a permanent policy of preparedness" were to be adopted to safeguard the nation.

4

He gave his sons no hint of the evidences of popular devotion that greeted his public appearances: the long-drawn cheers, which his efforts to check seemed only to intensify; the cries of "Teddy! What's the matter with Teddy!"—and the responsive roar, "Nothing!" John Purroy Mitchel, New York's brilliant young mayor, seemed to speak for all the city's millions when, introducing him at a public meeting, he declared, "We all love him, we all respect him, we all honor him." When the Mayor added, "and there are many of us who would gladly follow his leadership on the field of battle," bedlam broke loose. At every meeting at which Roosevelt spoke, the response was as it had been at the height of his popularity during his Presidency. After the long years of banishment, he was back in the American heart. His audiences responded as to a melodrama, roaring its devotion as he appeared, delighting in his insistence that "we ought to decide whether we have a country or a polyglot boarding-house," applauding, shouting, waving American flags.

At a great meeting at Madison Square Garden at which he was explaining why the American people must fight the war to a finish, a voice in the gallery asked, "Teddy, why don't *you* get over there?"

"He wants to!" another voice answered, amid thunders of applause.

Roosevelt lifted his hand abruptly. "Just wait a minute. You asked why I didn't go over there?" Once again, a surge of applause. "You'll have to ask somebody else that question," he shouted, and his voice cracked comically. "I did my level best."

A voice: "You bet you did!"

"I asked not only to go over," Roosevelt went on, "but I came with a hundred thousand more men in my hands to help." He paused. "I found that, so far as I was concerned, this was a very *exclusive* war." Once more his voice cracked. There was a roar of laughter, followed by more applause. "And I was blackballed by the committee on admissions." More laughter, and more applause. In an instant he was again grave, and angry. "I tell you, you man over there, I have sent over my four sons."

The applause was like a great wave breaking.

"I have sent over my four boys," he repeated slowly, "for each of whose lives I care a thousand times more than I care for my own—if you can understand that, you creature!"

Chapter X

HIS BOYS were always on his mind and, once a week, or oftener, sitting at his desk in the library, facing the Laszlo pencil-drawing of Mrs. Roosevelt over the bookcase, he wrote each one. He was "immensely delighted" when he heard that Ted and Archie had been given positions in the line, Ted, as major, in command of the first battalion of the 26th Infantry of regulars, in the First Division; Archie, as lieutenant. It was not long before Colonel Harbord, Pershing's chief of staff, was writing their father that Ted had his battalion on the "razor-edge" of efficiency, and Ted's commanding officer, Colonel George B. Duncan, was commenting on the "good judgment, zeal, energy, devotion to duty" that were Ted's, and the "ability to handle his men" that made the battalion "second to none in the division." "Next to the Colonel," Archie wrote, Ted was "much the best officer in the regiment," an opinion which Ted's father "guessed" was "about right." As for Archie himself, Colonel Duncan wrote, he was "the embodiment of energy, a natural leader who brings out at all times the best efforts of his men." Heywood Broun, in the New York *Tribune,* reported the feeling at the front about the former President's eldest son: the initial prejudice against him among the regular officers, and the way he had lived it down.

Kermit, as captain in a battalion of Sappers, was finding life in the traditional Garden of Eden romantic and hazardous, taking part in the capture from the Turks of Tekrit, the birthplace of Saladin. "I am overjoyed," his father wrote. "Three cheers! you have proved yourself; you have made good. . . . You have actually taken part in a big phase of the greatest war in history; you have efficiently done your duty for the right in the times that tried men's souls."

Meanwhile, privates in the rear rank were writing home about

Quentin: "All those bum deals I spoke of are plumb gone now. We have a real man commanding us now, just like his father." "We boys would do anything for him," another soldier wrote. "He always sees that his men are taken care of before he thinks of himself."

The father at Sagamore read the tributes with swelling chest. "All the family," he wrote Quentin, "are proud as peacocks." "I suppose you are now hard at work learning the new type of air-game," he wrote his youngest. "My disappointment at not going myself was down at bottom chiefly reluctance to see you four, in whom my heart was wrapped, exposed to danger while I stayed at home in do-nothing ease and safety. But the feeling has now been completely swallowed in my immense pride in all of you. I feel that *Mother,* and all of *you* children, have by your deeds justified *my* words!!!"

In his hunger to share Quentin's experience, he took a plane-flight that gave the press and the public spasms of belated appre-hension. He took it in a two-passenger plane that was trying out one of the new Liberty motors at the Garden City training ground, flying with Lieutenant H. J. Blakeley of the U.S.A. Aviation Corps, over a half dozen Long Island towns at a 5000-foot elevation. He stole the ride when the "top brass," escorting him over the field, was at the moment looking the other way, and brushed aside the suggestion that he wait until the aviator had made a brief trial flight. He insisted, moreover, that the flight be long enough and go into sufficient altitude to test the motor to the full.

"It might be gently hinted to the Colonel," commented the New York *Times* next day, "that his fellow-citizens are not entirely pleased when he endangers, for no very pressing reason, a life that many of them value highly as a national asset."

Did they really so value it? He wondered. So far as he himself was concerned, his only valid excuse for living, was to continue earning a good salary until the boys came home and he could put Archie and Quentin on the road to a livelihood. "Then," he wrote Quentin, "I intend to retire. An elderly, male Cassandra-has-been can do a little, a very little, towards waking the people now and then; but undue persistency in issuing jeremiads does no real good and makes the Jeremiah an awful nuisance." "My real task is done," he added in a letter to Ted, "and most satisfactorily done, by Mother and by me—the raising of you four boys in such shape that we lift our heads with pride whenever we think of you, or whenever anyone asks after you."

"The people I most respect here," the Colonel wrote Archie, "now feel that what I did as President, or in any other way, does not reflect nearly as much credit on me as the fact that Mother and I were able to bring up four boys who have done as you have done." "You and your brothers," their father wrote Ted, "are playing your parts in the greatest of the world's great days, and what man of gallant spirit does not envy you! You are having your crowded hours of glorious life; you have seized the great chance, as it was seized by those who fought at Gettysburg, and Waterloo, and Agincourt, and Arbela and Marathon. Until you are an old man you will never be able quite to understand the satisfaction I feel because each of my sons is doing and has done better than I was doing and had done at his age—and I had done well. And of course this is preeminently true of you. I don't mean that any of you will be President; as regards the extraordinary prizes the element of luck is *the* determining factor; but getting in the class of those who have to their credit worthy and even distinguished, achievement—that's what I mean."

The frustrated man at Sagamore Hill took scarcely less pride in Eleanor, indeed, than in his sons. "You lovely, competent person," he wrote Ted's wife, "I delight in thinking of you with your French class of troopers in the evening, and of your care of the canteen—in the famous rubber boots, I hope—in the afternoon." The formidable boots she had chosen to take with her had become a family joke. "I hear from different sources that you are doing capital work. Apparently you are confidential agent and errand-girl not only for Ted but for much of his regiment. Kermit in his letters has exulted in Ted's intense delight in having you anywhere near him. This had a stiffening effect on Ethel, who glared defiance at me and intimated that she also would be among the elect—Gracie by the way,"—Archie's wife—"having written her that they would go over together in the spring; in which case, there will be various creches, run by industrious grandmothers, scattered over the country.

"Lord, won't it be good when we are all together again! It is dreadful to have those we love best go to the war; but it would be even worse if they did not go. Ethel writes from Fort Ogle-thorpe that she is now thoroughly awake to this fact, for Dick is

379

wretched because the four boys are across and he is not; and she says that now her one wish is to get him over."

2

The Colonel gave the boys and Eleanor warm glimpses of life at Sagamore, of Ethel (after Dick had departed for the front, to be division surgeon of the Second Division) coming back with young Richard and little Edith, delighted, as the Colonel wrote Quentin, in "seeing her children growing up in the house where she grew up," and of Gracie, coming for long visits, "the dearest girl, so intelligent, and with such character," the Colonel wrote Archie. "I really think that she enjoys being down here with two old people, in bitter winter weather, in this house on a windy hill."

The fact that Gracie was to have a baby made her doubly precious to the lonely father and mother on Sagamore Hill. "Mother and I will look after her exactly as if she were Ethel," the Colonel wrote Archie. "This is Gracie's home, and her children's, as it is yours, for all the lives of all of you; and hardly her own father and mother can feel a more tender fondness for her than I do."

Now and then Flora Whitney came—"darling Flora," the Colonel described her—and touched the lonely pair by her thought of them and by her fine courage. "The way that pretty, charming, pleasure-loving young girl has risen to the heights, as soon as the need came," the Colonel wrote Quentin, "is one of the finest things I have seen. By George, you are fortunate!"

When Flora casually mentioned to Ethel that she was hearing from Quentin only at long intervals, the Colonel sent his youngest a word of advice clearly born of experience: "Now, of course, you may not keep Flora anyhow. But if you wish to lose her, continue to be an infrequent correspondent. If, however, you wish to keep her, write her letters—interesting letters, and love letters—at least three times a week. Write, no matter how tired you are, no matter how inconvenient it is; write if you're smashed up in a hospital; write when you are doing your most dangerous stunts; write when your work is most irksome and disheartening; write all the time! Write enough letters to allow for half being lost." The letter was signed, "Affectionately, a hardened and wary old father."

"This is the 32nd anniversary of Mother's and my engagement," the Colonel wrote Quentin on November 17th. "And I really think

380

I am just as much in love with her as I was then—she is so wise and good and pretty and charming."

"The 'Lady Camel,'" he wrote Eleanor, "is very well, thank you." He was referring to a quotation from Charles Edward Carryl, that was current on Sagamore Hill:

> "As for the Camel, he's
> Ridden by families.
> Any load goes for me."

"She had rather forgotten about being a camel until the other afternoon when I mentioned it, and she instantly looked very pretty and felt very woebegone, and realized that she was mated to a dull-nerved, coarse-natured, unappreciative and non-understanding boor —a jovial boor, which made it worse—and that life stretched before and behind in a straight, monotonous, dusty road of uncheered duty. Then we *did* cheer up; and took a three hours row on the glassy Sound, in the boat with a chair in it—by the way, *does* the memory of the inequitably divided chairlessness of the picnic boat still rankle?"

Periodically, Ted's and Eleanor's children visited at Sagamore. "Cornelius is the youngest," the Colonel wrote a little girl, a stranger, Marjorie Sterrett. "He is only about two months old. He isn't as long as his name. But he will grow up to it. He is named after his great-great-grandfather who, when I was very small, over fifty years ago, helped teach me a Dutch baby-song. Little Richard is the eighth Richard Derby, from father to son, born here in America. He loves the bulldog—a nice, friendly, almost toothless bulldog. Little Ted is really Theodore IV; for my father was Theodore Roosevelt. He was the best man I ever knew; strong, fearless, gentle. *He* 'feared God and took his own part.' Gracie is four. The other day her mother was giving her one of her first Bible lessons.

"Her mother said 'Now, Gracie, remember that God made everything.'

"Gracie (*much impressed*): 'Did He make *everything*?'

"Her mother (*with emphasis*): 'Yes; everything!'

"Gracie (*after a pause*): 'Well, He didn't make my leggings fit very well; but I'm sure He meant to, so I won't say anything about it!'"

The babies possessed Sagamore Hill, and dominated it. "Gracie is the most winning little thing I have ever known," the Colonel wrote Eleanor. "She mothers the small boys, and is so sure that we all love her! The first evening I read her 'Peter Rabbit' and 'Benjamin Bunny,' while Mother as an interlude read her 'Little Black Mingo.' Gracie felt that to have us read alternately prevented monotony. Ted's memory was much clearer about the pigs than about me; he greeted me affably, but then inquired of a delighted bystander—Mary, I think"—Mary Sweeney was a beloved Irish maid —" 'What is that man's name?' At supper, in pure friendliness and from a desire to encourage closer intimacy, he put the question to me direct, in a deep voice. Gracie explained that I was Grandfather (adding that she had two Grandmothers, who were twins) and that Ted was Theodore Roosevelt 3rd. I endeavored to explain that I was the first of that name; but the effort was a failure.

"This afternoon I took the three down to that haven of delight, the pig pen; I trundled Cornelius in his baby carriage while Gracie and Ted alternately carried and did battle over my long walking stick. We fed the pigs with elderly apples; then we came to a small rick of hay down which I had to slide each of them in turn until I finally rebelled; then halted so that each might get a drink of water; 'and so homeward,' as Mr. Pepys would have said."

Ethel's and Dick's children delighted their grandfather no less. They were "the dearest small persons imaginable," he wrote Dick. "Richard is so manly and friendly, and amuses himself, and is adored both in the house and in the stable! In the case of Shady, the adoration is accompanied by some reserves, as Richard makes his life haggard by busy and officious affection. Edie is about the dearest one-year-old baby I have ever known. She loves me very much if there is no one else more attractive around! At any rate I offer an agreeable relief from the monotony of the crib or the little pen on the floor, and she hails me with little soft out-stretched arms, and of course my heart is like water and I can't resist taking her up. Now she generally comes down to breakfast and crawls actively round the floor; and Richard, as soon as he has finished his breakfast, also drops hastily on all fours and joins in the all-four scamper, to Edie's intense delight; and Shady, no matter what his desires, is included in the game." "Richard is the manliest, busiest little fellow imaginable," the Colonel wrote in another letter. "I am of course of second-rate importance in his life, my chief useful function being to give him a lump of sugar as soon as we come down to breakfast (which is apt to be hand in hand while we negotiate the stairs) and then to have him hold the strainer while I pour hot milk into my coffee—a feat full of possibilities. But when I was away for six days the little fellow asked me on my return:—'Weren't you homesick for me while you were away, Grandfather?' As for Edie she is such a darling that I want to take her up and cuddle her all the time; she smiles and laughs and crows and waves her little arms and legs and is most alluring."

The Colonel's impulse to pick up the baby was not encouraged by Ethel or her mother. One afternoon, on the piazza, he had snatched the little girl up from her kiddie-coop when Mrs. Roosevelt came unexpectedly from the house. "Now, Theodore!" she exclaimed in exasperation. "Do you know what you've done? Now someone will have to hold that baby the rest of the afternoon."

"All right!" the Colonel responded. "I'll hold her!" And he did, rocking, all afternoon, while he discussed the state of the world with successive visitors.

When, late in 1917, the Colonel gathered a number of his magazine articles into another book, for which Mrs. Roosevelt gave him the title, "The Foes of Our Own Household," the volume was inscribed "To our sons and daughters their mother and I dedicate this book." "Daughters," the Colonel wrote Eleanor, included daughters-in-law, "and Flora shall have her copy with a special inscription to show that she is included among those of whom I am most proud."

As the Colonel and his lady sat before the fire in the library, winter evenings, surely they asked themselves, if not each other, would, in the words of one of his letters to Ted, all their "young Vikings" come back and "gather around the old hearthstone?"

Chapter XI

THE IDYL of the amiable grandfather sliding children down a hayrick, until even his boundless energy and enthusiasm cried a halt, gives no hint of the warrior laying about him with a battle-axe at what he called the "folly and complacent sloth" of the Powers in Washington. His editorials and speeches calling public attention to the nation's failure to prepare for the war which had been an obvious possibility for almost three years, were getting under the skin of the inefficient in Washington and of the partisans of the Administration throughout the country. They sought to shrug off his discomforting truths with the query, "Why cry over spilt milk?" The Colonel's answer was simple and direct: "We wish to be sure we do not spill it again."

But his critics were not thinking of the future. With the exception of the officials who knew well enough that what he said was true but couldn't afford to admit it, they were what the Colonel called "nice, shortsighted people," obsessed by the idea that, in wartime, a loyal citizen "stood by the President," whatever he did or left undone, and that a man who criticized the President was, by that fact, a traitor. The "bleat," as Roosevelt described it, took the form of "quavering or incoherent protests" against every effort to point out the damage done by the nation's unpreparedness; against his demands for speed and more speed in making rifles, artillery, planes, cargo-ships; against his insistence on the danger in the sentimentalism that kept the government from declaring war on Germany's allies. Roosevelt was criticizing the President! Dreadful! The "bleat" became drama when a Texas mayor called Roosevelt a "seditious conspirator who ought to be shot dead," and declared that the Abilene editor who published his articles should be "tarred and feathered." The editor, in a "Retort Courteous,"

384

offered the mayor and his "tar and feather expedition" a welcome that would "not be lacking in hospitality or warmth," and heard no more of him.

The truth was that the war effort seemed to the Colonel to be emulating both the tortoise and the crab.

"Our national army, the draft army, has only begun to learn the rudiments," the Colonel wrote Ted in November. "The spirit of the men is simply fine; but the shortage in even the most necessary arms and equipment is appalling." He cited an artillery regiment that still had "only wooden guns and *wooden horses*! Imagine trying to train men for modern warfare with such equipment! The infantry regiments average about one rifle to every four men, taking the camps all the way through; and most of them have had no target practice whatever. When the most elementary training is thus lacking, you may imagine how little has been done in the real war training of the kind that is needed at the present day."

Day after day, week after week, he pleaded with the Administration and with the public to face the realities, to speed up the war—and to learn what the "present shameful shortcomings have to teach about the need of a permanent defense policy." Across his desk he had one of the broomstick guns with which the recruits were being drilled, as he set down the cause and effect of "Broomstick Preparedness." One cause: Wilson's ridicule of the advocates of preparedness, in his Annual Message of December, 1914. Another: his 1916 presidential campaign on the slogan, "He kept us out of war." The effects: "broomstick rifles, logwood cannon, soldiers without shoes, and epidemics of pneumonia in the camps." He did not, he declared, dwell on these matters to blame anybody. "I dwell on them in order to wake our people to the necessity of learning the lesson they teach."

"But I can only talk or write," he wrote Ted, "and it is only the doers who really count. The trouble is fundamental and two-fold. The Administration has no conception of war needs or what war means; and the American army has been so handled in peace that the bulk of the men high up were sure to break down in the event of war. If three years ago we had introduced universal military training, if we had then begun to build quantities of cannon, machine guns, rifles and airplanes, and if, two years ago, we had begun an extensive series of large scale army manoeuvers, we would have made all our blunders and suffered all our delays at a time when they did not count—and the war would have been over now. Well, I am not merely wise after the event—I advocated all this at the time! Which is a pointless boast."

2

"I often feel fairly sick with impotent rage at my inability to make the authorities show wisdom and efficiency," the Colonel wrote Archie, "and the people are so foolish and uninformed that I am obliged continually to hold myself in, because if I tell anything like the whole truth they simply don't believe me and I do harm rather than good. But," he added, in a letter to Quentin, "I am the only man, seemingly, who dares try to wake our officials out of their stupor of fatuous complacency, who dares to point out a few of our more vital shortcomings, and endeavor to get them remedied and to speed up the war. The horrible delays, mismanagement and inefficiency about the army have been matched by what has been done in such matters as shipping, transportation and coal. Nine tenths of wisdom is being wise in time! We ambled deviously into this war without one particle of preparation; and we are paying a bitter price now."

He was immensely heartened when none other than the chairman of the Senate Military Affairs Committee, George E. Chamberlain of Oregon, a Democrat, brought the shortcomings into the open. "Congress is investigating the work of the War Department," the Colonel wrote Ted, "and, of course, has instantly found that all that I have said was true."

As Congress and the public gradually became aware that something was desperately wrong with the conduct of the war, the Colonel swung his mace with accelerating vigor. "Tell the truth and speed up the war! The American people wish the truth and can stand the truth." Anyone who objected to fearless exposure and criticism of the governmental shortcomings—which must be exposed if they were to be corrected—was a foe to America and a friend to Germany. Roosevelt set down the cost of unpreparedness in dollars and cents, and in the more precious values of human life: men in the camps—selected for physical fitness—coming down with pneumonia at six times the rate of men, women and children, of all ages and conditions, contracting the disease in New York City; and, of every three attacked, one died. Doubtless, he admitted,

386

administrative blundering was partly to blame. "But the prime cause is the failure to prepare in advance."

Day after day, Roosevelt hammered at four points: Face the facts of the national unpreparedness, tell the truth, speed up the war, establish universal military training as a permanent policy. He said the same things over and over in different words until they sank into the public consciousness and became a part of it without anyone fully recognizing how it had happened. Incidentally, he missed no opportunity to show up the Administration's incorrigible complacency. When, the middle of January, in the face of a powerful German offensive, the Secretary of War remarked comfortingly that "the French and British armies can be relied upon to withstand the shock," Roosevelt gave a snort that might have been heard across the country, quoting Artemus Ward's willingness "to sacrifice all his wife's relations on the altar of his country." "This statement of Mr. Baker," he pointed out, "absolves us from all necessity of commenting on his ingenuous defense of a system of preparedness which leaves our small army at the front with no artillery except what we get from the French and an army at home with batteries made out of telegraph poles and logwood."

For all his assertions to the boys of his general "uselessness," he admitted in a letter to Kermit that he did "fulfill a modest function, that of telling disagreeable truths which ought to be told but which it is very unpopular to tell and which nobody else will tell. This is a factor in making the Administration do about a fifth of what it ought to and could, instead of only a twentieth. But I tend to be regarded as merely a scold. I am no longer in touch with the dominant currents of the American stream of purpose and perception—I can't say 'thought' for there is uncommonly little of it at present."

The attacks on Roosevelt increased in bitterness. The German-language newspapers, with a few honorable exceptions, were spewing vitriol, cloaking, under effusive laudations of the President and his Secretary of War, their hope to see the inefficiency perpetuated.

"Hearst is now hand in glove with the Administration," the Colonel wrote Archie, "and he has been yelling that I ought to be imprisoned and that the authorities are merely debating as to what action about me they shall take. Lord, how I wish they *would* try to act against me! I am not in government employ, and there is nothing I would more eagerly welcome than any action by the government that would make my voice carry farther as I demand the speeding up of the war and specifically point out our delays, inefficiencies and shortcomings."

Barring such luck, he was granted the next best thing. The New York *Times,* the most influential newspaper supporting the Administration, took up his fight. Nine months after entering the war, the *Times* admitted editorially, America was giving her allies no effective military aid. "All our bustle and stir doesn't hide the fact that, through incompetence and lack of organization and system, we are far behind in our preparations to supply rifles, ammunition, machine-guns, airships, uniforms."

"I am heartsick," the Colonel wrote Belle, "over the delay, the blundering, the fatuous and complacent inefficiency and the effort to substitute glittering rhetoric for action."

The unrest in Congress and the country regarding the conduct of the war reached its climax in a speech which Senator Chamberlain made at a public meeting in New York. The military establishment of America had "fallen down," he declared, "because of the inefficiency in every bureau and department in the government of the United States." The next day the Senator introduced a bill in the Senate to create a war cabinet. The President countered with a blast denouncing Chamberlain's speech as "an astonishing and absolutely unjustifiable distortion of the truth," endorsing the Secretary of War, and opposing any change in the conduct of the war.

In the Senate "the pent-up fires of discontent," which, in the words of the New York *Times* correspondent, had for weeks been smoldering in Congress, "burst out in a flame of oratory." Other Democratic leaders supported Chamberlain with charges that corroborated the sharpest criticisms that Roosevelt had made regarding lack of arms at the front and sanitary conditions in the camps. Senator Stone, of Missouri, who depended for his political life on the German-American element of his state, and, as one of the "twelve wilful men," had helped filibuster the Armed Ship Bill to death a year before, ignored the Democratic source of the attack on the War Department and precipitated a storm by declaring that the Republicans were seeking to make political capital out of the war. He singled out Roosevelt as the arch-villain, denouncing him as "a menace and obstruction to the successful prosecution of the war," "the most seditious man of consequence in the country" and —"whether willingly or out of sheer madness—the most potent agent the Kaiser has in America." Roosevelt, Stone declared, had his eye on the Republican nomination in 1920, his heart was "aflame with ambition" and his pretended patriotism was a fraud.

Lodge rose to Roosevelt's defense. If the former President were as treasonable as Stone declared, why did the Administration not prosecute him? "He is visible; he can be found. He is also audible and—this is what makes his crime—he is also readable."

3

Late in January, 1918, the Colonel went to Washington to support the Republican leaders in their efforts to speed up the war, arriving with Mrs. Roosevelt at the Longworths' two days after Stone's blast. "Do you think it would be worth while," he said in his familiar staccato tones to the correspondents who crowded about him, "to say—if they want to arrest me—that I am here?"

A steady stream of politicians of both parties beat a path through the snow to the house on M Street, that day, and the days following. With them came justices of the Supreme Court, ambassadors, army and navy officers of all ranks, editors, scientists and a host of unclassifiable personal friends, all eager to feel the revitalizing touch of his presence. "I was kept on the jump, literally, without a minute's intermission," the Colonel wrote Quentin. Newspapermen besieged the house. Alice, leaning over the banister, counted thirty-three, at one time, "fairly stacked" in the small hall.

The atmosphere of the capital was tense. The White House gave out word that the President was "confident" that his Administration would "weather the storm" and would defeat both the war-cabinet proposal and the plan to create a department of munitions. Let the public withhold judgment; they would find that everything was all right. On the floor of the Senate, Chamberlain pointed out in respectful terms that the President did not know what he was talking about, countering the presidential accusation of "distortion" with incontrovertible evidence, gathered by his Committee. The agonizing story he told of unpreparedness and blunders, illness, neglect and death in the training-camps, sent shudders of horror through the Senate Chamber and reduced a number of senators to tears.

At the Press Club, the same day, Roosevelt asserted his right to criticize the conduct of the war, incidentally shredding the senator from Missouri, who had attacked him, and quoting Woodrow Wilson, the authority on congressional government, on the need of public criticism, *contra* Woodrow Wilson, the President of the United States, fretfully shielding incompetence. "Tell the truth," he told the listening journalists. "If conditions are good, tell the truth. If they are bad, tell the truth. If they have been bad and become good, tell the truth." The full telling of the truth would wake the American people up to a sterner realization of the task before them and consequently to "a sterner resolve that, cost what it may, every deficiency shall be remedied, every wrong undone, every failure by government officials turned into an achievement and success."

It was a crisis in which factionalism obviously had no place. In the Longworth drawing-room, men who, not six years before, had torn each other's hair out, chatted amicably while they waited in patience for a chance to talk things over with "the Colonel." All brought him the same story. Republicans in Congress and in the country, Democrats, dissatisfied with the conduct of the war, and others who had never had strong party affiliations but were interested in public affairs, found they were all thinking the same thoughts, but were "inactive and inarticulate for lack of leadership." "He sounded their views and they sounded his," the Washington *Post* reported. Roosevelt's were clear and precise and, as they unfolded, Alice noted that backbones stiffened. That night, at a Republican caucus, his proposals were adopted as party policy.

"No doubt seems to remain," said the New York *Times,* "that Theodore Roosevelt has become the leader of the Republican Party."

It was one of the high dramatic moments in a life packed with drama. Roosevelt had been rejected by the Republican leaders in 1912 against the expressed will of the voters in successive state primaries, and rejected again in 1916, not because he failed to see the issues confronting the nation, but because he saw them too clearly. With no organization behind him—for the remnants of the Progressives had been finally eliminated as a political factor a year and a half before—he had won his way back to leadership by the realism of his thinking, the passionate earnestness of his convictions. At the Longworth house, "standpatters" and "progressives," on speaking terms for the first time since the mid-term elections of the Taft administration, were asking one another why the obvious candidate of the reunited Republican Party in 1920 should not be Theodore Roosevelt.

Alice noted that, much as the same thought occupied her own mind, it did not seem to occupy her father's at all. "I am not in the least concerned with your supporting me either now or at any future time," he said, in effect, to the men he conferred with. "All I am concerned with is that you should so act that I can support you."

Chapter XII

FEBRUARY SET IN, bitter-cold. "Sagamore is just as warm as it ever was in cold weather," Mrs. Roosevelt wrote Mrs. Cowles. "We have plenty of coal but a bird cage is hard to heat."

"The North Room is closed by gaudy portieres," the Colonel wrote Quentin. "We keep the logs blazing in the library and find it cozy and comfortable." He loved the cold season for the open fires it made necessary, and liked nothing better than to poke up the logs. "I do think, Theodore," Mrs. Roosevelt would say, "the fire would burn better if you didn't fuss with it so much." But it did no good.

The Colonel was not well, and Alice had come up from Washington to spend the night. She was "as amusing and interesting as ever," he told Quentin. "She and Ethel and Mother have passed an evening of absorbing conversation to which I have listened like a pleased old owl."

Such moments of relaxation were rare. Fires in him were raging not only against Wilson but against destiny itself. "It is a very unjust world in which my sons and their wives and their mother and I have to pay for the slothful and utterly selfish ambitions of a cold-blooded and unprincipled demagogue," he wrote Archie. "History *may* never discover it; but when the war is over I shall write a full and truthful record of why we went in so late and so unprepared, and of the incredible baseness which lay behind."

He did not finish the letter. "Father wants me to send this off to you," Ethel scrawled in pencil at the foot of the page. "He was too ill to finish."

The recurring Cuban fever which had taken a malignant form during the Colonel's exploration of the Brazilian jungle had caused an abscess in his thigh. He was taken to Roosevelt Hospital where, next day, he was operated on for the original abscess and for two abscesses in his ears. A bulletin, that night, declared the operations successful, with no "unpleasant results." But, in the course of the day, an inflammation developed in the left inner ear. A mastoid operation might be required. In that case . . .

The public was gripped by a sense of danger greater than the bulletins indicated, and seemed, literally, to hold its breath. A poignant message at the top of the New York *Tribune*'s editorial column expressed the popular mood: "Theodore Roosevelt, listen! You must be up and well again. We cannot have it otherwise. We could not run this world without you."

For twenty-four hours the issue hung in the balance. If anyone caught the irony of the shadow of death falling across Roosevelt's triumphant return to Republican leadership, there is no record of it.

The crisis passed, the fever moderated. Three days after the operation, the Colonel was said to be on the road to recovery. The New York *Times,* which was inclined to be critical of him, expressed the "heartfelt rejoicing throughout the country," speaking of "an inspiring, a compelling force," the value of whose service, over the past three years, in arousing the people of the United States "to a sense of the national peril and of their duty," was "beyond all estimate."

Jack Leary of the New York *Tribune,* admitted to Roosevelt's room for the first time, remarked, "You had us worried, Colonel."

"I wasn't worried about myself," he answered. "I was thinking of my four boys. I tell you, I am mighty proud of my boys and"— he paused—"just as proud of my two fine girls."

"I have taken a somewhat sardonic amusement in the real panic that affected a great many people when for a moment it looked as if I might not pull through," the Colonel wrote Kermit. "They have been bitterly against me for the last three and a half years and have denounced me beyond measure. But when they thought I might die they suddenly had an awful feeling that maybe I represented what down at the bottom of their hearts they really believed to be right."

By the middle of February the doctors announced that the "alarming symptoms" of Roosevelt's illness had disappeared. The same day a group of "progressive Republicans," flushed with their victory in electing a young Indiana politician named Will H. Hays to the chairmanship of the Republican National Committee over the candidate of the Old Guard, let it be known that the selection of Theodore Roosevelt as the Party's standard-bearer in 1920 was a "certainty."

The Colonel took that kind of thing with a grain of salt. He was reading Mommsen's history of Rome and Mahaffy's "The Empire of the Ptolemies," which might give any man perspective and freedom from illusions. Besides, on the same day he had had word that Archie had been promoted to captain, which was much more important.

"I hated to have you worried in any way," he wrote Archie. His one wish throughout his illness had been "that it were in my power to guarantee the safety of one of you boys by any such trivial business as this." He was "a thousand times more worried about darling Gracie," who was about to have her baby, "than about anything that could possibly happen to me."

"Really I feel slightly impatient," he wrote Quentin, "over there being any anxiety about *me* . . . it's about you and the other boys that we have to think, and not about utterly unimportant troubles of their elderly civilian kinsfolk!"

"The chief reason I wished to get well was in order to resume my work of endeavoring to get my country to exert her great, but lazy and unprepared strength as speedily and effectively as possible," the Colonel wrote George V of England, in response to a message of sympathy that the King had sent him. "For the last three years and a half I have been preaching to my fellow countrymen their duty as I saw it; they finally saw it the same way but always two years behind-time as regards each phase of the duty; and nine tenths of wisdom is being wise in time. It is maddening to see Russia break and Germany stride nearer triumph because my country failed to prepare."

2

The war picture was darkening, when, early in March, the Colonel returned home from the hospital. Back at his desk in the study where, through the big window, he could see the snow still drifted high against the portable snow-fence that lined the driveway, the Colonel wrote an article for the Kansas City *Star*. It was time to "gird up our loins, bend every effort, exercise all our forethought. . . ." "If we had prepared as we ought to have done . . ." It was the old refrain. Spilt milk, to be mopped up and forgotten? Mopped up, yes, but never forgotten. Failure to speed up the war, to build cargo-ships, to produce cannon and planes with the utmost efficiency "may cause us as much trouble in the future as our past failure to prepare has already caused us."

Now, with all four boys at or near the firing-line in France or the Near East, the war became for the father and mother at Sagamore Hill, a brooding presence, by day and by night, in every room, at every meal. Word came that Quentin had been down with a severe case of pneumonia. Then it was Archie who was in the news.

"Early this morning the newspaper men told us you had been given the *Croix de Guerre*," the Colonel wrote Archie. "Then the War Department notified us that you were slightly wounded; then we received Ted's cable that you had been hit in the leg by shrapnel and your arm broken. . . . Ethel called up darling Gracie on the phone; naturally her pride and anxiety were even greater than ours. Fortunately your letter to her, saying that you had seen in the Paris *Herald* about the birth of your small son, had just come—what became of our various cables I have no idea."

At luncheon, that day, Mrs. Roosevelt ordered a bottle of Madeira brought. "All four of us," the Colonel went on—there was a guest besides Ethel—"filled the glasses and drank them off to you; then Mother, her eyes shining, her cheeks flushed, as pretty as a picture, and as spirited as any heroine of romance, dashed her glass on the floor, shivering it in pieces, saying, 'That glass shall never be drunk out of again,' and the rest of us followed suit and broke our glasses too."

"Mother bears herself, as she always does in every crisis," the Colonel wrote Ted, "with as fine gallantry as any heroine of history. After all, I don't wonder that her sons have turned out as you four have turned out."

"I can't begin to say how proud we are of you," he wrote Archie. "Our pride even outweighs our anxiety. You, and your brothers, by what you have done during the last year, have more than justified our lives. . . . Whenever I say what our people *ought* to have done, I think of what you *have* done; and I hold my head high. . . . I have received dozens of newspaper clippings and scores of letters about your wounds and the cross. I really think that our people generally felt a genuine pride in your 'proving your truth by your endeavor,' and thoroughly understand my pride in you; and a good many felt that, inasmuch as you were going to recover, they were rather glad that one of *my* sons had the dangerous honor of being among the first to be wounded in battle."

<h2 style="text-align:center">3</h2>

Imprisoned at Sagamore by the effects of his illness, the Colonel chafed at the picture of America, a year after its entrance into the war, "still merely an onlooker" while the German armies drove toward Paris. The nation owed "this ignoble position," he wrote in the Kansas City *Star*, to "the folly and the procrastination" of the government, "its inveterate tendency to substitute rhetoric for action," and its unwillingness to "cry over spilt milk" long enough at least to prevent more milk being spilt.

Why, oh, why, would the government not quit boasting, and act? Let it push the shipping program by night and day. Let it give France and England the men they "so sorely" needed. "Our government has delayed until the Allies have been brought to the brink of disaster. Let it act at once lest the chance for action pass completely by. Let Uncle Sam not be put in the position of the sub who only gets into the game just before the whistle blows. Above all, we must not so act as to rouse suspicion that this attitude is due to deliberate shirking on our part."

He was exultant when the news came that the American Expeditionary Force at the front had been put at the disposal of the French and English military leaders. "All Americans who are proud of the great name of America," he wrote in the Kansas City *Star*, "will humbly and reverently thank Heaven that at any rate the army we have at the front is not to remain in the position of onlooker."

"I suppose this means that Ted and you," he wrote Dick Derby, "and perhaps Quentin, will all be, where you will all wish to be, in the thick of as heavy fighting as the world has ever seen. Well, it is wearing anxiety to us who are at home, the having all of you over where the peril and the honor lie; but we wouldn't have you anywhere else for anything in the world."

"What has befallen you I have no idea," he wrote Ted, "but of one thing I am sure, my first-born son, that, no matter what the conditions, you have borne yourself with the utmost courage, coolness and efficiency."

Roosevelt was hailed as "the next President of the United States" when he rose to make the keynote speech at the Republican State convention at Portland, Maine. He spoke in an atmosphere made tense by the news from France. "If we do not speed up to aid our Allies . . ." He pleaded for speed, for round-the-clock work in ship-building, for preparations for an army of five million. The war was going to be won by "brains and steel, not by kid gloves and fine phrases," and must be fought "without flinching" to "a peace of overwhelming victory."

Incidentally, he gave his audience a strong dose of Progressive doctrine. "I wish to do everything in my power," the Colonel wrote William Allen White, "to make the Republican Party the party of sane, constructive radicalism, just as it was under Lincoln. If it is not that, then, of course, I have no place in it."

The convention accepted everything he said as Party gospel, and cheered him so the windows shook. They shook, it happened, in newspaper offices clear across the country. It was strange, in a war, commented the New York *Evening Sun,* "to see the impulse, the leadership, come from without the national Administration. But the fact is undeniable, and becomes more and more insistent, day by day." The New York *Tribune* went a step further. Categorically it declared that Theodore Roosevelt would be "the Republican candidate for President in 1920."

The Colonel wasn't greatly interested. "All that is near to me in the male line, is in France," he said to a friend. "If they do not come back what is the Presidency to me?"

5

For the first time in his life, the Colonel was finding sleep hard to capture and hold. As President, he told a friend, he had always been able at night to throw off the day's worries. "But now," he said, "I wake up in the middle of the night, wondering if the boys are all right, and thinking how I could tell their mother if anything happened."

The Colonel and Mrs. Roosevelt looked at each other across the dining table they had bought in Florence on their honeymoon, speaking of casual things, and thought, "How will he—how will she—bear it, if something happens to one of the boys?"

As he strode to the library after the meal, and she followed to take up her sewing again before the open fire, their footsteps echoed through the empty house.

A friend, who had seen Archie in the hospital in Paris and came to Sagamore to tell his father about it, commented to Roosevelt on how well he himself was looking after his own hospital experience.

The Colonel's reply seemed completely alien to his character. "I feel as though I were a hundred years old, and had *never* been young."

6

"Spring has fairly begun. The frogs are noisy in the ponds, the robins and song sparrows and redwing blackbirds are in song; the maple buds are red and the willow tips green; the first mayflowers and bloodroot have appeared."

"Apparently the great German offensive has begun on an enormous scale against the British front," the Colonel wrote Archie. "It is a bitter thought to me that it is only our folly during the last three years, and especially during the last eighteen months, that has prevented us from having at this moment in France a couple of million fighting troops, fully equipped with guns, airplanes and everything else; in which case there would be no German offensive, no hideous loss of life, and peace on our own terms."

But not even in the past six months had the Administration shown any "real appreciation" of the situation, devoting "their chief thought, not to preparing with the utmost energy to fight, but to adroit oratory, to futile intrigue, and to a damaging flirtation with the Russian bolshevists." The worst of it was that "so many educated people are such utter fools as to be taken in by it and complacently to announce that, after all, we have done very well, that 'words count more than bullets' (actually, this sentence is rather a favorite among the more zealous of the Government's defenders), and that by the moral majesty (i.e., fatuity) of our attitude, we shall impose peace on strong and unscrupulous armed men."

"It is very difficult for me to hold myself within any bounds at

398

all," Roosevelt admitted to Ted, "when over here the people responsible for our shortcomings not merely lie about them or complacently excuse them but actually boast about being unprepared and hold up the fact as something meritorious." But, even after the revelations of the Senate investigation, the Administration's supporters were sure that all was well and wanted to hear nothing to the contrary. The Delaware House of Representatives so far forgot the Bill of Rights as to come within one vote of passing a resolution calling on the Attorney General to proceed against Theodore Roosevelt because, in his Portland speech, he had "severely criticized the conduct of our National Government." In the United States Senate, a bill was introduced, punishing by imprisonment or fine any "contemptuous or slurring language against the President."

Roosevelt snapped his teeth. Were Americans subjects or citizens? "I am an American and a free man. My loyalty is due to the United States, and therefore it is due to the President, the Senators, the Congressmen, and all other public servants only and to the degree in which they loyally and efficiently serve the United States." If the law were adopted he would "certainly give the government the opportunity to test its constitutionality." The bill was passed but without the offensive clause. "No human being has questioned successfully the truth of anything I have said in criticism of the Administration," Roosevelt wrote a Western correspondent, "and every opponent, therefore, must either take the ground that mendacity is better than truth, or else that we have in this country the Hohenzollern doctrine of *lèse majesté*."

Chapter XIII

"*HERE,* spring is now well under way, although the weather is cold and gray," the Colonel wrote Quentin. "The woods are showing a green foam; the gay yellow of the forsythia has appeared; the bloodroot spangles with brilliant white the brown dead leaves of the hillside across the wet hollow by the frog spring. Mother is well, and so charming; and very brave. I have ceased to fret at my impotence to do anything in this great crisis; I rejoice that my four sons, and Dick, are playing the great part; and I putter round like the other old frumps, trying to help with the Liberty Loan and Red Cross and such like."

Spring, indeed, was in the air. On the first anniversary of America's entrance into the war, President Wilson delivered an address in Baltimore which revealed how divided his mind had been in the conduct of the war. He had had reason to believe, he declared, that the peace aims he had proposed had made an impression on the statesmen of Germany, but the terms which its military leaders had imposed on Russia had shown him that, in the minds of Germany's rulers, only force counted. "In this moment of utter disillusion," as he described his own mental state, he called for "Force, Force to the utmost, Force without stint or limit, the righteous and triumphant Force which shall make right the law of the world, and cast every selfish dominion down in the dust."

The New York *Tribune,* next morning, reduced the eloquence to eight blunt words: "Now, thank God, we are in the war!"

In Washington, praise of Wilson's emergence from "illusions" was mingled with memories of a speech Roosevelt had made in 1916, in Detroit, the stronghold of Henry Ford's pacifist propaganda: "Either we must surrender our rights and, at the same time, our self-respect, or else we must be ready to defend our rights

400

with a hand trained to the weapons of free men and a heart steeled to that stern courage for the lack of which the possession of the softer virtues can never atone." Members of the Senate and House were reported in the Philadelphia *North American* as saying that the principles which Roosevelt had been "so zealously upholding" had been "vindicated by the President himself," and "finally adopted" as the national policy.

The Colonel himself had no comforting sense of achievement. His self-disgust, in fact, deepened as he suffered vicariously the privations and dangers of his sons. "I feel to my finger-tips," he wrote Ted, "the fatigue and hardships and privation and discomfort and danger and suffering. . . . But the sternly wonderful thing is that in the great days you have been able to play a part equal to them. . . . You have made good in really extraordinary fashion; and I, who have done nothing in this war, walk with my head high because of the honor you four have won."

"Old Teddy sits with shining eyes," wrote a Western editor, "watching his sons hazard their lives for honor and duty."

"And it's true!" the Colonel wrote Eleanor. "I can hardly express my pride."

In New York, the Colonel ran into his friend, Finley Peter Dunne, the famous "Mr. Dooley." "Well," exclaimed Dunne with a grin, "the first thing you know your four sons will put the name of Roosevelt on the map!"

"They have done it," the Colonel exclaimed in a letter to Ted, "and if I *had* to choose, I would rather have had you four stand at Armageddon even than stand there myself. You, personally, are now in the position of greatest danger; but when the trumpets sound for Armageddon only those win the undying honor and glory who stand where the danger is sorest."

In every letter to his sons he contrasted their effective action with what seemed to him the futility of his own.

"The only thing I take a real interest in is the war," he wrote Ted, "and I loathe being unable to *do* anything, and therefore merely *speaking*." But, he exclaimed, in another letter, "the Administration never moves unless it is forced to by public pressure, and public pressure can as a rule only be obtained by showing the public that we have failed in doing as we should do; for as long as the public is fatuously content the Administration lies back

401

and does nothing. However, there really is some sharp discontent that in this great battle we should count for so little."

2

The German drive swept on toward Paris. Field Marshal Haig declared that the Allies stood "with their backs to the wall." In an article in the Kansas City *Star*, Roosevelt snatched the phrase and waved it like a banner, exulting in "our . . . gallant fighting men overseas" and lamenting the "scandal" and "reproach" to the nation "that they are so few."

Once more, his anger against the Administration blazed like a blow-torch. If the Administration now "repented of the cruel wrong" they had done in not preparing in advance, "we could afford to wrap their past folly and evil-doing in the kindly mantle of oblivion. But they boast of their foolishness, they excuse and justify it, they announce that they feel pride and delight in contemplating it." The Secretary of War had spoken of "the happy confusion" of the war preparations. "Therefore, it is for us, the people, to bow our heads on this, our penitential day; for we are laggards in the battle, we have let others fight our quarrel, we have let others pay with their shattered bodies for the fire in their burning souls."

"I have *some* effect in hurrying up the war," the Colonel wrote Archie. "They are afraid of me, and they do endeavor to hurry up the troops, to hurry the building of ships, guns and airplanes, and to make ready for reasonably serious effort, just in order to neutralize what I say. My constant pounding does, in this round-about fashion, produce some small results—better than nothing."

"The war-spirit of our people has steadily risen," he wrote Ted. "One amusing result is that the President has announced that he intends soon to come out for universal military training!"

"I do not think that anything would ever have been done at all," he wrote Dick, "if we"—he was referring to the following he had built up in Congress and the press—"had not fairly flailed the Administration into reluctant and dilatory, and too often inefficient, action. . . . The breakdown in the air program and gun program has been lamentable. We shall remedy all these things in time; but at every point we are from one to three years late; and we shall never deploy more than a quarter of the strength we ought to develop."

402

Early in June, the Colonel was in Ohio giving his gospel of Americanism undiluted to an audience mainly of German stock, stirring their pride in America, "a new nation with a future such as no other nation in the world has before it, if only we, the men and women of today, do our full duty, and bring up our sons and daughters to do their full duty as Americans and as nothing else." The next day, at Des Moines, Iowa, he was pointing out the necessity of seeing the war through to a "knockout." Wilson was showing signs of seeking a negotiated peace. "Unless we knock out Germany," the Colonel declared, "we will have to fight again, probably within the lifetime of men now old, certainly within the lifetime of those now young."

The man permitted to fight only with the spoken and the written word felt a kind of grim satisfaction in the physical suffering that, on these speaking tours, his poisoned body forced him to endure. On his way to a meeting in St. Louis, he developed erysipelas in his left foot. By the time he reached Chicago, he had a high fever, and was in considerable pain. He was urged to cancel his engagements, but refused and only grudgingly consented to let a physician accompany him on the next lap of his journey. At Omaha, he stayed in his room all day, preceding the meeting at which he was to speak, but he rallied himself that night and spoke with his customary vigor.

"Don't let any one fool you by talking about a patched-up peace," he said, "a peace that will be a credit to everybody. There can be no peace creditable to everyone in this war."

In the train that evening, exhausted from the fever, the heat and the strain of a speech into which, for an hour, he had poured all his mental and spiritual energy, Roosevelt told Jack Leary, the New York *Tribune* correspondent who was on the train, how glad he was that he had not let the fever stop him. "I think I'll get over this thing by just fighting it. Anyway, I've got to go on. Such meetings as this tonight are worth some sacrifice."

He still had a fever when he reached St. Louis, but managed to deal vigorously with the local committee which wanted him to denounce the German-American mayor as pro-German. Roosevelt, scenting a political feud, demurred. The Mayor, he said, must be asked to introduce him. He might be all that his critics asserted, "but I don't propose to condemn him without giving him a chance. As mayor he should introduce me and is entitled to introduce me. If he declines, then, by God, I'll pillory him. But not till he's had a chance."

A reporter of the *Globe-Democrat* noted that Roosevelt showed signs of illness, faltering as he mounted the speaker's stand in the Colosseum that night. But, as the band swung up, "the sick man of a moment before became suddenly well, strong, virile, and full of fight, the Teddy of other days, the idol of the American people."

The Mayor gave Roosevelt a resounding introduction, without reservations. Facing an audience of twelve thousand or more, made up largely of German-Americans, Roosevelt, as his custom was, gave them his doctrine of Americanism and fight-the-war-to-a-finish, in a dose stiffer, if possible, even than he gave the ordinary audience, free of inherited German pulls. "Any man who seeks to soften, explain or dilute his Americanism isn't an American at all. There is no such thing as a 50-50 American. . . . We cannot have a divided loyalty in our government any more than we can have a divided loyalty in our marriage."

"I preached the straightest kind of doctrine on Americanism," the Colonel wrote Ted, when he was back at Sagamore, "and on putting the war through, by hard, downright fighting, by the use of millions of men in the fighting line, with ample number of guns and airplanes; and I was cheered to the echo. Our people are waking up."

Three days after his return home he was on the road again. The abscess in his leg which had laid him low four months before, was acting up, but that was nothing, he said. He spoke at Trinity College, Hartford, Connecticut, pointing out to the five thousand gathered under the campus elms that the censorship, "unpleasant as it has been at times," might well be extended to cover "grandiloquent boasting" of what Americans were going to do in the war. Since he had been accused of liking to preach, he went on, and as the day was Sunday, he presented a text from the First Book of Kings, Chapter XX, verse 11: "Let not him that girdeth on his harness boast himself as he that taketh it off."

"Last Fall we were announcing that there would be twenty thousand airplanes with Pershing's army in the Spring, and the boast took in our own people. It took in the Germans, too, but, unlike our own people, they built airplanes to meet it."

Send over planes, he pleaded; send over men. Think in terms of an army of five million; ten, if necessary. Translate words into deeds. The Gettysburg Address, he reminded his audience, had been "made possible only by the men who had fought there. Make the Gettysburg speech *after* the battle of Gettysburg, not before."

The audience cheered. Audiences always did cheer. But what, the Colonel was thinking, did it amount to? "Our people," he wrote Archie, "still prefer washy untruths to the truths they ought to hear. . . . The only way I can help in speeding up the war is by jarring loose our governmental and popular conceit and complacency. I only wish I carried more weight."

4

He carried more than he thought. Hammering, day after day, on his two dominant themes—speed up the war effort, beware of a peace based on theory, sentiment and pious hope—he was building up a public opinion which was making itself heard. He complained to Mrs. Cowles that his mail had increased to 5,000 letters a week.

In his determination to get his message across to the man on the street Roosevelt was inclined to paint the picture in blacks and whites without much shading, and, in his effort to be heard above the din of machinery or marching feet, his voice at times seemed even to his friends a little shrill. There was, indeed, an almost frenzied note in his adjurations for speed, speed, speed, his laments for the "folly" of the past, the "complacency" of the present, the fierce, exaggerated (one must believe) denunciations to his friends— never in public except by inference—of Wilson. He was fighting not only for his country with all the fire of his passionate being; he was fighting for his boys and for their wives and children, fighting not only the Kaiser and his hosts on land and sea and in the air, but—definitely, hotly, persistently—the President of the United States; fighting with a kind of berserker rage that would not forget, would not forgive, the past, seeing his boys in deadly peril and suffering privation and pain.

The partisans of the Administration called him a "common scold," who was embittered by the fact that he himself was not in the White House. But they did not deny either his facts or his conclusions. Under the pressure of the millions who had come to recognize and to trust his sense of the realities, the Administration, indeed, generally did, six months or a year late, what Roosevelt had demanded. Extreme, intemperate, almost apoplectic, as he sometimes appeared, the man who had been in the political scrapbasket, four years before, was actually calling the tune both in the White House and on Capitol Hill.

The Republican politicians took notice. Early in July, a former Progressive from California and a typical hard-boiled professional politician from Connecticut met with the Colonel in the library at Sagamore Hill to ask him whether he were prepared to run for the Presidency in 1920. The Colonel, looking odd and unlike himself in his stiff white shirt-front and dinner-coat, answered, yes, he would run, "if the people want me, but only if they want me. I will not lift a finger for the nomination. I will not make a contest for it. It will have to come to me. It would be worthless on any other basis."

"Colonel," said the professional with the assurance of a man who had his facts in hand, "it will be yours, without strings and on your own terms."

Shortly after, in Albany, Raymond Robins ran into William Barnes, who had been New York State's reactionary Republican "boss" and in a libel suit, three years before, had tried in vain to destroy Roosevelt forever as a factor in American political life. "I suspect," Robins remarked, "we are going to nominate TR in 1920 by acclamation."

"Acclamation, hell!" answered Barnes. "We're going to nominate him by assault!"

The Republican organization, it happened, needed the Colonel for its own survival. Once more, the Party in New York was badly divided, and the only man who could unite it, the leaders were saying, was Roosevelt. They begged him to run for governor. His election, they told him, would be assured, and was there traditionally a better step to the Presidency than the governorship of New York? Roosevelt, absorbed in the war, was reluctant to be imprisoned in a job. But his friends and, more importantly, the leaders who had been his enemies—Taft, Root, Nicholas Murray Butler, Barnes, and the men in industry and the press who were their

406

backers—now recognized that the man they had conspired to defeat, four elections in succession, was their only hope.

Roosevelt was moved by the urgency of their pleas. If revenge was sweet, here was honey on the lips. . . .

Chapter XIV

"*THE COUNTRY* is beautiful beyond description," the Colonel wrote Ted in June. "It is the high tide of the year, with tree and flower and bird." "I speak occasionally and write occasionally, and render what small help I can in speeding up the war," he wrote Dick. "It amounts to very little; deeds, not words, are all that count now; and the justification for my existence is furnished by you and Ethel, by the three older boys and their wives, by Quentin and Flora."

The flag that hung in the window at Sagamore had five stars— the fifth for Dick—and the Colonel glowed when he quoted Belle's comment on it: "Heavens, what it means to hold one's head up proudly these days. It's the Great Glory!" "There," he wrote her, "spoke a daughter of America who is true to her faith!"

"Quentin has at last been able to get to the front," he wrote Belle on the first of July, "to fly in a fighting plane, apparently with a French squadron. So he is now in the post of peril and honor. Flora is very brave." Quentin had begged Flora to come to France to marry him, and she had been determined to go, with or without her parents' consent. Her father and mother had presented no obstacle, and the Colonel had promised that he and Mrs. Roosevelt would, if permitted, cross the seas for the wedding. "Flora is a trump if ever there was one," the Colonel wrote Quentin. "That pretty little girl has a strength of character that is really extraordinary."

"She rings true metal under trial," he wrote Belle. "Quentin is indeed fortunate—as are my other three boys!" The Colonel pulled the few wires that were available to him in a hostile Administration to have what he called the "idiotic ruling" against wives or fiancées of officers going to France, suspended in Flora's favor. "Life is a very perilous adventure now for those whose lives are worth living," he wrote Ted, "and, on every account, I hope she and Quentin can be married. It is well to have had happiness, to have achieved the great ends of life, when one must walk boldly and warily close to death." Unhappily, the Department stood by its ruling. Flora could not go; and the Colonel scored up one more grudge against what he liked to call "those creatures" in Washington.

Kermit had been given the British Military Cross for gallantry in action in command of a light armored battery, and had been discharged from the British Army to enable him to join the American army in France, and he was now captain in an artillery regiment. "Now all my four sons," the Colonel wrote Archie, "are fighting under our own flag." It was a load off the Colonel's mind. "The last five years," he wrote Ted, "have made me bitterly conscious of the shortcomings of our national character; but we Roosevelts are Americans, and can never think of being anything else, and wouldn't be anything else for any consideration on the face of the earth. A man with our way of looking at things can no more change his country than he can change his mother."

Archie's condition had proved to be worse than the doctors had thought, one arm being paralyzed; but he was resisting all efforts to send him home. Gracie came to Sagamore for a visit, bringing "wee Archie, Jr. . . . such a sturdy mite," the Colonel wrote Archie, "with an absurd resemblance to you when you were small. I am allowed to hold him, as I am an expert in holding small babies. Gracie was sitting with Mother and me on the piazza," he added, "when we saw Ethel coming up the lane, leading your steed of long ago, Algonquin, with Richard riding him—Algonquin being now shaky in every leg. It seemed so funny and pleasant to have the children of all of you doing what you yourselves used to do, twenty years and over ago."

Ted had been promoted to lieutenant-colonel, and was continuing to win golden opinions not only from high officers, from Pershing down, but from enlisted men whose glowing tributes reached the American public through the press. A stranger sent the proud father an excerpt from the letter of a friend serving under his eldest son: "My major . . . the best man I ever met . . . utterly fearless . . . as big as his father. . . . There isn't a man or an officer in this outfit who wouldn't start to take a message to Berlin tonight if he asked it."

"Lord, how well Ted has done!" the Colonel wrote Eleanor.

Edith Roosevelt's pride in the boys was less articulate than her husband's but no less reverent. For the first time since she had left the White House, she emerged for a moment from her cherished seclusion, to send a message, as poignant as it was brief, for nation-wide observance of Mother's Day: "Four sons in the fighting line are my epistle, written on my heart and read of all men."

Eleanor, meanwhile, "*looking* like a very pretty Dresden china shepherdess and *acting* like the most efficient woman of affairs," as Mary Cadwalader Jones wrote the Colonel, was making a remarkable record of her own. She had been the first woman sent overseas by the Y.M.C.A., had helped organize the first Leave Area in resort towns all over France. Pershing subsequently recognized her work through a special citation, and the French government gave her the Palms of the Academy.

"I hear of you continually," the Colonel wrote, "and really, Eleanor, the admiration expressed for what the boys have done is no stronger than the tributes paid to you for your administrative ability to accomplish results. I doubt if I have ever known of such hearty and universal commendation being expressed for difficult work of a kind peculiarly apt to excite friction." He spoke of a letter from General J. Franklin Bell, who had written admiringly of the boys, "but fervently proclaimed his loyalty to you as standing even ahead of them."

"I rage at my impotence to be of substantial service to all of you at the front," the Colonel wrote Ted, "and as for you and your brothers, I do not know whether I most keenly feel the pride I owe to what you four have done at this crisis, or the bitterness I feel that, while you face inconceivably wearing fatigue, hardship, work, responsibility and deadly danger, I sit at home ignobly in comfort and uselessness."

2

The Colonel's pride and anxiety were deepened when the New York *Times* reported that Ted had been cited for "conspicuous gallantry" on two occasions, first in repelling a German assault, and next in making an assault, when he had stayed with his troops after being "gassed in the lungs and in the eyes almost to blindness."

"Of course," his father wrote, "our pride even surpasses our anxiety. . . . You have won high honor by rendering great service. . . . John King, the Connecticut National Committeeman," he added in another letter, "has just written me that the Congressmen feel that what my four sons have done makes *me* a person of consequence! It is the sober truth that for the last year my strongest title to the regard of my fellow-countrymen has lain in the gallantry and efficiency of you four boys. And Dick stands alongside you."

"Ted had a rough time," the Colonel wrote Mrs. Cowles, "but is now all right; Archie's arm is still bad; Kermit was bowled over in Rome by malarial fever, but I hope he is with Pershing now."

That moment, in midsummer of 1918, at the height of the German drive, with all the boys, except Archie, in dire peril, was the moment a Western editor, denouncing Roosevelt, chose to state in his paper that "All his boys have got good jobs as aides to officers in France where they can take good care of themselves or get just a little bit wounded."

An unknown friend, Victor P. Buell, in McAlester, Oklahoma, wired Roosevelt the story, asking him to wire back the information he must have to put the editor in his place. Purple with rage, Roosevelt replied, "All four of my boys are in fighting positions in the line at the front. No one of them is an aide to any officer." He gave the record of citations, medals and wounds received. "Any man who is guilty of such foul and infamous slanders as those of the editor you quote about gallant American soldiers at the front, whether my sons or the sons of any one else, is an unspeakable, contemptible cur."

3

On the Fourth of July, the press reported from France that patrols from American pursuit squadrons in an unnamed sector had engaged in some twenty combats and brought down seven enemy planes. Among the airmen taking part, ran the story, was Quentin Roosevelt.

A few days later, the *Times* mentioned Quentin as one of fifteen fliers in combat, northeast of Château-Thierry, with twenty-one members of Richthofen's "flying circus." Four days later, the same paper announced that "Lieutenant Quentin Roosevelt brought down his first German airplane this afternoon."

"The last of the lion's brood has been blooded!" the Colonel exclaimed in a letter to Ted.

One late afternoon, ten days later, the Colonel, dressed in the knickerbockers and loose shirt that was his usual costume at Sagamore Hill, was in the library when a familiar lanky figure and cadaverous face appeared at the door. It was "Phil" Thompson, assigned by the Associated Press to cover Sagamore Hill, and a friend of all the household. He held a copy of a heavily censored cablegram to the New York *Sun*: "Watch Sagamore Hill for—"

"Have you any idea, Colonel, what it means?"

The Colonel gave a quick look toward the hall, then strode to the door and shut it quietly. "Something has happened to one of the boys," he said. "It can't be Ted or Archie, for both are recovering from wounds. It's not Kermit, since he's not at the moment in the danger-zone. So it must be Quentin. His mother," he added, "must not be told until there is no hope left."

He took the newspaperman to the door, then, with iron self-control, dressed for dinner and the customary evening of reading and casual talk with Mrs. Roosevelt in the Trophy Room.

The following morning before breakfast, Thompson was again at Sagamore Hill with a message in his eyes that made words unnecessary. The Colonel led him out to the piazza, and heard the verification of his calculated assumption of the night before. Quentin had been attacked by two German fighters and had fallen with his plane inside the German lines.

The Colonel strode up and down the veranda in silence. "But— Mrs. Roosevelt!" he cried, at last, in low tones. "How am I going to break it to her?"

Abruptly, he turned and entered the house. When he reappeared a half hour later, he had in his hand a brief statement for the press that Thompson had asked for: "Quentin's mother and I," it ran, "are very glad that he got to the front and had a chance to render some service to his country, and show the stuff that was in him before his fate befell him."

When Mrs. Roosevelt came out of the house a few hours later, her eyes were shining and her voice was steady. "We must do everything we can to help him," she said to Thompson. "The burden must not rest entirely on his shoulders."

The stricken father had agreed to give the keynote address at the Republican State Convention at Saratoga, two days later, and proceeded with grim determination to keep his promise. "It is more than ever my duty to be there."

Isaac Hunt, who had been in the New York Assembly with Roosevelt almost forty years before, noted, next day, the look of agony on his friend's face as he mounted the platform. The bedlam that broke loose when he appeared subsided only in response to Roosevelt's lifted hand, asking quiet. His manner, as he began to speak, was subdued, but, as he warmed to his theme, the old fire and vigor asserted themselves. What he said was in effect the same as he had said to a dozen other audiences, with particular stress on the future: "the task of rebuilding and upbuilding" after the peace was won, a new relation between capital and labor, steering "between the anarchy of unregulated individualism and the deadening formalism and inefficiency of wide-spread government ownership."

In the middle of his prepared speech, the grief that was in his heart came to unplanned expression.

"The finest, the bravest, the best of our young men have sprung eagerly forward to face death for the sake of a high ideal," he said, laying his manuscript aside, "and thereby they have brought home to us the great truth that life consists of more than easygoing pleasure, and more than hard, conscienceless, brutal striving after purely material success; that while we must rightly care for the body and the things of the body, yet that such care leads nowhere unless we also have thought for our own souls and for the souls of our brothers. When these gallant boys, on the golden crest of life, gladly face death for the sake of an ideal, shall not we, who stay behind, who have not been found worthy of the great adventure, shall not we in our turn try to shape our lives so as to make in this country a better place to live in for these men, and for the women who sent these men to battle and for the children who are to come after them?"

Roosevelt refused to see anyone after the meeting. The governorship? He would think it over. A cablegram had come from Eleanor saying that the report of Quentin's death was "absolutely unconfirmed." If the report proved untrue . . . When Roosevelt returned to Sagamore Hill he found a cablegram from Dick, saying that a fellow flier believed that Quentin had landed safely inside the German lines and was a prisoner. Pershing sent a similar report.

For three days the issue hung suspended.

Roosevelt had promised Henry P. Davison, head of the American

413

Red Cross, to receive a Japanese Red Cross delegation at Sagamore Hill on the afternoon of July 20th. He welcomed the members in the Trophy Room in a thoughtful speech dealing with the relations between the two nations. "It was not simply a routine affair," Davison's son Trubee, who was with the party, said afterward, "but one that required concentration and an accurate statement of events and dates." Alice, who, true to her custom when trouble hit the family, had instantly come on from Cincinnati, served tea while her father took his guests about the room, telling stories associated with his trophies.

As the delegation was about to depart, young Davison took the Colonel to one side. "I can't leave without asking you what hope you have for Quentin."

"I received this telegram from President Wilson just twenty minutes before you arrived." It was a warm and sympathetic message confirming the report of Quentin's death. Davison recalled, years later, this "most magnificent exhibition of self-control and courage" that he had ever seen.

Shortly after the door closed upon the visitors, a cablegram came from Eleanor saying that Ted had been wounded, and was with her in Paris. The *Tribune* headline next morning gave the grim picture: "THEODORE, JR., IS WOUNDED; QUENTIN DEAD." From the semiofficial Wolff Bureau in Germany came word, the same day, that "the earthly remains of the brave young airman" had been "buried with military honors by German airmen at Cambrai, at the spot where he fell."

That day, Will Hays had luncheon at Sagamore Hill. "I am glad you did not speak of Quentin," the Colonel said to his guest as they returned to the library from the dining room. "Edith could not have stood it." His voice suddenly quavered, as he added, "I don't think I could have stood it myself."

The next day, Sunday, in all the Protestant churches of Oyster Bay and at every mass of St. Dominic's Roman Catholic Church, prayers were offered for Quentin and the members of his family. In the town's service flag with its 321 stars, a gold star in the border reminded the townspeople that one of their own had, in his father's words, "paid with his body for his soul's desire."

"I went with Edith to the early communion service," the Colonel wrote his friend Robert P. Perkins. "It was exactly a year since, on Quentin's last Sunday before sailing, she had gone to communion

414

with him. Poor stricken Edith is very, very brave; but of course now and then she breaks down for a minute or two. . . . Well, we have to abide the stroke of fate without overmuch whining. When I was in the hospital last winter I used to grin at my own futility in wishing that it were possible for me to act as offering to the gods, and save some one of my boys from suffering or death, by dying myself. There is nothing whatever that is dreadful in the death of the old, but it is very dreadful to see the young stricken down in their golden morning."

"Flora is utterly heartbroken, of course," the Colonel wrote Ted. "She is young, and time will mercifully heal her sorrow; but she has had her golden dream and it has proved only a dream. If only she could have married Quentin! Thank heaven, you other boys have wives and children. The fine gallantry of Quentin's death has stirred our whole people; I have never known such widespread expressions—in editorials, in speeches, in articles—of pride and sorrow and admiration." "I would not for all the world have had him fail fearlessly to do his duty," the Colonel wrote Belle, "and to tread his allotted path, high of heart, even altho it led to the gates of death. But it is useless for me to pretend that it is not very bitter to see that good, gallant, tenderhearted boy leave life at its crest, when it held Flora, and such happiness, and certainly an honorable and perhaps a distinguished career."

"Well, it is very dreadful," the stricken father wrote Archie, "but, after all, he died as the heroes of old died; as brave and fearless men must die when a great cause calls. If our country did not contain such men it would not be our country. . . ."

President Arthur T. Hadley, of Yale, in a letter of sympathy, quoted Napier's line about the English officer at the storming of Bajados: "None died that night with greater glory; yet many died and there was great glory." The Colonel took the volume from a shelf in the library and read the account of the storming to Mrs. Roosevelt and Alice. It was one of the great feats of valor of the ages, the Colonel was thinking as he read, yet already his four boys had shown that they "had the right to stand on the honor roll beside the bravest, in that or any other battle of recorded history."

Once more, King George sent a warm message of sympathy. In his reply, the former President told of Ted, "gassed once" and "now in hospital with a bullet through his leg," Archie, "badly wounded by a shell"; both "cited for gallantry"; Kermit, "with your army . . .

given the Military Cross . . . now with our army under Pershing. Unlike most of their fellow-countrymen they had prepared in advance! They sailed from our shores over a year ago; their mother and I knew their temper and quality; and we did not expect to see all of them come back."

"If this war goes on," the Colonel said to a visitor, "none of the boys will come back."

Mrs. Roosevelt overheard the words, and went white. But he repeated them on other occasions, and did not lighten thereby the burden of her own dread.

It was a way he had thus to imagine the worst, so that anything short of the worst, when it came, might find him prepared.

Chapter XV

THE COLONEL took Mrs. Roosevelt for a fortnight to Islesboro, Maine, where Ethel and her children were spending the summer. Sagamore was too full of associations for grief so fresh and raw, and little Richard and Edie were balm upon their bruised hearts. "Little Richard was Quentin's favorite among all his small nephews and nieces," the Colonel wrote Dick. "He loved Uncle Quentin (the other day on the piazza at Sagamore when we heard an airplane he said to me 'perhaps that's Uncle Quentin') and he was so glad to see his Grandmother and so affectionate with her that it almost seemed as if he knew. . . ."

"In time of trouble," the Colonel wrote Belle, "the unconsciousness of children is often a great comfort."

When the grandparents returned to Sagamore Hill, Alice was on hand to welcome them and help them face the ordeal of reading Quentin's last letters. "He was at the fighting front, very proud and happy," the Colonel wrote Belle, "and singularly modest, with all his pride, and his pleasure at showing his mettle. . . ." "He had a fortnight or three weeks," he recalled, in a letter to Eleanor, "when he stood on a crest of life which cannot even be seen by sordid and torpid souls who know neither strife nor honor nor love, and who live forever in a gray fog at the lowest level. . . . Peter Dunne's remark about the four boys putting the name of Roosevelt on the map is no joke now."

Amid the grief of the homecoming was happily a message indicating Archie's imminent return. "The goose writes with obvious sincerity," the Colonel wrote Eleanor, "that he feels like a slacker and a loafer and has 'never been in any real fighting.'"

Archie arrived early in September. "Colonel Roosevelt stood on his porch at Sagamore Hill yesterday afternoon and beamed," the New York *Sun* reported next day. "Out in the yard, Captain Archie

Roosevelt, invalided home from France because of his wounds, was playing with his five-months-old baby, which he had seen for the first time a few minutes before, while beside him stood his young wife. The Colonel was dee-lighted."

"I prize his return most for Gracie's sake, and then for Mother's," the Colonel wrote Ted and Eleanor. "They have far more time in which to brood than I have; for, although I have very ugly doubts as to the value of my work, I have to do it, and it keeps me very busy."

2

The truth was, that a father's grief had not paralyzed the natural-born leader's impulsion to lead. He had refused the nomination for the governorship. "My whole heart is wrapped up in this war," he wrote Ted, "and in what is to come after; my whole pride and interest is in you boys and your wives; and I just could not wrench my mind off to a wholly different track."

But, if he could not engage in a political free-for-all, he could speak, he could write.

With a German peace offensive clearly in the offing, following the German defeat in the second battle of the Marne, and some "glittering proposal" probable, of "a league of nations to end all war," the Colonel pleaded for "that excellent variety of wisdom colloquially known as 'horse sense' " in dealing with a league aimed to lessen the number of future wars and diminish their area. "But let us never forget that any promise that such a league will definitely do away with war is either sheer nonsense or rank hypocrisy."

In successive articles, speeches and public statements he fought the idea of a negotiated peace. He had reason. Since early in January, when the President had set forth the famous Fourteen Points as the basis of a peace settlement, he had in other public addresses offered the Central Powers even more seductive terms. With consummate adroitness the addresses drove a wedge between government and people in Germany and Austria, and the Colonel was chided, even by his friends, for not joining in the enthusiasm, at home and abroad, for the "great moral leadership" which Wilson was acclaimed as exercising.

The Colonel recognized the leadership but found its moral quality dubious. What he was seeing was the President of the United States promising the Germans, in behalf of the Allies, what, Roosevelt was convinced, he could never in the world deliver; namely, millennial attitudes of magnanimity and self-abnegation such as the Twelve Apostles, seated around the peace table, might have found difficulty in maintaining, and Wilson himself did not pretend to practice in his own relations with political opponents. The Colonel was sensitive about practice lining up with preaching, and performance validating the promise. And here was Wilson, with no thought apparently of the responsibility involved, or the effect of possible disillusionment on the disheartened and demoralized peoples of Germany and Austria, luring them to an acceptance of terms which any appreciation of the realities, in a world torn by four years of war, might have shown him that even his own people, separated by the Atlantic from the battlefields and the ruins, would never accept and carry through.

The President, moreover, was making impossible pledges at home, also, promising the American people "the establishment of an organization of peace which shall make it certain that the combined power of free nations will check every invasion of right." Could Wilson, could any man, follow through on that *shall* and that *will*?

The Colonel could not directly challenge the President on his promises without appearing to throw a monkey-wrench into the delicate machinery of peace negotiation. So, instead, he exhorted the public to a "fight to the finish," pleading for the "manly virtue" of "making performance square with promise," and pointing out the dangers in peace-making by rhetoric and—when the German Chancellor, Count Hertling, started making addresses, too— "by competitive rhetoric."

He received a "strength-to-your-elbow" shout from a wholly unexpected source. A letter from Pershing, marked "Personal and Confidential," ended with a passage indicating that the general in command of the American Army in France was not at all sure that the Administration could be trusted to carry the war through. Let the nation move forward with all its strength and not allow the war to drag, Pershing urged, lest the public, losing interest, "fall under the spell of pacifist dreams and possible pacifist action."

From Taft, with whom Roosevelt had been reconciled that summer, the Colonel heard in a similar vein. He had talked with Wilson and become convinced that, if the Germans made the slightest concession, the President would make peace. The only thing that could prevent it was the whip of American public opinion.

419

In October, the Colonel went west on a speaking-trip for the Fourth Liberty Loan, and from Maryland to Montana built up resistance to the President's efforts toward a peace that would leave Germany free to start another war. "The only way to make a Hun feel friendly," he told a Nebraska audience, "is to knock him out. Don't hit a man soft, because he will come back and hit you hard. Put this war through right, so that no nation will look cross-eyed at you." As for a league of nations, fine!—in addition to, but, under no circumstances, as a substitute for, the preparation of the nation's own defenses. "Uncle Sam must, in the last analysis, rely on himself for his safety, and not on scraps of paper signed by others."

"Everywhere I found the war spirit steadily strengthening," the Colonel wrote Ted and Eleanor, "and the great crowds of men and women eagerly responded to my insistence that we should fight the war through until we secured an 'unconditional surrender' from Germany. . . . Then I got home and three days later Wilson turned one of the most shameless somersaults and, after having insisted that he would never submit to a 'negotiated peace,' started to negotiate one."

"It is a sad and dreadful thing to have to face some months or a year or so of additional bloodshed," Roosevelt wrote in the *Star*, "but it is a much worse thing to quit now and have the children now growing up obliged to do the job all over again, with ten times as much bloodshed and suffering when their time comes."

In the *Star* the Colonel delivered one hammer-blow after another in behalf of honesty, realism and fair-dealing, analyzing the President's proposals and tearing them to shreds. "What are the Fourteen Points?". . . "Further Consideration of the Fourteen Points" . . . "Fourteen Scraps of Paper." Did the President himself really know what they meant? Or care?

There was that item, for instance, about the removal "of all economic barriers and the establishment of an equality of trade conditions among all the nations." Obviously, Roosevelt pointed out, that meant that the United States "could have no tariff of its own."

A Democratic senator queried the President about it, and was informed that the section in question did not place "any restriction upon the free determination by any nation of its own economic policy."

If that was what Wilson meant, Roosevelt asked, why had he

said the exact opposite? If anyone in private life entered into a contract and tried to repudiate it by interpretations of that sort, there was "not a court in Christendom that would not adjudge him guilty of having used language with deliberate intent to deceive."

3

"It has been beautiful October weather," the Colonel wrote Belle. "Rather cold but clear and the foliage radiant." "The fall glory is fading now," he wrote Ted and Eleanor on October 27th, "but it is still very lovely. . . . I am sixty years old today. I hope that when you two come to this age you will have had as happy a life as I have had; and above all I hope that your children will have given you the same cause for pride that you, Ted, have given me; and that *your* sons' wives will be as you have been, Eleanor, for whom I feel such fond affection and in whom I take such deep pride."

During the preceding week, he added, "Wilson has been adroitly endeavoring to get the Allies into the stage of note-writing and peace discussion with an only partially beaten, and an entirely unconquered, Germany. . . . Wilson is at heart a pacifist, cold-blooded and without a single scruple or conviction. . . . My duty is to oppose him where he goes wrong . . . and, in a reasonable number of cases, I make him go fairly right. He has, however, I am thankful to say, come out into the open and made a frank party appeal for the Democratic Party against the Republicans; and this at least makes the fight more comfortable."

4

Roosevelt had been asked to deliver the Republicans' answer to the President's appeal, and, the day after his birthday, in New York, before a crowd that packed Carnegie Hall, he gave it.

He was received with the usual tumultuous enthusiasm, and responded with the customary clicking of the famous teeth and the waving of his manuscript. His speech was a bitter two-hour-long attack on Wilson such as would have been impossible in wartime if the President had not himself reconvened the "politics" he had proclaimed as "adjourned." Roosevelt pointed to "the most rigid party test" which the President had applied in his appeal for a

Democratic Congress. "He explicitly repudiates loyalty to the war as a test. . . . He asks for the defeat of pro-war Republicans. He does not ask for the defeat of anti-war Democrats. On the contrary, he supports such men if, although anti-war, they are pro-Administration. He asks not for loyalty to the nation. He asks only for support of himself."

"Rub it in, Teddy!" cried a voice.

"We Republicans," he went on, "pledge ourselves to stand by the President as long as he stands by the American people, and to part company from him at any point where in our judgment he does not stand by the people. This is the people's government, this is the people's war, and the peace that follows shall be the people's peace."

The New York *Sun* reporter spoke of the "great shout of approval that crashed from Carnegie Hall and was heard by thousands" unable to get into the building.

"Wilson's first note to Germany wakened a storm of angry protest," Roosevelt wrote Ted and Eleanor a few days later, "whereupon he instantly turned his usual somersault, and is now as old 'Ithuriel, resolute and grim,' for unconditional surrender," thus having, the Colonel added in a letter to Rudyard Kipling, "double-crossed the Huns instead of the Allies."

5

The Colonel said nothing in his letters of the pain he was suffering. A severe attack of lumbago, an outgrowth of the sciatic rheumatism he had suffered at intervals in damp weather during the past months, put him to bed shortly after his return home from the Carnegie Hall meeting. He crept out only long enough to vote on November 5th, but from his bed next day issued a restrained hallelujah over what he called, in a letter to Ted, the "stinging rebuke" given the President in the election. "He is in excellent spirits," said the *Times* correspondent, which was obvious.

He had won his four years' war with Woodrow Wilson. But his exultation was premature. He was not reckoning with the Dark Angel even at that hour just over the brow of the next hill, or with leaders less firm, experienced and farsighted than he, and less sensitive to America's responsibility in a world of nations and peoples cut loose from old moorings.

Mercifully, he was conscious only of the triumph.

"We did an unparalleled thing," the Colonel wrote Kipling, "and took away the Congress from him, on the issue that we stood for forcing the Germans to make an unconditional surrender. I took a certain sardonic amusement in the fact that whereas, four years ago, to put it mildly, my attitude was not popular, I was now the one man whom they insisted upon following and whose statements were taken as the platform."

The letter about the election that the Colonel wrote Ted was in Mrs. Roosevelt's hand, even to the signature. She added a postscript of her own: "Father is flat on his back with his gout . . . having a horrid, suffering time."

That day, the Colonel went to Roosevelt Hospital in New York, to be near his physician. During the seven weeks that followed he was able to be out of bed, though rarely out of a chair. He was warned, in fact, that, like his gallant sister, Mrs. Cowles, he might be confined to a chair for the rest of his life. He let that sink in. "All right!" he said. "I can work that way, too."

He returned to Sagamore Hill on Christmas Day. "The sciatica got the best of me for a time," he admitted to neighbors who greeted him on his arrival, "but I'm all right now." "It will be a couple of months before I am in any kind of shape," he wrote Ted, "but this happens to be the very time when I do not care to speak or to take an active part in politics."

Meanwhile, the war had ended. "Ted moved Heaven and earth to get to the front and to get Kermit to the front," the Colonel wrote Kipling, "and just three weeks before the end they went back to the first division, Ted as Lieutenant Colonel commanding his regiment, still limping, but able to hold his job, and Kermit as Captain of Artillery in the same division."

"I know Father will be glad," Ted wrote his mother, "that all of his family that are in physical shape were in front lines fighting when the bell rang and the curtain went down on the play."

"Time does not seem to help me," Mrs. Roosevelt wrote Mrs. Cowles, "to face the fact that Quentin will not come home with the others. . . . Quentin's birthday, Thanksgiving and Christmas, so close together, have made hard weeks. Now I shall fight on with more courage."

Eleanor returned from France, rich in honors, "pretty and dainty and happy," her father-in-law wrote Ted, "but dreadfully homesick for you. Of course I was enthralled with everything she had to tell. Well, next Xmas I hope we shall have the whole family, for three generations, gathered at Sagamore Hill!"

Once more, early in January, Eleanor went to see the Colonel. Speaking of Ted's war record, she said what, in effect, Ted had said to his boyhood friend, the Oyster Bay ancient, when he was thirteen: "Ted has always worried for fear he would not be worthy of you."

"Worthy of me?" the Colonel answered. "Darling, I am so very proud of him. He has won honor not only for his children but, like the Chinese, he has ennobled his ancestors. I walk with my head higher because of him. I have always taken satisfaction from the fact that, when there was a war in 1898, I fought in it, and I tried my best to get into this one. But my war was a bow-and-arrow war compared to Ted's, and no one knows that better than I do."

The first Sunday in January he and Mrs. Roosevelt were alone at Sagamore. He had been accustomed, since his return from the hospital, to spending the greater part of each day downstairs, but that day he stayed in bed, in the northwest bedroom, reading aloud to Mrs. Roosevelt or listening while she read, writing Kermit and spending long periods just luxuriating in the joy of being home with this dearest and most exhilarating of companions.

"The last attack of rheumatism was a little better," Mrs. Roosevelt wrote Ted. "Everything had been adjusted. I had a good nurse, and James Amos. He had a happy day. People came in and I went down to see them.

"Father was in your old nursery and loved the view, of which he spoke, and as it got dusk he watched the dancing flames and spoke of the happiness of being home, and made little plans for me. I think he had made up his mind that he would have to suffer for some time to come and with his high courage had adjusted himself to bear it. He was very sweet all day. Since Quentin was killed he has been sad, only Ethel's little girl had the power to make him merry."

Mrs. Roosevelt, sitting at a table beside him, completed the solitaire she was playing and was about to leave the room when he looked up from the book he was reading and said, apropos of nothing, "I wonder if you will ever know how I love Sagamore Hill."

At five o'clock next morning he was dead.

In Lieu of Footnotes

IF SOLOMON had ever expressed his thoughts on the making of many books in terms of his philosophy of seasons he might have arrived at the conclusion that there are books that cry for footnotes and books that cry for the omission of footnotes. "The Roosevelt Family of Sagamore Hill" seems obviously to belong in the latter class. It is primarily a story; a story of a man and his wife, the house they loved and the six children they brought up in it; and the fact that it is a true story—authentic to the last quoted word, so far as the records reveal—seems no reason for arresting the reader's eye with an asterisk and forcing it to the foot of the page to read in small type the proof that the author is an honest man. In a day when too many biographers let fancy take over where research falters, it may be said that the reader has a right to ask for evidence that the author is not getting his Muses mixed. But, to the discerning, the best evidence is always implicit in the text, and in this book the author has gone out of his way to make sure that it is unmistakable. Incidentally, the author's notes and the photostats of the newspaper accounts that contributed to his story will be available to historical students in the Roosevelt collection in the Widener Library at Harvard.

There are two or three statements, however, which may demand a reply to the historian's inevitable query, "Now where in the world did he get that item?" There is, for one, the story of the early quarrel or misunderstanding between Theodore Roosevelt and Edith Carow, and the manner of its ending. The author picked that up thirty-four years ago on a grassy butte in the Bad Lands of North Dakota, from Mr. Roosevelt's former ranch-partner, A. W. Merrifield, at that time a resident of Somers, Montana. Mr. Merrifield had it from Mr. Roosevelt himself, on a hunting-trip in the summer of 1886, and told it under the impact of a letter of introduction written in long-hand by Mr. Roosevelt some six months before his death. The taciturn hunter and cowpuncher of the 1880's who served as U.S. marshal of Montana during Mr. Roosevelt's administration, was an honest man with a good memory but no particular imagination, or, if he had had it, any incentive for exercising it in this case. His testimony, therefore, is as dependable as secondhand accounts can ever be expected to be. The late Mrs. James Russell Parsons (née Fanny Smith) gave the author other details of the early friendship of Mr. Roosevelt and Miss Carow. The date of their engagement—not previously recorded—is authenticated by Mr. Roosevelt himself in a letter to his son Quentin, written on its thirty-second anniversary, November 17, 1917.

The amount of Mr. Roosevelt's patrimony is stated in a letter from William T. O'Neil, of St. Regis Falls, N. Y., to his wife, dated April 13, 1883, reporting statements regarding his finances which Mr. Roosevelt had made to Mr. O'Neil.

The Sagamore maid's dire mixup of guests of divergent tastes was told to Miss Ethel Armes of the staff of the Theodore Roosevelt Association, thirty years ago, by one of the visitors involved, who had come with others to ask Mr. Roosevelt to address the Hamilton Club in Chicago. The confluence at Sagamore of the parsons and the politicians is confirmed by an item in the New York *Herald* of July 24, 1898, reporting the visit to Sagamore, the previous day, of the Hamilton Club group, including Senator William E. Mason of Illinois and of a delegation of Oyster Bay ministers seeking to make arrangements for the town's "jubilee" in honor of its returned hero. Happily, as the book was about to go to press, the author received final corroboration of the story. Mr. Hiram S. Cody of Winston-Salem, N.C., sent him a photostatic copy of a letter, written, August 27, 1898, to his father, Arthur B. Cody, by the latter's brother, Hope Reed Cody, one of the delegates of the Hamilton Club who visited Sagamore Hill that hot August day. The letter confirms to the last detail the story recorded by Miss Armes. The story of the call of the two newspapermen at dawn, following Election Day, 1900, is from Edward Marshall's article, "The Truth about Roosevelt" in the *Columbian Magazine* for June, 1910.

Historians will want to know where the author got the text of the telegram from the Secretary of War, Elihu Root, which was handed to Mr. Roosevelt just below the top of Mount Marcy on September

13, 1901. The message is one of sixteen which an employee, Mike Breen, of the Tahawus Club received at the "Lower Works" of the Club during the day preceding President McKinley's death and scrawled on slips of paper which he sent by messenger to the Club's "Upper Works" where the Vice President was staying. Mrs. Breen generously permitted the author to have photostats made of these messages; the photostats are now in the Roosevelt collection at Harvard. Other details of the Mount Marcy trip were contributed by the late Beverly Robinson or the late James MacNaughton who wrote an account in the Tahawus Club guest book. Some details are from an address by Mrs. Roosevelt at Theodore Roosevelt House, New York, in 1933. The terse message from Mr. Roosevelt to his wife, announcing President McKinley's death, was taken down by Mr. Breen on a slip of paper later pasted into the Club's guestbook. Mr. Roosevelt's *to be or not to be* on the question of a third term in 1908 is derived mainly from a long letter he wrote his friend, the British historian, George Otto Trevelyan, June 19, 1908.

The answer to the hotly disputed question of Mr. Roosevelt's initial reaction to the outbreak of the first World War, was given the author wholly unexpectedly by Associate Justice Felix Frankfurter, in his chambers in the Supreme Court Building in Washington, on March 17, 1953. The account of Mr. Roosevelt's final outburst of devotion to Sagamore Hill, some twelve hours before his death, was given by Mrs. Roosevelt to Mr. Everett Colby who quoted it in a memorial address at Newark, N. J., on February 9, 1919.

Whatever else in the book is new to history is drawn from family letters—Mr. Roosevelt's, first of all, published and unpublished, to his family and friends, the unpublished made available to the author through the generosity of Mr. Roosevelt's daughter, Mrs. Richard Derby, his son, Mr. Archibald B. Roosevelt and his daughters-in-law, Mrs. Theodore Roosevelt, Jr., and Mrs. Kermit Roosevelt. The author is indebted to Mrs. Derby also for permission to see Mrs. Roosevelt's letters to her sister, Emily Carow; and to Mr. W. Sheffield Cowles for permission to see Mrs. Roosevelt's letters to his mother, Anna Roosevelt Cowles, the entrancing "Bamie." For much engaging family history the author is indebted to the "Princess Alice" of fifty years ago, Mrs. Nicholas Longworth, Mr. Roosevelt's daughter by his first wife, Alice Lee; and to another, whose friendly cooperation has already been cited, Mrs. Eleanor

Alexander Roosevelt, widow of Brigadier General Theodore Roosevelt, Jr., whose gallantry on the Normandy beach is a "hero-tale" worthy of a place with those others that his father told in the early 1890's. The elder Mrs. Roosevelt's "Baby Journal," now in the Roosevelt collection at Harvard, provided tender or amusing details. Her account book, in the same repository, tells the year-by-year story of the family expenditures but leaves obscure the history of the family income, ever slightly breathless from the outgo's importunate pursuit.

For the *feng shuey* story the author is indebted to Major General Frank R. McCoy who had it directly from Mr. Roosevelt. General (then Captain) McCoy was military aide to the President at the White House and remained his cherished friend until Mr. Roosevelt's death.

Thanks are due, furthermore, to Mrs. Arthur Guiterman for permission to quote from her late husband's rhymed review of Theodore Roosevelt's "Letters to His Children"; to Mr. Wallace Irwin who has generously allowed the author to quote passages from "The Ballad of Sagamore Hill" and his mock-heroic epic, "The Teddysee"; and to Mrs. Vernon Howe Bailey for permission to reproduce her late husband's drawing of the house on Sagamore Hill.

Finally, the author bears witness to his indebtedness to the late Miss Nora E. Cordingly, the able and devoted curator of the Theodore Roosevelt collections at Harvard, and to Thomas Little, her successor, for untiring help in facilitating his researches, as well as to Miss Luella Horton and Miss Helen MacLachlan who, over a period of five years, successively translated his hieroglyphics into the legible symbols of the typewritten page.

H. H.

Index

Abbott, Ernest, 303
Abbott, Lawrence, 303
Abbott, Lyman, 238, 244, 303
Adams, Brooks, 50
Adams, Henry, 29
Ade, George, 267
Africa, 277, 278, 280, 281, 283, 289, 291, 296, 353
Alexander, Eleanor, 278; her marriage, 289. *See also* Mrs. Theodore Roosevelt, Jr.
Allies, The, 396, 397, 418, 422; and war purchases, 358
Alsop, Mrs. Joseph W. *See* Corinne Robinson, 2nd
American Ambulance Hospital, Paris, 343
American Historical Association, 329
American Olympic Team (1908), 247
Amos, James, 147, 148, 321, 424
Andover School, 331
Associated Press, 363, 412

Bacon, Robert, 243, 296
Bad Lands, the, 8, 13, 64, 303, 330, 348
Baker, Newton D., 362
Baltimore, Md., 308
Barnes, William, Jr., 93, 406
Bayliss, Charles, 100
Belford, Rev. John L., 44, 84
Belgium, 342, 343, 344; German invasion of, 340
Bell, Gen. J. Franklin, 410
Beveridge, Sen. Albert J., 338, 340
Bigelow, W. Sturgis, 246
"Big Stick," 236, 334
Birthplace of TR, 9, 330
Bishop, Joseph Bucklin, 223, 299
Booth, Charles, 341, 342
Boris, Grand Duke, 164, 165
Brewer, Dr. George E., 114, 120
Bridgeport, Conn., 166

Bristow, Joseph N., 202
Broun, Heywood, 377
Bryan, William Jennings, 94, 162, 319, 342, 349, 355, 372
Bryce, James, 347
Buffalo, N. Y., 108, 116
"Bull Moose Party," 310, 311. *See also* Progressive (Bull Moose) Party
Bullen, Frank T., 162
Bulloch, Anna (aunt of TR), 6. *See also* Gracie
Bullock, Seth, 31, 263, 293, 365
Burnham, Frederick R., 365
Butler, Nicholas Murray, 406
Butt, Archie, 193, 281, 283, 312

California, 242, 334
Cameron, Sen. James Donald, 175
Cannon, Speaker Joseph G., 210, 249, 277
Canton, Ohio, 90, 126
Carey, Robert D., 365
Carnegie Hall, 73, 421, 422
Carow, Mrs. Charles (mother-in-law of TR), 20, 25, 30, 31
Carow, Edith Kermit, 3, 4, 9, 10. *See also* Mrs. Theodore Roosevelt
Carow, Emily (sister-in-law of TR), 14, 43, 136, 258, 320, 331
Casino Theater, 317
Cassini, Count, 164, 165
Cathedral School, 128, 248, 260
Cats: "Tom Quartz," 249; "Slippers," 249
Chamberlain, Sen. George E., 386, 388, 389
Chanler, Winthrop ("Winty"), 330
Chapman, Frank M., 238
Chattanooga, 220
Cheney, Albert, 66, 170, 171
Cheney, Amy, 66, 67, 68, 190, 194
Chestnut Hill, Mass., 16, 21

429

432